yours,
Robert Straud.

Robert Stroud.

Lt. Robert Stroud,
Warden's Office

Robert Stroud

Your loving Son
R. F. Stroud
P. S. Remember this is my last card and
I will not try another hand,

Respectfully and Gratefully yours
Robert Stroud
17431 Brol dthin.

Robert Stroud   Bob   Robert Stroud

Date aug 30th 1909
Prisoner's Signature.

Robert Stroud

Reg No. 6744 ...Cell... Hospital ...Detail...
Name R. F. Stroud

No: 17431
Stroud

Yours loving Brother

Robert Stroud

Robert Stroud,
#17431.

Gratefully,
Robert F. Stroud

ALSO BY JOLENE BABYAK

Eyewitness on Alcatraz

BirdMan

The Many Faces of
Robert Stroud

Jolene Babyak

ARIEL VAMP PRESS
Berkeley, California

Library of Congress Catalog Card Number: 94-94179
ISBN 0-9618752-2-4

Cover design by David Bullen
Cover photo courtesy of the
San Francisco Maritime National Historical Park.

Ariel Vamp Press
P.O. Box 3496
Berkeley, California 94703

To Bobbie,
and the too many little kids
just like him.

TABLE OF CONTENTS

Introduction   1

Part I
Grand Illusion   5

Part II
The Prevailing Winds   25

Part III
Meet "John Pain"   51

Part IV
Cage Bird   85

Part V
Cell House Suite   127

Part VI
The Birdman of Alcatraz   151

Part VII
Broken Promises   191

Part VIII
Marketing the Birdman   243

Epilogue   273
Source Notes   281
Bibliography   314
Acknowledgments   317
Index   320

Photographs appear following page 184

Introduction
Further into the Mystery

I was already fascinated by the Birdman when I heard about the bullet holes.

I had grown up with "crazy" Stroud stories. My father, Arthur M. Dollison, was transferred to Alcatraz as a Bureau of Prisons employee in 1953. When I was seven years old, in 1954, we moved onto the prison island as part of a civilian community of two hundred people. By then the old man had already been there for twelve years. It was his forty–fifth year in prison. I knew about the Life in solitary confinement sentence, his two books on bird diseases and his mail–order bird business at the U.S. Penitentiary at Leavenworth, Kansas. As I got older I heard about the suicide attempts, the prison manuscript he was writing. And then the movie, *Birdman of Alcatraz,* came out.

But not until three decades after he died and after the U.S. Penitentiary at Alcatraz closed and became a National Park, did I hear about the bullet holes.

Although Stroud never took part in the May 1946 escape attempt and shoot–out, the corner near his cell—cell 41—was allegedly marked by more bullet holes from guards shooting into D block than other cells.

I asked a National Park Ranger to open the utility access corridor behind D block. D block was the segregation block, walled off from the main cell house. It frequently held a score or more of aggressive, escape–prone, violent, sometimes irrational convicts—and Stroud lived there the first six years he was on Alcatraz.

Think of a cell block as three stacked strips of metal boxes. The utility access corridor is the backstage of the cell block. It lies between the back of those cells and a wall separating segregation from the main cell house. From the catwalk you can climb a ladder to the top of the cell block.

In '46, nine seriously–injured prison officers had been captured by six armed, would–be escapists and were locked in two cells
in the main cell house just outside the segregation door. It was
thought by others that the armed convicts were holed up in segregation, and guards were outside the building shooting point–blank
into D block. Later, grenades were launched. The assault continued
for twenty or thirty hours—despite that many prisoners in segregation were uninvolved.

Stroud later testified that his cell was singled out for bombard-
ment. "A boat pulled out in the bay about half or three quarters of
a mile," he said. "The man was watching me with binoculars. And
they started firing some kind of explosive grenade in my cell."

It didn't make sense that they'd be shooting at him.

He'd killed a guard at Leavenworth, but it'd been thirty years.
Other prisoners on Alcatraz had killed officers; Rufus "Whitey"
Franklin, for one. It didn't appear that they aimed at his cell. Nor
was Stroud as famous as he would become. He was known among
prison officers for his unusual Life sentence and his privileges, and
among bird lovers for his two books. He was cantankerous, bitter
and considered an agitator. But those weren't reasons enough to
warrant such a deadly response.

As we walked along the mesh metal catwalk—Stroud's was the
second to the last cell on the top tier—we stopped at the back of each
cell and flashed the light. Although they had long since been
plugged up, bullet holes were clearly visible—perfectly round,
pencil–sized punctures with powerfully curled, charred edges. We
flashed the beam against the wall. Slugs which had penetrated the
sheet steel had grazed the concrete. It must have been terrifying in
those steel boxes with a violent storm of bullets and grenades
ricocheting around their heads. But there weren't many bullet holes;
half the cells had one or two. Some didn't have any.

We moved down, counting the few bullet holes along the way,
and closed in on the last two cells.

As we stood at the back of cells 41 and 42, it was sobering. We
counted a *score* of bullet holes. And the concrete behind those cells
was as chipped and pummeled as the moon's surface. We climbed

a ladder to the top of the cell block and flashed the light up there. The walls were riddled with bullet holes.

Perhaps as many as fifteen or twenty more.

Clearly a fusillade of bullets was concentrated in that corner. There were more than a dozen windows into which officers could aim their shots. Yet many of them had aimed in that particular corner.

The bullet holes told me one thing: it was an explicit statement that not all bitterness from behind prison walls raged from convicts. But it said something else too. Somehow Stroud had collected more enemies among men who knew him and more admirers among those who didn't than any prisoner I ever heard about.

It was as if he wore a different face for each person.

He wrote later that officials were using this escape "as an excuse for liquidating all the men in D block, and my name headed the list." But it also seemed as if he had cast prison administrators in the role of his father, who had wanted him dead.

Ultimately, those bullet holes became a symbol. In the years after 1946, Robert Stroud would become the most famous federal prisoner in America, "a genius," who was clearly rehabilitated, whose scientific achievements had proven it, and who clearly wanted to get out of prison.

And the bullet holes were tiny punctures in that well-crafted image.

                                    ❧   ❧

Part I
Grand Illusion

Robert F. Stroud grinned for photographers on a warm, late April day in 1962. He stood outside a Kansas City, Missouri courthouse during one of his last public appearances. The Burt Lancaster movie, *Birdman of Alcatraz*, was just being released, and curiosity about the real Birdman was at an all–time high.

At seventy–two, his face was white—not pale—*white*, and he was completely bald. He weighed one-hundred–and–thirty–eight pounds and looked frail and gaunt and elderly—not like a killer. His delicate, wire rim glasses made him look intelligent and sage, like Mahatma Ghandi. When he smiled, he looked like an impish old grandfather whose only desire was to play with his grandchildren, and relax. His escorts, U.S. Marshalls, were solicitous, keenly aware that they were with a legend. Despite that, Robert Stroud was handcuffed.

As he walked into the courtroom surrounded by his entourage, all eyes were drawn to them. For some, it was difficult to pick him out; slowly it dawned on them that he was the old man in the ashen face and the big suit. There was something ironic about his appearance. Strangely enough, with his hawked nose and his head hunched forward, he actually looked like a buzzard. As he sat down at the table with his back to the crowd, his skinny neck and bald head looked like the neck and head of a newly–hatched, naked bird. Although some may have chuckled about it, others were genuinely disappointed: he didn't look like Burt Lancaster.

Sitting in the court room that day was writer Thomas E. Gaddis and his wife, Martha. Gaddis had never seen Robert Stroud until this moment. For the last decade, however, he had been personally involved in Stroud's life, writing the book, *Birdman of Alcatraz*, from which the movie was taken. While the bailiff was occupied, Gaddis was summoned by one of Stroud's attorneys, Stanley A. Furman, and he quickly walked to the plaintiff's table. Fifty-four years old, impeccably dressed—almost dapper—Gaddis was idealistic and something of a raconteur. A former probation officer in Los Angeles, he had quit his job to write the book. To some in the government, he was making a living from Robert Stroud's plight. He received royalties from the book and movie, and was emotionally involved in getting Stroud released. The summer of 1962 he would participate in news conferences around the nation to promote the movie. Tom Gaddis was in deep. He would even write a dissertation about Stroud for a doctor of education degree.

Gaddis was thrilled to be meeting his hero. The old man turned, flashed a smile and quickly said, "I know who you are." Gaddis was astounded, his daughter, Phyllis E. Gaddis, said later. Although the bailiff quickly shooed him away, the author revered the moment as "almost romantic."

By 1962, the Birdman of Alcatraz had been in prison for fifty–three years and was the most famous prisoner in America.

Convicted originally of killing a man in 1909, he then fatally knifed a prison guard in 1916 for which he got Life in solitary confinement. Despite that the sentence was illegal, Stroud was forced into permanent segregation without a job—a status he held for the next forty–three years. During most of those years at the U.S. Penitentiary at Leavenworth, Kansas, prison authorities allowed him to keep canaries to occupy himself, which led to his study of bird care.

From those days in the 1920s, Stroud's fame as the "bird doctor" had steadily grown. At first he was only known to a small national audience of bird lovers. Then in the 1930s a couple of influential newspapers printed the story of the convict who raised canaries in his cell, calling him the "canary prisoner." Stroud became known equally as well for his Life in solitary confinement sentence.

The convict's accomplishments *were* remarkable. His first book, *Diseases of Canaries*, 1933, was the first pet bird disease book published in the United States. His second, *Stroud's Digest on the*

Diseases of Birds, 1944, was a four–hundred–and–eighty–four page tome on every aspect of bird care. Illustrated with eighty–six of his own drawings, Stroud's *Digest* seemed to be stunning proof that the prisoner had spent his time well.

After two decades of bird–breeding, and running a research lab and a mail–order business from his cell, the prisoner's birds were suddenly snatched up and he was quickly transferred to the U.S. Penitentiary at Alcatraz. Although situated beautifully in the center of San Francisco Bay, Alcatraz was the nation's maximum security federal prison. Stroud was again placed in segregation. Later, for an eleven–year stretch in the prison hospital he was maintained in *isolation*.

Although Stroud was actually the "Birdman from Leavenworth," he resided on Alcatraz when author Gaddis heard about the Bird-man and began researching his life story. Thus Gaddis was pro-vided with one of the most memorable book titles of the century—*Birdman of Alcatraz*. Published in 1955, the book became a best-seller, and gave Robert Stroud a wide, national audience.

Numerous articles followed Gaddis' bestseller. In 1957 the prestigious magazine *Scientific American*, quoting Gaddis, cited Stroud's "distinguished career in the study of bird pathology," despite living "in solitary confinement longer than any other pris-oner in the Federal prison system." *Newsweek*, in 1958, wrote about the rehabilitation of Robert Stroud "from convicted murderer to eminent scientist," stating that officers "were under strict orders" not to talk to him. The public became increasingly aware of him. Prominent articles followed in *Life* magazine and newspapers throughout the nation.

Titles like the "The Strange Saga of the Caged Birdman" or "The Agony of the Caged Birdman" offered up drama and pathos. Gaddis even got a little carried away. "[Stroud] faced the prospect of isolation unto death," he wrote in *Coronet* magazine, "which has turned prisoners into human vegetables."

In 1959, Stroud was transferred to the Medical Center for Federal Prisoners at Springfield, Missouri. Although he was still on close custody, he was out of isolation, and actually living quite contentedly in a unit with other men.

Three years later, in 1962, the baton of publicity was handed to Hollywood. Actors Burt Lancaster and Karl Malden, who starred in the movie, *Birdman of Alcatraz*, held press conferences in cities where the movie opened—sometimes with Gaddis, and Stroud's lawyer, Stanley A. Furman. They were selling the movie, the book and the man. Lancaster was said to speak "almost in grief of the fifty–two years Stroud has spent in prisons, forty–three of them (believe it or not) in solitary confinement."

The public latched onto the phrase "solitary confinement," thinking that Stroud seldom saw another human face and was prohibited from talking. Most were unaware that Stroud was no longer in Alcatraz.

Millions flocked to see the movie.

In the first scene, shackled convicts are being transported to the penitentiary at Leavenworth, Kansas, in an over–heated, poorly–ventilated train car. Lancaster, playing Stroud, his face set in angered indignation, smashes a window for a little air, and the cons rise up and cheer, thus setting the tone for the entire movie.

The film quickly dispenses with Stroud's second killing, of the prison guard, and focuses on his long, drawn–out sentence. It's the story of a rebellious convict who pulls himself up from a third–grade education into a veterinary pathologist—from inside his tiny cell. Telly Savalas' character, Vito, an impulsive, street–wise but dumb convict, is designed to lend dignity to Lancaster's portrayal of Robert Stroud. "What a face—like a pan full of worms," Vito says in thick Brooklynese about a woman he once knew. "Stacked? She would make your tongue hang out."

Lancaster is kind and caring. In one astonishing scene the camera focuses for two minutes on a nest of five eggs as one egg rocks, then cracks open. Finally, a naked baby canary flounders out of its shell. "Vito," Lancaster calls out, "you're a grandfather!"

Time is truncated now, and Stroud is seen with scores of cages lining his cell walls. He courageously battles unknown bird diseases—and loses. A prison doctor tells him there are no known cures and Stroud becomes frantic. Even his first bird—a sparrow he found in the prison yard—dies. Formerly grudging guards are saddened.

Then, one by one, Stroud cures those diseases—aspergillosis, avian septicemia, avian diphtheria, even fowl paralysis. The movie doctor calls him a "genius" who taught himself "hematology, histology, anatomy," a man "who knows more about pathology and bird anatomy than any man alive."

Suddenly, Stroud has aged gracefully, transformed into a patient, immaculate, wizened scientist.

There's family. Thelma Ritter plays Stroud's mother, Elizabeth, a determined, jealous woman with whom Stroud is unusually preoccupied, yet who ultimately rejects him over another woman, Stella Anderson. Stella (played by Betty Field) falls in love with Stroud, helps him sell his bottled bird remedies, then dutifully bows out when the self–sacrificing prisoner orders her not to follow him when he's transferred two–thousand miles to Alcatraz. ("I could get some spy glasses and look at your cell," she protests.) It's the stuff of which the 1950s were made.

Although aggressively bitter in the beginning reels, Stroud's defiance is lifted to righteous indignation. He has one enemy in the movie—not himself, not the prison guards—but the Bureau of Prisons, portrayed symbolically by Karl Malden. "You rob prisoners of the most important thing in their lives," he yells at Malden in a core scene, "their individuality!"

As the movie ends, Stroud is transferred to the Medical Center for Federal Prisoners in Springfield, Missouri. He appears nonchalant, even amused and humble despite his forty–some years in "solitary confinement." Edmund O'Brien, (who, as author Thomas E. Gaddis, narrates the film) meets the old man. In the movie, Robert Stroud is obviously rehabilitated. Yet, over a view of Alcatraz, a tag line announces that he is still in prison.

The Birdman *of Hollywood* made supporters of everyone. It was a prison classic. It even may have had a subtle, psychological influence over the fate of Alcatraz—which shut down the next year. But its influence for Robert Stroud was immeasurable.

He had been transformed from a multiple killer to a genius and an avian pathologist who had discovered and cured thirteen bird diseases. Perhaps as many as *one-hundred thousand* people signed petitions in 1962 asking President John F. Kennedy to release the Birdman from prison. They assumed that his intellectual achievements proved he was rehabilitated.

Thousands of others wrote letters to officials asking for the release of the Birdman. "I have seen the *Birdman of Alcatraz* three times," one woman wrote, "and each time I see it, I'm more compelled to plead for freedom for Robert Stroud."

"I wish you would release the Birdman of Alcatraz," another reasoned, because "he appears too old to commit crimes any more."

Nearly everyone was moved by the celluloid version of the Birdman's story. Among them was a young man fresh out of law school, Richard M. English, who was so impressed that he located Stroud's attorney, Stanley A. Furman, and offered his services pro bono. English served on Stroud's legal team the last eighteen months of his life. "He was completely rehabilitated," English said from his home years later. "He would have been no danger to society whatsoever."

English wasn't talking about Burt Lancaster. He was talking about the Robert Stroud he'd met face–to–face.

The people in the courtroom that April day in 1962 would have agreed with the young lawyer. But for different reasons. They had *only* seen the movie or read Gaddis' book. That Birdman had authority, integrity and moral seductiveness.

The courtroom was crowded with people standing at the back and in the aisles. U.S. District Court Judge William H. Becker took his seat at the bench and looked around. He gazed at the old man, his attorneys, the government lawyers and beyond, at a room full of curious people. He struggled to look impassive. "There were many women who were obviously from the bird–loving fraternity," he wryly commented later. "A lot of them had hats on with stuffed birds mounted on them."

Judge Becker called the room to order.

The question of whether Stroud was to be released from prison was not the issue at this hearing. Stroud had gone to court claiming that prison authorities were interfering in his attorney–client privilege. He alleged that the federal Bureau of Prisons had intercepted his letters to his attorneys; that they refused to allow him to negotiate a revision of his book, *Stroud's Digest on the Diseases of Birds;* and had forbidden his attorney from negotiating the revision. He also claimed that the BOP wouldn't let him publish a third book he had worked on for more than a decade, his lengthy manuscript on prison history.

Stroud wanted to show that the Bureau of Prisons had woven a net of interference and persecution around him since 1920, when he had been given his Life in solitary confinement sentence.

This court appearance, and two others in March and November of 1963, were Stroud's last; he was entering his fifty–fourth, and final, year in prison. In the courtroom, in fact, stood a slowly dying man.

As he walked to the witness stand, you could have heard a pin drop. All eyes were riveted on the ghost–like presence known as the Birdman. He put his hand on the Bible and his voice could be heard clearly throughout the courtroom. Stan Furman began to question him.

Furman was a courtly, impish, real estate attorney in his mid–forties. Initially he had represented Gaddis, when Stroud sued him over a breach of contract involving the *Birdman of Alcatraz* book. Like everyone, Furman became intrigued with Stroud's life story, and when the suit was settled, he began representing Stroud.

The old man had lots of lawyers over the years. Often his relationships with them were contentious, especially as he grew older and felt more familiar with the law. During the seven years of their relationship, Furman had represented Stroud at several parole hearings, two executive clemency attempts and two suits and their appeals. Although Stroud was still in prison, the lawyer had won him several important judgments. They both felt clemency was still possible. Their relationship was animated, cordial.

"Stroud was having the time of his life," Furman said later. "He was enjoying the publicity, and finally getting somewhere."

In the courtroom Furman asked about the letters written to his attorneys which Springfield authorities had returned. He asked about his manuscript on prison history. The bald, angular old man responded in a strong voice. His answers were articulate and straightforward; he was obviously intelligent. Judge Becker later said Stroud appeared modest and plain spoken. Furman felt he was "a man of great pride and sensitivity." The issues in the courtroom that day weren't life–and–death issues; the audience was excited, nonetheless. Their sharp image of Burt Lancaster began to fade, to be replaced by the pale old man now sitting before them.

Furman asked if Stroud wasn't the most important expert in the world on bird diseases. Stroud's reply was candid and matter–of–fact. "No, since the invention of antibiotics, everything I have written has become irrelevant."

Suddenly there was an audible stir in the courtroom; this was not what the audience expected. "You could see the air leak out of all the bird lovers," Judge Becker later said.

But the candor was typical Stroud, who always considered the naked truth to be an excellent defense.

In 1909, for example, after killing a twenty–three–year–old man over a $10 payment to a woman, Stroud marched into the police station and stated, "I shot a man." His supporters later were beguiled by this confession, thinking that his self–defense plea was supported by his honesty. Similarly, after the 1916 murder of a guard in the Leavenworth mess hall, Stroud wrote to his father, "I have never given any reason for doing it, so they won't have much to work on, only that I killed him, and that won't do much good, for I will admit that."

It was what Gaddis called Stroud's "pathological candor."

Sometimes his honesty was comically perverse. In 1961, when Stroud was about seventy years old and before the court on a motion to dismiss his 1918 indictment, he was asked why he wanted to get out of prison. According to U.S. Attorney Wilbur G. Leonard, he "confided to officials of our court that his principle interest in being released was to kill a number of individuals on his list and he had so short a time" in which to do it.

Court officials were stunned. It was not the typical comment of a man who wanted out of prison.

"He got into trouble by *not* being a liar," Furman admitted, chuckling.

And now he was saying that his scientific accomplishments, his research, his cures of septic fever and avian diphtheria—the focus

of the entire movie—was all out–of–date, as if what he had done
didn't matter anymore.

Nobody wanted to hear that. They wanted him to be the
double–murderer who had transformed himself into an eminent
veterinary scientist. Some of them no doubt owned copies of
Stroud's *Digest* and they swore by it. They could no more separate
the myth from the real Robert Stroud, as Stroud once put it, than
"cut a string so that it has only one end."

When interviewed thirty years later Furman hadn't remembered any ladies in the courtroom wearing stuffed bird hats, but
then, his back was to the courtroom audience, and anyway, as he put
it, "I wouldn't dare contradict the judge."

According to Becker, however, who faced the audience, the
sporty ladies in their bird trappings were devastated. "Some of
them didn't come back after lunch," he said.

At recess Stroud ordered raw meat, raw vegetables and a bowl
of tea. When it came, he began to eat, and those around him avoided
staring. The old man picked up food with his fingers and shoveled
it into his mouth. Either he hadn't been given utensils or else had
developed the habit of not using them—no one was sure. He chewed
and talked in a noisy animation. "His table manners were just about
like a boar pig," former Alcatraz officer Bill Rogers had once said.
"He practically got down in his food."

Stroud was apparently unaware on every level of how he
appeared to others. "He'd lived by himself for so long," said
Clarence Carnes, a former Alcatraz prisoner who had been in D
block with Stroud for two years. "His mouth would hang open and
his lips would droop." Morton Sobell, convicted of espionage at the
time of the Ethel and Julius Rosenberg case, agreed. Sobell regularly ate with Stroud at Springfield, adding, "We were usually alone
in the dining room. The other inmates shunned him." Even Stroud
admitted that his table manners were "atrocious."

Despite the public image of a man of immaculate personal
habits, the real Robert Stroud was a slob.

Throughout his life Stroud was rebuked for his personal habits.

Earlier when he had his birds, he had scores of cages in his cell—each filled with single–sex or pair bondings, fledglings, or recovering birds; each requiring daily attention in food, water and sanitation. Birds alighted on his clothes or flew around his cell, defecating frequently. Ashes and cigaret butts, water, seed shells and bird droppings littered his cell floor. Books, pamphlets and magazines were strewn about; he had seed in bulk, a microscope with slides, papers with drawings, and dead birds on which he performed autopsies. He was sloppy and careless when experimenting with sulphur, dyes and iodines. His cell was difficult to inspect, unsanitary, and according to officers, sometimes stank.

Officers frequently battled with him to clean up but Stroud could have cared less. At least one doctor at Leavenworth blamed a serious bout of pneumonia on his unsanitary living conditions.

He was no better at Alcatraz, or at Springfield, where he accumulated papers and note pads and smuggled food into his room.

In many ways Stroud didn't resemble the heroic movie portrait. He was far more eccentric, for example, and overly concerned about his bodily functions. Because of his two decades of medical research and his long self–absorbed years at Alcatraz, he often demanded food prepared to his specifications, based on his own medical diagnosis. He drank bowls and bowls of tea to avoid uremia, of which doctors could find no evidence.

For years he claimed he had Bright's Disease—in 1915 he petitioned for a commutation because he claimed he wouldn't live out his sentence. He lived. And doctors later saw no evidence of it. He demanded medicines for other illnesses of which there was no basis. Doctors found no evidence of "nephritis," "gout," "hyperthyroidism," "pellagra," or "other diagnosis he had in the past made on himself."

When Stroud felt ignored, he became petulant, and complained to the Bureau of Prisons in Washington, D.C.

"Within the last six months his complaints have been confined to his teeth, stomach and kidneys," reported one Alcatraz doctor in 1950 to the BOP director in a long memo detailing Stroud's health issues. "Concerning his kidney complaints, it may be said that they were bizarre and confusing and did not follow any set pattern."

It would have been comic, if it weren't so tragic. He frequently battled himself into a corner, as if to justify his victimization.

About his teeth, he had complained to Washington that the Alcatraz dentist refused to make him a denture. When queried, the warden explained in a memo that the dentist couldn't fit the denture until Stroud had a tooth removed—which he had refused.

It was a ruse he often employed.

Stroud was disdainful of the doctors and medical technical assistants who worked at Leavenworth, Alcatraz and Springfield; he felt he knew more than they did and derided them when they didn't find evidence of his diagnoses. They in turn, were sarcastic. In one memo, the chief medical officer and a physician called over from the U.S. Marine Hospital reported examining Stroud at Alcatraz: "Showed a 61–year–old white male, complaining of epigastric pain radiating up the right shoulder and left flank pain which HE says is pyelitis. His urine is not cloudy, however, and he has had no fever."

Prevented from reasoning with Stroud, who could have a massive angry determination, doctors gleefully noted his shortcomings. Stroud attempted suicide at Alcatraz in 1952. In a report, Chief Medical Officer Dr. Meltzer wrote, "With his usual egotism he pronounced that he intended to cut his femoral arteries and accomplish a rapid exsanguination, however, Stroud's knowledge of anatomy is . . . deficient . . . and he did not come anywhere near cutting any major vessel."

Besides wrongly diagnosing his own complaints, officers felt Stroud had other bizarre ideas. He shaved his entire body—the real reason why he was bald—and did so weekly for at least a dozen years.

In fact, the man who returned to the courtroom for two subsequent hearings on March 28, and November 7, 1963, in no way resembled the tidy, buttoned–down actor in the movie.

In the movie Burt Lancaster portrayed Stroud as abnormally preoccupied with his mother and in love with Stella Anderson. In real life Stroud was preoccupied with his mother, but he was clearly, preferably homosexual.

That was far too brazen for the times. While homosexuality still hasn't reached full acceptability today, it was a much more shocking concept to most Americans in the 1960s. Culturally, 1962–63 was still in the '50s—the days of J. Edgar Hoover, when, ironically, to be a homosexual was "subversive," and subject to job dismissal. Careers were ruined on the mere rumor of homosexuality.

Even in prisons, where same–sex relations were common, authorities battered men with labels like "homo" and "deviant."

The U.S. Parole Board in 1962 viewed Stroud's homosexuality *second only* to the possibility of his getting involved in another serious crime as a reason why they wouldn't parole him. Such an attitude reflected the public's fear and ignorance. "He was just a homicidal homosexual," a prison officer once spat out, as if the two were equal. Worse, in the eyes of some personnel who only saw homosexuality in the context of heterosexual bonding, Stroud took the female role. He was a "catcher" in prison parlance; not a pitcher, but a catcher. To them it meant he wasn't even a man.

Stroud's sexual preference didn't come up much in Gaddis' book or the movie, or the press conferences held across the country to advertise the movie and promote sympathy for the prisoner. When his homosexuality was revealed, supporters made sure it fell within the context of poor prison management and a what–do–you– expect defense. In fact Stroud had been homosexual all of his life. Writing in the third person, as he often did, he claimed that he "was ravished at the age of eleven by a circus roustabout,

> *Whom, when it was over, he thanked, saying that his only regret was that it had not happened at a much earlier age and immediately sought out a boy of like tendency but more aggressive who had previously sought his cooperation on a number of occasions.*

Stroud was ahead of his time; he was not ashamed of it like you were supposed to be. He was an advocate, and among prisoners who tolerate homosexuality to a wider degree, that was an embarrass- ment. But Stroud crossed over every line. He proudly called himself a "pederast," a man who prefers sex with boys. Among prisoners who place children on a sacred pedestal, that was an outrage.

Apparently, he seldom missed an opportunity to tell everyone how good it really was. Philip R. Bergen, former Alcatraz officer, who maintained a cautious respect for Stroud, felt on more than one occasion even he was propositioned.

"Stroud was such a floozy," Bergen quipped.

The old man actually had very few opportunities, given his forty–three years in segregation—he didn't cell with others, didn't go to the yard or shower with them, and didn't have a prison job. His actual experience was limited to his early years, 1909 to 1916, and his last years, 1959 to 1963, at Springfield.

Only two years before the Becker hearing, when Stroud was seventy years old, he was caught naked in preparation for an act of sex with a much younger male inmate at Springfield. People didn't know whether to be more shocked by his age or his nakedness. Reports stated that he readily admitted he was about to do it, and that it was his idea. When he was taken before the associate warden, the old rapscallion repeated that it was his idea.

Officials were anxious to suppress Stroud's two–thousand page manuscript on prison history because some of it contained descriptions of sex between men. Worse, Stroud even had a terrific, unabashed flair for description. "A little blond, wavy–haired, dimple–cheeked darling that had not yet had his first shave," he wrote about a prisoner early in his life, "sweet enough to hang on the Christmas tree."

In another passage he wrote, "Albert was by no stretch of the imagination a good looking boy while he had his clothes on. He worked with the writer in the tailor shop in 1915. He had protruding teeth, a rough, homely face blotched with acne, and a reputation of being one of the most brazen prostitutes in the prison, so the writer did not give him a tumble."

While prison authorities were not responsible for Stroud's sexual proclivities, they did aide and abet his pornographic writing. Think of it—Stroud had already written two books on avian diseases while occupied at Leavenworth. At Alcatraz his bird business was finished and he held no job for almost seventeen years. So he wrote reams of stories—some pornographic. In isolation, fantasy is often the only outlet; Stroud's drive pushed him to write down those fantasies. In a sense, the Bureau forced him into the corner, then condemned him for being there.

They refused to see that, however. In the Becker hearings, the government attached a short story written by Stroud as an example of an "indescribable piece of filth." In it, Stroud portrayed two brothers, aged nine and fifteen, engaging in a tough bout of Saturday morning sex, ending in coitus. Homosexual prose was underground in those days; very little involved incest and kids. In 1962, it would not have set well with the ladies in the courtroom. Or the public. By introducing a short story involving homosexual childhood incest prison officials hoped to suppress the entire manuscript.

Although the Bureau of Prisons was acting on its mandate to protect the public, there were other reasons as well. In prison, sex between violent men frequently ends in killing. Some cons operate on a if–I–can't–have–you–I'll–kill–you mode. Prison authorities could do little to stop it and preferred keeping it out of the public trough to avoid criticism. Secondly, Stroud had already murdered two men in trivial arguments. No one knew if he would kill again but he was an aggressively defiant man with a short fuse. In his writings not a hint of regret existed. It wasn't just the homosexuality, or the fact that Stroud was focused on adolescent boys. He had proven to be a predator. In a chilling passage describing sex with others when he was a teenager, he wrote, " . . . all boys on the road did as the writer suggested."

The Bureau did not want that immortalized.

Yet, in their paternalism and fear, and their attempt to keep Stroud from the limelight, they overlooked their best weapon: Stroud himself.

Stroud's writing had punch, energy and humor, and he could sound reasonable. "The man who can fight his battles with a typewriter and printing press does not have to use a battle axe or stiletto, and to do so is stupid," he wrote. "It is often possible to hurt a man more by making him publicly ridiculous than by chopping his head off, and it is not nearly so messy."

But his blunt reasoning was a foil, like the righteous indignation Burt Lancaster portrayed to make you forget he had killed two men. Stroud *had* used a "stiletto." He had used a gun on an unarmed man. Interspersed between observations about prison life, his birds and comments from his personal philosophy, there were bleak, manic repetitions of sexual encounters, and callous remarks about his killings. In other less reasonable words, he could also say he "blew his brains out," or admit that he "kept knives within easy reach of my hand. . . "

He could say, as he did in a letter about a business proposition, that he liked "to deal with all the cards on the table, face up, where I can give a split–second 'yes' or 'no' to any proposition, even one involving life and death, and many times in my life I've been called up[on] to do just that."

Considering that he had killed twice, his comments were cold, high–minded and remorseless.

"Hell, they didn't want Robert Stroud pardoned," said former Alcatraz prison officer Joseph Landers. "They wanted Burt Lancaster pardoned."

Perhaps the people in the hats, whom Judge Becker said didn't return after lunch, began to get an inkling that all was not what it had seemed. That the grizzled old stick of a man who wrote pornography about pre–pubescent boys was not quite the portrait they had come to expect. And just suppose, that if they had been able to go to all three Becker hearings in 1962 and '63, and if they had read the complaints and the supplemental complaints and the government's response and their attachments (and if they could have stayed awake through all of that), they might have seen not just one face of Robert Stroud, or the other, but the full tableau. They might have seen that here was a man with a pretty large ego— *a very large ego, in fact*—who relished a fight more than the outcome. A man who needed to fight in order to stay alive. A man who needed someone on whom to focus his wrath.

That person—who was not present at the proceedings but very much a part of the accusations—was the director of the Bureau of Prisons, James V. Bennett—Stroud's arch enemy.

To Stroud, Bennett was a "bureaucrat," an epithet to be spit out like overworked chewing tobacco. He called him "one of the most vacuous and shallow–minded executives it has ever been [my] misfortune to meet." Stroud's ability to turn a phrase increased a notch when he disliked someone. Later, by inference, he called Bennett "a bureaucratic nincompoop as free from original ideas as a frog from hair."

Bennett was a powerful man in Washington. By 1962, he'd headed up the Bureau of Prisons for a quarter of a century, serving under four presidents. Not a physically impressive man, he was five foot seven, had a weak chin, splayed feet and a Howdy–Doody appearance. But he almost single–handedly organized the entire federal prison system in his thirty years as director, and his grip on his appointment was second only to J. Edgar Hoover's.

Stroud and Bennett had a history of butting heads. In 1931 when Stroud was deep in his Leavenworth bird breeding business, the newly–organized Bureau of Prisons issued an order prohibiting businesses by prisoners. Stroud and his mother fanned a grass roots letter-writing campaign to embarrass the Bureau into backing down. Bennett, then assistant director, was dispatched to negotiate with Stroud and returned in humiliating defeat. A few years later, in 1937—the same year Stroud was first eligible for parole—Bennett became director.

Thereafter, for the rest of his life, Stroud toyed with the director's authority. Bennett made the rules. Stroud broke them. Bennett carried out Stroud's segregated status. Stroud used it to whip up wide public support. Bennett silenced prisoners to reporters—to stop the dime–store sensationalism. Stroud got Burt Lancaster to star in a film about his life.

By 1962, Stroud's supporters felt that Bennett had become personally caught up in a powerful grudge.

Indeed, Bennett was the keystone to the government agencies—the offices of the Parole Board and the Pardon Attorney, the federal courts, even the Executive Office—that kept Stroud behind bars.

"I spent some two–and–a–half hours with Mr. Bennett," Attorney English commented in 1991. "He was a very nice man. I'm sure he was generally a progressive man. . . . And [he] listened to my pitch. But it went in one ear and out the other. . . . He was *never* going to let this man out of prison—alive. And he won."

English was right. Bennett was not about to recommend release because of a sentimental book. In 1958, Stroud's attorneys initiated a petition for executive clemency, and Bennett's response to the U.S. Pardon Attorney was bureaucratic in tone;

Personally, I would raise no objection to the commutation of his sentence, but I do think there are many other life termers in our institutions who are far more deserving of relief than Stroud and who I feel sure would live out their days much more usefully if released. Until some action is taken in their cases I could not recommend Stroud's release.

By the time of the Becker hearings, all the big issues in Stroud's unusual life had been fought—he'd been saved from the gallows; he'd gained permission to publish his books; he'd been released from his lengthy segregation; and his dream of a movie about his life had finally been realized. This hearing, in all of its pettiness, was the end of a lifetime of acrimony between the prisoner and the Bureau. It was not their finest hour—Bennett's or Stroud's—but their final, niggling hour.

At the core of Stroud's complaint was a motion to prohibit the government from interfering in his attorney–client rights.

Furman believed that a pattern of interference had been going on for years. They attempted to show the Bureau's interruption and confiscation of Stroud's mail to his attorneys, Bennett's under-handed maneuvering during a court case involving a Constitutional protection and the deliberate use of misinformation by the Department of Justice.

But the flashpoint became Stroud's *Digest* revision. Stroud believed that if he could reissue his book along with the Burt Lancaster movie, he would realize a lot of money. Although Bennett permitted the revision, he hedged his approval by allowing Stroud to negotiate with only one publisher. Stroud had two publishers on the string for over two years. When the approved publisher dropped off, he focused on the second publisher and brought in Furman to negotiate. Bennett curtly removed Furman from the negotiations and had Springfield authorites return Stroud's mail.

In Becker's court room, government attorneys charged that Stroud had no intention of revising his manuscript, and that his negotiations only served to delay revising it. "He has never so much as put pen to paper," the government lawyer wrote, arguing that Stroud had spent his time negotiating "the sale of rights to something which does not exist."

The attorney had a point. Stroud's plan for revising the four–hundred–and–eighty–five page medical veterinary book was simplistic. He expected to take ninety days to revise it, tearing out each page, taping it to a sheet of legal–sized paper and correcting it in pencil along the margins. Never really a good scientist, by 1962, Stroud was hopelessly out of touch with veterinary medicine. He spent two years negotiating on a book he erroneously thought he could revise in ninety days.

Although this was the crux of his case, during the course of the hearings, Stroud introduced several new complaints. "My motion is so drawn that we can easily broaden the issue," he had written earlier to Furman. "I am sure this thing will be bigger than you ever dreamed."

At his second hearing he attempted to challenge his two homicide convictions which had occurred almost a half a century earlier. When that failed, he alleged cruel and unusual punishment as a legal basis with which Judge Becker could dismiss his sentence. Becker overruled, writing that Stroud's treatment at the Springfield Medical Center for Federal Prisoners was "much more gentle and kind than a convict could ordinarily expect." Stroud accused the Bureau of Prisons of holding to arbitrary, vague standards regarding approval of his manuscript on prison history. He argued that he should be allowed to read Gaddis' book about himself. He alleged that he had been the "victim of defamation" and "invasion of privacy by Bob Hope; Bob Hope Enterprises, Jack Benny and NBC" because of an apparent skit that had aired, and he believed his right to sue would be denied by the Bureau.

The purpose of all this was to confuse, lengthen the proceedings and maintain his public forum. But there was something else going on that was more central to Stroud's personality.

Stroud needed an enemy. It was the challenge that hooked him. One could be either victorious or victimized. Neither outcome mattered much because the battle itself was the intellectual challenge and the emotional charge.

Bennett, however, had become an all-too-willing enemy. From his point of view Stroud was a murderer who had consistently threatened others, whose bird breeding business had been a cover for a moonshine still and who had kited letters and manuscripts in his bird cages. Bennett even kept a prison shiv in his desk—a sharpened steel blade—which he frequently exhibited to reporters claiming that it had been made by Stroud to kill him. He was sick of the book, the movie and the articles—none of which got the facts straight—and sicker still of the minions of bird-brained, letter-writing supporters. And he let it get to him.

From Bennett's perspective, Stroud only wanted to keep his name before the public. Bennett had Stroud's letters returned because he was convinced Stroud's allegations were being passed on to Gaddis, who was deep into a nation–wide campaign to get Stroud out of prison.

In the course of two years of allegations, briefs and three hearings held both in Kansas City and Springfield, Missouri, Judge Becker sorted out the real from the rogue issues and ruled mostly against the Bureau of Prisons.

Ultimately, prison authorities were required to turn over most confiscated correspondence. They agreed to meet with Stroud's attorneys to determine the ground rules for his future relationship with them, to let Stroud read Gaddis' book and to allow Furman to negotiate Stroud's *Digest* revision with the second publisher.

Becker did not rule on the Jack Benny–Bob Hope sling, nor did he overrule the Bureau on their right to approve Stroud's manuscript on prison history prior to publication. In fact, Becker expressed confusion over the status of the extensive manuscript. "In some instances," he wrote, "it was unclear whether the plaintiff had been denied privileges or had assumed they would be denied." It turned out to be the old ruse. Only one copy of Stroud's manuscript existed. He had refused to forward it to Washington without keeping a copy and claimed they had refused to copy it.

Judge Becker separated the two squabblers and authorized a copy made without cost to Stroud. The prisoner could then submit it to the Bureau for their approval.

Stroud walked out of the court room on November 7, 1963, smiling once again. He had fought his battles with a typewriter and had proven that he was treated differently and unfairly. His bitterness was vindicated. He had won one of his only victories.

It was a short–lived victory, however. Ultimately he would not get what he had fought for. Within days, his manuscript on prison history was copied and submitted to Bennett for approval. But it was all he had won—the right to *submit* the manuscript for Bureau approval. Bennett subsequently denied permission to publish.

And while revision of *Stroud's Digest on the Diseases of Birds* was permitted, it was never revised. It was published again, however, and as of 1994 was still available for purchase. (There is one good reason why a veterinary medical book written in the late 1930s, and never revised, is still in print in the 1990s: on the back cover is a picture of Burt Lancaster.)

Instead, within two weeks, on November 21, 1963, one day before the assassination of John F. Kennedy—ironically, the man whom his supporters thought might someday pardon him—Robert Stroud died of a heart attack at age seventy-three.

None of this was anticipated, however, in Stroud's celebratory mood as he stood talking to reporters and photographers the day he left the courthouse a mere two weeks before his death.

Stroud had always shown the world many faces. When he turned one way, he could appear genuine, grimly humorous, even warm; when he turned the other way, he appeared menacing, moody and explosive. Which face was the real Stroud?

A photographer snapped a picture of the smiling old man and it was widely reprinted.

How could anyone who saw that face believe the quiet rumor that Robert Stroud was a sociopath?

ಶಿ   ಶಿ

Part II
The Prevailing Winds

Few photographs exist of Robert Stroud as a boy. One, taken around 1900 when he was about ten years old, has him casually sitting on the stoop of his home. Behind him on the porch stand two women; possibly his mother, Elizabeth, and his next oldest half–sister, Mamie.

The women are dressed in blouses with leg–of–mutton sleeves and long full skirts, and they stare hard and unsmiling at the camera. The kid is smiling, though. In other pictures when Bobbie, as he was called, was this age, he had a doleful expression, prominent ears and a tall, gangly body. But here his lop–sided grin and tousled dark hair gives him an all–boy eagerness and curiosity that seems contagious. Perhaps it's because of the small black dog he holds snug to his side.

Bobbie's oldest half–sister, Minnie, who probably took the picture, stood back to get the whole house in the frame, because that's the real subject of the photograph. The family's new house was a plain, one–story, two–bedroom, one–bath cottage on 22nd Avenue near downtown Seattle, Washington. Built in 1900, it was typical of the hastily–built cottages that accommodated the hundreds of thousands who thundered west after the discovery of gold in Alaska—just as the Stroud family had.

It was tiny. The parents slept in one bedroom with the baby, while the two older girls and Bobbie slept in the other. Or perhaps by now, Bobbie slept on a cot in the living room or in the attic.

Not photographed was his baby brother, Marcus, nor their father, Frank Stroud, who by this time might have been in Alaska seeking his fortune. Nonetheless, the picture was mailed to one of Elizabeth's siblings in Illinois, no doubt to reassure everyone that the Stroud family was doing well out West.

And from the looks of things, the Strouds *were* faring well. Elizabeth had her four children—Minnie, an adult, and Mamie, also approaching twenty, both from a previous marriage; plus twelve-year–old Bobbie and four–year–old Marcus, both of whom were her and Frank's boys. And now they had a home.

Everyone back home knew that Elizabeth was a determined, hard–working woman, a careful, passionately devoted mother to whom respectability meant a lot. In one letter she described a brown dress she had sewn for Minnie, made with a slight train and overskirt drapery, faced with bright red silk and finished with seven rows of machine–stitched red thread. She wrote about Mamie, who was seventeen "but everyone thinks she is fourteen," who had "female trouble" and no longer wanted to go to school because she hated it so. Elizabeth didn't use the term "retarded," but relatives knew something was wrong.

Elizabeth complained modestly that she was "worked to death in a vain struggle to keep my children as presentable as others," and took in sewing to help with the family finances, because "It don't pay to let [the children] feel that they are in any particular [way] inferior to others."

Of course they had troubles typical of any family at the turn–of–the–century. Frank had had typhoid in 1897 and then Baby Marcus came down with a horrible eczema, and Bobbie got typhoid; three years later, they were still trying to recover financially. Then Frank had invested money in some old mines in central Washington which proved to be nothing "but a hole to sink good money." And now he had the Alaska fever.

"I do not anticipate a fortune," she wrote resignedly. "I've almost lost all hopes of ever having any thing but a bare bread and butter existence." Looking at the photograph of the newly pur-chased house, however, it didn't seem like empty cupboards were hidden there.

There were *hints* of problems. In a letter written on New Year's Day in 1900, for example, Elizabeth detailed every item her chil-dren got for birthdays and holidays, and breathlessly remarked at how "foolish" the children were in getting her gifts "to the limit of their pocket books." But she left out Frank's gift list entirely. In fact, when you analyzed it, Frank didn't rate a mention unless it was negative.

And Bobbie? The one she would later call her favorite? Bobbie got one sentence—his gift list—and that was it. Nothing at all. As if she had withdrawn her love out of momentary spite. The baby was the "best looking," Minnie was teaching and liked it, Mamie was so proud of her gold watch. Frank was sending money down a hole. A ten–page, hand–written letter and not a thing about Bobbie.

Nonetheless, that wasn't enough to make an impish, all–boy adolescent, sitting on the stoop hugging his dog, end up a multiple killer.

There had to be something else. You had to tear back the layers of Victorian respectability, look beyond the picture of modest prosperity, and part the curtain of generations in order to see an undercurrent of anger, deceit and abuse that sabotaged all four of Elizabeth's children.

Because it began generations back, like it always does, when accidents of fate and personality fall together and resonate like a tuning fork.

The reverberations were set in motion at the time of the Civil War, when Elizabeth was just three years old.

Her father, John Franklin McCartney, left to join the Union Army, and her mother became increasingly sick and in 1864 died of tuberculosis. Suddenly four–year–old Lizzie and her one–year–old brother, Marcus, were orphaned; the two were farmed out to relatives for several years while the war dragged on and while McCartney went on to law school. Thus, at the age of four, little Lizzie became a surrogate mother to her baby brother—teaching him, protecting him, punishing him. Even then she was described as looking "sober," and why not? She felt abandoned. She never really got over it.

Eventually, McCartney married again, reuniting his two children, and he and his new wife, Minnie, had ten more children. Lizzie, as the oldest, with a lot of child–rearing experience behind her, was now expected to help out with all of her half–siblings. It was a sacrifice of her childhood.

Lizzie's father, Robert Stroud's maternal grandfather, John McCartney, may have been only five–foot–seven–inches tall but he had an imperial bearing and was a proud, remarkable man. A swarthy, tanned Scotsman, with a neatly trimmed, dramatically silver beard, high cheekbones, hooded eyelids and arched eyebrows, McCartney had arrived in Metropolis, Illinois, with only a few cents in his pocket and had become a prominent lawyer.

Metropolis is known for being the fictional setting for *Superman*. In the last half of the nineteenth century, McCartney was probably the nearest thing to Superman the town ever had. He owned and published two newspapers at various times and founded several banks. He ran for political office, campaigning on radical issues—that black men should have the vote, for example, and that females as well as males were entitled to higher education. McCartney was opinionated and judgmental. He hated liquor and was an early member of the Prohibition Party. Naturally, such an outspoken, political lawyer had enemies. There were rumors that he made his money off pension–seeking war widows. He was easily goaded into fist fights and legal suits. In one delicious slander in 1869, he was described by a political rival as "slouching around in all his greasy vanity." Eventually he became so successful that he bought several hundred acres of lovely farmland and built a five–story, twenty–three room brick mansion for his wife and twelve children. When he died in 1908, his estate was said to be worth more than a million dollars.

Vane or not, McCartney was revered, respected and perhaps feared by his children. He was demanding, especially to those children who were not properly submissive. And Elizabeth, who was the first born and had already learned self–reliance in the face of hardship, as one of her cousins once said, "was a headstrong young woman."

Indeed, she had become a charming, coy, always socially polite, iron–willed, dominating woman. She had been given the task of caring for others without recognition and she continued refining this role the rest of her life. The woman who would one day persuade the President of the United States to commute her boy's death sentence, had learned early to manipulate and use guilt to up the ante. She had had eleven little brothers and sisters on which to practice, and no doubt her sense of entitlement clashed with her father's will.

She had mixed feelings about McCartney. Eventually she drummed into her own children's heads that they had come from proud McCartney stock. Indeed, Stroud often bragged about him. But she also carried a bitter story about him. In Stroud's interpretation, she was "as much a victim as I am." He wrote, "what I really blame and hate is the system and the church th[at] built it and most of all the people who hold it—If it had not made your father a dirty, double crossing, hypocrite—a narrow minded bigot, you never would have been brought up the way you were . . ."

Elizabeth defiantly left home at age nineteen in 1879 and, instead of seeking higher education and against McCartney's wishes, married a thirty–year–old farmer named Henry C. Shaffer. Although she grew up with a highly successful father, she married men of lesser stature and then derided them for not achieving what she thought she deserved. The Shaffer marriage was a disaster; they were quarrelsome and bitter. Nonetheless, they had two children.

Minnie was born in January 1881. She was a pretty, bright, excitable child but sometimes possessed of an other–worldly calm. Mamie Emma, born December 30, 1883, was slow to learn, thin and awkward. She lacked the natural beauty of her older sister. Perhaps in another family or in another era she would have received better attention, but she was mentally disabled, and emotionally scarred as well. Even before she was born, according to divorce papers, Henry Shaffer occasionally struck his wife.

Divorce proceedings began two years after Mamie was born and lasted until she was five and Minnie was eight. Elizabeth charged her husband with adultery and took her two children to live with family and friends. She became a little more convinced that men only betrayed and abandoned women.

Disappointed, socially–embarrassed, with two emotionally fragile children, Elizabeth quickly found another man. Within six months of divorce, on April 25, 1889, she married Frank Stroud.

"I have a distinct recollection of it," Minnie said years later. "It was quite an event."

That wasn't the half of it. The newlyweds moved west within two months of their marriage, and everyone in the Stroud household quickly learned about living with an anxious dread.

"My father was a wastrel scion of a once wealthy and powerful southern family," Robert Stroud wrote in his tense, highly–charged style, "who, through his devotion to slow horses, fast women, and red whiskey had accomplished the financial ruination of his family and reduced himself to the status of a day laborer before meeting my mother."

Robert Stroud's father, Benjamin Franklin Stroud, is a mysterious, shadowy character. We have only Elizabeth's and Robert's comments on their hatred for him, Minnie's skimpy references and almost no demographical or sociological history. It's as if he appears suddenly to traumatize the family and then just as suddenly disappears from the records.

Born in 1858, he may have been the only son of Benjamin and Sarah Stroud, who were either from Indiana or Kentucky. Frank was fickle. He studied briefly to become a doctor, then abandoned that when he became infatuated with a cousin who was studying engineering. When his father died, leaving a large plantation and a "family fortune" in his immature hands, he quit school altogether.

If the story as it came down to Robert Stroud is true, then it's easy to understand why his father spent half his life seeking the easy money. He resembled a riverboat gambler—neatly dressed, handsome, with big ideas and a roving eye. "He was a nice–looking young man when I married him," Elizabeth explained about Frank years later. They impressed each other—Elizabeth with her cast–iron will and emotional pull, and he in turn with his dark good looks, daring sense of adventure, schemes and lies.

The first few months of the new marriage were exciting. Frank swept up his new wife and two girls and boarded the transcontinental railroad for a journey half–way across the country to the frontier town of Seattle, Washington. They shared the same dream—to find their fortune in the new country. It was a real honeymoon.

By then the northwest was experiencing exciting changes.

Less than four thousand people lived in Seattle in 1880, but because of the rail connection and the Alaska gold rush, by the time the Strouds arrived 1889, nearly forty–three thousand people lived there. By 1900 the population would double to more than eighty thousand. Ten years later, two–hundred–and–thirty–seven thousand were in residence. According to family legend, the Strouds arrived two days after the 1889 fire that nearly destroyed the city.

It was a symbolic new beginning for everyone. Frank found a job in the office of a coal mining firm, the girls were placed in nearby schools and Elizabeth set up housekeeping in a rental cottage on 22nd Avenue, just down the street from where they eventually purchased.

But things changed suddenly when Elizabeth discovered she was pregnant with Robert. That meant another mouth to feed. Frank was furious. The dream of quick money faded.

"[He] became very angry and insisted I destroy the unborn babe," Elizabeth wrote to President Woodrow Wilson twenty–five years later. "Because I refused to commit such a crime, his treatment of me the whole period of pregnancy was abusive and insulting in the extreme, keeping me in a state bordering on insanity the entire period."

She was more bold during testimony in 1916 at her son's murder trial.

"He got medicine and insisted on my taking it and he did everything—he knew a great deal more than I did—to destroy this child before it matured," Elizabeth said.

Abortion was illegal then and procedures were not widely known in the staid middle–class. Frank Stroud probably gained what information he knew from talking with prostitutes.

"How long had you been pregnant at that time," asked General Louis C. Boyle, Stroud's defending attorney at the time.

"From the time he first discovered such was the case, at nine weeks on."

"Until when?"

"Until the last three months before he was born. He ceased then."

"During your pregnancy, what was your relations to your husband—I mean sexually. This is a plain matter, you will have to talk up. Did you have sexual relations with him?"

"Oh yes."

"Under what circumstances?"

"Under the most distressing, if I might say."

"How long did that condition continue while you were carry-ing this child?"

One could almost hear the withering disdain: "Whenever I would submit, Mr. Boyle."

Diabolically, Elizabeth and Frank were perfect for one another.

He had a low tolerance for frustration, she could be frustrating. He was attracted to her because of her dependability, but then became the disobeying child. She withheld sex; he got drunk. She could bait. He could beat.

Elizabeth had made another disastrous mistake. Frank Stroud proved to be a chronic alcoholic and physically abusive. "I have a very distinct recollection," Minnie testified later through clenched teeth, "of months on a stretch when he was never sober."

The two parents fought one another, threatened, twisted the children's fears and affections, separated frequently and reunited to play out their individual childhood traumas. In another era she would be called "co–dependent." They remained married for twenty years.

"After these relations ceased during pregnancy," General Boyle would ask Elizabeth in testimony, "then did he cease his conduct in reference to sexual matters?"

"He never, really ceased up until the birth of the child, but whenever he was not gratified he went outside," she replied.

"How do you know?"

"By my own eyes, Mr. Boyle. He brought a woman right into our immediate neighborhood and lived with her."

"What effect did this have upon your mind?"

"Well, very distressing. . . . I was so upset and so worried I told him if he didn't remove her from the neighborhood I would burn them out."

"That was while you were carrying this boy Robert."

"Yes, sir."

Elizabeth delivered her third baby, Robert Franklin Stroud, at home on January 28, 1890, exactly nine months and three days after the two parents were married. Even before birth, Robert Stroud no doubt felt the effects of shame, fury, rage, anguish and violence.

Things did not get better. "When the child was born he completely ignored it," Elizabeth explained later to President Wilson in letters pleading for her son's clemency from the death penalty. For reasons which Frank may not have even understood, he hated and refused to pick up his first–born son.

It was a pre–verbal message the baby got with every breath. Many decades later Stroud wrote (in his typical third–person narrative), "Taught to hate father before he was two years old by the mother repeatedly in his presence accusing the father of wanting him aborted, cursing him at the moment of birth," drumming into his head that he was unwanted, unloved, untouchable.

Predictably, little Bobbie was sickly. He had convulsions while teething, and contracted pneumonia at age two. Elizabeth, who easily shifted her attention to each new baby at the expense of her other children, closed in on the boy and smothered him with care.

"As he grew, the father became abusive toward him and often beat him," she continued in her letters to the President, "and threatened to kill, not only the child, but the entire family, in his drunken frenzy."

Elizabeth blamed her husband. Robert blamed Elizabeth. In truth two deeply disturbed parents clung together and scapegoated this particular child—a pattern that is seen over and over again.

Each parent had a special device for wielding power: with Frank it was chronic verbal attacks, threats, systematic intimidation and severe punishment. It's well established among psychology professionals that abusive fathers often spawn excessively violent sons. In Robert Stroud's case it was more than a passing truth. "He violently hated his father," Stroud wrote about himself later,

and resented the fact that his mother would not take legal action to compel his father to provide for the family or give him carte blanche to do the compelling, which he would gladly have done with a pistol.

Yet current thinking in psychology points to emotional abuse as often more damaging to a child's well–being than physical abuse because it is so invasive and causes such deep, haunting scars. Scars of this type were underway long before Robert Stroud had words to describe them, essentially before memory. And they continued as he got older.

Elizabeth, on the other hand, punished by withholding love and used guilt to manipulate. She forbid certain emotions, isolated her troubled children from normal social interactions, overprotected them and enrolled them in her own bitterness.

"My every thought was tempered by her teachings and prejudices," Stroud was quoted by *Washington Post* reporter Eve Edstrom, "and my life was a series of disasters."

But there was more to it than that. Lots of children grow up in abusive homes and don't become multiple killers. Bobbie lacked an essential ingredient for a kid in a damaging family situation. He had no normal adult role models. Instead, both of his half–sisters were troubled.

By 1900, when he was ten, Minnie was nineteen and already having emotional problems of her own. Relatives have called Minnie's letters "wonderfully imaginative," and a cousin recalled her as "gifted but mentally unbalanced." As a child she saw everything, but in testimony later, she couldn't articulate beyond generalities the disturbing family scenes she witnessed in both the Shaffer and Stroud unions.

She had a difficult relationship with her half–brother most of their lives. Given his increasing defiance, and the scapegoating by his parents, she targeted him without realizing it, and blamed him for much of the family discord. Trained as a teacher, Minnie got out of the house early, and Bobbie was secretly pleased. She eventually married and had two of her own children. When Stroud went to prison she wrote to him occasionally but there is no record of any visits. She finally broke with him, and for several decades they did not correspond.

But Minnie could not escape the effects of twenty years of intense emotional cross–fire. She became increasingly disturbed. In 1932, when she was fifty–one years old, she was committed to a mental institution as a manic–depressive. She never recovered. In 1939 Stroud requested permission to write to her because she was dying of tuberculosis. She died at Western State Hospital in 1941, eight years after being committed.

Mamie, of course, was no help to Bobbie as an adult role model. The seventeen–year–old who acted fourteen was as emotionally disturbed as Minnie. Although most people who remember her only knew her late in her life, it's clear that even in her youth her mental disability only complicated the emotional struggles.

Only one letter from her exists in the Stroud files. Written in 1921 to Warden Biddle at Leavenworth, it underscores her gentle helplessness: "Mr. Bibble, I hope this little note find all well and may wish for a happy Christmas and new year to you and yours and all the offericels and inmates and also the City of Leavenworth [sic]."

Furman remembered conversations with her that descended into babbles. A distant cousin, Howard Faughn, remembers when he was a child that Mamie spoke rapidly, in half sentences. "She stared a lot," he said. "She had that look in her eye." Mamie remained dependent on Elizabeth all of her life, living at home until Elizabeth died in 1938, then hanging on alone in the house in Metropolis—outliving nearly everyone.

Of all his siblings, Stroud cared the most for Mamie; she appealed to his need to protect the unprotected. He wrote to her as if she were capable of fully understanding everything he said. When he received money from the Burt Lancaster movie, Stroud remembered her with a cash gift.

Nonetheless, she was emotionally absent during his childhood.

Bobbie, in fact, grew up in a bunker full of people who were wildly intelligent, mentally deficient, morally adrift and emotionally disturbed. There simply was no normal adult around him. His grandparents were two–thousand miles away.

His teachers were either uninterested, unimpressed or intimidated by his increasingly churlish, distant and defiant nature. "The child was never like other children," Elizabeth admitted, not understanding how she overprotected him. "[He] never cared to play with others; kept to himself and seemed to be brooding."

Little Bobbie Stroud remained outside of normal human contact as if separated by glass.

Yet even that might not have turned a child into a multiple killer.

If you imagine an inverted pyramid with two converging lines representing paternal and maternal bloodlines leading finally to Robert Stroud at the apex, then you begin to grasp what messages fell to him and led to his killings.

Elizabeth was strong and came from proud stock, but she was an obsessive, embittered woman who was also frequently humiliated and abandoned by weaker men. As Bobbie grew, she enlisted him in her hatred, teaching him that men were weak, too sexually driven, threatening and that they ultimately abandoned women.

It's been hinted even by Stroud that he was a victim of incest. True or not, it's sufficient to realize that Elizabeth placed more importance on children than adults—indeed, she held adult males in low esteem. And, to her, children were more important as love objects than adults. Stroud's tendency to seduce boys was simply an acting out of her message.

Elizabeth kept everyone in a state of dependency by accusing them of their shortcomings and then maintaining that only she could save them. When her children didn't perform to expectations, or showed anger or caused trouble, she dismissed them with a cold, calculated silence.

She frequently exaggerated so much that her statements crossed into lies. Although being a divorced woman was a social liability in those days, and referring to oneself as a "widow" is understandable, in Elizabeth's case it had its punitive side as well; it is in fact how she felt about the people she eventually broke with—that they were dead. Years before Frank died, she referred to herself as his widow. And she could get others to perpetuate those lies; during the opening statements at Stroud's third trial in 1918, the defense attorney called Stroud "a widow's son," although Frank would not be dead for ten more years.

More telling, after Elizabeth broke with her son many years later, twice she darkly described herself as the "widow of Robert Stroud."

In other words, when she broke with someone, her tendency was to kill him off.

As to Frank, he conformed to type as Elizabeth presented it. He was a chronic and dangerous alcoholic who beat women and children and who abandoned his family many times. This was undoubtedly a message he got from his own family.

Frank also used deceit and death as a means of banishing people. On his death certificate he is listed as a "widower," although Elizabeth outlived him by ten years.

But more importantly, Frank was childish, jealous, embittered and tyrannical (and Robert Stroud's only male model), a man who frequently threatened to kill his own family, and whose only means of settling disputes was through violence.

Elizabeth promoted the idea that "the only grain of comfort" she could "extract from the crushing disgrace" she and her other children felt because of Robert's killings was the knowledge that her son "was not all to blame but was paying the penalty of his father's sins." Fairly sophisticated stuff in psychological circles in the early 1900s. But it was a denial of her own role in the blame.

Banishment by death was a psychologically acceptable means of disposing of problems. This crucial message was like a tidy little pendulum clicking off killing like clockwork.

Although Bobbie had remained the baby in the family for eight years, by 1898, Elizabeth gave birth to Marcus McCartney Stroud—named after her brother. Marcus was a chubby, dark–haired baby whom Elizabeth felt was precocious and cute. Frank also took a liking to this boy.

Now Bobbie could see how differently he was treated, and he resented it.

Predictably, he reacted to his mother's intense devotion to the baby and his father's new interest by becoming sick. At age ten he contracted typhoid.

Over the next few years a series of long illnesses resulted in a closer association with his mother—a double–edged sword. It's clear she instilled in him a strong conviction of honor, righteousness, a sense of importance and history. She drummed into him an infatuation with honesty. But there was a hitch. Truth could be used to yield to a larger, private morality.

At her knee Bobbie learned the value of emotional manipulation to achieve his life's goal. And increasingly, he began to resist anyone's authority over him—a cancer that drove his psyche and shadowed his entire life.

It didn't take much. Bobbie's intelligence and defiance was all Frank needed to explode.

If the little kid brought home a stray dog, Frank snapped. More mouths to feed. More money. Within minutes the two were into a violent quarrel. Frequently their shouting came to blows. Once after Frank knocked him down, Stroud wrote, he "came up out of the dirt with a rock in each hand. The first one hit him in the chest hard enough to break two ribs. He treated me with respect after that."

About the time Bobbie and the two women were photographed in front of their cottage, he claimed he had already tried to kill his father. He'd also tried to kill himself, writing that he drank "known polluted water" because he knew he wasn't normal.

Marcus, who escaped the worst of the family trauma, later commented on the distinct difference in treatment he got from his father compared with his older brother. There are reasons for this. When Frank became drunk and threatened to harm the boy, Bobbie intervened, and by the time Marcus was six Frank had left the family.

But Marcus had several coping mechanisms typical of a sibling of a violent offender. He watched his defiant older brother end up in violent quarrels with their father and learned to get his way by being compliant and accommodating. It had lifelong consequences.

Throughout his life Marcus always seemed to be searching— changing jobs, working schemes. As a kid he delivered newspapers, then worked in a foundry. In the 1920s he was on the fringe of show business, becoming a Houdini–type vaudevillian known as "The Great Marcus." In the early 1940s he was personnel director in a "radio and television institute," then his letterhead announced that he was Stroud's "agent." In the 1950s he became a general manager of a water softener company and then a salesman. He moved frequently, and over the years resided in Seattle, Washington; Juneau, Alaska; Kansas City, Missouri; Metropolis, Illinois; Los Angeles, California; Chicago, Illinois; Minneapolis, Minnesota;

Sacramento, California; and Honolulu, Hawaii.

Out of embarrassment perhaps, he changed his name to Lawrence Gene Marcus, or L. G. Marcus, and encouraged people to call him Larry. Although no one could remember much about him, a cousin, commented that "We were never fond of him. He was not rated very highly."

His writing was a little befuddled, his focus a little muddied, but he meant well. Much of his early adult life Marcus was pushed around by his older brother, frustrated by Stroud's provocative defiance and largely unappreciated. Their's remained a stormy relationship. Marcus visited Stroud in prison, wrote letters to him, tried to follow Stroud's unending demands, gave him advice that was generally ignored, broke with him, and returned when the publicity geared up in the late 1950s and early '60s.

Marcus didn't show for Robert's funeral in 1963 and sued the estate for his portion of the publication rights. Eventually he lost touch with the family, and died at age seventy–eight in Honolulu, Hawaii, on April 19, 1976. He was survived by a wife but no children; his remains were cremated.

Robert Stroud derided his brother endlessly, and was overheard many times boasting that if he'd been outside in Marcus' shoes, he'd have made a million dollars. When they were kids, however, Stroud protected him. In fact, protecting those who were younger and weaker became a lifelong characteristic of Stroud's, as if he were compensating for his own vulnerability.

As a child Bobbie hated school and, using his frequent nose bleeds and headaches as a reason, would refuse to go.

He was focused, however, and quick, bright and had a good memory. It's been said that he practiced card tricks for hours. He was also self–absorbed, stubborn and a poor listener. Like most kids, he disliked being confined in the classroom. Moreover, he thought he was smarter than most of his teachers. And he could not be dominated. Yet, it's likely his performance didn't match his considerable expectations. His grades didn't match his ego. He was impatient, rough, angry and egocentric.

It was always said that he quit school in the third grade, and this may have been an exaggeration Stroud himself perpetuated to

underscore his high innate intelligence. Because, from what Elizabeth has said, and what Stroud later testified to, he quit at age
thirteen or fifteen, or, as late as seventh or ninth grade.

By then he was regularly hanging out along the Seattle wharves
with longshoremen, sailors and fishermen, day laborers, alcoholics
and prostitutes. At age thirteen he was arrested for larceny. He had
already begun experimenting with sex by then. Sex with boys was
apparently easy; with girls there had to be a condition. He wrote
that he was "unable to function normally with a member of the other
sex unless she became the aggressor." He later testified that he
began having sex with older women at age thirteen.

At fourteen, according to prosecuting attorney Fred Robertson,
he was soliciting business for "women of the underworld."

Then around the age of fifteen, he contracted a malarial–like
disease which left him "very delirious and there was days he laid in
a stupor," Elizabeth said. "Naturally he fell behind in his classes,
and this developed in his quitting school. I could not get him to go
any more.

> *Finally under the advice of the doctor* [Elizabeth con-
> tinued in court testimony], *I sent him out in the country on
> a milk ranch, as we called it. The doctor suggested that
> the association with cattle would be good for him. He
> started growing so much you could see from one Saturday
> night to the other. At the age of fifteen, he had reached his
> present stature. There seemed to be no strength with his
> growth. Just like a weed raised up in the swamps.*

About the same time, 1904–05, Frank Stroud left Elizabeth
and, flaunting social mores, began living with a married woman
named Mary Martin. Elizabeth had been augmenting the family
finances for years by taking in sewing. Now she garnered the wages
of her oldest children.

The separation left Bob, as he now preferred to be called,
"dominated by three women in a household where petty bickering
had become a habit. Naturally I cut out from under as soon as I was
big enough."

Stroud took off. His explosive temper had always been held in check by his mother. But now, away from her, and away from any consistent adult voice, at age fifteen, Stroud became his own man, and began, as psychoanalyst Alice Miller has said, "living out hatred," to ward off the knowledge of his own fate as a victim.

No records exist of this period of his life, but various sources fill in the gaps. In one article many years later, told by a fellow Springfield inmate, Stroud reported that he walked in the snow from Sedro Woolley to Anacortes, Washington, where he got his first lesson on how to scam for food.

Thereafter he began hitching rides on railroad cars.

In 1905, the Metropolis, Illinois, newspaper reported that "Master Robert Stroud" dropped by for a visit. He met his grand-father, who by now was a seventy–year–old doyen of rather stern and illustrious proportions. Given Bob's serious tone, he and McCartney may have gotten along. But Bob was a fifteen–year–old kid with considerable experience, little insight and a great deal of hidden anger; he may have been disturbing.

Worse, for McCartney at least, who believed everyone should get proper schooling and make the most out of his life, Bob was a kid out of school. McCartney was probably dismayed that one of his grandsons—a kid of obvious intelligence and cunning—was tramping around the country instead of in school.

McCartney was no doubt shielded from most of his nephew's thoughts. Bob spent a lot of time with one of his aunts, whom he said was five–foot–seven, two hundred pounds and had never been with a boy. "Had I stayed a little longer," he wrote many years later, "I would have made love to her."

Although none of the remaining eleven aunts and uncles who lived near Metropolis would have said as much to Bob, among themselves, it's likely they talked about Elizabeth's difficulties with husbands and kids. This was the whispered stuff among the adults—their children were only vaguely aware of the talk about their cousin who would one day be the black sheep in the family. "I was married before I knew the man existed," said second cousin Howard Faughn.

When the pressure got to be too much, cousin Bob left Metropolis.

He later wrote that he was arrested after dropping off a freight train, probably about this time, in an unknown southern state, where he experienced his first taste of American prisons. "On the way to jail," he wrote,

> *I saw a chain gang of about thirty barefoot women, clothed in single, thin cotton garments, sweeping the main street under the direction of two male guards, one of them armed with a shotgun and the other one with a revolver on one hip and a coiled blacksnake hooked to his belt and hanging over the other hip. About half of them were white.*
>
> *My second disillusionment came when I reached the jail, which consisted of a large room containing four or five rows of open steel cages. Men were housed on one side, women on the other, and neither had any privacy. There were children in the jail as young as nine years old.*

He met other "bindle stiffs" on the road, hoboes, vagrants, what are today called the homeless. He hopped the freight cars, sometimes sitting in warm cars with other males, or sometimes he'd "blind baggage," a far riskier ride between the engine and the passenger car.

Hopping trains meant stealing food, or working a day for a meal, or begging. It meant uncertainty, adventure, but cold nights in doorways, pissing in alleys; it meant an occasional homecooked meal from a sympathetic woman or a relative, or it meant pork and beans at the county jail.

Somehow the passage of time has given this era a more romantic quality than it deserves. Riding the railroads meant avoiding the "railroad dicks" who'd smirk and invite a kid to jump off a moving train or suffer arrest. There were other hazards. The gangly youth now known as Bob Stroud had the personality of a leader; he was smart, cynical, fascinating and sometimes vicious. Most of the men he met on the road were not as cunning or as wily.

Stroud's visits home were always short. The reunions and separations were painful to Elizabeth and disruptive to the other children.

When back in Seattle for a time, Bob got into more trouble. "Why, myself and another young fellow stole some copper there," he said in testimony later. "It seemed to be the consensus of opinion if they would send me to [Alaska] they would take me away from my associates I was running with . . ."

By 1907 Bob Stroud took a job as a section hand for a railroad building company in Alaska. Elizabeth sent two postcards to her sister in Metropolis that year. The postcard scenes are of Alaska, and she briefly noted that Bob was living "in that frozen country" and "seems to like it." Alaska was still a wild country, just a few years beyond its Yukon gold rush days. Stroud said later that it had "none of the social bonds that exist in the states." He felt that the high population densities in cities forced people into separate "casts" divided by strict social and moral rules. Alaska was free of all that.

He had other reasons to feel free; he testified later that he began taking morphine regularly.

Prison records indicate that he was convicted of larceny in Katella, then moved on to nearby Cordova, along the southern coast of Alaska. Elizabeth Stroud said he met a woman named Kate Dulaney aboard a ship on the way back to Juneau, in the southeast Alaska panhandle. She convinced him to take up residence in Juneau, where he attempted to earn money as a peanut vendor and ran a little "restaurant" chow line.

Stroud contracted pneumonia, and legend has it that Kate Dulaney nursed him back to health. She was older than Stroud— maybe by some twenty years. According to Stroud's own theory, she was the aggressor in the relationship and he was able to have sex with her.

Stroud's "restaurant" didn't pan out. He didn't have enough business, and there was no money for supplies. He began to buy stolen supplies from the railroad stores and authorities suspected that Stroud had organized the fencing himself. Convicted, he served ninety days.

In 1908, John Franklin McCartney died and was saved from the humiliation of his grandson's first murder.

Elizabeth had filed for divorce in 1907, but Frank promised to

move back home and support the family, and the suit was dismissed. He became abusive again, however and remained a few
weeks, then left for good.

Finally, in 1909, Frank filed for divorce, claiming the impos-
sibility of living with Elizabeth because of their different tem-
peraments. Elizabeth filed a counterclaim, citing his adulterous
affair, his drinking to excess and his reluctance to support the
family despite his prosperity as a coal merchant. Indeed, he had
purchased several pieces of property which he kept hidden from her
by placing it in the name of a third party.

In the 1909 decree, Elizabeth got all the property and Frank got
a $50 bill. According to a city directory soon thereafter, she was the
widow of Benj. F. Stroud.

Frank moved to California. He settled in a little town near
Sacramento called Omo Ranch. When he received a request for
financial aid after his son's second killing, Marcus claimed he
refused, muttering, "Let him die." But after Stroud's sentence was
commuted in 1920, Frank wrote to California Representative John
B. Raker. It is the only note by him ever found and a sad testimony
to his own self–esteem. "If it had not been for the help of all of you,"
he wrote on April 23, 1920, "my son would have been buried today
and at any time that I can be of any service to any of you, I am
always ready, of course I know that a man of my calibre could not
be of much service to gentlemen of your standing."

Frank wrote to his son only occasionally while Stroud was in
Leavenworth. In an amusing note years later, Stroud wrote that his
father had visited him once and they considered what a mess Frank
had made of both their lives. At least cynicism was a trait they had
in common because they decided that, given both their fates,
patricide might have been a "swell idea."

Frank's last years in California remain obscure. He never
remarried, lived alone, never purchased property, appeared only
twice in the precinct registry, left no will and died either a "book-
keeper" or a "lumberman."

According to federal prison reports, he died of starvation in
1927, when Stroud was serving his eighteenth year in prison, and it
may have been how Stroud sarcastically described it. Indeed,

Stroud wrote years later that his father "died of malnutrition because he would not accept charity, and drove away people who want[ed] to take him to a hospital with a gun as long as he was strong enough to hold it."

But a California death certificate places Frank Stroud's death in 1928, of a cerebral hemorrhage. A tiny note appeared in Stroud's prison file in 1928, a note that was sent by him as a telegram to the El Dorado County Hospital in Placerville, California, where Frank died. "No money available for privat burial [sic]."

There is no record of where Frank Stroud is buried. He was seventy years old when he died, and in keeping with the family pattern of denial and deceit, he had let it be known that he was a "widower" with one son living in Indiana. Stroud, of course, was imprisoned in Leavenworth, Kansas, at the time, and Marcus was in Chicago, Illinois.

Robert Franklin Stroud was a murder waiting to happen.

The kid was by now a rough–cut six–footer approaching his nineteenth birthday. His face was angular, lean and grizzled. He probably ate poorly and indulged in morphine; at six feet he was a scrawny one–hundred–thirty–six pounds.

In Juneau he and Kate renewed their friendship with a twenty–three–year–old Russian bartender named F.K.F. Von Dahmer who called himself Charlie Dahmer. They had known him in Cordova. Dahmer was an unknown in Juneau; like Stroud, he had been there only a few months.

According to the *Daily Alaska Dispatch*, Dahmer, Stroud, and Kate Dulaney—who also called herself Kitty O'Brien—had been seen drinking together the night before the killing. It was presumed by the newspaper that Dahmer had become too amorous of Kitty, and Stroud later went to settle the score.

The legend from Gaddis is that Stroud was in love with her, Dahmer had given her a black eye and she begged Stroud to kill him.

The rap from U.S. prison reports was that Stroud was her pimp and Dahmer hadn't paid the full price for her services.

For whatever reason, at about 7:30 p.m. on January 18, 1909, with long, angry strides, Stroud walked the three or four blocks to Dahmer's shack.

He never adequately explained what occurred inside Dahmer's shack that night. But shots were heard by a neighbor, who saw him run quickly out of the cabin, and who asked, "What's the matter in there?" Stroud muttered, "Nothing." The neighbor, getting no response from Dahmer's residence, hurried to the authorities. In the meantime, Stroud strutted into the police station and calmly told the surprised officer, "I shot a man." Indeed, he had.

An autopsy, conducted by Dr. L. O. Sloane for $50, concluded that the lethal bullet entered Dahmer's head about an inch–and–a–half in front of the left ear, then burst out his abdomen. Sloane concluded that Dahmer was shot while prostrated. Another physician, Dr. Boggs, concurred. A reporter for the *Daily Alaska Dispatch* theorized from the inquest that Stroud struck Dahmer over the head with the gun and a bullet exploded from the chamber to hit the wall. Once Dahmer had fallen, Stroud squeezed the trigger a second time, execution–style.

The money involved was less than $10.

Although Stroud was an avid talker all his life, although he filled scores of legal–sized note pads with his comments on his life in and out of prison, although he published two books, and had written a third manuscript before he died, he was uncharacteristically tight–lipped about both his murders. He explained nonchalantly in his manuscript, that ten days before his nineteenth birthday, "the writer called upon this man and killed him." He also wrote: "I was living with a woman.

> *A man she lived with years before I met her beat her up. My mother always taught me that a woman who is good enough to sleep with is good enough to protect. I took a pistol and blew his brains out.*

Both Stroud and Kitty were indicted for first degree murder. Each claimed that Dahmer owed them money. She told authorities that she had urged Stroud to kill the Russian, then later recanted, claiming she was "unconscious and hysterical and incapable of understanding what I said." Stroud claimed the killing was self–defense; Dahmer had reached behind in his pocket, and Stroud assumed he had a gun.

According to the *Daily Alaska Dispatch,* both Robert, (who ironically was initially identified as *B. F.* Stroud) and Kitty appeared "indifferent," and "unmoved." Neither "betrayed much nervousness during the time they were in the courtroom."

Stroud was too stunned to react, or else he didn't care. "I had a great many interviews with Stroud during the time I was representing him," wrote Thomas R. Lyons later. Lyons represented Stroud during preliminary hearings but then was appointed District Judge in Fairbanks and left the case. "When I first called on him at the Federal jail, he was greatly emaciated and seemed to me to be hardly mentally responsible. . . . I am satisfied that he was not then normal mentally. He seemed to have little or no appreciation of the enormity of the crime with which he was charged."

If Stroud was momentarily stunned by his own deed, he was certainly not mentally incompetent in the legal sense. Stroud told a different story—many times—a story of deliberate murder. He once faced a prison clerk on Alcatraz who wrote up an annual report on his behavior and attitude, and readily admitted that he had killed Dahmer, calling it "justifiable homicide." Later still, staff psychiatrist Dr. L. Moreau, at the Federal Medical Center at Springfield, wrote,

> *He described the scores of violence in his life—the killing which constituted the original offense, later the stabbing of a fellow–inmate and then the stabbing and killing of the officer at Leavenworth—in detail and with an apparently sadistic pleasure, repeating the acts symbolically with vigorous motions then laughing.*

These admissions and descriptions may have been Stroud's mischievous baiting and defiance of authority. Throughout his life, he never skirted responsibility for any of his deeds, especially his killings; his sense of honor prevented that.

But there was something else. Supporters have often pointed to

Stroud's surrender to authorities in this case as evidence of his innocence and support for his contention of self–defense. Gaddis even called it Stroud's "curious mixture" of complete justification and acceptance of responsibility. This is a profound misreading of the man.

He may have been too dazed to realize what would result from his conviction—it was his first killing and possibly shocking even to him—but he fully admitted killing Dahmer because he felt Dahmer *deserved* to be killed. And he was the man to do it. The man "with the character to commit serious offenses." All his life Stroud was consistent in this regard: he did not avoid the responsibility but he would not accept the blame. He felt no guilt. In Stroud's mind, Dahmer had brought it on himself.

At the hearings he may have felt nothing.

Upon learning of her son's crime, Elizabeth sailed to Alaska on the *SS Jefferson*. She alternately invented excuses for her son's behavior, blamed her no–good husband and felt that Robert must have been justified. Stroud aided her in this interpretation. In time, she would weave a fabrication that would spring him from full blame. Later she called him a victim of a "bad woman of the dance halls." Kitty had urged him to do it. "My poor boy," she was quoted as saying, "infatuated with her, under her influence but chivalrous and brave, pleaded guilty to save her."

It's not possible to know when Stroud began hating his mother, but at this time he was still gladly under her powerful influence. On Friday, February 5th, Stroud and Kate Dulaney were taken to the courtroom for their pleas, and Stroud's attorney asked the court for a postponement until Monday, because the *SS Jefferson* had not docked yet and Elizabeth was delayed. Robert Stroud wanted his mother present at his pleading.

After Elizabeth arrived, Stroud entered a plea of not guilty to First Degree Murder. His attorneys asked for a change in venue and suggested Valdez—across the Gulf of Alaska. Valdez was a remote, wild region, the northernmost ice–free port which was difficult and dangerous to get to. Such a trip offered a chance for escape and the town could have served up a more lenient jury.

The court agreed to a change, but to nearby Skagway along the panhandle. Abruptly his attorneys waived Stroud's rights to the change in venue and withdrew his not guilty plea in favor of a guilty plea for manslaughter.

First Degree Murder in Alaska Territory was punishable by the death penalty or life in prison. Stroud evidently became convinced that he could hang. Stroud was also "determined to save Kitty," Gaddis maintained, and by eliminating a trial it would be difficult to try her.

That might not have been the case, however. The prosecution's evidence was damning. A witness had agreed to testify that Stroud stated he intended to kill Dahmer. That, plus the coroner's report, Stroud's confession and testimony of the witness who saw him emerge from the cabin could have been sufficient to establish a guilty conviction of First Degree Murder. Moreover, Kitty may have been convinced that it was in her best interest to testify against Stroud in exchange for dismissal of her own murder charge.

Stroud didn't plead guilty to manslaughter to save Kitty. She turned evidence in exchange for her own life.

Manslaughter in Alaska then was punishable by one to twenty years. Stroud was given twelve years.

For Elizabeth McCartney Shaffer Stroud and her son, 1909 was a rough year. At age forty-nine, she was granted her second divorce. Her son, of course, began his first days in prison in August that year.

But Bob Stroud would fall even deeper into trouble and eventually receive a sentence that most people would consider worse than death.

№   №

Part III
Meet "John Pain"

Stroud differed from other child abuse victims who grow up to become multiple killers because he had acute powers of observation, a talent for writing and an incredible ability to enhance his world while buried in a tiny concrete cell.

That didn't show on August 30, 1909, when he was dressed out in the rough, woolen, horizontal stripes. But prison guards could sense his powerful, unforgiving will.

Before them stood a man who was beginning a twelve–year sentence for manslaughter in the U.S. Penitentiary at McNeil Island, Washington. He was a square–shouldered, intense nineteen–year–old, whose ears, his most prominent feature, stood out from his head like flags in a stiff wind. In the Commitment Log, filled out the day he arrived, he was described as six feet, one–hundred–thirty–six pounds, dark brown hair, fair complexion, light blue eyes. His left eye was narrowed a bit by skepticism, his large lips set in a sullen grin. The clerk thought a moment, then wrote, "intemperate." Stroud looked like all the other tough guys.

Stroud's intensity was palpable; anger mixed with a sense of betrayal, fear and boredom; he'd already spent seven months sitting in a territorial jail. Now he would hit hard labor.

Thirty years later in a short story, which won him an honorable mention in a nation–wide prison contest, Stroud called his alter ego, "John Pain." He described him with "lips curled in a half sneer," a man with an "uncontrolled contempt for the ignorance of men over him." That was what guards saw, and would continue to see for the next ten years.

But Stroud was also depressed that day. They shoved the property release form at him and he signed with a heavy, flat, almost horizontal slant. He was Number 1853.

McNeil Island, in Puget Sound, Washington, had been a federal territorial jail until 1907, when it became the third federal penitentiary in the nation. Sentences from Alaska Territory crimes were also served here. Today it is a state prison, but for many years it was one of the oldest federal prisons in the nation.

By the time Stroud arrived, the original cell house was already old and filthy. It was a concrete palace, three stories tall with barred windows. Ten years before he arrived federal examiners had complained that its porous floors, which had been damaged by hobnailed boots—shoes with sharp thick nails to protect the soles— were impossible to clean.

Stroud was led through the door and "stumbled down four or five steep and deeply worn stone steps leading to the floor–level of the cell house," he remembered more than forty years later. "Everything was incredibly filthy."

Like most prisons at the time the cell house was poorly ventilated; it had a stench that he would remember all of his life. The dead air stank of unwashed men and the night buckets used for toilets in each cell. He was racked into a little cage that was a "black, evil–smelling cavern."

> *The gloom, the chill, the filth, the rutted floors, the stench of the night buckets, the silence, almost like that of the grave, fell upon my spirits and reduced them to the lowest point in my experience. . . . I was frightfully lonely, frightfully miserable."*

His cell was typically small; he could touch both walls with his arms outstretched. His window was tiny and covered with wide, flat bars which emitted little light. "Only directly in front of the windows was there enough light to read by," he wrote. "On dark days, reading would be impossible." Stroud would spend fifteen hours a day here. In time he would double–cell.

The bunks were so wide in the narrow cell, that when one man moved around, Stroud wrote, the other had to lay down.

Sundays were the worst. ". . . At least nineteen hours of every Sunday was spent in the cell," he wrote,

So it was important that the two men coupled up together in a box four feet wide, nine feet long, and seven–and–one–half feet high, were congenial and considerate of each other's rights and feelings. It was only by going on sick call, to regular chapel services and Sunday school that a man could avoid spending twenty–two hours of each Sunday in his cell.

He had entered a world with which he was at least familiar. Prisons, then as now, were filled with the same assortment of normal, emotionally immature, mentally incompetent or pathologically disturbed men he'd already met. Most were liars, thieves, drunks, drug addicts, con artists, bank robbers, drifters, embezzlers, murderers, rapists or sociopaths. A few were judges, bankers, preachers, government workers or foreigners. Some claimed to be doctors (although they couldn't remember where they got their medical degrees). Some were illiterate. One or two were lawyers or engineers. Some were sick with the "pip," the "syph," or the "sump." Some were violent, predatory homosexuals; others were brazen queens "catching" for any big guy who could protect them. Perhaps the biggest minority—the ones who were not coming back—had been caught in a simple transgression that could put anyone in prison. *All* were innocent, they told each other, and they could prove it. Most had been betrayed, bum–rapped or cold–cocked and with every re–telling they became more convinced of their innocence.

Stroud had hung out near the wharves. He'd ridden the rails. He'd made friends with the safeblowers and pickpockets alike— with the" yeggs," "dips," "fences," "hop heads" and "moochers" he met on the road, and the Yukon boom town gangs with their pimps and prostitutes. He spoke the language. He could signify. He knew the code. It wouldn't be that different.

Except one thing that would always grate, "Obey all orders," he read from a sign on the wall that first day, "instantly without question."

When Bob Stroud entered McNeil in 1909 he was barely literate. His spelling was poor, his grammar rough, and his sentences ran together without much punctuation. He had moved as far from middle–class society as possible.

Decades later, he wrote about these early years in his long, unpublished manuscript on prison history. By then, he had taught himself to write well enough to publish two books; learned enough law to submit writs to the courts; become familiar with biology, chemistry and ornithology; and moved into studying French, Italian and Spanish, even attempting to read books by Victor Hugo and Baudelaire in the original language. He had rejoined society, in a sense, by moving his middle–school education into a college–equivalent aptitude.

Throughout those intervening years behind bars he saw reforms come and go. He saw the thieves and illiterates of the 1910s and '20s meld into the gangsters and kidnappers of the '30s, and meld into the organized criminals and racketeers of the '50s. He saw the three independent federal prisons at McNeil, Leavenworth and Atlanta fold into the federal Bureau of Prisons which by 1944 included twenty–nine institutions nationwide, all controlled by a central office in Washington, D.C.

He was in his sixties when he wrote about his imprisonment at McNeil. He sat on a hard back chair with his legs kicked up on the bed with a board on his lap, writing on yellow legal pads. Large, bright security floodlights lit up the exterior building at night and shone through his window, allowing him to write long after the cell lights had dimmed and all other prisoners were forced to go to sleep.

Those early prison years, as he described them, were an almost schizophrenic era in which guards and cons worked within a framework of gentlemanly honor and unscrupulously severe punishment.

"Hard as some of those old dungeon–type prisons were," he wrote typically,

> *one of the best things about them was that no one had the time or inclination to live the inmate's life for him. He was forced to stand on his own two feet and fight for what he*

got, but within the narrow limits of his own little world, he
enjoyed a mental and moral freedom unknown in federal
prisons today.

The "mental and moral freedom" Stroud claimed to have enjoyed from 1909 until 1916 was little more than his remembering those years through a thirty–five year nostalgic filter, back to a time when he was living in the main prison population; back to the 1920s even, when he gained enormous power while still in segregation. Before 1930, when the Bureau of Prisons, which became his nemesis, had organized.

Director Bennett allowed Stroud to write his manuscript on prisons so long as he didn't write about anything occurring *after* 1930. Being honorable, Stroud mostly complied. But he used his forum to state unequivocally that prisons in those early days were far superior than later examples. It was an argument tainted by his feelings of injustice at the hands of the Bureau of Prisons. He couldn't see through his own bitter veil. Instead, he wrote, "In those days men with the character to commit serious offenses,

were never ridden by the guards, nor would their superiors
permit it. Such men, if left alone, go on and follow prison
routine, naturally. They cause no trouble. If not left alone
or treated fairly, they may cause bloodshed. It was the
constant, petty troublemaker who was ridden to death by
the guards.

Call this cheap psychology if you will, it paid off. No
matter how serious the offense, no matter how severe the
punishment, when that punishment was over, it was over;
and the book was closed. The prisoner was made to feel
that there was nothing personal in his treatment; that he
had brought his punishment on himself; and that he had
paid the debt in full. It did a great deal to prevent lasting
bitterness.

It wasn't that those prisons were superior. They weren't. Treatment was far more arbitrary, conditions more harsh and punishment more cruel. Neglect, abuse, overcrowding and boredom were normal. But the entrepreneurial sort, a maverick like Stroud, could extract enormous privileges, as he put it, "by the simple process of doing as he pleased and then making his conduct legal by the argument of status quo."

In those days, convicts at McNeil moved in lockstep, a system of marching "nuts to butts" which set the regimen for the entire prison. Work was hard labor—breaking rock in the quarries, working in foundries or in the steam power plant. The lucky, the wealthy and the snitches often got the better sewing jobs.

Silence was observed at meals, at work and while marching. Convicts could only talk quietly to their cell mate. They quickly learned to talk out of the sides of their mouths, or with hand signals.

At meals prisoners sat on bolted–to–the–floor benches facing the same direction. All needs were made known to guards by hand signals. There were no knives, no salt and pepper. The races were segregated.

Working conditions for guards were also atrocious. Men were required to work twelve–hour days, six or seven days a week, and if a guard wanted a day off he found his own replacement. It didn't make for pleasant company.

Recruited from rural America, guards were underpaid, often poorly educated, blunt and sometimes brutal. In many cases they were second–or third–generation prison employees. They bought their own rifles and paid for their own ammunition. There was no insurance if a man died in the line of duty. Bribes, blackmail and protection were not unknown, and guards sometimes acted as "mules" to pass money or drugs on the galleries.

They wore high–collared, dark wool suits handmade in the prison tailor shop at their own expense. The stand–up collars on their jackets had gold–block letters, "U S P," for U.S. Penitentiary, embroidered on the sides. They wore military style hats, and regulation "sneak" shoes. They may have looked like little postmen in their uniforms, but the sight of one standing in the hallway striking his shiny black club in the palm of his hand while silent prisoners marched by would dispel that thought.

Clubs were part of the guard's uniform: long, black, wooden

police billies, or short, buck–shot filled, leather–wrapped saps. Either one could do a lot of damage. The McNeil Island Rulebook of 1911 told guards to remember that "the prisoner, however disposed to abuse and violence he may be, is wholly within their power and largely at their mercy." While this was intended as a caution against abuse, it also gave a subtle permission.

For a convict to move closer than ten paces towards a guard was forbidden, and approaching without permission was a grave offense.

Spanking a man with a thick, wooden, knotted board, attaching a twelve–pound ball and chain to his ankle, chaining him standing at his bars, dripping water down his throat, or hosing him in the face until he fainted, were *standard* methods of punishment in state and federal prisons throughout the United States. Solitary confinement was always accompanied by bread and water diets, sometimes for so long that the prisoner's life was endangered.

Dentists were non–existent. At McNeil at this time there was no hospital, and Paul W. Keve, in his book *The McNeil Century*, wrote that "most of the time the guards applied their own home remedies." Stroud agreed; in a lively, and perhaps slightly exaggerated account, he wrote, "Medical attention was of the sketchiest.

> *There was usually a more or less skilled convict who could administer purgatives, narcotics, and swab and suture wounds or apply crude splints to broken bones. Aching teeth were pulled, often with forceps made in the prison blacksmith shop, and without anesthetics. In fact, any prison inmate back in those days who could not stand to have a tooth pulled or a minor operation performed without an anesthetic or without crying out was looked upon as a weakling and a crybaby. On one occasion the writer underwent a forty–five–minute operation to remove a cut and frozen tendon from the palm of his hand without anesthesia or narcotics.*
>
> *. . . At some prisons there were arrangements for bringing in outside surgeons in serious cases, but the red tape was so involved that the inmate usually died before*

the permission could be obtained. As a result, prisoners often attempted to and did save the lives of their otherwise doomed companions by performing major operations upon them, following the technique from a textbook propped open on the patient's chest during the operation.

Don't laugh! The writer has seen major operations upon the abdominal cavity performed in just that manner by a safeblower working without gloves and with a cigarette in his mouth while ether was being used as an anesthetic, and he has seen the patients make uneventful recoveries—man is a very tough animal.

Wardens and their assistants were politically appointed; when the governor came in, so did a new warden. For that reason they were independent and more colorful in their methods of maintaining order. The "mental and moral freedom" Stroud heralded amounted to living within a system which was not yet organized, presided over by officials who met their own needs in unique ways.

O. P. Halligan was a typical warden. "The King," as cons called him, presided over McNeil from 1905 until 1919. He was a sweet–faced, almost cherubic Irishman who was disliked by some staff and hated by most cons. One employee called him "stupid and ill–bred," and even Stroud wrote, in his short story about "The King" written in 1939, "By listening carefully and replying in grunts and monosyllables, he gained a reputation of great wisdom." Halligan was rumored to have taken sexual advantage of at least one female prisoner and one guard's wife. He was also said to be very cautious of his prisoners; he was constantly accompanied by two terriers, said to be trained as burglar alarms to run in front and warn him of approaching cons.

Stroud saw him as a comical, vain man who believed in harsh discipline and practical solutions. Halligan's was a turned–around world where fist fights between cons were encouraged and possession of a postage stamp a capital offense. If "The King" or his deputy warden were present, Stroud wrote, men could fight until one of them gained an advantage, then the fight was stopped and they were asked if they wanted to shake hands. "If they shook, that was the end of it, there was no report."

A sense of fairness prevailed among guards and cons then, which was unmatched, Stroud argued, by administrators and guards after the creation of the Bureau of Prisons in 1930. "It was looked upon almost as bad to steal from a guard," he wrote.

If a guard did anything sufficiently serious to a convict, the convict was considered justified in hurting him physically in any way possible, but it was considered very poor sportsmanship to injure him through his possessions or property.

One can imagine Stroud writing, then pausing and smiling as he wrote, "So long as professional thieves and murderers made up the bulk of the population, such things were seldom done. But with the influx of soldiers, pimps, drug addicts, square–johns, bootleggers, and petty thieves there had been a distinct lowering of the moral standards . . . "

But Halligan knew what his worst enemy really was: adverse publicity. "[It] might force him out at any time and he knew it," Stroud wrote,

so the worst offense any inmate could commit was that of having stationery or a postage stamp or attempting to smuggle a letter out of prison. Money, opium, morphine, whiskey, cigarettes, cigarette papers were minor offenses. Postage stamps which might mean uncomplimentary publicity were serious, very serious, offenses, for there were usually men in every prison who could turn such a connection into a good account if they wanted to.

Prisons were strapped for money then as now. Administrators often negotiated with businesses in town to lease prison–labor, leading often to incredible abuses. Convicts became contract workers with quotas, and those who didn't make quota were at times treated so harshly that maiming or death resulted. It wasn't personal.

But, also, men often created their own employment by trades

with other prisoners, or by skills they had picked up. Stroud told of one man who gathered crime stories from convicts, wrote them up and sold them to magazines; of another who was so successful at making stuffed animals that he employed five convicts. Men made beaded handbags and silk pillow cases and even silk bedspreads, "one of which was purchased by Marshall Fields for $1,800," Stroud wrote. In this world, cons could keep small pets. Birds, especially canaries, were said to be favorites among Lifers. Mice and rats were also trainable.

Convicts often were allowed to eat as much as they wanted. "On one occasion, when I was very hungry," he claimed, "I ate thirty–seven pork sausages at one meal, and I never ate less than three steaks or six mutton chops at a meal."

Rules for prison visitors were much more lax. They were allowed to bring in food and necessities and hand them to convicts face–to–face. Opium and morphine came in frequently by this method, and according to Stroud, some wardens didn't care, as long as it calmed prisoners, and reports of it didn't get out of the prison. "But drugs did come into the institution in small quantities every day," he wrote.

> *Many an addict received a letter every evening, lifted the stamp and licked his daily dose of morphine on its back. Morphine came stored in handkerchiefs. . . . Paper, however, will hold larger quantities of morphine than cloth, so some addicts merely ate their letters.*

In such a wide–open setting a man like Robert Stroud could wield enormous power. But all the pieces weren't in place yet. The challenge now was to overcome boredom, and the shame of his own ignorance.

Stroud began by studying math and reading. He also began to read about Theosophy.

Combining karma, past lives, communication with the dead and planetary science, Theosophy was enjoying some controversy about that time, and it reminded him of his early childhood belief in reincarnation.

Elizabeth claimed that as a kid Bob saw things other people didn't. "On one occasion he come in telling a long story about grandmother," she said later in court testimony. "He had *never* seen his grandmother. [But] she was there, he had seen her, and talked with her." Theosophy also appealed to Stroud because it allowed him to form his own moral code and assign responsibility however he wished.

Stroud was a quick study. He was bright, focused and almost fanatical in absorbing as much as he could. Yet his self–guided instruction lacked discipline. He skipped over what he didn't want to learn, and made incomplete associations. He learned at least enough to dominate others verbally. His belief system was so protected, however, that when others disagreed, he became angry and dangerous. John Pain, indeed.

Stroud apparently caused no trouble for two years. Then he lashed out.

According to Gaddis' doctoral dissertation, Stroud quickly became "a hardened, long–term, high–status inmate" by "making knives, attempting escape, and breaking rules." Gaddis essentially blamed the prison environment, ignoring that the hate that surrounded Stroud before he was even born achieved its greatest reach while he was in prison.

In Gaddis' popular book, Stroud's knifing incident at McNeil was romanticized—almost a Robin Hood tale: "After two years and four months of hard prison regime," he wrote, "Stroud began to break rules. Working in the kitchen, he secreted food and took it to his cellmate. A short–term prisoner who also worked in the kitchen observed this and . . . at a parole–board hearing, this inmate informed on Stroud. . ."

That story does not jibe with Stroud's court testimony, nor letters written by Warden Halligan.

According to cross–examination at his later murder trial, Stroud answered, "Why, this other prisoner and myself were doing a little business in morphine in the prison.

He happened to get sore at me and informed the warden
. . . [and] colored it up a little. And the warden inquired

*about it and I explained it the best of my ability. After that
I learned it was the warden's intention to use some of my
remarks against other people in prison. That would place
me in a position I didn't like. I blamed the other man for
placing me there and we met up this day I had a small pen
knife. And we went to it.*

"The King" told another version. But given his political position, it is probably the most suspicious of the three. He wrote that
Stroud believed he was about to be escorted to another prison and
wanted a chance to escape, and so had asked prisoner Adolph E.
Henry, the hospital orderly, for some poisonous drugs "to use as
'knock–out drops' for the Deputy U.S. Marshals." Henry came
straight to the warden and snitched it off.

Whatever the truth, there was a debt to pay.

On November 1, 1911, Stroud struck Henry in the back with a
knife. As Henry ran, Stroud got off a few more thrusts. A physician
reported that Henry received seven stab wounds in his back, shoulder,
upper arm and buttocks, one of which penetrated the pleural cavity.
(He sutured them without anaesthesia.)

Stroud reportedly told Halligan he "had intended to kill Henry
and regretted being unsuccessful," but later passed off the stabbing
as an attempt to scare Henry.

Halligan also said that he learned from a "reliable source" that
Stroud intended to kill two other prisoners, Westman and Battan.

"Stroud borrowed the doctor's pocket knife to cut some meat,"
Stroud himself wrote years later in a plea for executive clemency.
Then in his off–handed deadpan humor, he finished, "The meat was
the orderly."

Stroud was reduced to stripes, shot back to third–grade status
and confined to his cell. As was customary, he was handcuffed
standing at the bars during the day, and fed a diet of bread and
water. He was not advanced to second grade and taken out of stripes
for four–and–a–half months.

Halligan was anxious for Stroud to be tried for assault to
commit murder. Several letters exist in which he states that he
wanted to send him to Leavenworth because McNeil was over-

crowded. But there was another reason why he was anxious to get Stroud to trial. "It would be appreciated," "The King" wrote on April 1, 1912, in a note that is contained in Stroud's files, "if this case can come to trial at an early date as the prisoner's health is suffering by reason of the manner of confinement."

Stroud was given six months for the knifing, but he lost fourteen–hundred–and–forty days good time—almost four years which would now have to be served. He was transferred to the U.S. Penitentiary at Leavenworth, Kansas. Things were getting grimmer. "If anyone had told me that the day would ever come when I would feel regret at leaving that cell house," he wrote, "I would have thought him mad."

On September 5, 1912, he was photographed at the U.S. Penitentiary in Leavenworth and given number 8154. By now the mug shot revealed a twenty–two–year–old, gruff–looking con with anger in his eyes and mock on his lips. He was tightly coiled, bitter and defiant, which among cons translated into a dark charisma.

Leavenworth penitentiary differed from McNeil Island only in locality. Rising above the flat, hot, dusty plains in east central Kansas along the edges of an indifferent, conservative, dun–colored town of Leavenworth, the penitentiary was the most maximum–security prison in the nation and one of the biggest employers in town.

Called by cons the "Big Top" because of its domed capitol, Leavenworth was opened in 1895. It was a walled city; it had its own power house, its own water tower, factory shops, a farm and a cemetery known to cons as "Peckerwood Hill." It was also consistently overcrowded. And in September, when Stroud arrived, it was oppressivley hot. Six months of every year, in fact, the cell house was a concrete hell where the top tiers could radiate over a hundred degrees and where the humidity regularly shook hands with the devil. Stabbings at Leavenworth weren't as big a problem as pulmonary diseases.

Warden Robert W. McClaughry was in command when Stroud arrived. The warden was a uniformed, armed, practical taskmaster, one of the last Civil War holdovers and chiefly known for introducing fingerprint identification to the Justice Department. The two men actually had a tiny connection; the warden had been an Army paymaster during the Civil War and had signed the discharge papers of Captain McCartney. Stroud undoubtedly did not know that. He called him "one of the hardest of the old–time prison wardens." McClaughry's guards were armed with rifles and pistols and they carried canes with steel tips that "would split a man's scalp like a knife," Stroud wrote,

> *and it was so much easier to knock a man down than struggle with him. That there were many guards who accepted this view was evidenced by the number of white turbans always to be seen in the sea of heads in the big dining room.*

McClaughry was replaced by Warden Thomas W. Morgan in 1913. Morgan reflected the future of prison administrators; he wore a suit instead of a uniform, and served during a reform era. He attempted to set up Leavenworth as the "model prison of the world." He allowed a convict–newspaper to be published, he brought in a phonograph and a motion picture machine. He allowed "lady" singers, tango dancers and pianists to entertain. A large brass band regularly played during meals in the prison dining room.

Yet the two men were enemies. Stroud never let a good hatred go by. He called him a "cheap, grafting, psalm–singing hypocrite," and said that he "most bitterly and undoubtedly would have killed him had the cards broken just a little differently." But then, Morgan was in charge when Stroud pulled the knife out of its sheath, fatally stabbed a guard, and sullied, for the moment, the model prison reputation. "I was in no hurry about killing Morgan," Stroud also wrote later,

> *however, it would be stupid to kill the man without bringing his administration into disrepute, and it would be fun to see how much less I could make of that administration. Being of this turn of mind, I would not overlook any good*

opportunity. The day might come where I could catch the
man alone for an instant, so I made it a point to keep one
of my knives within constant reach of my hand.

Morgan wasn't the only man for whom Stroud had a knife
waiting. Stroud seldom minced words. In one document, he called
the Captain of the Guards, John M. Purcell, "the best trouble man
the writer has ever known. A man he hated and twice came within
a hair's breath of killing." Nor was he veiled in his contempt for
others who crossed him. But he sometimes took credit where no
credit was due. He wrote of the occasion where he "*saved* the life
of a guard and himself,

> *by grabbing the guard's arm just as the guard was going*
> *to strike the writer with a blackjack at a time when the*
> *writer had four witnesses to the unprovoked attack and*
> *ten inches of steel within easy reach of his hand.*

Within four months he was written up for "talking and laughing"
in the dining room—a prison rule he knew well. Two months later,
he was escorted to the hole for making a hacksaw blade. The
following September, he was caught with a pipe–cutter, a hammer
and chisel in an apparent effort to escape from a utility tunnel. In his
manuscript he wrote, "One afternoon while I was working in the
powerhouse, a steam line burst,

> *I volunteered to work on repairing the break, and I*
> *worked two hours overtime, until about 6:00. It was a*
> *mean and dirty job . . . After completing the job I was*
> *given a shower, clean clothing, then taken to the kitchen*
> *and given a special supper of sirloin steak, and put on a*
> *list for extra tobacco that week. I did not have to ask for*
> *any of these things. I had not expected them. I had vol-*
> *unteered for the job because it would enable me to look*
> *certain parts of the prison over with a view to escaping.*

The next month Stroud wanted to see the deputy warden.

After their meeting Fred Zerbst wrote on a note that still exists in Stroud's prison files: "Wants to attend school and study higher mathematics. Record bad. No."

One year later, Zerbst was beginning to sound like a curmudgeon: "Wants to play Viola: No!"

By 1915 Stroud was working in the tailor shop. But he took lots of sick days and Warden Morgan didn't consider him a valuable worker. Other reports indicate that Stroud was surly, once threatened to put a guard "in the morgue in twenty–four hours," and tried to coerce "young unsophisticated kids" for sexual liaisons.

Stroud continued the schooling he had begun at McNeil. He read more about Theosophy and wrote long letters to his mother about his beliefs. When Morgan introduced correspondence courses, he enrolled in mechanical drawing, mathematics, structural engineering and strength of materials. Elizabeth told a Kansas City reporter many years later that her son had earned three diplomas, and according to the *Topeka Journal,* he eventually graduated "with high honors" from the extension school of Kansas State Agricultural College. But there are no records to substantiate either statement.

Stroud's grasp of mathematics and engineering principles, however, so impressed one of his college teachers, that the man apparently visited the prison to meet the convict.

Stroud, in fact, could master anything he tried—particularly if he had a model before him. He took up painting, for example, and became quite good. Elizabeth, who had moved to Alaska after her divorce, claimed that Stroud's greeting cards were good enough to sell, and helped with her finances. One of his large portraits, a copy of a painting of Queen Louise of Prussia, hangs in a small public library in Sabetha, Kansas. Although the woman is romantically depicted and somewhat idealized, her eyes are direct and compelling. Later drawings of Stroud's included in his *Digest*—particularly if they were copies of drawings from other books—are quite detailed, graceful and true to life. His free–hand drawings are more crude, yet even they show a talent.

The ease with which Stroud could master whatever he tried was amazing—and increasingly a part of the problem. Stroud needed a challenge like he needed an enemy. The goal itself was not nearly so attractive as was the challenge. And a clear path with no obstacles was no challenge. He needed something to overcome, someone to push against, a system to defy, a pot to stir up. He needed revenge. And revenge could only be got by overcoming adversity and defying authority.

In 1915, there were no real challenges, no real obstacles. He was a good artist, he was quick at math and could master engineering courses. However unconsciously, he saw nothing but long, boring years ahead of him—years in which he was trapped behind bars able to accomplish everything far too easily.

He still believed that he had unusual powers. In 1915, he wrote to Elizabeth,

> *I wished a Stroke of parallisis* [sic] *on a man last summer who was in perfect health. I was bound by my word that I would avoid trouble with him and while I realy* [sic] *had nothing against him I wanted him out of my cell and would have made trouble if I hadnt* [sic] *of give[n] my word—— forty-eight hours after I expressed the wish he was in the hospital with the Stroke——I have had the same thing happen fifty times with people and things—— The funny thing is when I am in that state of minde* [sic] *I can never wish any thing good, Or any thing directly for my self.*

By then Stroud had sunk to one of the deepest depressions of his life. He expected to do seven more years on his original sentence, and he began to talk of suicide.

In a letter to Minnie in September 1915, he wrote, "I have been a fool for seven long years. I should have killed myself the night I kill[ed] Russian Charley." He told her he was trying for a presidential pardon. In this early application for commutation, found in the U.S. Pardon Attorney files, Stroud argued that he had "Bright's Disease," a chronic inflammation of the kidneys, and would not live out his sentence. Writing to Minnie, he waffled between hoping he had a chance with President Wilson and realizing that his record was not that convincing. After he was turned down, he wrote again, "I have tried my last and I shall now start to do what I should have done seven years ago. 'That is to die' and I shall do it the first time I have the chance."

Stroud's threats were idle talk.

"... I can't live this way much longer," he wrote to his mother in October,

> *and if you could know my real state (which only I can know) you would not blame me if I quit for I have heard you say that you always thought that death [was] better than the loss of mental balance and you would not ask me Mother Dear Would you? to accept what you considered the worst of the two.*

Elizabeth asked him to be patient, suggesting that he might get out next year. But the pressure was mounting and Stroud needed release.

"Mother I should feel very badly if you were to pass away," he wrote March 25, 1916, ostensibly in response to a guilt–ladened comment she had made earlier. The letter was written in two sittings, one day and the morning before the event that would stir up the trouble he sought. The entire letter—much more than reproduced here, full of pain and remorse—became an exhibit at the trial;

> *but you know that I can see very littel [sic] left in life for either of us—you have had the best of me tho at that for you had the pleasure of your youth the satisfaction of a family—I have for years longed for a family and a home where I could be happy but that like every thing has been denighed [sic] me—I guess Minnie will never write to me again. I have tried my best to insult her in my last letter— she told me about Arthur Krahn standing a chance to get life in Walla Walla. She spoke of it as tho she thought that it was just the thing—well she know [sic] what I think—I have wished a peace [sic] of hard luck on to her which she hasnt [sic] a chance to avoid and that is that she will some day know what her word "life" realy [sic] means—She will for the chance[s] are 100 to 1 that that kid of hers will go*

wrong for neather [sic] *of its parent[s] know enough to*
help it go right—I feel sorry for the boy—I must say good
by Mother Darling A Kiss for my littel [sic] *sweet heart*
who I love better than life —

Minnie eventually got her hard luck. She learned what "life"
meant when she was committed to a mental hospital. But Stroud did
not wait to *wish* Guard Andrew F. Turner dead.

At noon the next day, on Sunday, March 26, 1916, about a
thousand convicts dressed in Sunday issue blues were marched into
the Leavenworth dining room. Hidden beneath Stroud's prison coat
was a steel shank with a filed blade at least five inches long.

The dining room was approximately two–hundred–and–fifty
by a hundred–and–twenty–five feet. It held exactly twelve–hundred
seats, arranged in three long columns of rows with five seats each.
Each man sat at a bolted table facing the back of the man in front of
him. Stroud was seated near the front, in the center of five seats.

Each column was separated from the other by a six–foot–wide
aisle in which guards patrolled, clubs in hand. Captain John M.
Purcell sat at the front.

At the back, as they did at every meal, a twenty–six piece brass
band played music to drown out the silence. Legend has it that the
band was playing "In Paradise" when it happened.

Events leading to the killing are unclear. The most consistent
version is that the night before, Saturday, March 25, Stroud discovered that his nineteen–year–old brother, Marcus, whom he
hadn't seen since the boy was eleven, had come all the way from
Alaska to take a course in nearby Kansas City. Marcus had attempted to see Stroud but had arrived on a non–visiting day and had
been turned back.

"He had fruit, candy, nuts and messages from home," Stroud
later told the court.

"Saturday night at supper being in deep thought about my
brother," he continued, "and rather wild with joy, I broke a prison–
table rule. Mr. Turner leaned over and took my number."

Stroud knew exactly what that meant. In prison lingo, he was going to get a "shot," and he would not see his brother.

In *Birdman of Alcatraz*, Gaddis described Guard Andrew F. Turner as a "stocky, muscled, large–fisted man of thirty–nine," who was five feet, eleven inches, weighed a hundred–and–eighty–five pounds, was born in Arkansas and had a limited education.

According to testimony, however, Turner was between twenty–six and twenty–nine years old. And, in what is probably a wedding photograph introduced into evidence (perhaps to prejudice the jury), Turner looks anything but a stocky, muscled, large–fisted man of limited education. With soft, round features, rimless spectacles and curly brown hair parted in the middle, he appears, in fact, quite sophisticated. "Damn!" exclaimed former officer Bergen when shown the photograph, "he don't look like a prison guard."

Evidence was introduced that Turner made prisoners "nervous." According to a prisoner named Wallace, Turner's idea of proper authority was not to report a man, "but to do it personally." Convicts apparently had spread a rumor that he had been transferred from Atlanta for fatally beating a prisoner there.

Whether the story is true or not cannot be ascertained. Gaddis portrayed Stroud and Turner as having several angry encounters. "Stroud kept watching Turner whenever he was around, in common with other convicts," he wrote. But in Stroud's writings there is little evidence that he hated Turner on sight, as Gaddis has said. Years later Elizabeth embellished the story about a guard, "who beat an old man into insensibility. He took an intense dislike to my son. He taunted him, presecuted him, threatened to kill him, called him names that are known among men as killing words. One day he started to club my boy and my son killed him in self–defense."

If Stroud and Turner did have words—indicating a personal feud between them and therefore better grounds for Stroud's self–defense plea—Stroud didn't take advantage of it at the first trial. He was asked,

Q. Something has been said with reference to your having some trouble with Guard Turner at the laundry where it is said you said he pulled you down on the laundry steps.

A. That statement is not true.
Q. Did you have any trouble with Guard Turner at the
laundry or any other place?
A. No, sir.
Q. Did you ever have a talk with him other than that
related to the jury?
A. No, sir.

Stroud raised his hand for permission to get up and two men
stood to let him out. It wasn't unusual for a convict to ask to get up,
but it was unusual to talk to a guard. Turner, who had walked on,
now turned around and faced Stroud. No one was sure what Stroud
said, either "Did you shoot me?" or "Are you going to shoot me?"
  Turner replied. In testimony later, Stroud said he then told
Turner "I am trying to explain about my expecting a visit," and
Turner said, "Go on you cocksucker,"

and [he] reaches for his club with his right hand. As he
reaches for his club I see that he is mad and I begin to lose
my own temper and reached for the knife at the same time.

The encounter lasted less than twenty seconds. "I turned
around and saw prisoner Stroud and guard Turner standing talking,"
testified Officer E. E. Whitlatch in the first trial, "I started to move
up the aisle and I saw Stroud grab for Turner's club."
  With lightning speed Stroud reached with his left hand, pulled
out the knife and plunged it into Turner's chest. His aim was
deadly; the wound was two inches from center and five inches deep.
It struck Turner's heart, and he was instantly paralyzed with a loss
of strength from a sucking wound. He hitched, and slumped to
the floor.
  Alarmed, nearby prisoners stood up and waiters stopped cold.
Guards froze, afraid of a riot and fearing for their lives. Captain
Purcell raced to Stroud. Turner went into cardiogenic shock—pump
failure; his heart rate accelerated, his blood pressure dropped and
his arteries constricted.
  Stroud didn't bolt for the door. Instead he stood, dazed, until

Captain Purcell cautiously approached him, demanded the knife and took him to solitary. Guard Turner was carried from the dining hall, and within eighteen minutes he was pronounced dead.

In six–and–a–half years Robert Stroud had broken most serious prison rules. He had been caught with knives, with hacksaw blades, he had attempted to escape, he had knifed a prisoner and he had threatened to kill guards. These things would remain on his record the rest of his life. Now he had killed a guard.

"We came cheap in those days," said Bergen. "They'd give the widow a small pension plus so much for each kid—it wouldn't have amounted to much."

That killing made Stroud a marked man for life.

Stroud got his catharsis from depression. "I guess you know by this time that I killed a guard Sunday noon," he wrote to his brother three days later. "I am at present in solitary confinement. I am getting along very well and in fact feel better than I have in some time. The reason for it is that my mind is at rest."

He explained later to the court that after "that thing" occurred "a feeling came to me of courage, that I had absolutely nothing to fear; that I would be taken care of."

"What about your conscience?" General Boyle, Stroud's attorney, was to ask in the first trial.

"That does not bother me," Stroud replied.

"Why not?"

"Because I don't see where I have committed any moral wrong in that case."

In a letter to his father and later submitted as evidence, Stroud explained, "The guard took sick and died all of a sudden. He died of heart trouble. I guess you would call it a puncture of the heart. Any[way] there was a knife hole in it."

Boyle was to ask in the courtroom: "What is your understanding about right and wrong of civil law—who is the judge of that?"

And Stroud had replied: "The right and wrong of physical actions can only be judged by yourself. Your own higher conscience toward your Master."

In fact, he felt confident. "Now don't worry," he had written his mother from his cell on March 31, 1916,

> *you know what I was up against in Juneau – well the*
> *people here are not neer* [sic] *as much affected as they*
> *was in Juneau as neer* [sic] *as I can understand and I have*
> *an even better deffence* [sic] *than I had there. . .*

But Elizabeth Stroud *was* worried; this was her son's second killing. As she had done before, she packed up and left Alaska for good. Arriving in April, she settled in nearby Kansas City, Missouri, and remained eighteen years.

Genteel, polite—almost obsequious—the fifty–nine–year–old mother of the prisoner now wore wire rim glasses and combed her almost–white hair in a tight bun. Older Leavenworth officers, who remembered seeing her walk up the long road to the penitentiary, thought of her as a "real lady." But she quickly buried any impression that she might be a pushover; Elizabeth still had her flinty determination and indomitable will.

Her starring role was only now about to begin. She hired the lawyer, and decided that her twenty–six–year–old son would plead insanity.

Although Morgan reportedly called her a "wealthy woman from the Klondyke," Elizabeth cajoled everyone in the family to help with her cause. "I've succeeded in raising money by mortgaging my interests to the other heirs," she wrote later. She sold her house and the land which she had wrestled from Frank, and garnered the wages of her children. According to a family friend, Mamie washed clothes "six and seven o'clock in the morning until twelve o'clock at night" to obtain cash for Stroud's defense.

Elizabeth claimed to be without means, and used this to her advantage. Her meager allowance and good name became two of the chief arguments in her application for presidential clemency.

Stroud was not happy about the insanity plea; it struck at the heart of his ego, but he bent to her will. Although himself an iron–willed, threatening and bitter man, he was no match for his mother.

The first trial began in May 1916, and Stroud entered a plea of insanity and self–defense.

Boyle placed him on the witness stand and immediately moved into rich territory. "Is there any influence, anything that counsels you, your spirit or your mind?" he asked.

"The Master or Agura," Stroud answered. He explained, "Why, there is a theory, Masters that exist on the high plane of existence, and very seldom manifest themselves on the physical plane, but they take a vast part in the affairs of the physical plane, and their services are for the betterment of mankind."

"Are the Masters spirits or men?"

"They are men who have developed to the Agura head."

"Agura?"

"Yes, sir; they are reincarnated. They have absorbed all the knowledge that this sphere could give them," Stroud answered. This was Theosophy, a blend of spiritualism, pseudo–science and religion not widely known.

A few questions later, Boyle asked, "What is your idea about obligations to moral and civil laws as distinguished from this obligation that you have spoken of?"

"Why, the civil laws are a body of chance more than anything else, and the only moral laws that are without defect would be the laws of nature."

"Well, who was the arbiter, and who is to determine what those are?"

"Why, Devos of Carmen," Stroud replied.

"How are you to learn that?"

"You learn them by experience and instruction from your Master."

Much later, Boyle asked the question whose answer was calculated to show the jury that Stroud himself had no responsibility in determining Turner's fate. "What was it that brought it on the victim, then?"

Stroud replied, "Some influence of the Master, as near as I can explain."

Although Stroud answered directly and with clarity, Boyle led him in a direction which to the layman could only be interpreted as the rambling of a mad man. Boyle did not dwell on the exact details of the knifing—particularly whether Stroud had grabbed Turner's hand that held an upraised club. He simply elicited Stroud's Theosophical beliefs. Stroud didn't try to hide anything when questioned. He admitted that his "religious views are brought into this case for light on the sanity question."

But insanity, its causes and affects were not widely understood in 1916. Although psychiatrists occasionally used words like "psychopath," more often they spoke in terms of "moral insanity," or "criminal degenerate." During the trial, for example, several psychiatrists referred to Stroud as being "of the degenerative class."

Doctors thought mental illness could be determined by physical appearance, and much of their examination consisted of measuring ear lobes, head size, shape of hands, feet, palate and testicles. Five doctors for the defense examined Stroud. Dr. Lindsay L. Milne's testimony was typical; he stated that Stroud's testicles were "soft, somewhat atrophied, [with] a very pronounced varicocele on the left side," meaning that his left testicle had enlarged veins. His testimony agreed with that of Dr. Clarence C. Goddard, who said, "[Stroud] has the dome head of a paranoid. His testicles show perversion. . . " The doctors testified that perversion could not be determined by head size alone, nor by the size or shape of a man's testicles, but that together with insane deeds, perversion could be confirmed.

One doctor on the stand hinted at the real motive of Robert Stroud. "He is a law unto himself," Dr. William F. Kuhn pronounced, perhaps the most accurate statement made about Stroud during three years of trials.

The psychiatrists' comments were augmented by the McCartney family, who testified that no less than seven close relatives were so insane they had to be committed, and several had subsequently died in those asylums.

Government attorney Fred Robertson was having none of this. He wrote that Stroud "not only is of sound mind, capable of appreciating the quality of his acts, but that he is a young man of more than the ordinary mental capabilities." In another letter he damned Stroud with high praise, calling him ". . . a conspicuous example of a man with a wonderful mentality. . . "

In the trial, Robertson quizzed Stroud on his early sex life, his crimes in Seattle and Juneau, his first murder, and his knifing at McNeil Island. He elicited the fact that Stroud had never pled insanity before.

Stroud admitted on the stand that he had not been able to "wish" misfortunes on people "fifty times or more," but only two or three times.

Mostly, however, Robertson got Stroud to talk about his correspondence courses—mathematics, strength of materials, structural engineering, physics—at which the prisoner had excelled. The fact that intelligence has nothing to do with emotional instability was too sophisticated a point for the jury in those days. Robertson had shown that Stroud was a bright, sane, logical, talented individual.

In other testimony, the fatal scene was described.

Guard E. E. Whitlatch testified that he saw Stroud grab for Turner's club. Another guard named Beck testified that Stroud grabbed Turner's wrist with both hands. This actually strengthened Stroud's self–defense plea; a reasonable person might conclude that Turner had broken free of the convict's two–handed grip, was about to strike, when Stroud, forced to protect himself from club blows, pulled his shank and stabbed Turner.

The jury, however, was in no mood to forgive Stroud for having a knife and using it. The testimony about his prior behavior, his previous killing, and the defiance of his act in front of more than a thousand prisoners was overwhelming. They concluded that Stroud had not acted in self–defense, nor was he insane. He was pronounced guilty and sentenced to hang.

Elizabeth was stunned.

Boyle uncovered an error, however. Judge John C. Pollock hadn't instructed the jury that they could also convict *without* the death penalty. Elizabeth took the verdict to the U.S. Circuit Court of Appeals and won. The case was sent back for re–trial.

The second trial began in May 1917. Insanity was dropped and self–defense became the sole plea.

This time, Whitlatch testified with a more studied version.

Although it's not possible to know what was conveyed by Attorney Fred Robertson to his witness, the guard carefully forgot several things. He now claimed he had never seen Stroud grab Turner's club and didn't remember saying he had. This tarnished Stroud's self–defense plea.

Even worse shenanigans by the prosecution were to come. Robert Stroud had an uncanny ability to get people to go to unusual lengths to see that he was punished. Warden Morgan, for example, reported that Stroud was unmanageable during the trials, bragging about the murder, threatening to kill another guard and struggling violently whenever he was moved to or from the courtroom. The prosecution suspected Stroud of deliberately trying to manipulate guards into retaliation, thereby making his self–defense plea stronger.

At the same time, Stroud claimed there were attempts on his life by guards. In a letter to prison officials, U.S. Attorney Fred Robertson said that Stroud had charged them with trying to poison his food. Stroud also claimed guards tried to tempt him with an unloaded gun once, when it suspiciously fell into his lap as he stepped from a car to go to the courtroom.

It was the type of animosity that would exist between Stroud and administrators for the rest of his life. Exaggeration, outright lies and manipulation existed on both sides. Stroud had a propensity for causing men to over react in clearly punitive ways. He had begun to replicate the Stroud family dynamics in the men who were in charge over him.

Convicts were not allowed by law to testify in court, for example. In the second trial, in a mockery of justice, Robertson *pardoned* five prisoners as they walked into the courtroom. Defense, of course, was prevented from using the same tactic. They were not even allowed to present prisoner testimony.

Stroud was convicted again—this time sentenced to Life.

Elizabeth marched the second verdict all the way to the U.S. Supreme Court. On February 18, 1918, the trial was nullified on errors and returned to the District Court in Kansas for a third trial date. According to Gaddis and Judge James C. Logan, who also wrote a doctoral dissertation on Stroud, the case caused procedural changes in Federal court trials. Prisoners were allowed thereafter to testify in the courtroom without pardons.

A third and final trial was held in May 1918. Stroud was really gambling this time. It was the challenge; he wasn't happy with Life, and even though he was still up for the death penalty, he wanted to try for an acquittal. In this trial Whitlatch testified that he "didn't see his club at all," and claimed he didn't remember ever saying anything else. "You never have gotten your testimony the same way twice, have you?" the defense attorney accused, "Is that the fault of your memory, you think?" Whitlatch answered with a curious non sequitur, "I have not been memorizing it at all."

Beck also recanted his original testimony.

Stroud lost again.

"On that double hand–hold justice depended," he proclaimed before sentencing, calling upon the good name of his best defender;

> *my mother knows the truth. I was innocent of murder. For myself it matters little, but in justice to her belief in my innocence I challenge the attention of every fair–minded person of these facts.*

He was given the death penalty.

"Jury out less than one hour," Warden Morgan gloated in a telegram to Atlanta.

Bob Stroud had stirred up the pot a little too much. On June 28, 1918, it was ordered that he be returned to the U.S. Penitentiary at Leavenworth, "and held in solitary confinement until Friday, the 8th of November next" whereupon he would be executed by hanging.

Elizabeth took the case back to the Supreme Court but this time she failed. There was a stay of execution and then Judge James Lewis decreed that Stroud would hang on April 23, 1920.

Elizabeth now had one route to save her son—the President of the United States.

Woodrow Wilson was by then bedridden with a stroke. His wife, Edith Bolling Wilson, was largely attending to him as well as to the affairs of state; she carried notes from Secretary Joseph Tumulty to her husband. It's been portrayed that Elizabeth had an audience with her and convinced her to persuade the president to commute Stroud's sentence. Nothing in the Wilson presidential papers, however, or in early articles, indicates that they even met.

Elizabeth proved to be very politically adept, however, as well as a good actress and an appealing, modest, forthright mother. She did get to presidential secretary Joseph Tumulty, and he was highly influenced by her appeals.

Elizabeth's case rested on two legal issues: that guards Whitlatch and Beck had changed their testimony, and that her son was mentally incompetent from a family which had more than its share of insane people.

She had another, more successful argument, however, to which Tumulty bowed: she pointed out that she and her other children had sacrificed *their* lives to gain justice for her son. Indeed, most letters from supporters sent in the winter of 1920 to President Wilson stressed her fine traits and enormous sacrifices as much as they did her son's mental incompetence. Typical was the comment by attorney George Kelly, ". . . However much her unfortunate son may deserve the extreme penalty, yet she ought not to be made to suffer more."

In a memo to the president, Tumulty urged him to commute the prisoner's death sentence. Believing that there was a strong streak of insanity in the family, Tumulty underlined those family names Elizabeth had mentioned. The presidential secretary also pushed forward Elizabeth's emotional argument. "With the money she has made by her needlework," he wrote plaintively to the President, "she has paid the cost of these trials." Like many of Elizabeth's statements, there was less truth than drama.

But these were dramatic times. In Leavenworth, Stroud claimed to reporters to be indifferent about dying, while his mother was in Washington pulling all the strings.

Mrs. Stroud, however, had a formidable enemy in U.S. Attorney General A. Mitchell Palmer.

Palmer was heatedly against the commutation. Tumulty quoted him saying that Stroud was a "moral degenerate," who "should be destroyed." Palmer stated his main argument, "Other guards have been killed and the prisoners in some way have escaped the penalty justly required for such crimes. It is therefore, highly important, both as a matter of necessary example and strict justice, that the sentence be carried into execution."

Palmer lost this battle though. Wilson signed Stroud's commutation order, sentencing the convict to "Life imprisonment in a penitentiary designated by the Attorney General."

It was a bitter blow to Leavenworth officials, who felt that guards were now vulnerable to other killings. And it was a bitter irony for Stroud, number 8154, who was still serving time for his 1909 manslaughter conviction and his prison assault with intent to commit murder. His new Life sentence for Turner's killing wouldn't begin until February 28, 1922. He wouldn't be eligible for parole until 1937.

Nonetheless, Stroud wrote years later in a fantastic claim that he had a burst of energy after the commutation.

> *At first, five minutes walking was all I could stand at one time, but within sixty days I gained forty pounds, and none of it was fat, and no one would have believed that I ever had a bad kidney. I remained on the diet of rare beef, raw fruit, milk and candy for one year. At the end of that time I was in the best health I had ever enjoyed in my entire life. I could stand on my fingertips and pick up a handkerchief off the floor twelve times. I could do a dozen pushups on any two fingers of each hand or on my thumbs alone. I would drag my bed, books and blankets, and build the pile up until it was even with the nipples on my chest, then jump over that obstruction until I had cleared it twenty straight times. I would put one foot on my wash basin, spring up and grab my radiator, which was twelve feet from the floor, and chin myself twelve times with either hand.*

Whoever ordered that Stroud remain in solitary confinement for life can no longer be determined by documentation. But it came down day one.

On Saturday, April 17, 1920, in a short notice in the *Kansas City Star* entitled "Stroud Won't Be Hanged," it was reported that

Leavenworth Warden A. V. Anderson "received a telegram from Attorney General Palmer this afternoon" indicating that Stroud's death sentence had been commuted.

The three–paragraph news item ended with the comment— presumably raised by Anderson—that "The commutation of the death sentence brings a problem before the prison officials. They are afraid of trouble if they place Stroud in a working gang with other prisoners. He also is a trouble maker for the guards. Yet he can't be kept in idleness the rest of his life."

The next day, the *Star* wrote a longer piece entitled "Stroud To Be Isolated." It said that Stroud had been read the contents of Palmer's telegram, and Warden Anderson was quoted saying, "Unless some other provision is made, Stroud will be kept in the segregated ward during his sentence, which is for life. He will never be permitted to associate with other prisoners and will be allowed only the customary half–hour each day for exercise in the court. He will be given the ordinary task each day of breaking a certain amount of rock, a provision taken to safeguard the health of all prisoners confined in the isolation ward. He will not be able to see visitors other than members of his immediate family."

That Stroud would be isolated was understood by other reporters meeting in Anderson's office that day. "It will be hard," a reporter for the *Leavenworth Times* wrote on April 17, "to keep him in idleness the rest of his life."

There are several possible suspects behind this order.

In June 1917, Assistant Attorney General Larrin Graham wrote that Stroud should be placed in segregation and given no opportunity to obtain another weapon, and this has several times been cited as the original order. When Judge James Lewis pronounced sentence in 1918 he decreed that Stroud "be held in solitary confinement until . . . hanged by the Marshall until dead." Although he probably didn't intend that Stroud remain in solitary until death, this too has often been used to justify Stroud's unusual confinement.

But a finger "dipped in blood," as Stroud would say, pointed to one man, and only one, who could have done it—Attorney General A. Mitchell Palmer.

And Palmer may have had a unique reason to demonstrate

his displeasure.

High–toned, moralistic and possessed of enormous self–confidence, Palmer could be considered a man of "greasy vanity" like Stroud's grandfather was described. He was a heavy–set man with very white skin, white hair, and a high caliber of pride, prowess and capability. Well–organized, a strong public speaker and a Phi Beta Kappa, he had family ties back to the days of William Penn.

He entered politics early and learned its lessons well. He rose to become head of the Alien Property Bureau during World War I, a department organized to seize German–owned property in the United States. It was a position that would test even the most honest of men, and Palmer apparently failed. His biographer, Stanley Coben, wrote that he was accused of passing around "a gigantic gravy bowl to his friends and political associates." Coben described him as walking a fine line between the legal and illegal, of being highhanded and closing his eyes to the dishonesty of his associates.

Historian Richard Gid Powers was more blunt. He accused Palmer of being "avaricious and up to his elbows in political profiteering."

Despite the accusations, Palmer had delivered Pennsylvania voters for Woodrow Wilson, and in repayment Wilson appointed him Attorney General in 1919. He was Attorney General only for three years, and it was Stroud's dumb luck to be up for commutation during that sliver of time.

The prisoner's commutation bid fell into the maelstrom that was 1919, in which the spirit and hope of the American people were drained out of them in a whirlpool of disappointments. The Great War had ended with a body count of more than eight–and–a–half million; President Wilson failed to win support for his League of Nations and became bedridden from a probable stroke; Prohibition had begun, making the sale and transportation of liquor illegal— and suddenly profitable; even the National past time—baseball— had been sullied when the Chicago White Sox fixed the World Series.

Inflation, unemployment, strikes and riots were at a crush in the summer and fall of 1919, and much of the blame was placed on foreign agitators and communist sympathizers.

"Too many people had free speech in this country," Palmer

once said, and after a bomb exploded at his own home, killing and maiming the dark–haired perpetrator, his accusations became more shrill. "Fully 90 percent of the communists and anarchist agitation is traceable to aliens," he declared. A. Mitchell Palmer was at the helm of what became known as the "Red Scare," which reached its zenith in the Fall and Winter of 1919–1920.

In fact, Palmer had his eyes on the 1920 presidential nomination, and he thought he had his finger on the public pulse. It was Palmer who gave a little–known Washington, D.C., lawyer named J. Edgar Hoover his first big assignment. Hoover became head of an anti–radical campaign, and reported directly to the Attorney General's office.

Acting within a presidential vacuum, in November 1919 and again in January 1920, Palmer and Hoover organized nationwide raids in which suspected communists, anarchists, Russians and other aliens were arrested—without warrants—and thrown in jail. More than four thousand were arrested in January 1920.

Known as the "Palmer Raids," the round–ups were one of the most flagrant violations of civil rights in American history. Most of the charges were dropped because of illegal search and seizures, illegal arrests and lack of evidence. There were reports of police brutality, of women and children being held behind bars, of foreign–speaking men unable to understand the charges against them. It turned out that many of those arrested were immigrants who had joined political clubs for purely social reasons.

Palmer was yanked before a Congressional investigating committee and skewered in the press. He tried to recoup his political loss by predicting a nationwide May Day demonstration, but it never materialized.

Stroud's neck was in the noose just at the moment when things were not going well for the Attorney General. Palmer's authority and power were quickly dissipating and it was apparent that he was losing his grip on the presidential nomination. He was not about to lose a little battle over an unknown guard–killer.

The breach of civil liberties that he practiced on a mass scale was duplicated in Stroud's case. The Palmer telegram that Warden Anderson read to Stroud has never surfaced along with Stroud's prison records. But judging from the news reports, there can be no doubt that it decreed "solitary" for life. This was a unique breach of legality based more on Palmer's political boondoggle. But there was another, much more *personal* reason.

It was an old, favorite, often–repeated family tale that Palmer's great–grandfather, Obadiah Palmer, was on his way home from a Pennsylvania Quaker meeting one evening in 1813 when he stopped by the home of a great landowner by the name of Daniel Stroud.

In Stroud's home, Obadiah met another visitor named Sarah Van Vleit to whom he was attracted. Daniel Stroud eventually offered Obadiah Palmer a job, and with his employment secured, Obadiah asked Miss Van Vleit to marry.

They settled on Stroud's land in a little town which became known as Stroudsburg, Pennsylvania. They named their first son— Palmer's grandfather—Charles *Stroud* Palmer.

The Attorney General had grown up in Stroudsburg; he graduated from Stroudsburg High School. In 1900 he was elected President of the Stroudsburg Democratic Club. When he would retire in two years (after his meteoric descent into ignominy) he would return to his beloved Stroudsburg.

Stroud is a fairly common family name in the United States and there was probably no relationship between the prisoner and the Palmer ancestry. But the connection is too ironic to be ignored. The convict's sully of the good Stroud name was rich for revenge.

Stroud would never know the probable reason why he was given such a harsh, uncompromising sentence. Were it not for the common family tie, Palmer might not have stooped to attend to such a small detail as the commutation of a guard–killer at a time when he was so busy trying to keep his reputation intact.

Although Life in solitary confinement was a flagrantly illegal sentence, that point would not be ruled in Stroud's favor for forty years. And, ironically, throughout most of those years, it would prove to be an advantage for him.

&a.&a.

Part IV
Cage Bird

In 1920, the Leavenworth segregation building was called "isolation" or "solitary confinement." It stood by itself in the yard, entirely separate from the main prison building. A small, fenced-in exercise yard was hard against the main south wall.

The deputy warden's office was located in this building and beyond his office, through an iron-barred door, were the segregation cells. The first cells were for men who temporarily cycled in and out for fights, smuggling or breaking other institutional rules. The second floor cells were permanent segregation—for escape attempts, assaults, rapes and murders. Stroud celled here with other segregated prisoners.

"Pretty rough 'solitary'," officer Philip R. Bergen called it, "very depressing, shabby, dingy, with a dungeon-like appearance."

Arthur M. Dollison, who began his probationary year as an officer at Leavenworth in 1938, remembered these cells as large and stark—without furniture or fixtures. "There was a small drain in the floor," he said, "and a tiny, tightly-grilled window on the back wall up near the ceiling." Each cell had two doors—a regular barred cell door and a massive solid door with a small window-like opening so an officer could peer in before unlocking and opening it. The solid door could remain open or be closed, depending on the prisoner's behavior.

The dinginess and the poorly lit cells were only part of the atmosphere. Men here had forfeited nearly all privileges; they held no jobs, ate in their cells and spent much of their time in idleness. You could have scraped the tension off the walls.

This was the place where human misery and defiance coagulated; where bad-tempered, erratic and crafty convicts were locked deep inside a prison within a prison.

These cells were filled with defiant, assaultive men, many of whom were "doing it all," drug addicts with "dreary expressions and pinpoint pupils;" multiple killers like Stroud; violent, torturous rapists like Carl Panzram—it wasn't personal, he just wanted to kill boys for the sexual thrill of it; cagey escape–artists like Roy Gardner, guard killers like Manuel Ono; all of whom—except Panzram, who was executed—eventually wound up on Alcatraz.

Talk among these men was filled with racial and sexual slurs, guard baiting and hatred. Sometimes the yapping and ranting descended into quarreling and silence. Men broke into screaming rages, keeping everyone awake all night. Even Stroud "could wake up the whole cell house cursing." Some of the guards were no better; some were hard–core bigots, some liked to incite; most showed little sympathy or interest. Open hatred existed among the prisoners for the guards and sometimes it was the other way around as well. Stroud wrote that he hated one guard so much that he had "borrowed a knife and had lain awake night after night waiting for McKean. Had he ever gotten [sic] a hold of McKean's arm the writer planned to break it over the bars and cut it off."

Mainliners viewed the men serving long, hard time in segregation as martyrs. Stroud remained here for the next twenty–two years, becoming its longest, most martyred and most famous occupant.

In the early days he painted, smoked cigarets, studied and paced. Outside, in the decade since he'd been imprisoned, many changes had occurred. The automobile had moved from being a novelty to a necessity. Telephones, electricity and indoor bathrooms were now standard household amenities. Moving pictures theatres were everywhere. The Victorian age had given way to the era of the flapper, when women bobbed their hair, wore shorter skirts, drove cars, went to college and had jobs. Soon they would vote. The first "world" war had erupted, in which airplanes dove and tucked while gunners shot down enemy planes.

When that Great War raged, prisons filled with Conscientious Objectors, "reds" and rebels, and there was a distinct improvement in the quality of conversation on the tiers. Aside from that, life inside Leavenworth underwent little change. Everyday was just like the last, and would be just like the next.

Legend has it that while alone in the yard one day in 1920, Stroud found a fallen nest with a pair of baby sparrows. He may have hid it in his jacket and smuggled it into his cell. At first he hand–fed the baby birds on his own prison food. Soon he was covering the exercise yard looking for insects. Feeding and observing them took up entire days.

No one thought much about it. Other Lifers had had pets before. Stroud could keep his birds.

He was patient and curious, with nothing else to do. He rolled countless Bull Durham cigarets, smoked them to the nub, ground them out on the concrete floor and watched the babies grow. Because he ate and slept in the same room, he became a keen observer of their behavior.

As he brought them into adulthood, they began flying around his cage, chirping, defecating and shaking their feather dust. Here were cell mates who didn't talk back and yet provided him with hours of involvement.

Later one of the sparrows became sick, and while he watched curiously, it flew down to the concrete floor and attempted to peck at it. Stroud decided that the bird wanted to eat dirt, and he wrote in his second book more than two decades later that he asked a guard to bring in a box of fresh dirt. (His words: "I sent for some loam.") The bird died before the loam arrived, but its mate, who had also taken sick, ate twice her weight in dirt and recovered within three days. Stroud felt that soil was somehow vital to a bird's health, and he called this observation, "the first fact of therapeutic value to crown my early experiences with birds."

He asked for and got a canary—not an unusual request to grant in those years when federal prisons operated independently and wardens were politically appointed. He built his first bird cage out of a wooden soap box, his mother said, using a broken piece of razor blade he concealed after a guard issued it for shaving.

By 1921, Warden Morgan had been gone for two years. A former county sheriff, Warden A.V. Anderson, had also now been replaced by Warden William I. Biddle.

A familiar face in Leavenworth county since he arrived as a kid in 1879, "Billy" Biddle had started out as a cub reporter on the *Leavenworth Times*. Under the tutelage of "Colonel" D. R. Anthony, one of the colorful Kansas "pistol–packin'" publishers, Biddle became editor, eventually working for the *Times* an accumulative sixty years. More importantly, Biddle managed several of Anthony's political campaigns and early on gained acceptance in county and state Republican committees.

Thus nicely positioned in political circles, Biddle was appointed to the board of directors of nearby Kansas State Penitentiary. A Quaker, Biddle served on the board during a reform era, when prison stripes, lockstep, the famed "water cure," and the contract system were all abandoned. Kansas also became the second state in the nation to try prison parole.

Biddle's eventual appointment at the federal penitentiary in 1921 was obvious and logical. And also a tremendous benefit for Robert Stroud. Politically astute, reform–minded and a civic booster, Warden Biddle liked to put a nice sheen on every story.

He presided at the prison at the end of a nation–wide reform era when the public became acutely aware of poor conditions and exploding populations. On his first day, June 1, 1921, Leavenworth was already overcrowded at 1,721 convicts. By mid–1925, 3,345 convicts were housed there. Men were sleeping on cots in the basement and along the corridors. Breakfast was hardly finished before lunch began. Yet Biddle, in an April 1925 letter to a private citizen inquiring about Stroud's welfare, called Leavenworth "the largest and finest institution of its kind in the world."

Ever the publicist, Biddle gave tours, and according to Stroud's later writings, every tour ended at the segregation unit where Stroud entertained visitors with tricks he taught his canaries. The smartest bird would come when he called, or hang upside down on his fingers. Since Biddle and his newspaper had already made mileage out of Stroud's murder trials and death sentence, it was important now to refer to Stroud as the "rehabilitated double–murderer," thus his own reputation would be enhanced.

Biddle conducted these tours anywhere from one to seven times a day, Stroud said, at least twice a week for six years.

Stroud maintained that he built his privileges by doing as he pleased then claiming a precedent, but that doesn't give Biddle enough credit. Biddle impressed his visitors; tit for tat, Stroud got most of his requests.

And he asked for more canaries. Now he needed permission to buy bigger bags of seed and supplies for more cages. By 1922, he was getting alcohol with which to clean his cages. Then he needed *cooked* food. According to a Stroud letter, early administrators allowed officers to cook food for his birds every day in the Guard's Mess. After the Guard's Mess was moved to another part of the institution, Stroud claimed he was given a "blow torch and furnish[ed] with gasoline" to prepare food in his cell. No matter how much other prisoners complained, Stroud's privileges were justified, by him and everyone else, on the Attorney General's sentence.

And everyone was fascinated by the birds.

Canaries were among the most popular caged birds in the 1920s and '30s. Although parrots, toucans, cockatoos, mynahs and parakeets were not unknown, canaries were famous for their rolling, liquid songs, their piquancy and zest.

Ranging from five to eight inches in length, often highly colored, canaries had been bred in Europe since the sixteenth century. Germany was famous for its Hartz Mountain singers; England and France for their birds with beautiful colors and elegant bearing. Smartly colored birds such as the London Fancy, the Silver Spangled Manchester Coppy, the Cinnamon Yorkshire, and the Golden Spangled Canary competed with American Roller canaries and Crested Warblers. Breeders called their enterprises the "Harmony Aviaries" or the "Caruso Aviaries," after their top singers.

Stroud joined an active coterie of canary fanciers who formed local clubs, attended concert tours of singing champions, bristled over the finer points of songsters and knew absolutely nothing about avian diseases. In fact, the convict would become one of the most vocal and unusual members of this ardent community.

He subscribed to the *Roller Canary Journal and Bird World,* which was published in nearby Kansas City, and began breeding common canaries.

"I was on my way," he wrote later, "from one male and five

hens, I raised almost one–hundred birds and began to think about the serious problem of selling them."

Elizabeth eventually moved to Kansas City, Missouri, about forty miles from Leavenworth. She lived alone at 1216 Campbell St., until Mamie joined her in 1922. In 1923 they moved to a duplex at 1353 E. 10th St., residing for eleven years in what is now downtown Kansas City. Mamie took a job as a gluer in the Pearson Paper Box Company. Elizabeth worked for almost a decade at the Interstate Casket Company, sewing satin casket liners. Her only day off was Sunday—not a visiting day at Leavenworth—but the warden usually allowed her to visit anyway.

She wore a path down the penitentiary hall. Now sixty years old, she was grandmotherly in appearance—plump, with a soft powdered face, moist bright eyes behind gold wire–rim glasses and white hair that was held in a bun. Obsequious, eager to please and polite to a fault, she wouldn't think of inconveniencing anyone and projected a high–minded, heartfelt integrity. In beautifully hand–written letters to wardens asking for permission to visit her son, she would underline words to drive home the point: "I think you know," she wrote to Warden Biddle in 1923, "*I* would not attempt to smuggle anything contraband into the institution." In another letter dating from the early '20s, she asked to bring ice cream. ". . . But, as I am sure you know, I will not try to slip anything contraband in to the institution, and it seems to me so very nourishing and refreshing during the summer."

She was anxious to give her son his every wish. "My Dear Mr. Biddle," she wrote the warden,

> *In the list of articles we are permitted to send to our loved ones for Christmas you list cake. Bob never, even as a small boy, cared for cake but was always very fond of cream puffs with real cream in them. I am hoping you will permit me to substitute cream puffs for cake, when I bring over my Christmas treat. . . . I was allowed to bring him a dozen a few years ago.*

In a letter to Biddle's successor in 1927, asking to bring her son an Easter Lily, she pointed out that Biddle had allowed it before. She ended it, "Will you kindly let me know as soon as possible so I can make my plans according to *your* rules."

She was complimentary and flattering. In 1929, she wrote to Warden White, "It means so much to me to know one who understands human nature and its many weaknesses and can deal justly under most trying conditions, is in authority over him."

Sometime in the mid–1920s, Elizabeth began carrying out cages of canaries which she took home to sell. Later, Stroud smuggled out letters in those cages.

Not much was known about birds in those days, and what was considered good judgment then is now largely discounted.

Stroud began experimenting with various types of bird seed. He found high concentrations of mustard seed in some bags, which the birds rejected, and a lot of dusty, moldy seed. He became so knowledgeable about seed that he would eventually tell breeders that he ordered "a small red German Rape, a good grade of Morocco Canary, Hemp, and a mixed tonic seed they put up for me on my own formula." He began buying seed in bulk, mixing up his own formula and advertising it for sale in bird journals.

Probably his greatest initial accomplishment was alerting amateur bird breeders to the dangers of moldy seed. Once a fungus called aspergillus, much like green bread mold, becomes established, it attacks the lungs of birds and can become fatal. This fact was well known among poultry breeders, but perhaps not widely understood in amateur bird circles.

He learned quickly to keep breeding records, noting the parents, the number and condition of their babies, his best songsters, and what problems occurred.

As his flock increased, he had bigger management problems. After an early lice outbreak, he ordered lice powder and inspected and powdered his birds once a week. He also ordered disinfectants and washed each cage once a week. "Bath houses are all numbered and cups are all thoroughly disinfected," he wrote.

As prison administrators, guards and other segregated convicts watched with amazement, Stroud's simple hobby grew into an
industry needing not only disinfectants and bulk seed, but drugs,
solutions, insecticides and more cages for isolating sick or breeding
birds and raising babies. Once he gained permission to sell his birds
by advertising in the local *Roller Canary Journal*, he encouraged
his buyers to act as agents for other sales.

He requested more and more items. "Sir," he addressed a letter
to Warden Thomas B. White, who had replaced Biddle in 1926,

> *I would like to send this order. I need a new pan to wash
> my cages in. The on[e] I made two years ago is so badly
> rusted at the corners that it is about to go to pieces. I also
> need 4 new nest boxes, as in mating 12 hens and with only
> 12 boxes I have no chance to clean them. It is for these
> purposes I wish the steel. The moth balls I use to mix with
> my seed and bird food during hot weather to keep insects
> out of it. 1 lb. last[s] me about 2 years for this purpose.
> The brads I need in making shipping cages.*

Although years later in a newspaper article he passed off his
bird business as "the most drudging chore, one that I was willing to
undertake only because it was one avenue opened to me, and they
were *my* birds," that was the defiance in him talking.

During this time, when he was in his thirties, his breeding and
selling endeavors became a passion. He built cages out of cardboard at first, using rolls of tape. Some were embellished with wire
bars and later, some were even roofed with tin from large tin cans
from the prison kitchen. By February 1930, he was requesting and
getting "tubes and dishes to grow germs in." In 1931, he requested
material to construct a steel cabinet.

From common canaries, Stroud moved to pedigreed birds,
advertising "Fancy Pedigreed Glucke Rollers." By "scientific
breeding" he originated a strain that combined beauty and song.
Later, an avid fan named Fred Daw, who corresponded with Stroud
for more than twenty years, claimed that Stroud crossed the Red
Hooded Siskin and the common canary, creating a new breed which

by 1939 was "sweeping the country."

Anyone stepping across the ancient threshold of Leavenworth segregation would be smacked by the incongruity of a chirping aviary down the corridor. Stroud sat, with a cigaret in his mouth, working at his desk. Colorful birds perched on his shoulders, on his cell bars or window bars, filling the air with song, and bombing his concrete floor with guano.

Very quickly the cell began to smell.

Indoor aviaries require constant attention—daily change of water, food, tray bottoms, periodic cleaning of cages, toys and floors. Birds defecate every fifteen minutes. The larger the aviary, the bigger the need for cleanliness. Even one Kansas summer day missed and Stroud's cell reeked.

Describing the conditions in his cell, he wrote,

> *his hands, face and clothing were smeared with paint, since he is one of those persons who cannot work with anything without getting it in his ears. There were a hundred birds flying around the cell, and there were bird droppings everywhere, even in his hair and ears. Since he was a chain smoker, not addicted to ash trays, there were cigaret butts all over the floor.*

Guards frequently admonished him to clean up, and he gave them grief. "This prisoner, Stroud, does not want to believe that you were over here inspecting the building," wrote one guard to Warden White in a letter from Stroud's file. "And he thinks that the guard in charge is trying to get rid of his birds by making him keep his cell clean. . . . I would appreciate it very much if the warden would inform this prisoner that he is required to keep his cell as clean as the other prisoners."

Stroud continued writing more requests for his needs, and ignored guards who badgered him to tidy up his surroundings. When he didn't get what he wanted, borrowing a technique from his birds, he would "squawk my head off."

Stroud was busy and feeling important. By now he was selling his good stock singers for $7–$10 each, and his show quality birds were $25 and up. Later he bragged that his prize birds were $50 or $75. He claimed that in one three–month period he sold $900 worth of baby birds. Even some administrators appeared proud of his business. "He has a great variety of birds at various prices," one warden wrote at this time. "No doubt you will hear from him . . ." There were problems however; although Stroud claimed he did all right one year, he lost $1000 worth of birds to disease.

Stroud's descriptions of the first avian diseases he encountered are too generic to determine exactly what he was seeing. Apparently healthy birds suddenly dropped from their perches, panted like they were feverish and quickly died, one after another.

It's likely that the first diseases he encountered resulted from poor nutrition, poor management and improper sanitation. If left unattended even a short time, bacterial overgrowth in feces can contaminate fresh food, water and then the feet and beaks of birds. Birds already compromised by nutritional deficiencies or other diseases are soon subject to secondary bacterial infections.

And like all breeders, Stroud was searching for champion colors and crested warblers, purchasing canaries from other breeders. Thus he was constantly introducing potentially sick birds into his own flock. With few quarantine methods, he was compromising his birds.

Stroud attempted to find answers in the literature for the diseases he was seeing, but there simply was no literature. He did find books dating to the 1860s and '80s—"pet care" books which were devoid of real information and riddled with misinformation.

Canary Birds, written by Mary Wood and published in 1869, is typical. Clearly written for a privileged audience—Wood advocated warm milk and bread "and every now and then a little bit of sponge cake soaked in sherry wine"—it is charming and simple and woefully inadequate on diseases.

The major bird disease term was "Decline," which resulted from an "unnatural diet," Wood said, and could be cured by feeding the bird spiders or placing a rusty nail in the drinking water.

Frequently the cure was worse than the disease. Birds have an important gland under the tail which secretes oil used by the beak to coat the feathers to protect from rain. If this "rump gland"—now called the preen or uropygial gland—becomes clogged, Wood suggested prying it open with a needle then applying unsalted butter and sugar. It'll cure the disease, she warned, but destroys the gland "and the next moulting season the bird dies for want of oil to soften the feathers."

Along with spiders and rusty nails as purgatives, and butter and sugar as a bacterial disinfectant, other cures consisted of olive oil, salt water baths, ice baths, castor oil, cod liver oil, watercress and chalk.

In *The American Bird Fancier, or How to Breed, Rear, and Care For Song and Domestic Birds with their Diseases and Remedies,* written by D. G. Browne in 1881, fanciers were told that if a bird develops a tubercle about the size of a hemp seed, to cut it off and anoint the wound with fresh butter.

Sweating, another disease, could be cured by washing the bird in brine several times a day, cleansing it with rain water and setting it out in the sun to dry.

Diseases were commonly named for their symptoms. In a disease known as "Rupture," the intestines "seem to have fallen to the lower part of the body, where they become entangled and turned black." Too much nutritious food is deemed the cause.

Rich food was also said to be the cause of Epilepsy. Browne suggested dipping birds frequently in cold ice water and giving them olive oil.

In *Canaries and Cage Birds* by George H. Holden, 1888, caster oil was recommended for treatment of consumption. A piece of rock candy was good for the disease known as "Loss of Voice."

Diarrhea was caused by too much green food, decaying food or old drinking water. A biscuit soaked in new milk, with chalk and powdered loaf sugar could cure simple cases. More serious incidences were treated with fifteen drops in the water of elixir of vitriol and a tincture of opium.

"Inflammation of bowels" was caused by too much stimulating food, or by bad drinking water. Treatment consisted of a change in diet, painting the bird's abdomen with turpentine, feeding it caster oil and a tincture each of opium and belladonna.

This author was more than generous. "If the bird is about to be given up," he wrote sympathetically, "a little brandy may be added to the drinking mixture as a last resource." Opium, belladonna and brandy would certainly usher the bird out in style. If all else failed, at least the aggrieved owner could begin the wake.

Stroud ordered the Farmer's Bulletin No. 1337 entitled "Diseases of Poultry" (published by the Department of Agriculture in 1925), but it offered little practical advice beyond recognizing diseases. Chicken pox, white diarrhea, cholera, fowl typhoid, tuberculosis, enterohepatitis, rose chafer poisoning and vent gleet were all the major diseases cited, and in each case treatment was considered futile. "As a rule," it advised, "when a bird becomes sick the best policy is to kill it."

That was the status of veterinary information on avian diseases in the 1920s—almost zero. Stroud no doubt read the books with a mixture of amusement and disgust, but with the growing realization that he could make his own discoveries and write his own book on canary diseases.

One prominent medical veterinarian book existed—*Diseases of Domesticated Birds,* by A. R. Ward, D.V.M. and B. A. Gallagher, D.V.M. (Gallagher had been the author of the Farmer's Bulletin pamphlet). Written in 1920, it was directed at professional veterinarians and contained over three hundred pages on diseases of turkeys, chickens and other farm fowl. Only one chapter—eight pages—concerned diseases of canaries.

Nonetheless, it became Stroud's bible. He obtained a copy and it influenced his research for the next twenty years.

The first disease Stroud encountered he called septic fever. Like nearly all canary diseases he claimed to have discovered, it was a common name in fowl diseases and discussed in Ward and Gallagher's book.

The disease struck suddenly after Christmas one year. One–by–one his birds dropped to their cage floors, panted, fluffed out their feathers and died. It was heartbreaking. Many of his babies had been hand–fed. He wrote later that he lost a hundred birds out of a hundred–and sixty in one outbreak, and began practicing the "kill and disinfect" method. "Every time he passed the bird cage," he wrote later,

> *even after it was too weak to stand on a perch, it ran to the bars and called to him, begging him for help he could not give. The suffering of this poor, dumb, helpless creature who had trusted him all of his life hurt him more than the death of any human being ever has.*

It was this disease that caused him to study bird diagnosis and treatment. In Ward and Gallagher, he read that the symptoms were loss of appetite and lethargy until the bird squatted in the corner of the cage and died. Death occured after a sickness of from twenty–four to thirty–six hours. The disease could only be diagnosed upon autopsy, when it could be seen that the spleen, liver and other organs appeared enlarged. There was no treatment.

Stroud began to perform autopsies. Following the diagrams in Ward and Gallagher, he first opened bodies of previously healthy birds to find the organs and see how they normally appeared.

Over the next two decades he performed many autopsies, eventually making drawings of organ systems and sections, cell structures, lesions and disease manifestations. Many of his drawings made it into his second book. Later, his supporters assumed that he had knives and scalpels available, but the record is unclear. Normally prisoners were not allowed to keep any cutting tool in their cells. Yet, according to a later government report, Stroud was allowed to have surgical instruments. Stroud himself claimed that he didn't have cutting instruments, on the other hand, and instead performed autopsies with his own unique method. "In at least ninety percent of the post–mortem examinations," he wrote in his second book, "nothing but my fingers were used because they were the only tools available."

Stroud was unusually observant and a quick study. In later writings, he advised breeders to make their own autopsies, asking the following questions:

> *As shortly after death as possible the body is picked clean*

and its condition noted. Were the feathers in good condition? Were they oily and elastic, dry and brittle, damp and doughy? Were they louse eaten? Were there any pinfeathers? Are the muscles well filled out? Is there any fat beneath the skin? Are there any sores, bruises or other abnormal marks on the skin? These are the questions the examiner must ask himself and answer before the skin is broken. The skin is then removed—you can tear it right off with your fingernails. Are there any red spots on the skull? Are there any hemorrhagic spots on the fatty tissue? Can you see the abdominal organs clearly through the peritoneum? Are there any dark red or yellow spots in the skeletal muscles? At this point the breast must be removed. You will be able to do a nicer job with a very thin pair of scissors, but you can easily pick it to pieces with your fingernails . . .

Stroud recognized the same symptoms that were discussed in Ward and Gallagher's book. He didn't know that their description was applicable to the last stages of *any* fatal avian disease.

In autopsy, he also saw that his birds had enlarged organs— further proof to him that he was seeing the same disease. But he disagreed with their findings, and set about to write a very convincing diagnosis.

In one of his first articles published in *Roller Canary Journal and Bird World* in September 1928, and in a later article in January 1932, he reported that septic fever was identical with roup, canker and bird pox, and one of the many forms of disease he called avian diphtheria. He also later suggested that psittacosis (a common parrot disease then making news but with no cure) was similar.

He wrote that the disease takes many forms and is hard to recognize. The bird pants, loses its voice, gasps for air, discharges a yellow–ochre diarrhea and dies. In another form, there may be painful sores, or large bumps on the head or blisters around the eyes.

Differing from Ward and Gallagher, Stroud definitely thought there was a cure. He invented it. He suggested breeders pay more attention to cleanliness, separate the infected birds, put salt in their drinking water, and "send for my specific at once." If they couldn't get his specific in time, he suggested they add three drops of potassium chlorate with the salts to the drinking water. He told them to open the sores and wash them out with a solution of potassium permanganate.

Other treatments included sodium citrocarbonate, dehydrated sodium phosphate and peroxide of hydrogen added to the drinking water.

"Stroud's Specific" was a medicine he developed which he began marketing in the late 1920s. It consisted of one bottle of "Stroud's Avian Antiseptic" (later called "Stroud's Salts No. 1") and another bottle called "Stroud's Effervescent Bird Salts." Selling for two dollars each, they were a mixture of dilute forms of sodium perborate, and citric acid and salt.

At least by 1928 he was attempting to market it. He asked for and obtained permission to print a letterhead—a fantastic privilege for a convict serving Life in segregation. On his letterhead, he claimed that "Stroud's Specific" would cure several diseases:

> In poultry: a positive and guaranteed control and cure for every outbreak of roup, bird pox, vent gleet, fowl cholera, fowl typhoid, bacillary white diarrhea and apoplectiform septicemia. In pet birds: septic fever, typhoid septic enteritis, cholera, apoplectiform septicemia, canary necrosis and contagious pneumonia in canaries, psittacosis and apoplectiform disease in parrots as well as a host of minor ailments.

Stroud came to feel that his specific was a miracle drug, and he tried to enlist others in its production. In a 1931 letter to the president of an advertising agency in Philadelphia, he wrote,

> This treatment is the only one known for the septicemic diseases of birds. It is based upon a newly discovered bio-chemical reaction . . . in the food and water . . . which destroys the bacteria in the blood. This reaction has escaped discovery in all the large bacteriological labo-

*ratories in the world for the simple reason that there is
nothing in the nature of the substances used that would
indicate that such a reaction is possible, and if possible,
that it would have any effect upon septicemic diseases.*
[Stroud clearly wanted someone to mass produce it for
him.] *. . . I am unable to protect my rights as they should
be protected, or to develope* [sic] *it by myself as it should
be developed. So naturally I would be willing to consider
any reasonable offer that would assure the commercial
development of the treatment under conditions that would
protect my interests.* [Although Stroud's writing and
spelling had clearly improved since 1915, he could be
felled by his own excitement.] *An interest in a product
that can be protected by a basic blanket patant* [sic] *and
that is specific for a whole line of hitherto incurable
diseases attacting* [sic] *all manner of worm blooded* [sic]
creatures has possibilities that do not come ones [sic] *way
every day.*

"Stroud's Specific" was marketed with a pamphlet entitled "A
Remedy for Avian Septicemias Affecting Poultry and Pet Birds."
Much of the information in his article on septic fever was contained
in this pamphlet. Later he would reprint the same information in his
first book, *Diseases of Canaries.*

And although he was no longer marketing the bird medicine by
1944, he recommended using it in his second book, *Stroud's Digest
on the Diseases of Birds,* to obtain "astounding" results. "During
the five or six years this product was on the market I was able to
cure hundreds of thousands of sick birds of dozens of different
species with it," he wrote.

Breeders were grasping for cures. By '33, Stroud had written
more than a half a dozen articles for *Roller Canary Journal and
Bird World* and *American Canary and Cage Bird Life.* Besides
writing articles on septic fever, he wrote about feeding experiments
and formula, about diseases such as aspergillosis, fowl cholera,
hemorrhagic septicemia, apoplectiform septicemia and bacterial
poisoning, he wrote about baldness in birds, and about how to

recognize diseases ("My Bird is Dead").

In ads he urged readers to contact him with their problems, calling himself "America's foremost authority on the diseases of canaries." Stroud, his fingers gripping his cell bars, repeated to anyone in isolation who would listen exactly how important he was. "The real reason my stuff goes over so well with the breeders," he would call out to other disgruntled convicts, "is that I know how bird people think, since I am one of them. I know the questions that have puzzled me so when I sit down to write I simply answer those questions."

Outside, people were convinced by his authoritative writing voice and the repetition of his name.

When magazine readers *were* skeptical of his claims, Stroud's replies were magnanimous and seemingly scientific. In one reply he suggested the reader perform several experiments to test his hypothesis. Yet the tests were so complicated that most readers would assume that he knew what he was talking about.

The skeptics were on to something, however. Stroud was stepping onto the hallowed grounds of medical quackery.

The main ingredient in his bottled bird cure—sodium perborate—is chiefly used today in bleaching waxes, ivory, straw and other fibers, and in laundry soaps and toothpaste. Its only veterinary use was formerly as an antiseptic mouthwash.

Potassium chlorate, another of his suggestions, is used today mainly in matches, fireworks and other explosives, and in the dyeing and printing of black on fibers. According to *Merck's Drug Index*, the standard authority on chemical compounds, it was also formerly used as a topical antiseptic, and in veterinary medicine, in dilute forms as an antiseptic mouthwash.

Potassium permanganate is a topical astringent, used in deodorants.

Hydrogen peroxide is a bleaching agent and an antiseptic.

Sodium citrocarbonate and dehydrated sodium phosphate are not listed as having any medicinal uses.

Thus, his medicinal "cures"—including his own "Specific"—were antiseptics. Although they might attack a local bacterial infection, they would have no affect on viral or parasitic diseases, nor any affect on diseases which are a result of a breakdown in the immune system.

And Stroud could not distinguish among bacterial, viral, parasitic or immune–system diseases in birds. No one could.

When Gaddis published his book, the causes of most avian diseases and the paths of transmission still had not been sorted out. In fact, Stroud's discoveries still looked valid, at least superficially, in 1962 when the Burt Lancaster movie was released.

The 1989 paperback edition of *Birdman of Alcatraz* recalled the "triumphant story" of a man who became a "world renown scientist while held in solitary confinement longer than any man in this century." It is a line worthy of Stroud's own hype.

This "scientist" was just beginning to make mistakes.

In the late 1920s, while Stroud was cleaning cages and breeding baby canaries, Carl Panzram was contemplating suicide.

A mass murderer who hated the world, Panzram took it out on little boys. By his own account in *Killer, A Journal of a Murderer* (which was put together by Thomas E. Gaddis), Panzram raped and tortured, and then killed. He once forced a man at gunpoint to rape another man. He wasn't very particular about whom he raped. "I rode them old and young, tall and short, white and black." Tough, dangerous and cynical, he was sentenced to hang for killing a Leavenworth guard. Thus Panzram served on death row in segregation with Stroud and his birds.

Panzram was scared of hanging, Stroud said, and he and others in segregation quietly counseled him on how to kill himself. While Stroud may have thought he was serving Panzram well, he and the other cons had ulterior motives—a suicide would be interesting and relieve tension. "Time and time the writer explained how simple and painless it really is to do a good job," Stroud wrote later, revealing that he passed a razor blade to Panzram. In a matter–of–fact tone Stroud urged Panzram to "press two fingers down into the groin until the throb of the big femur artery can be felt; work the fingers back and forth until the artery is brought against the skin; then cut it. Just a little nick," he explained, "a determined man could tear that thin skin and pinch the artery in two with his thumbnail."

Panzram apparently tried and didn't have the guts. "Crybabies," Stroud called him and others like him who were now filling up Leavenworth cells. Panzram was hanged in August 1931.

What Biddle had tolerated and encouraged, each subsequent warden was forced to accept. Not only did the prisoner have a cell–house aviary, a rudimentary laboratory and a mail–order business in resifted seed, medicines and baby birds, he was also developing a large correspondence.

As many as one–hundred letters from bird lovers written between 1928 and 1931 are contained in Stroud's prison file. People wrote asking about their sick birds, about canaries that suddenly stopped singing. Pet store owners, "America's bird breed-ers [who] went stark, raving, feather–mite mad" and even zoo keepers wrote for his advice.

Every letter required several administrative steps. First it was read by a prison clerk who then sent it to Stroud along with a "Special Purpose Letter" form, which required that Stroud ask for permission to reply to it. The form was checked by the clerk, signed off by the deputy warden, then returned to Stroud so he could reply. Once written, his letter was often retyped and a copy placed in his file. As his business grew, Stroud's correspondence became an administrative nightmare.

Stroud was also sending and receiving numerous telegrams. He was frequently boxing up birds together with seed and water for sales around the country, and just as frequently receiving boxes with sick, dying or dead birds for his diagnosis. Money was coming in by wire which had to be credited to his account by a clerk.

Each transaction required custodial and administrative atten-tion. Other segregated convicts had severe curtailment of their letter writing privileges; Stroud had *unlimited* letter writing privileges and his requirements were growing.

"Stroud had his light on just as long as he wanted," said retired officer Bill Sugg, assigned to Leavenworth when Stroud was there.

"He had a typewriter—it was unheard of!"

Unhindered by the normal routine of convicts in population, unemployed in prison labor, Stroud devoted full time to study. Paradoxically, he flourished in segregation. His business became his power base.

It's difficult to get a picture of his behavior at this time because annual prison reports before 1935 are either non–existent or have not been released by the Bureau of Prisons. Letters written to outsiders at this time—many of them women—are newsy and awkwardly warm, but provide some clues to his personality. He could be comically ignorant of his own contradictions, for example, writing to an admirer in 1931, "For without boasting, I come first in that field, without any near seconds."

Yet, his written requests to authorities were studiously obsequious and humble, as is standard among prisoners. When he didn't get his way he outlined his distress in highly detailed letters to the warden. Later, when the Bureau of Prisons was established, he wrote to the director in Washington. While legitimate avenues of complaint, Stroud was already getting more privileges than any other prisoner in the federal prison system—including mainliners at Leavenworth and minimum security prisoners elsewhere.

"See what can be done to put Stroud's mind at rest," came one sarcastic comment to one of his complaints.

If anything, Stroud seemed more tedious than dangerous.

Warden White took a more narrow view of Stroud's success than had Biddle. Although he allowed Stroud to publish articles and continue his business, White had a large institution to run and he wasn't attentive to the burgeoning needs of Robert Stroud.

Each bird was shipped in a box that also contained enough water for the trip. The box had to be mailed from the prison in a timely manner in order for the bird to survive.

Sometimes things bogged down and Stroud wrote to the warden, painfully explaining his problem in a conciliatory and logical fashion. "Now Sir," he wrote in one letter, "the people to whom I sell my birds have no idea that I am in prison. They expect me to live up to my word, and I try to do so. I don't like to be made to appear a liar and unreliable when I have lived up to my part."

White responded, in accordance to the usual dynamics in prison—authoritative and dismissive—but with tacit permission;

I have your complaint about the shipment of one of your birds, and will state that I am sure the employees here are giving you as much attention as they possibly can, and I am not going to interpose any interference. I don't care about being annoyed with your bird transactions. You will have to take the matter up with the officers concerned.

As long as Stroud was able to continue his business unchecked, he was tractable and fairly content. Although administrators might have considered him a nuisance, they obviously could live with it. But things were going to change. Stroud's canary breeding and advising business was going to take on missionary proportions.

Times were changing in the 1920s and '30s. What became the Great Depression was foretold by a stock market crash in October 1929. More and more Americans would be thrown out of work until, in some quarters, nearly twenty–five percent were unemployed. The painful economic downturn would last for more than a decade.

On top of that, a strong conservative streak pushed through the prohibition laws, ushering in one of the most tumultuous periods in American history. If Prohibition made the selling of liquor illegal and suddenly highly profitable, then automobiles and machine guns made bootlegging big business. Bank robbery, drive–by gangland slayings, crime syndicate assassinations and kidnappings for huge ransoms also became the crimes of choice. Newspapers and radio, eager to get the public's nickel, shouted out sensational headlines while the masses read and listened with fascination. Vicious thugs became household names: Bonnie and Clyde, John Dillinger, "Baby Face" Nelson and "Pretty Boy" Floyd.

To circumvent all this, the U.S. Government began legislating sweeping crime laws. Kidnapping, crossing state lines to avoid prosecution and bank robbery became federal crimes. The Federal Bureau of Investigation was established. The federal Bureau of

Prisons came into being at this time, which brought McNeil Island, Leavenworth and Atlanta penitentiaries under one organization centralized in Washington, D.C., ending the patronage system and making civil servants out of federal prison employees.

Sanford Bates became its first director. Then, both to end the contract system and employ prisoners, the BOP instituted "federal prison industries," headed up by none other than James V. Bennett.

The Bureau sent around a memo stating that beginning September 1, 1931, all outside businesses conducted by federal prisoners would be forbidden. Few cons cared—*except* Stroud. His business had grown into an institution and he now had a power base.

In the summer of 1931, Warden White stated that Stroud had to get rid of his birds. He began intercepting Stroud's mail, responding to Stroud's fans that his bird business had ended and the prisoner could no longer act as a consultant.

Stroud became outraged. He was carrying "between $400 and $1000 worth of birds" in his cell, he wrote in a letter pleading his case to old Warden Biddle, now retired, and he had $200 worth at his mother's address. "My cell is lined three rows high with wire cages, all nicely white–enameled."

When he angrily told Elizabeth that the government was stopping his business, the two of them mobilized. She went to the *Kansas City Star* and obtained an interview with A.B. MacDonald.

Kansas newspapers were quite influential at this time; William Allen White, who wrote for the *Emporia Gazette*, was a nationally known writer, and MacDonald enjoyed an equally healthy regional reputation.

A full–page, highly sympathetic, dramatic article appeared on Sunday, October 4, 1931. Entitled "The 'Canary Prisoner' is to Lose The Birds that Have Been His Only Companions for Years," it stated that Stroud would lose his business on October 16th. Elizabeth, profiled as the mother who was being supported by her son's endeavors, was pictured holding one of his homemade cages. In a curious photograph, Stroud is shown in shirt and loosened tie wearing a visor. Stroud, who has been "more than fifteen years in solitary confinement," asks "only to be allowed to keep his pets."

"He has been born again," Elizabeth railed. The pugnacious,

white–haired, seventy–one–year–old was now in her second wind. "In his cell now he has one–thousand high–class canaries, rollers and a crested warbler that he developed himself," she was quoted as saying.

Think of it. A thousand birds! No one questioned it. No one imagined—if it *were* true—that such a large aviary in such close confinement would cause an unbelievable stench. Stroud later claimed that he had an annual income of $8,000, which compared with the dollar's worth today, is a yearly salary of $70,000. These were quite fantastic exaggerations which were never really examined. People were fascinated and moved by the "solitary confinement" smoke screen.

Elizabeth called her son "the mildest, gentlest, most tender-hearted child I ever bore." She claimed that he was "given three diplomas in difficult mathematical and engineering branches" of Kansas State Agricultural College (now University); she reeled off his studies in music, poetry, religion, languages, the sciences and rhetoric. She said that he painted for six years in prison to support her until "he became almost blind—wearing out his eyes that I might eat and have a bed in which to sleep and a roof over my head."

The *Star* article also quoted E. J. Powell, editor of *Roller Canary Journal and Bird World*, as being impressed with Stroud. Indeed, Powell had published most of Stroud's articles, eventually published his first book, wrote letters to wardens on his behalf (referring to his organization as "this great Canary institution"), supplied names and addresses of subscribers to enlist in the support of Stroud's clemency, and even visited the prisoner on several occasions.

Conspicuously absent from the *Star* article which so prominently featured Elizabeth was any mention of a woman who was fast replacing her as the most important woman in Stroud's life: Della May Jones.

A subscriber to Powell's magazine, Della Jones had offered a pet bird as a third prize in a contest in which Stroud competed. After discovering that the winner was not only the "canary doctor" who wrote the articles but also a federal prisoner, she began writing to him about 1929. Some time after that, she walked the long entrance road to the massive, walled prison, announced herself to the tower guard and was let into the foyer, where the steel doors bolted shut with a deafening metal–to–concrete report. She was escorted into a room where she met Robert Stroud.

Intrigued and emotionally overwhelmed, Della Jones became the most well known of that cadre of lonely, adoring women who frequently latch onto infamous prisoners and multiple killers.

She was completely taken in. Like most women in similar situations, she began to rationalize his rougher deeds and romanticize his motives. "Bob killed the guard in prison," she told a reporter later, "because the guard was a bully and was mean to the prisoners and when he struck Bob, there was nothing else to do but defend himself. He wouldn't have killed the man in Alaska if he had been older in the ways of the world and had not been under the influence of a woman much older than himself."

She also passionately believed she could gain his freedom.

Later, when it became important, she would tell reporters that she was "attracted to his personality," and "fell in love with him." She claimed that she spent six thousand dollars on Stroud's business—good money during the depression—and her statement may even be true.

She was no threat to Elizabeth as long as she remained in Shelbyville, Indiana, and just wrote letters. But, according to Della's son, Fred Jones, she inherited a little money, left the family and moved to Kansas City to be near Stroud. Just before Christmas, 1930, she took the apartment next door to Elizabeth at 1345 10th St. They shared the same man. Now they shared the same porch.

Unlike the movie heroine who was an appealing, but asexual, widow, Della was described by prison officers and her own son as a large, plain woman who at one time weighed more than two hundred pounds. Poorly educated and unsophisticated, she was an antithesis to Elizabeth. Her letters were garbled, overwritten and confusing; they were full of misspellings—"mutch," "ment," and "possiable" instead of much, meant and possible. In a letter to Warden White in 1931, responding to his request to inspect a bottle of "Stroud's Specific," she stated that they had orders "wating."

She was eager and industrious, however. Throughout the years

from 1930 to at least until 1934, she consistently wrote twenty or
twenty–five letters to Stroud each month, amounting to hundreds of
letters—out–writing even Elizabeth. She wrote Stroud almost every day, and at times twice a day. He responded in kind. Letters
contained in his file show that their relationship hovered around
business schemes, the buying and selling of "Yorkshires, choppers
and fighters," his bottled bird cure, his forthcoming book and
getting endorsements and signatures for his clemency petitions.
The letters had a breathless, excited quality.

Moreover, they frequently communicated about bird sales and
deals by telegram—"Three for twenty–five OK will write Love Bob."

"No blues can ship whites OK if satisfied."

"Are you sick?" she asked so frequently it appeared to be a
coded message.

"Four available OK Two White on Blue Love Bob."

Stroud didn't suffer fools easily and wasn't always pleased. "It
is three weeks since you had Odenwald's offer," he wrote in one
telegram. "No excuse for not closing deal but if you don't, dare to
say so by wire by my expense Bob." Much later, when she was his
only outside contact, he would refuse to hand power of attorney to
her because, as he would tell a Leavenworth administrator, "she is
incapable of intelligently furthering such action." But by then their
relationship had fizzled. At this time, she was quite useful.

Elizabeth, as one can imagine, was not pleased at being pushed
aside for a younger woman. Through an obsequious veil, she
became bitterly jealous. Della and Stroud worked furiously together,
ignoring, or perhaps unaware of, Elizabeth's growing estrangement.

The same month the *Star* article was published, Della's by–
line appeared in a *Roller Canary Journal and Bird World* article
entitled, "An Appeal for Justice For One Who Has Given Years of
Valuable Service to the Canary Breeder."

For the first time it was announced that the author of all those
diagnostic articles was a convict serving a Life sentence.

> *Surely, you all know Robert Stroud,* [the article began] *but
> you have not known that this service came to you from a
> solitary cell; that the man who labored into the dead of*

*night, every night, that you who enjoy freedom might be
saved from worry and the loss of your birds, has never in
his entire adult life been free.*

The article was notarized as being written by Della. But it was
much too sophisticated for Della, and pure Stroud—with his
characteristic run–on sentences and emotional blackmail. Even the
notarization smacked of Stroud, who maintained that the appearance
of truth was a good defense. Stroud wanted readers to realize—
especially if his research had saved their birds—that *they* were
responsible for getting him out of prison. The message was hard–
hitting and domineering. At the end came quite fantastic instructions:

*Write to Warden T. B. White! Write to Sanford Bates,
Superintendent of Prisons, Washington, D.C. Write to
your representative in Congress! Write to both of your
United States senators! Write to President Hoover! Write
to your newspaper, or call it on the phone! Write! Tell
them what you think! You do not have to write long letters
or fancy ones. Just a few lines . . . But Write! Write! Write!
Talk to your friends! Talk to your family! Talk to your
fellow club members! Talk to your employer or your
employees! Talk! Talk! Talk! And tell them to write too.
You live in a democracy. Your opinion, if you will express
it is the ultimate law. If Stroud has grown too big for his
solitary cell there is plenty of room outside. Now what are
you going to do about it?*

Two months later—five days before Christmas in 1931—the
Denver Post ran a story entitled, "How The Hidden Life of the
Astonishing Canary Convict Was Disclosed." This time it was said
that Stroud had been in solitary confinement for *sixteen* years. Its
holiday appeal was even more touching. Stroud's mother spent
"$10,000" to save him from the gallows. "Now he must give up his
hobby—and her support—because of a new prison rule."

As the *Post* imagined it, Stroud's first killing occurred when a
"burly miner" sitting at a bar with a "boyish, naive" Stroud and the

"scarlet woman" he had befriended, roughly grabbed the woman. Stroud came out of his chair swinging. "He landed a blow with his right fist square on the miner's jaw," the *Post* continued. "The latter reeled. Stroud struck again, again and again. From every corner of the room men came running, but before they could reach Stroud the miner was unconscious on the floor. He never awakened."

The article asserted that later in prison, Stroud worked so hard at painting his greeting cards, that "he started to go blind. Could a worse tragedy have threatened?"

Once again it was said that Stroud did not want to get out. "He has asked simply to be allowed to keep his birds—so that he may be able to retain what joy he has been able to get out of a life that for most men would have been hopeless."

It was Robert and Elizabeth at their best.

In fact myths that surrounded Stroud for the next thirty years had their beginnings in the *Star* and *Post* articles, and later in another full–page article in the Sunday *St. Louis Post Dispatch*. These newspapers reached more than a million general readers in Illinois, Missouri, Kansas and Colorado. That, plus a tiny but passionate group of bird lovers who read the canary journals, started the first groundswell of what writer Charles Remsberg three decades later would call "the tambourine jangle of Stroud's Salvation band."

Despite what the newspapers reported, Stroud *did* want to get out of prison. And Della wanted him out, too. He wrote up a petition for a nation–wide drive for executive clemency which Della would manage, along with help from Elizabeth and E. J. Powell.

The petition asked President Herbert C. Hoover for a pardon "so that justice may be done."

Stroud's argument rested on the premise that his discoveries were so important that he should get a chance to develop them not because he deserved a second chance but "in justice to those whom he had served." It was shaky and irrelevant grounds.

We maintain that [justice] can not be done unless this man's claims concerning his discoveries are investigated by actual tests of his formulas under conditions that will protect his priority rights in them. We feel that the claims

made by this man are so important that, should they only
prove partially true, society, in justice to itself, must
request that he be given a chance to develop them . . .

This reasoning became the grounds for many later arguments
for Stroud's release: that his deeds had more than atoned for his
murders; that his discoveries proved he was rehabilitated; that even
if his scientific research was only partially right, it was so beneficial
to society he should be released.

Passionate letters poured into Leavenworth penitentiary, into
Congress, the Bureau of Prisons, the Justice Department, the Attorney General's and the President's office. "Why is that man in
prison?" one writer asked prison officials, and it seemed to echo
what everyone who had ever heard this story demanded to know.
Appointed officials looked like bullies, forbidding the prisoner's
rehabilitative efforts and attempts to support his seventy–one–
year–old mother.

"Have you a mother?" one anxious woman wrote. "Has the
governor a mother? Oh *Please, please* do not deprive this man the
satisfaction of feeding his old mother."

Then came the petitions. Hundreds of sheets with thousands of
signatures. Public officials were overwhelmed.

Here was the joke, Della Jones had said. People soon got tired
of answering all those letters.

The new Bureau of Prisons, with its fresh administrative
appointees, reeled from the furor that had been aroused. As head of
the new prison industries, Bennett went to Leavenworth to speak
with Stroud. It must have been an auspicious meeting.

Bennett, then thirty–seven years old, had a bland white bread
appearance.

Stroud, on the other hand, who was older at forty–one, and
taller at six feet, who had beaten the death penalty twice, had been
in prison for twenty–two years and in Leavenworth segregation for
fifteen, was currently at work on his first book (for which he had a
publisher) and feeling supremely confident.

He may have initially fooled himself into thinking that he was dealing with a gentle, benign bureaucratic assistant, but Bennett was anything but that. He had an iron will and an organized mind. Born in Silver Creek, New York, in 1894, Bennett was the son of an Episcopal minister. He graduated from Brown University and got a law degree from George Washington University. After World War I he was assigned to the U.S. Bureau of Efficiency, a department designed to streamline federal bureaucracy.

In 1928 he reported on a study of the nation's prisons. A little naively, but in tune with the times, he identified the goals of the organization as: "protecting the mails, preserving order on Federal reservations, suppressing counterfeiting and the like; prohibiting use of alcoholic liquors, suppressing the drug evil, apprehending automobile thieves and protecting women and girls." His writing helped produce legislation which formed the Bureau, and set up Federal Prison Industries, Inc.

In 1937, when Bates would retire, Bennett would become director. Although he had never worked in a prison even one day, he would guide the federal prison system in his vision.

Although the Bureau had begun with the three principal mens' prisons at McNeil, Leavenworth and Atlanta, Georgia, and one womens' institution, it was quickly granted appropriations for a new penitentiary at Lewisburg, Pennsylvania, a detention farm at Milan, Michigan, the Medical Center at Springfield, Missouri, and several dormitory–style institutions for short–term offenders. In 1934, Alcatraz would be folded in as the top–level "escape proof" penitentiary.

By 1944, under Bennett's leadership, the BOP would have twenty–nine institutions. When he finally retired in 1964, thirty-seven institutions existed across the nation. (Today that number has more than doubled.)

Bennett would institute a classification system with prisoners assigned to minimum, medium and maximum security institutions. He would support "experimental" prisons like the Federal Correctional Institution at Seagoville, Texas, a minimum security facility that looked like a college campus. He would institute career planning, skills training, job placement and group therapy programs. At the end of his career, he supported work–release—an almost radical concept for the times.

In short, Bennett was a progressive. In speech after speech he outlined the problems he faced directing an organization which attempted to rehabilitate men hidden behind concrete walls and barbed wire. He hammered away on the disparity of sentencing, on the bleak, cramped conditions and hopelessness in prisons, on the need for increased use of probation and other alternatives.

A shrewd man, he often focused on the poorer conditions in state prisons where money was scarce and the violent criminal case load was higher. Such criticism served to obfuscate problems in his own "big house."

Incredibly, he remained naive sounding, and his writings never lost their hint of fatuousness. He described the fear and vulnerability an incoming prisoner feels, "It is this moment of their deepest trouble that they find their need for honest guidance and friendly counsel," he wrote in his book, *I Chose Prison*. One imagines the "friendly counsel" given a convict in chains just off the boat at Alcatraz. Or how a comment like, " . . . I slept in as many cell blocks as possible to get an inkling of what life is like . . . " might sound to a convict in the Leavenworth dark hole.

He was a gentleman who preferred not to offend. He was the consummate lawyer who couched his comments, a tendency that led him to tone down a roguish alliteration in his book. In writing about Al Capone, whose work assignment was cell house sweep, Bennett said that the Alcatraz cons called him, "the man with the mop," an anecdote which didn't make sense unless you knew that the cons on Alcatraz delighted in calling the great mob boss "the Wop with the mop."

Bennett visited the bigger penitentiaries often and he tried to talk to all prisoners who requested it. He remembered many by name and could often recall their crimes and sentences.

A common complaint, however, was that he lacked cell house savvy. He was hidden "deep inside an impregnable castle," Bergen once said, "with layer upon layer of bureaucratic yes–men which officers, who were on the line, found almost impossible to penetrate." One of his first administrative orders in the late 1930s was a rule forbidding the carrying of blackjacks, nightsticks or clubs without authorization—a progressive ruling that did not sit well with most maximum–security prison officers. In short, Bennett was a liberal. And Stroud was a deep–dyed conservative.

In fact, they were exact opposites. Bennett hated to offend. Stroud relished offending. Bennett did things by the book and accomplished his tasks through channels. Stroud leapt over the heads of men who tried to block his plans. Bennett was trained in logic. Stroud battled his opponents emotionally, wildly encircling them, hitting with below–the–belt punches, jumping from casual goodwill to barely–disguised threats, confusing and wearing down his opponents.

Living in the dingy segregation unit where language was crude and corrupt, where men had descended as far as possible, where life seemed hopeless, Stroud fought for every privilege he could get. He had nothing to lose. He was on his own turf. He had precedent on his side. He had the *superior* anger. And he had a great deal of popular support.

In a head–to–head combat, Bennett had few advantages.

Neither man wrote about this first meeting, nor were there any illuminating notes from Stroud's file. Della talked about it though and she got her story from Stroud.

Bennett apparently told Stroud he would have to get rid of the birds. To which Stroud replied that he wanted out of prison then. Bennett retorted that he couldn't do that, only the President could, and asked if Stroud had sent in petitions. Hell no, I haven't sent in a petition, Stroud reportedly said. He'd sent in a thousand of them—each with a hundred names or more.

Bennett tried a different approach, telling Stroud that everyone in the Bureau had Stroud's interests at heart. Stroud was not convinced; he claimed he had seen some letters written by officials in Washington about him and they were not flattering.

Then Bennett made an incredible offer. He suggested that Stroud allow the Bureau to make him head of a bird business that they would operate as part of prison industries.

As incredulous as this sounds, it is supported by letters in Bureau files. White wrote to an inquiring citizen that same fall,

"The department is now trying to carry out this plan so he can continue to raise birds and instead of carrying it on as a private business of his own, to have the institution undertake to do it for him . . ."

Two weeks later White wrote to a congressman, ". . .we are just now trying to work out his problem in allowing him to keep his canary birds and set it up as an industry . . . "

Days later, White was more adamant. "It will be made an industry and he will be in charge of the production, sales, etc., under our care of course."

Bennett urged Stroud to think about this offer. They shook hands and Bennett left. Stroud thought about it and no doubt laughed. He ultimately refused. "He was getting pretty cocky about that time," Bergen said.

Stroud felt it was evident that the Bureau wanted to stall until everything died down and then make the conditions so hard it would be impossible for him to continue his business.

On October 31, 1931, White sent a letter to director Bates. Enclosing a copy of a letter from Della to Stroud together with a photostat copy of a petition, the warden told Bates that they were "preparing to launch another campaign, and from the looks of it, it will be bigger and better than the last campaign he waged." White warned of "another avalanche of letters to you, and in the end, will no doubt cause the President considerable annoyance."

Director Bates was frustrated. In November 1931, he wrote to U.S. Pardon Attorney James A. Finch, "It looks as though the President and yourself may have to decide whether the welfare of the Nation's canaries is of more importance than an attempt to keep human beings from being murdered."

Stroud did not have supporters in the higher ranks—then or ever. Finch replied, "I am thoroughly familiar with this case as I was the pardon attorney at the time the President commuted the sentence—contrary to the recommendation of the Attorney General—and anticipate no difficulty in dealing with the situation should further petitions be presented."

This little skirmish came at a politically sensitive time for the Bureau. Massive appropriations from Congress were needed to construct new institutions throughout the country, and congressmen were getting angry letters from their constituents about this one federal prisoner who was losing his only means of supporting his poor widowed mother.

In the face of this, the Bureau retreated.

The original memo had forbidden businesses by prisoners "except to the extent specifically approved by the warden." Stroud now became the only exception to the rule.

It was a major victory. It was his doing "as he pleased and then making his conduct legal by the argument of status quo."

On New Year's Eve, 1931, Stroud typed through the night. He wrote letters to fellow bird breeders—women—to whom he was familiar and chatty. He referred to 1931 as "one of the most eventful of my life, and the hardest year of work that I ever put in." He wrote to another that "the Christmas pressure has eased off now. . . . I got a dozen new birds yesterday and I have been watching them for signs of fever."

A few days later, he wrote that he was selling roller canaries at $10, unbanded ones for $7; he had a white and blue roller priced at $12. He was selling rape, hemp and canary seed for sixteen cents a pound, tonic seed for fifty cents per pound and mineral food for twenty cents a pound.

In 1931, Robert Stroud had made the powerful federal prison Bureau back down; he was the only prisoner allowed to keep pets and operate a mail order business from his cell. Leavenworth penitentiary was terrifically overcrowded in 1931, as it would be for at least another ten years. And Robert Stroud would soon have *two* cells.

More tellingly, he had now orchestrated the hierarchy of the federal prison system into the same family tune with which he was familiar. The new Bureau of Prisons—and, in particular, James V. Bennett—had taken on the role of Frank Stroud. Figuratively, at this moment, Stroud had become the ten–year–old who had "come up out of the dirt with a rock in each hand," throwing the first rock hard enough to break two ribs.

But the Bureau didn't necessarily treat him with respect after that.

Two years later, in 1933, Stroud's first book, *Diseases of Canaries*, was published.

> *The skeleton of a bird is a grotesque sight to ordinary eyes* [he wrote on the first page], *but to those of engineers it is a thing of great beauty, for nowhere else in nature does one find a better application of engineering principles. Lightness of weight, strength, and flexibility are obtained in a perfect manner. ... Another perfection of construction is the clavicle (wish bone) which forms a natural spring and prevents the powerful impulses of the flight muscles from forcing the wings to strike each other or dislocating the shoulders. It takes up the momentum of the wing perfectly and thus makes flight possible.*

Neatly organized and well–written, the book appeared to be what every breeder needed. It contained an extensive grounding in avian anatomy, feeding, vitamins, general management and moulting; it covered problems such as insects and accidents, as well as specific diseases which Stroud called septic fever, apoplectiform septicemia, infectious necrosis, hemorrhagic septicemia, nestling diarrhea and aspergillosis. It showed how to recognize symptoms and diagnose an illness and contained notes on bacteriology and drugs. It was edited by Herbert C. Sanborn, Ph.D. from Vanderbilt University, sold for two dollars and appeared to be a little gem.

Everything about the book made it seem the most important early work on bird diseases. Stroud's explanations are often brilliantly clear, forceful and elegant—leading one to understand that his hyperactive sentences have been toned down by extensive editing. *Diseases of Canaries,* in fact, appeared to be for the lay person what Ward and Gallagher's *Diseases of Domesticated Birds* was for the veterinary professional.

But there were provocative annoyances. Despite his impressive credentials, Sanborn was a philosophy professor and an amateur bird breeder who admitted that the study of bird disease was outside his specialty. And *Diseases of Canaries* depended on Ward and Gallagher for much of its information. In fact the book was organized precisely like Ward and Gallagher's book. Three of the four drawings were copies from their book. Even some paragraphs were closely paraphrased.

"The female generative organs consist of a single ovary and an oviduct situated on the left side of the abdominal cavity. The right ovary and oviduct usually fail to develop. Occasionally a rudimentary right oviduct is present," Ward and Gallagher wrote.

"The female canary has a single ovary and oviduct situated on the left side of the abdominal cavity. As a rule the right ovary and oviduct do not develop, but there are cases in which they are present in a rudimentary form," Stroud wrote.

"The feathers are complicated modifications of epidermic structure," Ward and Gallagher said.

"The feathers of a bird are a complicated modification of the skin cells," Stroud wrote.

In another example Stroud copied, he was clearly foiled. In the drawing of a bird skeleton, sketched while looking at a drawing in their book, Stroud wrongly identified the patella, which in both humans and birds is the kneecap. Stroud named it as part of the sternum, and it's easy to understand why. In their drawing the kneecap is drawn close to the sternum and it's difficult to decide where the arrow is pointing.

More importantly, however, once the reader ventured into avian diseases, the book suffered from the same problems as did Stroud's earlier articles. In fact much of the material was a duplicate of his magazine articles.

Thus he had not really advanced from his initial mistakes.

He advised giving the same solutions, such as hydrogen peroxide, potassium permanganate, sodium perborate, potassium chlorate, aromatic cascara and others which were simple stimulants and local antiseptics.

He advised giving birds salt in their drinking water, which we now know is toxic to a bird.

He even fell victim to some of the same silliness that occurred in books written in the 1860s and '80s. He claimed that apoplectiform septicemia—a term, like most of his disease terms, which is out of date today—was caused by sudden change in the weather. Diseases are caused by bacteria, virus, parasites, by genetic coding or a breakdown in the immune system, not by changes in the weather. He also erroneously thought that birds displaying sudden fits were actually experiencing hemorrhages in their brains—hemorrhages which he thought could be stopped if the bird was caught mid–flight and its head doused under cold running water.

He also advised giving "Stroud's Specific." By 1933, however, Dr. H. E. Moskey, D.V.M., the veterinarian at the Food, Drug and Insecticide Administration, had cited it as worthless, and officials at Leavenworth and the Bureau had refused to allow Stroud to market it further.

In short, although *Diseases of Canaries* looked impressive and partly represented an advance in bird care, its diagnostic evaluations and treatment recommendations were worthless.

None of this was known in 1933, however. The publisher, Powell, thought he had a winner. But the Great Depression was deep into its third year and book orders were not pouring in. Stroud received no money from Powell in 1933, and he filed a complaint with the copyright office over infringement of his contract. Stroud later said he got "not one cent" from the book, and he felt that Powell intended to "beat me out of it." He also hated the way the book had been edited, and pronounced it shoddy and poorly printed. Copies that are still in existence, however, are beautifully printed and have remained in good condition even sixty years later. Nonetheless, Stroud carried the grudge the rest of his life.

Years later, in 1938 and '39, in what may have been an honest attempt to generate sales, Powell reprinted verbatim several chapters in a series of articles in the renamed *Canary Journal*. Despite the fact that Powell promoted the articles as coming from Stroud's book, "a book every fancier should own," Stroud was further angered. By then he was calling Powell "a crook" and saying that he had been "gypped."

Whether Powell actually cheated Stroud, or whether the long arm of the depression killed sales, is not known. What is known is that Stroud was a life–long collector of injustices who always blamed everyone else.

In 1939 he attempted to sue Powell. The government replied that Bureau policy forbid suits by federal prisoners and Stroud responded by asking the Bureau to sue for him.

He typed out a three–and–a–half–page letter to the Social Service Unit in Leavenworth in which he laid out his plan. He suggested that they find out which printer published Powell's magazine and how many copies were printed. He wanted them to notify Powell that royalties were due for *each* magazine in circulation; he wanted them to remind Powell that he would be liable for "triple damages" for deliberate copyright infringement; he wanted them to demand that Powell give him a full–page apology and full retribution in thirty days; and he wanted them to warn Powell that if he didn't comply, the "proper authorities" would see to it that Powell would go to prison. Stroud also wanted a similar warning sent to the printer. He didn't want to make a claim against the printer, but he did want the printer "to know that if the claim is not settled he would be subject to prosecution for his part in the infringement."

"I think that this just about covers the matter," Stroud ended.

And there the matter did end; the Bureau would not sue a private individual on behalf of a federal prisoner.

Stroud couldn't let it drop, however and he got a little of his own back.

All of his life he made comments in a get–even tone which were bitter and irascible, but which, to another way of thinking, appeared mischievous and rascal. In the first sentence of his second book, in explaining why he had written it, he wrote that he wanted to take another step towards practical, effective avian therapeutics "since my former work, *Diseases of Canaries,* was hastily executed and badly garbled in the hands of the publisher . . ."

Other problems demanded Stroud's attention in 1933–34.

The Army was abandoning its military fort and prison on Alcatraz Island in San Francisco Bay and the Bureau was interested in turning it into the nation's most maximum security penitentiary.

Rumors race through all prisons at the speed of light, and in Leavenworth, the mill ground out lots of "names" going to Alcatraz: Roy Gardner, "Machine Gun" Kelly, Charlie Berta, Harvey Bailey, Albert Bates, "Blackie" Audett—and Robert Stroud.

He attacked as he had before. In January 1934, he wrote up another executive clemency application and smuggled out letters to be mailed to opinion makers.

One letter—signed by Della but, again, undoubtedly written by Stroud—protested that he was being shut down and shipped to Alcatraz. It stated that the prisoner "while held in solitary confinement, where he is still held" had discovered a "biochemical reaction that made the cure of septicemic diseases that had hitherto been incurable a simple matter." But that "jealousies created by the success of these discoveries" led to the order to curb his research.

The letter claimed that Stroud had found a cure for avian diphtheria, roup, cholera, psittacosis, apoplectiform septicemia, and that he discovered the mode of propagation in fowl paralysis.

"Any one of these discoveries," it was written, "made in a government laboratory at public expense, would be heralded around the world. But because they have been made in a prison cell, by a convict, at his own expense, under the greatest possible handicaps, every imaginable effort is made to suppress them."

Stroud repeated his assertions in his ten–page, single–spaced, typewritten petition for executive clemency. He wrote that he is "recognized throughout the entire English speaking World;" that he "successfully identified and classified every contagious disease known to attack canaries and other small birds;" that if the discoveries had originated in government laboratories they would be considered "among the most important of the century" but because they originated in a solitary cell "are suppressed . . . to the great financial loss of thousands of persons;" that his discoveries were so simple that it was "incredible that all our Government supported laboratories that have spent so many thousands of dollars in the study of poultry disease, without ever curing one of them, should have failed to stumble on it;" that poultry septicemic diseases "cost the American poultryman not less than $50 million per year . . . and the best our government laboratories have [done] has been to offer a few dubious serums and vaccines as preventatives;" that the prison bureau not only wanted to "wreck" his business but were "working a great hardship upon the world as well;" and that the government could protect his rights "only by granting him his freedom and full civil rights."

Stroud did not stop there. Now that he had learned to write, and taught himself far beyond his seventh or eighth grade education, now that he had forced the Bureau to his will and had published a book, he was entering a phase when long harangues, veiled threats, strident accusations and passionate disclosures were used to express his strong will and unshakeable belief that he was the savior of the bird world. His years of labor, he asserted, "could not be brushed aside by an airy wave of the bureaucratic hand."

Testimonials, some with writing as imaginative as Stroud's, poured into government offices. Dr. Herbert Sanborn, Ph.D., the philosophy professor who edited Stroud's book and admitted that he knew little about the science of bird diseases, now wrote that he was "astounded at the scientific knowledge which this man has acquired. ...He has discovered a chemical combination which is a cure for septic fever in poultry which he claims is identical with roup." A man named Lewis wrote to President Franklin D. Roosevelt that there was nothing more pleasant than having "a little tot run up to you with a carefree happy expression and cry out mummie dickey is singing again Ooo I'm so happy." Lewis was asking President Roosevelt to help "prevent Mr. Stroud's transfer to Alcatraz."

The petition for clemency and the testimonials would be enough for most, but Stroud went much, much further. He wrote up a contract declaring that he and Della Jones were husband and wife.

Once again Della marched out of Leavenworth with a juicy story. Local and regional newspapers printed the news, stating that Stroud was fighting a transfer to Alcatraz, and wanted a "Christmas Pardon."

"I am in love with Robert Stroud and I will do anything morally and legally right to gain his freedom," Della was quoted in the November 1933 *St. Louis Post Dispatch*. She immediately began referring to herself as "Mrs. Della Stroud."

Stroud based the legality of his marriage on the fact that the

U.S. Congress had never enacted a marriage law to supersede the Code of Napoleon which recognized marriages by contract and which had been in effect since before the 1803 Louisiana Purchase. It was quite a stretch.

Della's son, Fred Jones, later called their union "strictly a business deal." And although she claimed she filed the contract, no record was located.

The marriage worried the Bureau, however; on November 20, 1933, a telegram reached Leavenworth Warden Fred Zerbst. "We have received form letter signed Mrs. Robert Stroud stop Please wire whether this prisoner has been married."

Zerbst wired back that day, "Robert Stroud not married."

Nonetheless, the story had the weight of passion and drama.

Calling her "my constant aid and inspiration," Stroud explained his reasoning in his petition.

> *To my family I was an infant or moron to be pampered like a pet poodle, lied to, deceived and suppressed, every ambition discouraged by every means possible until I was constantly reduced to the brink of despair.*
>
> *. . . It is only natural that a sentiment should have grown up between us. We were mature humans unattached, of opposite sex, and working together with a common aim. We planned to marry if and when I was ever released. This plan did not meet the approval of my family, who did not seem able to understand that I was over forty years old and such matters was [sic] strictly my own business. I was confronted with the ultimatum of parting with this one most faithful friend, violating all faith she had placed in me, despoiling her of the money she had invested in my business and returning to the status of an infant, or parting with my family. There could be just one answer.*
>
> *In the present year, foreseeing trouble with the publisher of my book and realizing that the malice of my family for this woman would be sure to prompt them to join forces with the enemy who was trying to rob me, and who would do anything to destroy my one outside contact*

through which there was any possibility of him being brought to account, it appeared to me that the only right and honorable thing that I could do was to protect the financial rights of this woman (whom I loved) in her investments in my business by making her my wife.

This was the last straw for Elizabeth Stroud. She stated that Della had caused trouble between them. She scolded Della, saying that she thought the publicity was now harmful to her son's efforts to gain his freedom.

"I am sorry Mrs. Stroud feels put out about this," Della retorted. "I have spent $6000 of my own money in Stroud's bird business and in getting his book on canary diseases on the market. I am his manager in the sale of the canary medicine for which he developed the laboratory formula. I am his wife and I am proud to be his wife because he is a fine man, gentle, kind and certainly he had paid his full debt to the Government for his crimes."

Because of the public declaration of marriage, Elizabeth dropped her efforts at seeking her son's pardon.

There can be no doubt that this move by her was damaging. In 1934, Zerbst wrote to U.S. Pardon Attorney Finch,

I believe Stroud now is as dangerous as ever before, and this opinion is shared by the officers with whom he comes in contact. This opinion also is shared by his mother, Mrs. Elizabeth Stroud, who is devoted to him as only a mother can be, but she realized the situation as it really is. Mrs. Stroud only recently expressed her fears that, if released, her son would soon again be a serious menace to himself and to others, and that even her son's best interests are being served by keeping him as at present situated.

Elizabeth's betrayal could not be overcome. Although the Bureau refrained from sending him to Alcatraz at this time, his clemency was once again denied.

For Elizabeth, her son's marriage was a slap in her face—proving again that she had been betrayed and abandoned. To her thinking, she had devoted virtually her entire life to him—first as a protectorate against her husband, then as a life–long missionary. How she thought of him is reflected in many things she did—but none more poignantly than the fact that in 1933 and '34, in a darkly appropriate rubric, she listed herself in Polk's directory as the *widow of Robert Stroud.*

Both women moved from their adjoining apartments in 1934. Della moved to 1615 Summit, where in 1935 she listed herself as Mrs. Della Stroud. Elizabeth, now seventy–four, and Mamie, now fifty–one, moved to Metropolis, Illinois, returning after an absence of fifty–five years. Elizabeth seemed to have little purpose left in her life and she died of cancer three years later.

Robert never forgave his mother for her abandonment. From that moment he denigrated her as possessive, domineering and the seed of all his problems. He claimed to a prison psychologist late in life that she even tried to make him do things by hypnotism.

Correspondence between Della and Stroud "both inbound and outbound" was suspended on March 23, 1934, but prison reports in 1936 show that she visited Bob twenty–seven times that year alone. The relationship was coming to an end, however. Stroud was no longer able to sell his bird preparations and he needed her less to sell birds. Della eventually stopped writing, dropped out of the limelight and died of stomach cancer in the early 1960s.

Although Leavenworth administrators tried to get Stroud transferred to Alcatraz again in 1935, the Bureau refused to transfer him. He was better off in Leavenworth for now, they said.

          🙵   🙵

Part V
Cell House Suite

By 1935, the Leavenworth Birdman was forty-five, weighed one–hundred–and–eighty pounds and had a receding hairline. By now he had the pungent, nutty "gingivitis breath" characteristic of bacterial infection in the mouth—within ten years several of his teeth would lose their grip and have to be pulled—and that, with the stale smell of cigarets that clung to his clothes and hung on his words, gave him a strong presence.

Reports said he had been studying books about mathematics, physics, biology and chemistry for seven years. He was judged to be college equivalent in aptitude and given an I.Q. evaluation of one–hundred–sixteen. He was an accomplished oil painter. His correspondence list was large and adoring. The petitions and the articles about him caused Washington to recommend that he be given two cells—one for his birds and another for his living quarters and improvised laboratory—a virtual suite with an opening cut between them. Alvin "Creepy" Karpis, who was captured in the spring of 1936 for his part in a notorious kidnapping, stayed briefly in Leavenworth segregation before being transferred to Alcatraz. He was astonished to see Stroud emerge from the hole in his wall one day, "buck naked," with colorful canaries perched on his head and shoulders.

Weslyan University donated a microscope for Stroud's use in 1936. He later called this one of the most exciting moments in his life, opening up an entire new world for him. He began spending hours peering down the scope at blood and tissue samples.

Picture a poorly lit prison cell with a single bare bulb in the ceiling and a tiny window high on the back wall. According to Bergen the walls of Stroud's cell were stacked with bird cages "from floor to ceiling." The prisoner sat at a homemade table, his eyes glued to his microscope, a note pad to the side. "The first time I saw him he was looking through a microscope and totally ignoring us when we were introduced," Bergen remembered. "He was barefoot and stripped to the waist, in a pair of denim pants, with a green eye shade. He looked like anything but a scientist."

The green eye shade, like accountants used to wear to cut the glare from overhead light bulbs, became a kind of hallmark Stroud look. It followed him to Alcatraz and later to Springfield, and became so threadbare that sometimes it was held together with tape.

Stroud's microscope was only one indication of the celebrity status he had achieved. He had a steady stream of important visitors throughout his years of bird research. Mabel Walker Willabrandt, Assistant U.S. Attorney General from 1921 until 1929, visited Stroud several times on trips to Leavenworth as part of her duties to oversee the BOP.

Later, he had also caught the attention of J. Edgar Hoover, the young, dangerous director of the FBI who was just then riding high on the Karpis capture. Hoover purchased a yellow canary from Stroud to give to his mother. According to Leavenworth files, Anne M. Hoover even wrote to Stroud in 1936, possibly to thank him. But the "yellow canary" which they named "Jailbird," had moulted and was discovered by them to be a common sparrow that they suspected Stroud had dyed.

Hoover later delighted in telling audiences that even he could be fooled. But whether the canary had been color–fed and its new feathers had come in neutral, or whether Stroud had actually cheated Hoover is not known; the director was a notorious liar, the convict an occasional one.

"He was an historical figure in the Bureau!" Bergen said. Bergen was a senior officer at the U.S. Penitentiary at Lewisburg, Pennsylvania, in the late 1930s; he occasionally escorted transferring prisoners to Leavenworth, and this was his first glimpse of the Birdman. As was customary, he was usually asked first if he wanted something to eat. "And the second question was—'Do you want to see the Birdman?' Needless to say we always ate and we *always* saw the Birdman.

"Everybody had heard about Stroud! And we *knew* when we

got back to Lewisburg that all of our acquaintances were going to ask about the Birdman."

The attention didn't humble the prisoner any, who was now thinking about a second, much bigger, and to his mind at least, more important book. From 1936 until 1942, unencumbered by a prison job, Stroud worked in his improvised laboratory, making requests for more unusual items.

When he discovered that he couldn't cut tissue thin enough for microscopic observation, he built a microtome—an instrument capable of making extremely thin slices. Using glass, half–inch threaded rod, a tin can, scraps of sheet copper, black enamel, wood screws, an oak block, wax and a razor blade, he built an instrument, he bragged in letters, capable of slicing tissue at "two microns." A micron is one–millionth of a meter. Even if Stroud's homemade apparatus could slice that thinly, he had nothing with which to measure it. Yet this became one of the facts of his incredible scientific feat.

Judging from comments in his book, he was also allowed to have daily fresh eggs and fresh lettuce; he could get bone meal, meal worms, ground oyster shells, cuttlebone, lawn cuttings, and shredded burlap; large supplies of disinfectants, insecticides and louse powder; he had use of several hot plates with which to cook, and had storage cans.

He was also allowed a liberal use of solutions and chemicals— potassium iodide, zinc sulfate, copper sulfate, sodium fluoride, naphthalene, potassium chlorate, and numerous dyes which he ordered from the Du Pont Chemical Company, as well as denatured alcohol, methyl wood alcohol, glycerin, tartaric acid, sodium per- borate and iodine. He had thermometers, test tubes, slides and petri dishes; a collection of pet magazines, government bulletins, jour- nals and books on veterinary medicine, as well as books on biology and chemistry; and he had his own typewriter, paper, ribbons and envelopes. In one passage in his second book, which illustrates how far authorities were willing to accommodate him, he wrote,

Freehand drawing by the author made from tissue fixed in
mercury–iron solution and stained in toto with hematoxy-

*lin and phloxine, imbedded in paraffin and cut on a hand
microtome of the author's own construction.*

He still ordered seed in bulk and apparently, lots of it. In his
second book, he also wrote,

*Note: for the last three years, 1939, 1940, 1941, I have
replaced the egg powder with meat and bone scraps. My
present formula is as follows: Sunflower seed flour—
made by running fresh sunflower seed through a fine
grinder and sifting the resulting mass through a fine
screen, which will remove most of the hulls—resulting
from the use of five pounds of seed is mixed with five
pounds of dry ground bread; two pounds of ground rape
seed; two pounds of ground flax seed; two pounds of
ground sesame seed; one-half pound each of hulled oats
and maw seed; one ounce of salt; eight ounces of meat and
bone scraps; two ounces of cod-liver oil and one-half
ounce of wheat germ oil. This is thoroughly mixed
and stored.*

In 1937 he was granted permission to buy cotton, rubber
gloves, a hot water bag and a syringe. In 1938 there was a note from
Deputy Warden Shuttleworth that Stroud "complained because his
order for electric supplies was disapproved."

Even Stroud was somewhat incredulous at his privileges. He
wrote that he had been given enormous latitude by Warden Anderson
in 1920 which continued unchecked for many years.

*. . . For eleven years, I enjoyed the confidence of prison
officials to such an extent that I actually had tons of bird
seed and large quantities of chemicals and equipment
shipped into the institution and delivered to me without
the bags or boxes being opened. I could have, had I cared
to do so, had tommy guns and cases of explosives shipped
into the institution without risk of detection. Yet, this
confidence was never violated in the most minute detail.*

But officers worried that Stroud could bury some of his activities and comments from his manuscript suggest that he did just that.

All surplus matches were sent to me, and I soaked their heads off and recrystallized the sodium perchlorate they contained. Toothbrush handles had to be scraped into fine flakes with razor blades. The red phosphorus was soaked from the matchboxes. These substances, harmless enough by themselves, make, when properly mixed, a fulminating substance as sensitive as mercury fulminate and as powerful as nitroglycerin. These powders were stored in the talcum powder cans. The top of the can was removed, the powder dumped out, the stuff to be stored placed in the bottom of the can to within one–half inch of the top, then covered with a piece of toilet paper and the remaining space filled with talcum powder. When the time came, I planned to convert these talcum powder cans into hand grenades that would explode on contact by means of a rubber driven firing pin made from a nail that would be released by the force of the impact.

Nor could he resist boasting in the same manuscript that once guards "found in my cell two knives; three saws; a brace for a drill; a key I had just been filing on; and at last, after almost three years of searching, enough material to make four or five hand grenades—though I am not sure they ever figured that part out."

Whether his comments reflect his actual activities or merely swaggering cockiness is anyone's guess. It's clear, however, that the state of his cell was an irritation to officers who couldn't inspect it and didn't trust him.

Increasingly his bird breeding business also constituted a health hazard. In hot summer months, the fresh bird food attracted gnats, flies and mice.

"His cell was always dirty," complained retired prison officer Nova Stucker, who worked at both Leavenworth and Alcatraz. "You had to force him to clean it up."

Stroud was quite casual about it. In a letter to a friend he joked,

"For some insane reason, every once in a while I put something in a special place and then I can't find it for three or four years."

Art Dollison, who first met Stroud about this time, was much more impressed by his surroundings than by the man himself. Dollison was nineteen years younger than Stroud. Tall, thin, with cobalt–blue eyes and a quiet demeanor, he had graduated from Ohio Weslyan University in 1932 with a B.A. degree in Business Administration. He had a series of stop–gap jobs during the depression and was eventually forced to seek a job as a prison guard. The maximum–security prison was his first assignment.

He had heard about Stroud long before they met. Officers frequently groused about the convict's set up in segregation; officers complained that their own kids didn't get Stroud's advantages. In his probationary year in 1938, Dollison was occasionally assigned to a detail called, "Captain's Office Extra," and several times escorted Stroud from segregation to the prison movies. He found "a stern looking individual who didn't say a word from the time I picked him up until I returned him after the show."

But Dollison was struck by Stroud's privileges. "In a penitentiary that was built to house sixteen–hundred prisoners and in 1938 had more than three thousand, where men were sleeping in makeshift dormitories and in the basement of the cell house, where orderliness was extremely important, this man had two enormous connecting cells with all the fixtures and no solid door and an immense store of supplies and equipment. And the best thing you could say was that it was badly cluttered and smelled like a chicken coop."

Stroud, however, was immune from everyone's complaints. It was understood by everyone that his special sentence entitled him to more privileges.

"Without a doubt," Dollison said, "this man had more privileges than any prisoner in Leavenworth history. The only thing he lacked was permission to move about the institution without an escort."

Bergen saw an even more glaring breach of moral integrity. "The impression I had was that the institution was using Stroud and his birds as a publicity gimmick." He maintained that although the Bureau had been in operation for five years, "Leavenworth was still in the throes of the old patronage system and the wardens had not been totally brought over."

The Canary Prisoner was maintaining his status quo.

Despite his excess of privileges, Stroud was still complaining. In 1936, for example, he protested that he was not getting enough "Dobell's solution" which he felt he needed.

"The difficulty [is] that he wants to do his own prescribing," Warden Fred Zerbst wrote to the assistant director of the Bureau. Zerbst explained that Stroud wanted the solution "by the gallons," for the gum disease he was developing. But numerous dentists had assured the warden that it wasn't the proper remedy. It was a simple mouthwash, Zerbst explained. And Stroud was using it to disinfect his cages.

"Our medical personnel changes quite frequently and at first, these doctors do not always understand Stroud, who is highly emotional, unreasonable and dictatorial," he wrote. "Those who are not familiar with him sometimes displease him."

Stroud frequently battled with the medical and administrative personnel. They often refused to approve his medical and drug requests and differed with his self-diagnosis. "Unquestionably, Stroud knew a lot about birds," one Leavenworth report said. "It's hard for a layman receiving clerk, lacking such knowledge, to disallow some medical preparation ordered by Stroud without setting off his proven capacity for martyred protests of persecution."

In fact, Stroud flooded the prison and Washington with protests.

"This man has had numerous complaints throughout his entire period of incarceration and has been treated symptomatically for these complaints," the prison physician wrote in 1935. "He is bothered with chronic nephritis and chronic gastritis and has been receiving treatment for these conditions. He has had considerable trouble with his eyes, but at present is wearing properly fitting glasses. There is nothing serious or critical in his condition, however, he will, in all probability, require considerable medical treatment for his numerous complaints."

There's some indication that the conditions in which Stroud

lived actually contributed to his frequent illnesses. In his second book he said that he once lost four hundred baby chicks to aspergillosis. Aspergillus has been known to affect human lungs, and such a high proportion of birds infected with the fungus could have contaminated his environment, resulting in a severe respiratory ailment for Stroud.

Psittacosis is a serious disease in birds which Stroud did not consider contagious to man. But it is highly contagious and known to induce severe flu–like illnesses in humans. In Stroud's case, it may have led to a bout of pneumonia.

In 1942 he complained often of stomach and lung problems. Since he had a "rather serious pneumonia" that year, Leavenworth Medical director Dr. O. H. Cox had "repeatedly advised" him to be hospitalized for study and proper treatment. "He absolutely refuses to come to the hospital and while he does not seem to be getting worse, he continues to complain," Dr. Cox wrote, stating that Stroud's "self–medication [is] based on erroneous ideas." He noted that Stroud's cells were "unsanitary," and that his ailments could in fact be "caused by his own careless personal habits."

Not only did administrators feel trapped by his continuous requests, but they had to justify their denials every time he complained—necessitating more and more administrative and custodial bother. This further undermined their generosity.

By 1935 yearly reports were being generated about each prisoner. Officers, deputy wardens, doctors and sometimes psychologists evaluated each man's attitude, intelligence, health, church attendance, work and disciplinary habits, physical, psychological and emotional well being. Reports about Stroud not only offer a survey of his behavior but also reveal attitudes of prison authorities—illustrating how the two entities interacted.

That year, for example, an officer wrote that Stroud enjoyed his work and never complained, stating, " . . . for the last three–and–a–half years. . . he has been unusually well–behaved in his isolated situation." Yet the same official did not recommend Stroud for school attendance nor for transfer out of segregation.

Why? Stroud and Leavenworth penitentiary were locked in a battle of wills. Although it appears that he received no serious reports at Leavenworth—indeed, an early Alcatraz report stated that he had "no disciplinary reports while at Leavenworth"— Stroud became more and more of an administrative annoyance. Worse, instead of demonstrating appreciation, he became more and more demanding.

And like a bitter lover who grants far too many concessions to an unappreciative mate, Leavenworth penitentiary began to withhold its rewards.

The deputy warden in 1935 was succinct. "Stroud will always be a custodial problem and menace and should he be released among the other prisoners, he would probably be a disciplinary problem. Recommendations: No Transfer. Maximum Supervision."

There would be no reports of disciplinary problems for years but persistent remarks about his haranguing, his arrogance and overweening pride. In a comment that was not included in Stroud's prison reports but turned up in a 1958 Bureau of Prisons Summary Report, it was stated that a work report from November 16, 1936, said, "This man has a defiant nature. I have to keep him by himself at all times. If he has other men around him, I have experienced so often that he is an agitator, tricky and boastful."

Bad reports in jails, mental hospitals and prisons follow people around like long dark shadows. Once something is recorded, it becomes fact. Evidence of this is abundant in more than twenty-five annual reports about Stroud. The same stories get repeated, the same wording is often copied.

"Owing to the fact that he is well contented in his present condition," the 1935 report stated, "it is recommended that his custody remain unchanged."

Similarly, another report later recommended that Stroud should be kept in segregation because of his "vicious and aggressive trends." Much of his life officials would report him cheerful one year and a constant menace the next. Often the reports were more a reflection on how Stroud interacted with individuals. With some officers he was content, easy-going and talkative; with others he was demanding, self-righteous and arrogant. Yet each one of his moods was used to justify his confinement. His status remained unchanged year after year.

Stroud's attitude of entitlement also grated on prison authorities in Washington and lost him more ground.

When Bennett became director of the Bureau of Prisons in 1937, according to the *Washington Post,* Stroud wrote to him, asking for an additional five hundred square feet of floor space, preferably "on our side of the walls." He asked for a special mailbox for his business correspondence and a college–educated employee to aid him. He intended to pay for the assistant, he said, with his business proceeds. Stroud wanted a guard named Eckholdts to be his assistant and offered to pay him ten percent of his gross.

Always pushing to further his requests, he added, "Big men do not follow precedents; they create them."

Stanley Furman noted that Stroud used his bird business as a weapon. And the Bureau would never forget this insubordination.

That same year, on February 27, 1937, Stroud became eligible for parole. A 1936 annual report noted that he did not have a job waiting for him upon possible release and "will work for self."

It must have been a rhetorical question; Stroud was not about to be granted parole. But the exact reasons have never been revealed.

Curiously, his parole records are absent from his personal files. Although his files located in various archives throughout the country are thick with minutiae from 1909 until 1963, records on parole decisions are not included. When queried, the U.S. Parole Commission stated that the BOP kept parole records on individuals imprisoned prior to 1975. Yet a 1992 Freedom of Information Act request elicited no parole records.

According to Gaddis, Parole Board Executive Ruby M. Carr gave no reason for denying parole.

According to *Washington Post* reporter Eve Edstrom, who in 1962 was given access to prison reports, letters and perhaps even Stroud's manuscript, Stroud "made it clear that he would accept none of the usual conditions of parole. He wanted unlimited traveling privileges, wanted to decide where he would live, who would be responsible for him and what requirements would govern his activities." It certainly sounded like Stroud. Under such circumstance parole would be denied.

But there's another reason why Stroud wasn't paroled.

Informally prison officers and some prisoners have maintained that Stroud would not give up segregation, return to the main prison population and take a job. To do so would have lost him his emotional and intellectual power base. General prison talk has always maintained that Bennett offered him the choice of giving up segregation and trying out the main prison population but that Stroud refused. Parole, therefore, was out of the question.

Stroud may have guessed that he would never get paroled and therefore refused to toe the line. "I am neither a moron nor a sycophant, the only types they conceive worthy," he was quoted as saying about the Bureau years later, "but a man of strong character who in fifty years has not been broken and cannot be broken."

It was a further example of his need for a challenge, for an enemy to push against. Stroud only knew how to be *for* something, or *against* something. He didn't know how to simply *be*. He was now entering a phase, however, when he was losing more ground than he gained.

The prisoner continued writing to bird lovers and supporters who had become steady correspondents—people to whom he could easily show his chatty, enthusiastic, buoyant side. Yet letters to his family—people who had witnessed his bitter, manipulative, paranoid side—mostly had ceased.

His father had died in 1928. Letters to and from Della had ceased in 1936. His half–sister, Minnie, had not written to him since 1926. After she entered a mental hospital in 1934 they did not correspond until she was diagnosed with tuberculosis in 1939, and then only briefly. Marcus wrote infrequently and appears not to have written at all from 1929 until 1943. Mamie never wrote to him while Elizabeth was alive.

In fact, there seems to be no letter from *any* member of his family from 1934 when Elizabeth severed her relationship with him, until 1937, when she sent a note from Metropolis. Coincidentally or not, 1937 was the year she was diagnosed with uterine cancer.

On August 3, 1938, Stroud added Mamie to his correspondence list, saying, "I am expecting nature to take my mother off of it within the next few days. She is dying with cancer and has been unable to take nourishment for three weeks." Elizabeth died on August 19, 1938, at seventy–eight.

From 1938 until late 1942, while Adolph Hitler rearmed Germany in violation of the Versailles Treaty, took over Austria and Czechoslovakia, invaded Poland, France, England and Russia and eventually drew the United States into the second World War, Stroud sat at his desk, using his microscope and making extensive notes on what would become his next book. He was still surrounded by cages of birds.

This book would be far more involved and more authentic to his own voice than *Diseases of Canaries*. Indeed, originally it was going to be one thousand pages. It would contain everything he had ever learned, including information on cages, bird seed, breeding, moulting, sexing, every disease he had encountered, all the chemicals and drugs he had used, and more. He could now study blood smears and germ cultures to back up his diagnosis, in fact to bludgeon his critics; in one passage he claimed that he made over two thousand sections of one bird to discover its fatal illness.

Not only would this book cover septic fever, aspergillosis, fowl cholera, hemorrhagic septicemia and apoplectiform septicemia, but he would enlarge upon avian diphtheria, psittacosis and fowl paralysis.

His pencil handwriting—sometimes printed like old–world script, sometimes severely slanted, at times circular and scrambled—was driven from one note pad to another. When he completed one section, he typed up his notes. He made scores of drawings of which eighty–eight made it into the book—sections of a canary's kidney magnified six hundred times in which he identified "lesions of chronic nephritis," sections of an oviduct, of the male reproductive system, of leukemia cells and nerve tissue.

Because the book was never professionally edited, it would be a more accurate reflection of his personality, at times magnanimous, comical, ornery, puffed–up, patronizing and denunciating. In text that eventually made it to print, his writing could sometimes be unintentionally comical, such as his comment in the forward that "We all stand on the shoulders of dead men." Sometimes his humor was intentional. "Those of you who are not interested in microscopic work," he wrote in one passage, "can just admire my drawings and skip over the involved text."

Yet he tossed out opinions on subjects wholly unrelated to birds. "Much of our craving for drink, narcotic drugs and even swing music," he wrote, "is traceable directly to our overrefined diet of steam–cooked and processed food." In one footnote he said, "I have seen hopheads eat moth balls to break a morphine habit."

He *needed* to publicly discredit others whose ideas differed from his. Of one, Dr. Durant, he wrote, "and while I may have lacked some of his social and educational advantages in life, I have probably looked into the bodies of as many dead birds as he has, and cured a hundred to his one, or the one of any other man living." He was critical of veterinary doctors and the "generally slipshod looseness of expression of the medical profession," often making sarcastic comments—"and the 'vets' do not seem to have thought of an answer to that one yet."

He was boastful. "It may interest some readers to know that when this drawing was made I was suffering from lobar pneumonia and meningitis and was almost as dead as the sparrow was when he fell into my hands."

Many of his assumptions were not based on fact. In one passage he wrote about birds being afflicted by migraine headaches (a condition that does not exist in avians).

> *These symptoms are so realistic that they can be recognized by the observant breeder the first time they are seen. The only reason why the afflicted bird does not hold his head in his hands and moan is that he has no hands.*

His comments were sometimes chilling in their nakedness. "The best course," he wrote about an ailing bird, "is to choke it." His precise description of killing a bird by snapping its neck is cold.

"A child may like and need candy, cake and ice cream," he wrote in a paragraph about tonic–seed mixtures. "War conditions have shown us that a person deprived of these things will do absolutely anything to obtain them, sell their bodies or commit murder with equal readiness. . . "

Reading between the lines, it was quite possible to see that here was a man with a supremely casual outlook on the value of life. In writing about mating birds, he argued, "There are cases, however, where it is only by violating nature's laws that we can open the door for improvements. In such cases conduct your mismatings with your eyes open. Know what you are doing and why, and then have the decency to destroy the misfits you produce."

Yet he said over and over that his birds meant more to him than his fellow man.

> *Years of work, of study, of careful observations; the lives of literally thousands of birds, the disappointments and heartbreaks of hundreds of blasted hopes have gone into these pages; almost every line, every word is spattered [sic] with sweat and blood. For every truth I have outlined to you, I have blundered my way through a hundred errors. I have killed birds when it was almost as hard as killing one's own children. I have had birds die in my hand when their death brought me greater sadness than I have ever felt over the passing of a member of my own species.*

Indulgent, overlong, didactic, rambling, with wildly inappropriate digressions, and off–the–cuff opinions, this manuscript lacked the organization and professional restraint of his first book. It was, in short, a testimonial.

Stroud's conviction that he was the savior of the bird world was used to salve his badly shattered core ego and enhance his status. But it was also used to keep prison authorities from taking away his bird business. Letters poured in from people asking for help. Each one still required a "Special Purpose Letter" request, in which he described why he was replying. These were often barely disguised messages to prison authorities.

On December 1, 1941, he wrote, "This letter is in reply to one from a lady with a contagious disease in her flock. The enclosed letter, which she received from the Laboratory of the Missouri U and which she asked me to return, give[s] a good idea of how much they know about bird diseases and why my help is in such demand."

On January 3, 1942, he asked to reply to a letter. "The enclosure on psittacosis was sent to me by this gentlemen and he asked to have it returned. Since he wishes to discuss this subject before his bird club, but wanted to get my reaction to it. Something that is not hard, since I know this disease frontwards and backwards, and know that there never has been a proven case of human psittacosis."

". . . And if the condition is what I think it is," he wrote on another request, "I can probably cure the birds, providing it does not dye [sic] in the mean time."

On Feb. 20, 1942, he wrote: "This is in reply to a letter from this man concerning psittacosis and the difficulties some of the bird breeders are having because of certain pernicious influences interested in supressing [sic] birds. It happens that I have a little knowledge of the subject, since I have cured hundreds of cases of this disease, and can stop any outbreak in twenty–four hours."

Stroud was convinced of his importance and he obviously convinced many of those around him. His need to be right and to be a savior, forced him to brag so much that the sheer weight of his cockiness brought him down. In researching his letters, manuscripts and books, the same themes emerged again and again. Officers who had known him repeated statements he had made that could be found in his writings (which they had never read). Once he latched on to an idea he beat everyone over the head with it. This tendency led him to unbelievable comparisons.

"There is one essential to wining [sic] any fight whether you are using a test tube, a typewriter, or a tank," he wrote in a letter that was returned to him as inflammatory and never sent, "and that is [that] the spirit does not quit.

When a man quits or turns soft, he is whipped. The

tougher my problem, the tougher my attack. The more setbacks I have the more determined I become and the harder I work, and it is because of those very qualities that I have been able to whip every serious disease with which I have worked. I lost my first babies with brooder pneumonia in 1921. I cured the disease in 1938. I lost my first birds with fowl paralysis in 1928. I cured the disease in 1940. I lost my first bird with pneumonia in 1922. I finally worked out a simple and accurate method of diagnosis and a positive treatment only in 1941. Regardless of what we think of Hitler, and I had his number, completely, back in the '20s, before he gained power even in Germany, he is the best possible illustration of the effectiveness of a fix[ed] purpose. For, regardless of his personal qualities, he has a very effective singlemindedness. And if I have one good quality, it is the same kind of singlemind[ed]ness.

The same problems that medical doctors found in Stroud's self–diagnosis were rampant in his avian research as well: he knew much less than he assumed.

Stroud's most crucial blunder—the foundation upon which all of his errors rested—was that he was not medically trained. No matter how many "dead bodies" he dug into, no matter how good his descriptions of diseases were—and they were often quite good—no matter how many cell sections he sliced and drew, and no matter how many diseases he said he named and cured, he ignored the procedure by which all pathogens are isolated and identified—Koch's Postulate. Thus his basic research was seriously flawed.

Briefly, Robert Koch received a Nobel Prize in 1905 for his test used in diagnosing tuberculosis. His success in finding the bacteria was based on his discovery that an organism could be grown outside the body. This enabled him to examine the bacteria under a microscope and then transmit it to a healthy animal.

Once a pathogen causing a disease is isolated and transferred into a healthy body which then contracts the disease, one can say the disease has been discovered. This may take decades and involve many scientists. Stroud claimed to have discovered cures for thirteen diseases. He may have been looking at bacteria cultures, but he could not ascertain what he was seeing, nor could he isolate the organism and duplicate the disease in healthy birds.

Stroud, in fact, had the common problems of any researcher—he saw associations where none existed and he lumped together diseases of various origins. Ultimately he did not understand basic medical facts.

To illustrate his challenges—or the challenge for any non-medically trained person—it's necessary to explain some basic medical realities.

A common way to group disease is by causative agent—for example some diseases are bacterial, or fungal or parasitic; some are viral, and still others are a result of a failure of the immune system.

In humans, bacteria, fungus and parasites can all cause local infections which can often be treated locally. Nearly everyone remembers as a child having a skin wound dabbed with an antiseptic. Children often encounter ringworm, or head lice—both highly contagious. And diarrhea can be caused by bacteria, or be food related, and be treated with an antibiotic.

Most viruses, however, cannot be treated directly. The patient can spontaneously recover such as with the common cold or influenza, or die from a viral infection, or be prevented from exposure by vaccination. Nothing is going to cure it.

A breakdown in the immune system—such as cancer or acquired immune deficiency syndrome, is an entirely different invasive process of which even today we know very little. Some of these include genetic diseases, such as multiple sclerosis, which is inherited at a very basic cell level and seems to have a time–released mechanism. Heart attacks can be genetically or emotionally based, or be caused by improper diet and a lack of exercise. Other diseases may also have numerous triggers—various forms of cancer, for example, may have environmental, psychological or genetic links.

The challenge of identifying the cause of various diseases becomes even more complicated when a researcher takes a symptomatic, or a symptom–based identification approach, as Stroud did.

For example, a patient with acute diarrhea can have a bacterial infection, an influenza virus or even cancer of the colon. An antibiotic may wipe out the bacterial problem, but it won't kill a virus—*even though the patient may eventually recover.* And certainly, treating a cancer patient with an antibacterial will not cure that disease. But that same treatment may mask those symptoms, at least for a while, and when the patient dies several years later, death will not seem to be related to the diarrhea. This particular problem, the masking of illness, is characteristic of a bird who lives in a flock and often hides serious diseases from its community so that others will not kill it in order to keep away predators.

As if that isn't enough, a patient with cancer of the colon may also pick up a bacterial infection—causing diarrhea. A doctor successfully prescribing for the bacterial problem will probably miss the cancer involvement, even though it's still there, hidden, waiting to be diagnosed.

Until his time (and for many years after) no one had scientifically classified avian diseases, which Stroud was attempting to do. But because he didn't understand basic medical truths—that diseases have different origins requiring vastly different approaches—he lumped together a lot of them—almost as if he were mixing together Montezuma's Revenge, a flu virus and colon cancer under one diagnosis.

Clustering like this is common among pioneer researchers. Avian diphtheria, a disease Stroud studied and named, is a typical example. He called it "the hydra–headed chameleon of all bird diseases," which is acute, contagious and highly fatal. He stated that symptoms followed three different paths: bronchial, which included flu–like symptoms or sores in the mouth; external lesions, such as blisters or sores around the vent; and pox, which commonly caused sores around the beak and eyes of farm fowl.

He wrote in his second book that "diphtheria, roup, canker, fowl flu, vent gleet, septic fever, shipping fever, bird scourge, contagious bronchitis, contagious pneumonia, epithelious contagiosum, contagious catarrh, gapes, bird pox and possibly psittacosis," were "just a few of the names" applied to this disease.

Dr. Robert Schmidt, D.V.M., Ph.D., a nationally–known avian

pathologist in private practice and associated with the Consolidated Veterinary Diagonostics at Davis, California, counted "about a half a dozen different diseases" in this description. Dr. Schmidt, author of scores of articles on bird diseases, is a leader in the relatively new field of pet avain pathology. When shown Stroud's section on "avian diphtheria," he couldn't determine exactly what disease Stroud was seeing but he was able to separate out several terms. "We see pox [today]," Schmidt said, "And pox is a virus." In other words—not curable, but only innoculated against.

"And pox can be associated with any number of bacterial diseases," he said, the most important of which was an avian disease called psittacosis. "Psittacosis is not a virus at all, but a type of bacteria."

Psittacosis (pronounced sit–a–ko–sis) had made big news in 1929, when a large shipment of infected parrots was released, and many people throughout the world were infected and killed, including scientists working on isolating the disease. For some reason Stroud wrongly decided that humans were incapable of contracting it. And he erroneously thought he had a cure. Although the organism causing the disease (chlamydia) was isolated in 1930 in England, no cure was available until the tetracycline drugs in the 1950s.

Other diseases Schmidt recognized in Stroud's description are influenza, which is a virus that affects a variety of mammals and birds, and triclomoniasis ("canker"), which is a parasitic disease. The pathologist also noted that birds with sores in their mouths are often shown to have nothing more than Vitamin A deficiencies.

Thus, Stroud was linking at least one viral and two bacterial diseases with a parasitic disease and possibly a vitamin deficiency under one diagnosis.

Stroud devoted eighteen pages in his second book to "avian diphtheria," covering incubation, symptoms in all its various forms, morbid anatomy, examination, prevention and treatment. He included four drawings of the heart and lungs of infected birds, a drawing of a rooster's head showing lesions on the comb and wattle (taken from Ward and Gallagher), three drawings of birds with typical scabs or blisters, one of the typical posture of an infected bird, and a drawing of a lung section infected with bronchial pneumonia magnified four–hundred times. It was very impressive.

Dr. Brian Speer, D.V.M., felt that Stroud was largely describing a pox virus which has long been known to cause strangely variable clinical signs even in the same species—making it sometimes difficult to identify. A nationally–known veterinarian practicing avian medicine and surgery in Oakley, California, Speer agreed that Stroud was linking many types of diseases.

Stroud can't be blamed totally for making mistakes. But he compounded his errors by arrogantly pushing a treatment which was inappropriate in nearly every case, namely the same bubbly salt concoction he invented which was no longer on the market: "Stroud's Specific." Ten years had passed since he had been stripped of his privilege to market his bottled bird cures. Yet he persistently urged readers to buy it and if they couldn't obtain it—how could they?— he suggested they use sodium sulfate or sodium phosphate— treatments which Speer recognized were at best only antiseptics.

Thus any cure of any disease that Stroud clustered under the diagnosis of avian diphtheria would be entirely accidental. And if he was really seeing a pox virus, his treatment was complete- ly worthless.

Stroud claimed in his second book that hemorrhagic septice- mia could also be cured by "Stroud's Salts No. 1," and "Stroud's Effervescent Bird Salts." Thus he was linking even more diseases to his worthless treatment.

In the 1957 *Scientific American* article Gaddis was quoted as saying that Stroud had "embarked upon a study of fowl paralysis that was to last for years, and he set up experiments proving that the disease is developed and transmitted by green plant food." But even Gaddis was unaware that Stroud's experiments were not scientifi- cally controlled.

In this example, Stroud had purchased a pair of cinnamon canaries from a breeder in 1928 and noticed that one of the birds held its neck in an awkward position and seemed to have asthmatic attacks at night. He felt that whatever disease it was exhibiting was not contagious.

At the same time he decided to grow supplemental greens and seeds in the corner of his exercise yard. Because he didn't have soil, he mixed lime with cage refuge consisting of sand, seed shells and birds droppings, some of which came from the cage of the cinnamon bird. Later he fed the greens and seeds grown in this mixture to baby birds, and found that they also developed the typical neck position of what he now called fowl paralysis.

On the basis of his experiments Stroud determined that fowl paralysis was caused by a parasite capable of an independent existence in the soil, and, as Gaddis later wrote, was developed and transmitted by green plant food. Stroud went on to say that sulfanilamide was a cure for it.

Stroud was quite proud of himself, and clearly, later, Gaddis was, too. "The finest laboratory equipment money could buy," Stroud wrote in his book, "failed to work out a method for the control of fowl paralysis; though it may be egotistical for me to mention the fact at this place, I solved that problem with a couple of pails of sand and some bird droppings. And I did it at a time when I had never seen a microscope at close range."

Dr. Speer was skeptical. "I'd be very suspicious of some viral–neurologic disease being transmitted by green plant food," he said. Speer explained that head trauma, spinal fracture and calcium deficiency can cause paralysis. "Low blood calcium levels produce seizures, or lead toxicity produces seizures and sometimes paralysis. And there's a common form of cancer of the kidney that erodes up and eats into the sacrum and destroys the sciatic nerve, producing paralysis in one leg. . . . But there is no specific disease that we're currently dealing with that is induced by fresh greens alone."

He thought perhaps that Stroud might be passing on a virus, quite possibly a paramyxo family virus, which even today is "still challenging and difficult to isolate," Speer said.

If that was true, sulfanilamide, which is an antibacterial drug, would have no therapeutic effect.

Stroud had other basic research problems which were unavoidable. During autopsies, he often found hemorrhages in various organs. He theorized that the hemorrhages were the cause of death, and assumed that apoplectiform septicemia, a disease term that is not in use today but was making the rounds of the veterinary journals in his day, was caused by hemorrhages induced by egg–

food poisoning.

"A lot of what he saw was simply post–mortem change," Dr. Schmidt said. He explained that in death blood begins to "pool," and where it pools depends on how the bird is lying when it dies. Blood pooling occurs in the deaths of all animals, including humans. It is a form of decay, and except in cases of injury or stroke, is not the cause of death, but the result.

Moreoever, bacteria in putrefied food such as egg, does not cause death by hemorrhaging.

Another disease for which Stroud made numerous claims is aspergillosis—about the only one with the same name today. Aspergillus is a fungus much like green bread mold. Old dusty seed often contains aspergillus spores and once the spores invade the lungs of a bird (or a human), they can activate and produce a fatal disease. For more than a century it was known that breeders, like parent birds who chewed the seed before feeding it to their babies, had also succumbed to the disease.

Stroud thought he found a cure. While becoming fascinated with color dyes (he was using them to color–feed his birds, and later to stain smears for easier viewing under a microscope), Stroud discovered anthroquinone violet dye.

Stroud claimed anthroquinone would iradicate aspergillosis once it contaminated his birds. "It is possible to cure every case of acute, generalized aspergillosis," he wrote, by administering Du Pont's anthroquinone violet base. So sure of it he said, "I claim priority in the discovery of the therapeutic properties of this substance, since I was informed by the manufacturer that they had no information concerning its physiological properties."

He may have been onto something. Chemical dyes have long had medicinal links. Sir William Henry Perkins started the synthetic chemical dye industry in the mid–19th century when he discovered mauve while trying to find a cure for malaria. Today we know that gentian violet, a shiny dark–green dye, is an anti–infectant and effective against pinworms. Pararosaniline was used in the treatment of the disease schistosomiasis. Methelene blue, as people with aquariums know, is an effective treatment for a fish disease called ich. Some dyes may even have anti–fungal properties, such as crystal violet, which has been used to kill fungus in chicken feed. In fact, anthraquinone is one of the oldest classes of dyes and recently derivatives of it have been used as anti–cancer therapies, such as adrimycin.

But veterinary science has apparently not followed up on Stroud's theory of a dye–based cure for aspergillosis. There are a number of reasons. Given his haphazard diagnostic methods, it's not known if he was actually seeing aspergillosis. Secondly, birds don't usually manifest physical problems until very sick, therefore it's difficult to diagnose an early case—the only manifestation he could possibly cure with this treatment.

And even today, both Drs. Speer and Schmidt agreed, a late-stage case of widely–spread aspergillosis is all but impossible to cure.

Letters poured into Leavenworth anyway, fan mail from every state in the union. "I'm raising canaries for a living," one man from California wrote. "I have met with problems that can be solved only by Mr. Stroud—if he is willing."

"We sincerely believe that he will be our last source in trying to find a cure," wrote another.

In 1935, a man from Brooklyn, N.Y., wrote, "I have been informed that you have a patient at your institution who is considered one of the best birdmen in the world by bird fanciers. An engineer from Brazil . . . was my informant. . . "

In 1938 Stroud requested permission to write more than one hundred special purpose letters, most of them to bird fanciers.

The same year he was granted permission from Bennett to submit his manuscript to Harper Brothers Publishers and they turned him down. He tried several other publishers but was un-successful.

Stroud was still shipping birds in the early 1940s. In one request for four dozen birds, he was able to send twenty–two. He was giving advice to bird breeders on an almost daily basis. One man opened up a dead bird, removed the organs and sent them to Stroud for diagnosis. Stroud returned a telegram, "Bird's organs more like Typhoid than Fever one teaspoonful sodium perborate to each quart of drinking water to entire flock."

He was still getting requests to purchase copies of *Diseases of Canaries,* and now, even getting requests on his as yet unfinished *Stroud's Digest on the Diseases of Birds*.

In September 1942, a man wrote from the Department of Genetics at the Carnegie Institution of Washington, "I find it remarkable that research work should be done in prison especially under so many handicaps as he described. And I can state that at least some of it has been successful."

Over two thousand names, it was said, were contained in Stroud's correspondence card file. That is an exaggeration that Stroud may have perpetuated. But during a period of eighteen–and–a–half months from late 1940 until the spring of '42, Stroud wrote more than one–hundred–and–eighty letters, each letter requiring a special request form.

"He really requires a private secretary," one clerk complained.

Part VI
The Birdman of Alcatraz

By 1940 Stroud had been in prison for thirty–one years. He was now fifty years old. He had become institutionalized; adjustment to life on the outside would have been difficult.

He had just won honorable mention in a nation–wide federal prison contest with a story entitled "The King's English" about Warden Halligan at McNeil Island. Buoyant, he worked feverishly for the next two years on his second book, thinking that it would be seven hundred pages long and probably cost $22,000 to publish. "The book is coming first–rate," he wrote to a friend. "The new drawings are out of this world."

But on December 7, 1941, Pearl Harbor was bombed and the U.S. entered World War II, an event that would change Stroud's life as much as it did the lives of millions who now flooded recruitment centers around the country. As officers began to quit to join the armed forces, wardens faced operating overcrowded prisons with fewer men. Senior Officer Bergen, for example, who by 1939 had transferred from Lewisburg to Alcatraz, had his enlistment blocked by the warden. Dollison, who by 1940 had transferred to the Correctional Institution at Ashland, Kentucky, watched as officer after officer dropped out. War fever eventually became so great that at age thirty–four he, too, went on leave to join the Army.

Stroud was still commercially breeding canaries, still ordering large quantities of seed, research materials and medicines, still complaining about vague illnesses and receiving and writing large quantities of letters. War would change that. Leavenworth no longer had the man power to service him. Administrators quietly asked Washington to transfer him to a "small institution" for closer supervision.

There was only one small institution.

Early in the morning on December 16, 1942, officers walked into Leavenworth segregation, stood outside Stroud's cell and told him to get dressed for transfer. Although there may have been rumors of an imminent transfer, for security reasons, official action is sudden and immediate. Stroud probably guessed that he was going to Alcatraz. Once he dressed an officer hand–cuffed him, attached it to a waist chain and then bent down and fastened leg irons around his ankles.

A special medical report in October 1942 had stated that there was "no medical contraindication to his transfer to Alcatraz." The doctor hastened to add, however, that "should he be deprived of his privileges and be forced to give up the study of breeding canaries, he would cause considerable trouble." At the bottom of the report were the words: "Work: Permanent Isolation."

Surrounded by officers, one whose hand gripped the crook of his arm, Stroud was quickly shuffled out of Leavenworth's segregation. As was usual among men handling an impulsive and unpredictable guard–killer, there was little small talk.

Stroud boarded a train on a special Leavenworth spur and traveled for three days, getting his first glimpse of life on the outside in twenty–two years. It was immediately apparent that even in the small towns, the pace of life had increased dramatically since 1918 when he had last been out. Seemingly overnight automobiles had multiplied; streets were noisier and packed with women shoppers, soldiers or kids, all hurrying to get somewhere.

While he traveled, his two cells were inventoried and emptied.

"By slow degrees he became the center of a contraband moonshining business and a letter–kiting scheme," a BOP summary report later stated, explaining its reasons for transferring Stroud. "The dozens of cages, shelves of books and stacks of magazines he had been permitted provided concealment for these activities."

A list dated December 21, 1942, was drawn up. "In addition to a remarkable quantity of nuisance contraband," the Bureau report summarized, "there were numerous medicines whose principal component was alcohol, eighteen boxes of matches, fourteen packages of razor blades, two screwdrivers, one brace and bit, one pair of side–cutting pliers, one claw hammer, one carpenter's hand saw, one improvised hacksaw blade, electric wire and fittings and sheet iron scrap, etc."

Most of these were usable for the construction of boxes but what was he doing with a homemade hacksaw blade and packages of razor blades?

"The following contraband was also found in the cell: an improvised still for distilling alcohol, made from an old pipe, electric light bulbs converted into flasks, glass and rubber tubing, and heated by a homemade electric hot plate. This equipment was destroyed. Three–and–a–half gallons of mash (emptied into sewer); alcohol consisting of two one–quart bottles; one one–pint bottle; one partially filled gallon jug; one beaker at [the] still containing [a] small quantity; and other smaller quantities concealed in various ways. Some had been placed in lengths of glass tubing and the ends sealed. All the alcohol was emptied into the sewer expect one bottle held for evidence."

Stroud had boasted to officers enroute that he had been "cooking" 188 proof grain alcohol for twelve years, and once had sixty pounds of sugar in his cell without that "dumb bunch" at Leavenworth knowing about it. The officers, as Stroud knew they would, relayed this news to Washington and it was later quoted in a 1962 *Washington Post* article.

More alarming perhaps than alcohol production, which is commonly brewed in any prison, a separate report commented on another piece of contraband found in his cell. The report had a remarkable similarity to something Stroud would write in his own manuscript ten years later when he reminisced about the hated Warden Morgan of his early Leavenworth days. The 1942 report stated that "he carefully hollowed out a niche under one of the tables and put a stilleto–like dagger in it, so arranged that it could be taken out and used instantly."

Alcatraz Island dominated the beautiful San Francisco Bay like an armored tank in a field of daisies.

You couldn't sit in a restaurant along the wharf or hang on the cable car down Hyde Street and avoid seeing the morbidly fascinating prison. You couldn't sail the bay, or ride one of the tourist boats without drawing close to the 200–yard forbidden zone that surrounded the prison island. And if you were a chained convict on the eleven–minute boat ride, you couldn't help but feel the immensity of the island's reputation as the nation's most maximum–security prison. More than one prisoner cried on that boat ride.

"I'd lived in the Bay Area, and I never heard anything good about it," said James Quillen, who arrived as a twenty–two–year-old kid four months before Stroud. Quillen, in his 70s when interviewed, had pulled a forty–five–year sentence for robbery and kidnapping. He remained on Alcatraz for ten years. "You put on a tough guy exterior," he said softly, with some refinement for a man with such a past. "But you have to wonder, 'Is this where I'm going to die?' For years I thought this is where I'd die. I *still* get nervous when I think about it."

Although seemingly overnight Alcatraz had become the "dreaded penal colony," in reality its reputation had been seeping into the public consciousness since the 1860s, and references to the "devil rock" can be found in newspapers as early as 1890.

An Army fort dating from the Civil War era, it steadily became an ever–larger military guardhouse as other forts in the Bay Area sent their deserters and miscreants. When decency forced the Army to abandon its ramshackle, firetrap guardhouses in 1912 and build the large prison monument that stands today, the island was finally designated a prison. Over time, thousands of Army soldiers transferred in and out. Most were convicted for relatively minor military offenses—absence without leave, drunkenness or assaulting a superior officer—yet given fifteen– and twenty–year sentences. And while most men saw their terms drastically cut to a few months, they never forgot the stigma of being consigned to a fog–bound island with violent offenders and predatory rapists. And when most of them returned home, they told their families about that devil island.

Alcatraz was consistently an embarrassment to the Army. Even after military convicts built the cell house in 1912, the Army regretted it—it was the first thing that immigrants and tourists saw when they arrived on ships to the port of San Francisco. By the depression they were looking to unload it.

The crime spree of the 1930s and several widely–reported, vicious prison breaks, made the BOP decide to take over Alcatraz as its maximum-security penitentiary. Walter Winchell and the media shifted the public's attention from gangsters to G-men— famed government agents like J. Edgar Hoover and Melvin Purvis— and even James A. Johnston, the banker–turned–warden who was picked to rehab the military cell house on Alcatraz and open the federal penitentiary.

Thus, by the time the first reporters toured Alcatraz in the summer of 1934, a sizeable number of people throughout the United States had already heard about Alcatraz and quite willingly believed its suddenly notorious reputation.

Eight years after Alcatraz opened as the federal maximum–security prison and five days before Christmas in 1942, Stroud stepped onto the dock in leg irons and handcuffs. He was quite beefy then. "He is well nourished and looks well," the prison psychiatrist summarized in an early report, noting that he was six feet and weighed one–hundred–eighty–three pounds. Yet he had the pale, bloodless face of a Lifer. Creases between his eyes gave him a slightly tense look and his lips were precise and tightly–drawn. His hair was cropped short which accentuated his large, perpendicular ears. "Very, very pale," said Bergen, who by then was a lieutenant on Alcatraz and had wandered down to see him. "The skin on his hands and arms was almost white."

Although at age fifty–two Stroud was twenty years older than the average con who stepped onto the dock in chains, he was not the oldest. Fifty–seven men were over fifty years of age at the time they transferred to Alcatraz. The oldest, Robert Spears, had been sixty–six when he arrived. Nonetheless, Stroud was older than most and prisoners often referred to him as the "old man."

He was driven to the top of the island where the large cell house stood, and escorted into a side entrance, emerging into the basement. He showered and was given a new set of clothes. He became number AZ 594. Five–hundred–and–ninety–three prisoners had already been imprisoned on Alcatraz, and about half were still there.

By then, Alcatraz had found its niche in American prison mythology. When it had opened as the nation's maximum–security federal prison, Warden James A. Johnston and Bureau director Bates had shown reporters around. The dramatic placement of the island prison in the midst of cold, "shark–infested" bay waters, coupled with Johnston's intense attention to security details, the high number of officer–per–convict ratio, as well as the proliferation of weapons, pushed reporters to tag it as virtually "escape proof."

Indeed, Alcatraz's "escape proof" record remains mostly intact today. In its twenty–nine years (it closed in 1963), one–thousand–five–hundred–and–forty–five prisoners served time there. Only thirty–six, or about two–and–a–half percent, seriously attempted escape. Of those, thirty–one were brought back, dead or alive, and five disappeared (two in 1937 and three in 1962).

The tag "escape proof," nonetheless, was a challenge to early prisoners of whom a high percentage had attempted escapes in other prisons. In fact, statistics show another interesting pattern. In its short federal prison history Alcatraz experienced fourteen escape attempts. Of those, ten occurred by 1946. Indeed, by the time Stroud arrived in '42, six attempts had already taken place and four more would occur in the next four years. After '46, however, interest died down, and in the next seventeen years only four escape attempts occurred before the prison closed.

Thus, the island's reputation was constantly being tested in those early years, resulting in more and more media attention as a rock–hard, escape–proof penitentiary.

Another attention grabber was the small, select coterie of big–name convicts, most of whom had arrived long before Stroud.

An average of twenty thousand men were held in federal prisons throughout the country in any given year when Alcatraz was open. Approximately two–hundred–and–fifty of them, or about one percent, were housed at Alcatraz. Theoretically, they were the worst behaved one percent. Men weren't transferred to Alcatraz because of their crimes, but because of their behavior. Most were career prisoners who had served time since their teens and who represented every crime and act of mayhem known to man. Most had landed in other federal prisons first, then crawled their way through assaults, murders, rapes and escapes to land on Alcatraz. Most had also racked up detainers in state prisons and had decades to serve. Most were unknown petty criminals with a dangerous accumulation of criminal incidents and paranoid, defiant attitudes.

Only a handful were famous. But that roster read like a star-studded Hollywood blockbuster—Capone, Kelly, Karpis, Roy Gardner, "Doc" Barker, "Blackie" Audett, John Paul Chase and later, Mickey Cohen. Although nobody realized it then, those names were being woven into the fabric of American folklore. The gangster era with its colorful monikers—"Creepy," "Waxy," "Blackie," "Scarface"—its tough–guy sheen and outlaw attractiveness, still sells.

Al Capone, for example, had been implicated in scores of murders and had been imprisoned for federal income tax evasion.

At 5 feet 10 inches and two–hundred–and–fifteen pounds, "Scarface" had begun his eleven–year stretch at Atlanta penitentiary in 1930. It was said that he was still running his rackets through his lawyers, however, and in 1934 he was on the first train to Alcatraz.

On "the Rock" Capone was mostly docile and conciliatory— humble even. Big name convicts learned quickly that in prison it paid to be modest; younger punks and thugs got their kicks off the backs of the famous. After several trial work assignments Capone was given one of the more menial jobs in prison—cell house janitor. It meant that he rarely got outside the prison except to go to the exercise yard.

By the time the thirty–five–year–old mob boss was reduced to sweeping the cell house floor his life was mostly over. He'd already had two courses of anti–syphilitic treatment and was undergoing a third. It was too late, however. On February 5th, 1938, he went into convulsions followed by stuporous sleep and mental confusion. "During the next few days he became quite disturbed, noisy, restless," Alcatraz psychiatrist Dr. Romney M. Ritchey wrote, "and twice soiled his room."

When examined, the great Capone was distractible, unable to concentrate, his judgment and reasoning severely impaired. But he was definitely expansive. He told Ritchey that he planned to go "into charity work" after his release, and "will build factories and industries to furnish employment to everyone needing it." One could almost feel the excited presence of a parenthetical exclamation point. Capone evidently took a great deal of pleasure in relating his plans to Ritchey. The doctor diagnosed him as "psychotic."

Capone had already gone from Alcatraz when Stroud arrived, and instead of building factories to employ everyone, he sat out the rest of his life in Miami until he died of cardiac arrest in 1947, at age forty–eight.

Another big name from Alcatraz, "Doc" Barker of the infamous "Ma" Barker gang, had been killed in a 1939 Alcatraz escape attempt.

Alvin "Old Creepy" Karpis was still on Alcatraz. Karpis' reputation was made when J. Edgar Hoover tagged him "Public Enemy Number 1" for two big kidnappings in the 1930s. Although he was eligible for parole in fifteen years, Karpis would remain on Alcatraz longer than any man—almost twenty–five years—from August 1936 until November 1962. Karpis had a name to live down, however, and was often in scrapes with other cons. Later, at McNeil Island, he befriended a kid named Charlie Manson, teaching him to play guitar.

When the rumor hit that the Canary Prisoner had arrived, Karpis told everyone how he'd seen Stroud at Leavenworth. Later Karpis would say that Stroud had a "definite mental quirk."

Thus Stroud's arrival occurred after the dreaded name of Alcatraz had been burned in the public's mind by its underground reputation from the military era, its escape attempts and big–name criminals. Yet Stroud would remain on Alcatraz for seventeen years and rival Al Capone as the con with the biggest name. In fact, his name would be linked to the battleship–shaped island like an anchor—dragging it down into its final ignominy.

Stroud was quickly escorted up the stairs, entering into what one officer referred to as "the temple"—the cavernous, stealthily quiet concrete warehouse that contained between two and three hundred prisoners. He passed "Time's Square," the juncture between the dining room and the wide corridor known as "Broadway,"and the concrete floors were shined to such a high gloss that they nearly jumped out at him. The cell blocks were three tiers high and above them was a long bright skylight. Everything was painted light pink, with red trim. Alcatraz was more modern, cleaner and better lit than Leavenworth.

In fact, in 1942, Alcatraz was one of the most modern penitentiaries in the nation. Each cell had a toilet, a sink, a small metal fold–down shelf and seat, and a four–inch single Army mattress on a metal bed that was bolted to the floor. The bars on the cells were modern "tool–proof" steel. It was one of the only prisons—then or now—that maintained one man–one cell.

Modern or not, Alcatraz was designed as the federal punishment prison. When a man went to "the Rock," he had usually lost good time—accumulated years off his sentence that he now had to serve. At Alcatraz he had no privileges beyond food, clothing, housing and medical care. Work was considered a privilege, and the workday was short. In fact, time out of the cell was minimal—half hours for meals, yard time twice a week for a couple of hours, then back in the cell. Every new day would be exactly like the last. Every day ended at 4:40 p.m., when the last count was taken. After dinner at 5:00 p.m., men were locked down for the next fourteen hours. Lights out at 9:30 p.m. The nights were long and frequently troublesome. One man could keep the whole cell house awake all night— or at least until reinforcements were brought in to escort him to D block. At times the whole cell block rocked with a blistering frustration that could be heard in the officers' family quarters down the hill.

"It was a prison that was out to break you," Quillen stated firmly, "not rehabilitate you."

After a man acclimated to the close security and the tension of long confinement, adjustment to other penitentiaries would be difficult.

Three times a day most men were released from their cells and escorted to the dining room for a half–hour meal, but Stroud would never eat in the dining room. Twice a day, Monday through Friday, men were escorted to work details, but Stroud would not be assigned to a job. Once a day there was a sick–call line. Yet Stroud would not even see that.

He was taken through a door behind which was D block, where the activity level reached an almost comatose state.

"Old Saltwater" Johnston, who was warden in 1942, had either agreed with Director Bennett to segregate Stroud or took it upon himself as a mandate of the prisoner's Life in solitary confinement order. (The timing of Stroud's arrival suggested that Bennett and Johnston waited until after D block was completely renovated before sending him there.) Nonetheless, placing a man directly into D block was a departure from the norm. Stroud would skip quarantine—a thirty–day cool–out in a second–tier cell in the main cell house—and go directly into segregation, a status he maintained for the next seventeen years. Although he had few disciplinary reports at Leavenworth, his alleged concealment of razor blades, hacksaw blades, a dagger and possibly material for homemade hand grenades helped prolong his special status.

The warden was a tough man, but he was not like the beefy, officious wardens Stroud had seen in the past—men who were often photographed in military attire carrying long rifles. Instead, James A. Johnston had the air of a banker about him. He usually wore a three–piece, pin–striped suit with an ever–vigilant white handkerchief poking out of his chest pocket.

Johnston was sixty years old when he took over at Alcatraz, and sixty–eight when Stroud arrived. At five–feet–eight, with a shock of white hair, skin like refined wheat flour and round wire–rim glasses, Johnston had such a dignified presence that one newspaper called him the "diminutive czar." He remained warden on Alcatraz from 1934 until 1948.

It seemed as if he'd been groomed for the job. At age thirty–seven in 1911, he became warden of California's notorious Folsom Prison. A year later he was appointed warden at San Quentin—at the time more dangerous than Alcatraz. He proved to be a reformer—

abolishing corporal punishment and clothing stripes, installing farms and honor camps. In 1919, after studying law at night for several years, he passed the California Bar. A refined public speaker, Johnston was a member of the prestigious Commonwealth Club, which put him in company with powerful men. In 1925 he left public work to become vice president of the American Trust Company in San Francisco. But after the stock market crash, the bank failed. On January 1, 1934, he was appointed warden at the U.S. Penitentiary at Alcatraz.

Times had changed and so had Johnston. Although he still considered himself a reform warden, the rules on Alcatraz would now reflect a man who was fed up with violence. First he hand-picked officers from around the country. (One of his senior officers was Paul J. Madigan who later became the third warden on Alcatraz.) Staff would number one–hundred, for approximately two–hundred–eighty prisoners. "Damn near as many guards as prisoners," retorted Henry Floyd Brown, a prisoner who served there about the same time as Stroud.

Johnston reconstructed the old Army prison facilities, adding cyclone fences topped with barbed wire, towers, tool resistant bars, gun galleries and extra armaments.

He helped establish the rules which remained largely the same until Alcatraz closed. There was no commissary where prisoners could buy candy or cigarettes, no big–name entertainers to perform for them, no newspapers and, until 1956, no radio. Inmate personal property was limited and subject to frequent inspection by officers. Letters from home were read and retyped by a mail censor before the typed copy was delivered to the prisoner; letters by prisoners were censored and retyped. Visits were limited to a wife or blood relative once a month for approximately two hours. Reading, smoking, game playing and artwork were almost the only pastimes. There were virtually no out–of–cell evening inmate activities, and little else to relieve the long, boring hours confined in a cell. Movement to and from work, the dining hall, the basement shower, the hospital and yard was done in small groups, and after most such movements the men were counted. Inmates proceeded directly to their destination, without stopping for conversation with occupants of other cells, or fellow workers, and without dawdling to look out the window. Entering another prisoner's cell regardless of whether it was occupied was considered a very serious offense.

Ironically, such stringent rules were a safety feature for prisoners; fewer men were murdered or raped at Alcatraz because of the lessened opportunities.

Johnston brought back the silent system and for the first four years prisoners worked and ate in silence. But they rebelled and the rule fell in 1938.

In contrast to the stringent regulations and lack of diversity, Johnston hoped that prisoners would respond to a strong role model. For that reason, at the noon meal he would stand at the entrance of the mess hall when prisoners filed out—showing that he was available to every prisoner who wanted to talk to him. During one of these episodes a convict named Burton Phillips knocked him down and began kicking him. Although Johnston felt buoyed by the fact that officers *and* prisoners had pulled Phillips off him, it was said by officers later that he entered the dining room less often, and grew more distant from prisoners. Phillips was worked over pretty good by the officers, Dollison later learned, and he was escorted to D block.

Johnston shared one thing with all of his predecessors: the warden was God. On the boat—named the "Warden Johnston"— you didn't sit in the same cabin as Mr. and Mrs. Johnston without an invitation. On the job you didn't question his authority, overrule or ignore his orders. He appeared omnipotent.

The warden, his wife Ida Fulton Johnston, and their three daughters lived a few steps from the prison building in a seven–bedroom California–Mission style mansion built by the military for the commanding officer. Without a doubt, the family had the most spectacular view in northern California, overlooking San Francisco Bay, the bridges and the city.

But Johnston could seldom get away from it all. He needed all the traits of a prison reformer–banker–lawyer–czar. He had inherited a second–rate physical plant; he had to calm the fears of San Franciscans who were alarmed that the nation's most maximum security prison sat resolutely in their bay; he had to woo Washington politicians who would complain about the high cost of caring for such a puny number of prisoners; he had to administer officers who guarded the BOP's most escape–prone, often dangerous, unpredictable population.

Like anyone, Johnston may have been curious about the Canary Prisoner. But it would be some time before he would go to segregation and meet him; he wouldn't want to confer any status on the new prisoner.

Stroud was taken through the door into D block. It felt immediately different; it was darker and had a mausoleum–like chill. High barred windows were on one side of a wide aisle, and the other side contained three tiers of cells, each one bigger than those in the main cell block. Six cells on the flats were the closed–front isolation cells, or what the convicts called the "hole." Each of these had two cell fronts, a sliding barred gate inside, and a massive, solid steel door outside. When officers shut that solid door, a man was isolated in silence and darkness. These were the short–term, high–punishment cells for men who had committed institutional offenses. Since Stroud had never celled in one of these—and never would—he was technically not in solitary confinement, as he and others always maintained.

Although the second and third tiers of cells faced windows that overlooked San Francisco Bay, the view was restricted by unwashed glass, detention sash and tool–resistant bars, making the city appear more remote than ever.

D block was located along the windward side of the island. Winter and summer, gusts of wind were sucked through the Golden Gate to smack into the wall along D block. The entire building was alive with whistles and howls from Pacific winds, but segregation got the worst of it. Some officers spoke of walking the flats at night in their overcoats and sitting on the radiators to keep warm. Stroud was racked into a cell along the floor—the draftiest section—where he could be closely watched.

Before stepping in, he could look up at the gun gallery officer. Armed, clothed in a dark–gray woolen uniform and locked into a barred patrol walkway that ran the width of D block and through a door into the main cell house, the officer coldly looked back at this guard–killer and bird doctor.

As he stepped into his cell Stroud heard the same old clanging of metal on metal. His eyeglasses were confiscated and he immediately filed a request for their return. His file shows that he also complained that he was so cold he had to sit with a blanket over his legs.

As its name implied, segregation was different. Also called isolation, the "hole," seg, or what the Bureau would later call the "Treatment Unit" or T.U., D block was where men were confined to their cells twenty–four hours a day. They filled their time writing letters, playing checkers or chess, reading books or magazines, sleeping or talking quietly among themselves. Twice a week, if their classification permitted, they could go to the yard. Once a week they were taken out one at a time and given a shower—locked in a shower stall along the flats.

Not everyone in segregation was in punishment status. Some were worried that they could be killed by another con—because of owed favors, ill–conceived comments, raging animosity, "signifying" or eyeballing the wrong man—and sought protective custody. Others were forced into D block by circumstances.

Nonetheless, segregation was hard time for everyone.

Close security prisons were similar in one respect: the body of factual information was slim and the body of misinformation was voluminous. News from the outside was limited and censored. What information did circulate inside was often heated by rumor, innuendo and paranoia.

Prisoners weren't usually known to each other by their real names, for example, but by their prison names—nicknames given by other cons. Sometimes they didn't even know each other's real names. Staff members were given more derogatory names like "Big Donkey," "Meathead," "Slaughterhouse," "Big Stiff," "Ass Kickin' Fats," "Saltwater," "Big Stoop," "Fuck Face" or, in Dollison's case, "Weasel Eyes." Usually, but not always, it wasn't personal. Letters written to Dollison, who arrived on Alcatraz later and became the Superintendent of Industries, indicate that prisoners had only a vague idea of his name or how it was spelled.

Some prisoners even lost track of time or dates, relying on the daily regimen to mark the passage of hours. Days and even months could slip by.

But it could be worse in segregation. First, when a man went into D, it was usually for an assault, contraband or escape attempt. Going to seg meant loss of privileges such as a job, restricted diet and often isolation. If his behavior warranted it, a prisoner would be placed in a dark cell for as many as nineteen days. And often he'd be real stiffed about it.

Later, when he came out of the hole, officers placed him in a regular segregation cell on the second or third tier, let him brush his teeth and wash up. He could talk to the others in D block, but he couldn't see them. When he took a shower or went to the yard, one cell opened—his. When he returned, one cell opened—his. Consequently he only vaguely knew what cell he was in, and he had even less knowledge of where everyone else celled. By the time Jim Quillen landed in D block he was aware that Stroud was housed above him, but he didn't know where. In fact, Stroud had moved to the top tier, and was residing in cell 41.

D block was worse in other ways. Respect between officers and prisoners—a thin veneer at best—deteriorated here because of group mentality; nearly every officer was regarded as the enemy. Cons were hostile and rarely spoke more than a few words to them. There was one very simple reason: men who talked to guards at length were suspected of informing. As long as a prisoner and an officer were alone they could be civil and talk at length. But the minute another prisoner entered the picture, talk subsided.

"The minute you showed any particular attention to any given inmate," Bergen said, "he immediately fell suspect to the other inmates. Very few of them would talk to you."

Former prisoner Clarence Carnes agreed; if a con had a long visit with an FBI agent or a prison official, the others became agitated.

Thus, D block had its own code and its own cachet.

The most notorious insider in 1942—and for a long time thereafter—was Rufus "Whitey" Franklin, a man virtually unknown by the public but notorious among prisoners for killing officer Royal Cline with a hammer in a 1938 escape attempt. Franklin was emotionally unstable and violent. Although he was officially in solitary confinement—one of the six closed–front cells—he was on the regular line diet and his solid door was left open. Nonetheless, he was a cause celebre among other cons because of his long isolation status, and he was often used to whip up fervor against the guard force. Franklin was not returned to the main population until 1951, thirteen years after the guard killing. By then, Stroud had already served thirty–five years in segregation.

Stroud had learned from others—rightly or wrongly—that Bennett approved every move in and out of Alcatraz. Although wardens in all federal prisons were given plenty of latitude, and although assistant directors could transfer prisoners in and out of other institutions, Bennett apparently oversaw every Alcatraz transfer. To some officers, Alcatraz was known as "Bennett's island." Indeed, in his book, Bennett even called himself "a talent scout for Alcatraz." Stroud bitterly believed that this transfer to Alcatraz was a result of a "conspiracy within the Federal Bureau of Prisons," which in turn resulted from a "personal animosity . . . among high officials of the BOP" against him.

He began immediately to file a motion for illegal confinement.

Within six months he had filed a petition for a writ of habeas corpus. Although Alcatraz Associate Warden E. J. Miller asserted that Stroud was using the law "as pastime," this was his first legal assault on A. Mitchell Palmer's Life in solitary confinement order, and represented his extreme unhappiness at his transfer.

Stroud v. Johnston stated that Bennett and Leavenworth Warden Walter A. Hunter had a "personal animosity" against him. Stroud's paranoia about Bennett increased over the years. He later wrote his brother that he told Senator Langer of North Dakota, who visited Alcatraz one day, that "[Mr. Bennett] has twice attempted to have me murdered."

In *Stroud v. Johnston*, he argued that he had been held in "absolute solitary confinement" for long periods; that "solitary

confinement" was too vague and ambiguous to be properly interpreted; and that it was cruel and unusual punishment in violation of
the Eighth Amendment. He further argued that his transfer to
Alcatraz was illegal because authority to transfer prisoners had
been granted to the Bureau after his original sentence mandated
confinement to Leavenworth.

Stroud was capable of whipping up great sarcastic indignation
which often diminished his legal arguments. He wrote that he'd
been sent to Alcatraz "so that a new, different and more severe
punishment may be inflicted upon him, in order that the over
inflated ego and personal animosity of a bureaucratic penologist,
drunk with power, may be appeased . . ."

In a separate motion, he petitioned the court to order Warden
Johnston to produce fifteen D block prisoners—among them Rufus
Franklin and Burton Phillips—who would testify that his punishment "is different and greater than" their punishment. Stroud had
aroused enthusiasm among prisoners to testify in a San Francisco
court; nearly every Alcatraz con would willingly perjure himself
just to see the outside world for one day.

The petitioner did not have all his arguments lined up however.
He was forced to admit that he had been held at Leavenworth with
other men—not in solitary confinement—and that he had had
attained privileges far beyond the norm. Thus his own argument
that his confinement was absolute, cruel or unusual was struck
down. His third issue—that he was exempt from transfer because
the government's authority to transfer had been granted after he had
been confined—held no merit for the court. He lost. In December
1943 the Circuit Court of Appeals concurred with the verdict.

In the meantime, Stroud was busy with his book corrections.
Bennett had stood by his word that the prisoner could publish it and
Warden Johnston honored that commitment.

Although D block prisoners were given limited writing privileges, Stroud was allowed to edit his five–hundred page manuscript
and order special books and magazines. His cell, in fact, was once
again filled with legal pads, books and magazines.

He worked when others slept and slept odd hours. Thus he didn't always join the usual rumble of segregation conversations. At other times he couldn't avoid the gab fests and joined in.

"I've heard guys argue for one week that Joe Louis could have beat Jack Dempsey," said Clarence Carnes, who was in segregation during Stroud's time. "And Stroud would yell, 'What in the goddamn hell does it matter?' "

Listening to cons discuss the writing of Erskine Caldwell and Thomas Wolfe in D block one day, Stroud argued that they were both poor writers because of their liberal use of vulgar language. Stroud was a conservative. He maintained that anything could be written without vulgarity, and to prove it, he wrote a pornographic story involving two young boys who were brothers and lovers, passing it around to other cons. It was this story that was confiscated and used against him in the 1962 court battle.

A month after he arrived on Alcatraz, an article of his appeared in *American Canary Magazine* entitled "I Wonder." It's unlikely the Alcatraz staff was even aware of it.

"Many years before most of you were born," the article began, "a young man with an insatiable craving for knowledge, but no formal schooling, entered a United States penitentiary. Entered it with the firm resolve to add something useful to his knowledge every day."

Although the story omitted mention of the manslaughter and murder convictions for killing two men, it used the solitary confinement issue to keep the emotional focus on Stroud. "After four years under sentence of death," it said, "he found himself facing a life sentence in solitary confinement and in the hope of being able to earn the money with which to supply his small needs, he took up the breeding of canaries . . . " The narrative was by turns folksy and righteous. "I have never received one dime [of] royalty for this work," it said, ". . . Regardless . . . I have never slackened my pace in my study of bird diseases."

The article was a plea for money. Stroud wanted readers to finance the printing of the new book. Claiming that he had found "a cure for every contagious disease with which I have worked," he asked that one thousand people order the book for $5.00 each. If they didn't, he warned, "you will have contributed to closing the door to an understanding of bird diseases in your faces." When disease strikes, "you will cry in vain" for help that will never come because "laboratory workers do not work twenty hours a day or live, year in and year out, in their bird rooms."

On the same page was a half–page paid advertisement promising delivery of the book within ninety days—April—and calling Stroud "the most unusual researcher the world has produced since Louis Pasteur."

Although Stroud wrote "I Wonder," the ads were probably placed with the help of his brother, Marcus, who had suddenly reappeared in Stroud's life.

Marcus had by now changed his name to Lawrence Gene Marcus, and signed his letters L. G. Marcus.

After the early 1920s, when he had performed in Chicago vaudeville as "The Great Marcus" and had written his brother infrequently, Marcus had lost touch with Stroud. By 1943 he was living in Minneapolis, Minnesota, and working for the Electronic Radio and Television Institute. By then Stroud needed help getting the manuscript published, and thereafter, Marcus's letterhead appeared as, "L. G. Marcus, Agent for Robert Stroud."

File notes indicate that Marcus sometimes paid court filing fees for his brother, pacified Stroud and the Bureau when they had problems communicating, responded to letters addressed to his brother, had the manuscript typed, solicited publishers and finally ushered the printing. It was a thankless task. It appeared in a later correspondence that Marcus even loaned Stroud more than $15,000. Yet Stroud was critical of his brother, frequently calling him "stupid" and often claiming "I would have made millions if I'd been in his shoes." In a variation on that theme he wrote later that, "If I'd had anyone but Marc handling my affairs I would have been free years ago." But Stroud now needed him, like he had needed Della Jones years before. And, in his weaker moments Marcus may have been convinced that Stroud could make them both rich. Their association grew and he began thinking of moving to California.

Two more articles appeared in February and in April, "I Wonder Too," and "Don't We 'All Wonder Too'?" both written by fans. The texts of both also omitted mention of his serious crimes, yet repeated his "miraculous" accomplishments while working under impossible odds.

Ads now promised delivery of the book in sixty to ninety more days. Clearly, money was not pouring in. "The sooner the money is collected the sooner we can make delivery," the ads said.

By June it was apparent that sales were lagging. An announcement—"We Apologize"—promised the book by August.

In September, an ad guaranteed delivery by October. In October, the ad proclaimed finally, that "the presses are set to roll."

In December 1943, S*troud's Digest on the Diseases of Birds* was finally published.

Stroud did not endear himself to many in the Alcatraz staff that first year. In a March 1944 memo contained in his file, it was noted that he was "very lazy, evades work," was "resistant/obstructive" and a "defiant agitator." It stated that he "is dangerous and an agitator. Very outspoken against all government agencies." The doctor noted that he "complains at times of rather indefinite pains and believes he fully understands his health problems and wants to prescribe for himself." Associate Warden E. J. Miller described Stroud as "sarcastic" and noted that his "hatred for all officials was very plain."

Stroud was still proving he had two sides, however, and still proving that men saw in him what he wanted them to see; in the same report, the chaplain described him as "talkative, friendly, studious."

James V. Bennett also made news in 1944. A favorable article on him, entitled "He Took the Bars Off Prisons" appeared in *Nation's Business*. It described him as a progressive watchdog of crime and cost, noting that he held the fate of seventeen–thousand men and women in twenty–five federal prisons throughout the country. To show that Bennett was "no softy," the article also mentioned a story that Bennett related. It described an unnamed prisoner as a "double murderer in Atlanta prison" who had "worked up quite a little business in canaries" and who also had made a "beautiful little shiv" out of a file.

Bennett proudly showed the reporter a shank of steel now honed to a razor–sharp edge. He felt that it made the point. In years to come he would show the homemade knife to many people, some of whom weren't as impressed. "I have seen plenty of prison–made knives" Bennett was quoted saying in the article, "but this is the only one that was made for the express purpose of killing—me."

Stroud's Digest on the Diseases of Birds was an impressive book. Containing four–hundred–and–eighty–three pages of text, with an extensive glossary of terms, a section on drug dosages, scores of drawings and two indices, it appeared to be a thoroughly researched work. In it, Stroud discussed all the major diseases he had encountered, all arranged alphabetically. Individual diseases were broken down by history, origin, symptoms, morbid anatomy, prevention and treatment. Full explanations for scientific termi- nology and theories were given in layman's language. He drew pictures of blood cells in both normal and diseased samples, egg structure and formation, embryos, generative system and sections of many organs. He described his first experiments and autopsies that led to his early failures and eventual cures. He discussed other researchers' findings—albeit in mostly derogatory terms. Almost nothing, in fact, was omitted from this book.

On first glance, knowing that Stroud had conducted his studies while in a maximum security prison, it was difficult not to be impressed.

Although officers who had seen it described it as a plagiarism, they could not have known that nothing like it existed. The *Kansas City Star* called it "singularly complete and detailed," but muttered that "it might have been less vituperative." In part, they were commenting on his dedication, which made it into the first printing:

"To all of my friends," it began, "who by their kindness or encouragement have aided in making this work possible, and to all of my enemies,

whose mean, little, or thieving souls, actuated by bigotry,
jealousy, spite, sadism, vindictiveness, or ignorance, have
taken such keen delight in throwing what they fondly hoped
would be insurmountable obstacles across my path, but
who, by their very opposition, have stimulated me to greater
effort and greater accomplishment than would have oth-
erwise been possible for me, this volume is appreciatively
dedicated.

May the members of the former group, a group so large
as to prohibit the singling out of any select few for special
mention, enjoy all of the good things life has to offer . . .

I have no desire to name the members of the latter
group, since they all know their true place in my esteem,
nor would I extend to them the kind of good wishes they
have had for me; they have to live with themselves and
knowing themselves, that should be sufficient punishment.

Despite the dedication, the *1944 Biological Abstracts*, an industry annual of all scientific works published, credited the book
with numerous cures and original contributions, including,

iodide supplement to prevent losses of chicks at hatching;
sulfanilamide as a cure for fowl paralysis; anthroquinone
violet base as a cure for aspergillosis; cure of various
septicemic conditions with effervescent salt mixtures;
cure of uremia with warmth and diuretic preparations;
cure of avian diphtheria with effervescent salts plus so-
dium perborate.

More than a decade later in 1957, Gaddis was quoted in
Scientific American,

Stroud found that all bird infections of the hemorrhagic
septicemia group could be controlled by the same meth-
ods that were known to be effective in avian diphtheria; he
discovered and described a typhoid–like disease of ca-
naries; he demonstrated that apoplectiform septicemia,

which sickens poultry, was also a disease of canaries, and that the source of infection lay in egg material; he suggested the psittacosis was a pox–virus infection in modified form; he isolated and identified the organisms associated with three forms of pox–virus disease, demonstrating that most of the fatalities due to the disease were the result of secondary invasion.

These were quite fantastic statements of fact which were totally erroneous. But it's easy to see why otherwise rational men and women were taken in. Stroud's *Digest* was seemingly the most thorough and articulate book on bird care published to date in the United States. It would stand alone in the avian veterinary field for almost twenty years. In fact, some of his descriptions of disease signs were so detailed that when shown the book almost fifty years later, Dr. Brian Speer, D.V.M., said that he would "love to have records from many of my colleagues [today] that are that descriptive."

Yet, no matter how seductive, nearly every medical recommendation in the book was fallacious.

Only a discriminating reader, who examined the book in its entirety, could begin to grasp its problems, however. Differing from his 1933 debut, *Diseases of Canaries*, this book appeared odd, wordy, didactic, rambling and difficult to follow—one of the reasons why it may have been so convincing. So daunting to read, in fact, that Bureau of Prisons personnel who reviewed and approved the manuscript had missed one of the book's more diabolical highlights. In his glossary of medical and technical terms, Stroud had included the inexplicable and stunning item: "Sadism," describing it as "a form of sex perversion in which pleasure is derived from inflicting pain upon another. Anyone who takes a keen delight in the infliction of pain is designated a sadist."

The term is included in editions that are still available today.

Very few people were actually able to judge the book's scientific merit in the 1940s and 1950s. Veterinarians—whom Stroud derided for knowing nothing—were simply not specializing in pet birds. They were concerned mostly with farm animals—horses, cattle and poultry. "And every once–in–a–while," said Dr. Speer, "some brave soul worked on dogs or cats."

Dr. Schmidt agreed. "Nobody cared," he said. "There weren't that many pet birds around and those that were had no economic importance."

The *Journal of Avian Diseases*, largely regarded as the first professional journal on the subject published by the newly organized American Association of Avian Pathologists, only began in 1957—fourteen years after Stroud's *Digest* was published. And even its first issue addressed the diseases of chickens, turkeys, pigeons, pheasants and ducks. Canaries and parakeets were finally *mentioned* in an article on salmonella in 1962, and no other article on pet birds appeared in the professional journal until 1966. *JAD* never even mentioned Robert Stroud once, not even when he died in 1963.

In fact, veterinarians were given responsibility for the diagnosis and treatment of avian species only in 1960, when California finally included pet birds in the Veterinary Practice Act. And the man who is regarded affectionately as the "granddaddy of bird medicine," Dr. James Harris, D.V.M., a biblical–looking practitioner in flowing white hair and a long white beard who practices in Oakland, California, didn't begin his specialty practice until the early 1960s.

Veterinarians who specialized in avian medicine didn't have their own professional association until the Association of Avian Veterinarians organized in 1980, and even today they represent only a small number of veterinarians.

Thus the major push for research in avian pathology didn't commence until almost two decades after Stroud died.

Although Stroud had enlarged his experiments, completed more autopsies and used his microscope extensively, his research had not advanced beyond his first confusing and erroneous articles that appeared in 1928. His *Digest* not only didn't break any new ground, but it perpetuated diagnostic and treatment myths for several more decades. Yet no one could prove it in 1943. Neither could anyone disprove Gaddis in 1955 when he called Stroud a "renown scientist" in the *Birdman of Alcatraz*. Nor could anyone discredit the Burt Lancaster movie in '62 in which Stroud was called "a genius."

Robert Stroud went to his death thinking that his discoveries ranked up there with Louis Pasteur and many, many people throughout the country agreed with him. Still do, in fact.

The book can be ordered, as of this writing, from a publisher specializing in popular pet books. It's claimed that the book is sold because of it's historical value only, but no warning label is printed on the book. Thus, incredibly, Stroud's erroneous treatments more or less dating from the 1920s are still circulating. And specialists today consider most of his recommendations to be lethal.

Yet, despite Stroud's obviously questionable research, current avian veterinarians are far more magnanimous towards him than he was towards their predecessors. Although they consider his book a testimonial, they consistently cite his acute powers of observation and knowledge of the literature as well as his ability to persevere under incredibly poor conditions.

Dr. Harris, D.V.M., is one example. Although fascinated by birds as a child, his first articles on bird care appeared in 1974 and involved the treatment and rehabilitation of oil–soaked birds. Since then his practice has included nearly every aspect of avian medicine, and papers and lectures have addressed avian bacteriology, micro-biology and therapeutics, avian respiratory diseases, reproductive system diseases, extending into the human–avian bond, and pet loss and human bereavement. From 1972 until 1986 Dr. Harris was the surgeon and consulting veterinarian for the Departments of An-thropology and Psychology at the University of California at Ber-keley. He considers Stroud to be "as much a pioneer in medicine as the Zulu witch doctor," he said, "who figured that when one of his warriors broke a leg, that if you could stick it in mud and pull on it, you could set it." He felt that Stroud's limitations had only to do with the state–of–the–art of veterinary medicine at the time, and the limitations of his facility and equipment. "He made mistakes," Harris conceded, "but that's the history of medicine."

In fact, several prominent avian veterinarians feel that Stroud was, as Dr. Speer asserted, "way ahead of his time."

"He hit very clearly on one statement," Dr. Speer said as he picked up a copy of Stroud's *Digest,* turned to a page and read out loud, " 'And thousands of owners of pet canaries too lazy to take the trouble to learn how to care for their birds, imagine that when they keep a cupful of cheap stale packaged seed, and throw them a leaf of stale wilted, half–rotten lettuce once in a while [that] they perform their whole duty.' " Speer looked up, "Now that's a foundation statement for 1940."

Stroud knew that birds, as Speer put it, were "people with feathers," who needed a higher quality care than was commonly given at that time.

This was perhaps the prisoner's most valuable contribution. Experts giving papers at professional meetings have often cited Stroud in their introductions—not for his research—but for some of his observations on bird behavior and care.

Stroud was not an avian pathologist as he claimed in 1962. He was an aviculturist—one who keeps birds—or, at best, a trained observer and perhaps an early ornithologist—someone who studies birds as a branch of zoology. But his medical research was seriously flawed, his treatments were bogus and his cures overblown.

Nonetheless, he's still somewhat of a a hero. "An avicultural hero," Dr. Harris noted. Harris then concluded with some sadness. "But he had a tragic flaw. He failed the attitude test every time."

Stroud's attitude in prison was as obvious as the nicotined–stained fingers that gripped his cell bars when he called out in D block. He was living on the third tier by now, in cell 41, next to the last cell on the east side. He was allowed to keep a copy of his book, and he probably passed it around to other segregated prisoners, tying it to a string and dropping it down. Most of them exhibited only casual interest. A few officers looked it over. He tried to get the doctors to read it, and years later, he gave a leather–bound copy to his attorney, Furman.

Its publication coincided with a wire service article that appeared in newspapers throughout the country, which caused a small avalanche of protest letters to Alcatraz.

Then a tiny pamphlet appeared in 1945 by a group calling itself the "National Bird Protective League." Entitled "The Life Story of Robert Stroud," it stated that it was published because of the "demand of so many people" to read about the man who wrote the *Digest* "while confined in a solitary cell." The pamphlet looked very similar to pamphlets Stroud himself had printed in the early '30s for his bottled bird remedies. Moreover, the League's offices were in Minneapolis, Minnesota, where Marcus lived. Judging from this and the pamphlet's content, it's likely that Stroud wrote it, putting his own spin on what was fast becoming a legend.

The pamphlet mixed truth with fiction. "Because of a technical error in the wording of the commutation," it asserted, "prison officials kept Stroud in solitary confinement where he has been all these years and still is."

Written in the third person, the story conjured up a new version of the Turner killing. Turner "took a dislike to a young prisoner, a friend of Stroud's . . . and started abusing him. This young prisoner was unable to protect himself from Turner's abuse and free use of his club." Stroud had asked him to "lay off the kid" and as a result a fight ensued and the club–wielding guard was killed. "Stroud possessed one great fault," the pamphlet stated, "he was always trying to protect the underdog."

The pattern borne of Elizabeth and Robert was now established: obfuscate the killings to make the prisoner seem less culpable, play up his intellectual achievements to prove he was rehabilitated and tug at the heartstrings. Stroud quoted himself several times, most notably when talking about his heroic efforts to cure his birds' diseases,

> *This does not mean that I gave up the fight, but that I was now fighting with the same, cold desperation that had marked other incidents of my life, but with this difference: the same mental qualities that have in other crises of my life led to destructive action were now turned to a constructive end.*

Stroud's book, the newspaper articles and this pamphlet all hit the bird–loving public exactly where Stroud wanted them to, and for several more years Warden Johnston got letters from people condemning his treatment of Stroud and demanding that Stroud be recognized for having rehabilitated himself. People even tried to call.

Stroud would never see most of the protest letters, but he was allowed to answer some of the questions. And, as long as the book generated interest and he was recognized as an expert, he was relatively content. But, as 1945 turned into '46 and interest died down, there seemed nothing exciting on the horizon. His name began slowly disappearing from the news; he was clearly losing power. The pressure mounted and he began to amuse himself in other ways.

Jim Quillen met Stroud about this time. Quillen, whose prison name was "JQ," got himself to D block in April 1946 for digging a tunnel in an aborted escape attempt. After days in solitary, he was placed in cell 26 on the second tier. It put him there at a pivotal moment in Alcatraz history and within close proximity to the old man.

Quillen was twenty–five at the time, a tall, lanky, slow–talking, ruffled kid with an already scarred life behind him and a forty–five–year sentence in front. Modest and thoughtful when interviewed years later, he reminisced about Robert Stroud with some bitterness.

After dinner on the night of April 27–28, 1946, while Quillen was in a nearby cell, Stroud began yelling that his stomach hurt and he wanted the doctor. The D block officer took a long breath, called the control center, was told that the doctor was not on the island but the medical technical assistant was. When called, the MTA at first balked, suggesting that Stroud would settle down. After hanging up the officer told Stroud that the MTA would be up in a while. As time passed and the MTA didn't show, Stroud yelled again, louder this time, that his stomach hurt and he needed the doctor. A couple of cons joined in, demanding that the doctor be called.

The hapless officer got on the phone again and convinced the

MTA that he better examine Stroud or there'd be trouble. After a while the MTA was unlocked into D block and racked into Stroud's cell. Quillen, like everyone, could hear the commotion. He thought the examination was perfunctory and the MTA left. As soon as the assistant was gone, Stroud started up again. Several cons yelled out angrily to get back on the phone and get that doctor in here.

Part of their beef was the ever-present fear among captive men that a man could be ignored and die in his cell; nearly everyone had heard such stories or witnessed it. But some of it was because of the tension of constant lock up. D block cons were often excitable, impetuous, easily frustrated or violent. It didn't take a lot to get everyone riled up, Quillen said. "The guys were really on edge and everything was so contagious in that place."

Besides Stroud, Franklin and Quillen, a score of other prisoners were locked down, among them: Burton Phillips, who had walloped Warden Johnston; Jimmy Grove, who was serving twenty years for attempted rape, twenty for attempted murder and fifteen for murdering a con; Henri Young, a bank robber who'd tried to escape from Alcatraz along with "Doc" Barker, Rufus McCain and others in 1939, and was in D block for fatally knifing his buddy McCain in 1940; Harmon Waley, who had a forty-five year conviction for kidnapping nine-year-old George Weyerhaeuser and keeping him in a hole in the ground, in a car trunk and later handcuffed to a tree while he collected the $200,000 ransom. Many men hated Waley because he screamed for hours on end that he wanted a piano key board to play. William Dainard, whom Warden Johnston had cited for building two muzzle-loading pistols on Alcatraz, was there, along with Louis Fleish, of the infamous Detroit "Purple" Gang, and Sam Shockley, who was largely regarded as crazy and who was later executed for his part in an armed escape attempt. Altogether there were twenty-six men in D block, all of whom had caused trouble in the main blocks of prisons everywhere; men who felt as much pressure from confinement as did Stroud.

In a short while Shockley started yelling and then Harmon Waley. Soon the whole block was filled with an angry clamor, as men threatened to break up the place if the doctor didn't show.

"Stroud was great at inciting people," remembers Bergen. "He

knew exactly the words to use to get those nincompoops agitated.
We never overheard Stroud say to anybody—'break, burn, assault'—
anything which would have connected him with it. He was smarter
than that."

An angry MTA was again racked into the block. "The second
time he did a thorough exam," Quillen said, "and he couldn't find
anything." After he left, Stroud started yelling again, angrily
complaining that the MTA didn't know anything, that his stomach
hurt and he wanted to see a real doctor. By now it was known on the
block that the resident doctor had returned to the island, but had
refused to see Stroud.

The frustration in D block began to rise. Someone took his tin
cup and raked it across the bars, bellowing out the demand that the
doctor examine Stroud *now*. Others joined in. Within minutes D
block erupted into a screaming rage. "When they're making noise,
they're not dangerous," said Alcatraz officer Bill Long. "But they'd
rock the place pretty good." It continued for several tense minutes.

A quickly made–up "goon squad"—officers who are often
available for disturbances—was unlocked into D block. Once in a
while this kind of disturbance causes men to hose down convicts,
but this time they didn't. Guards shouted out that everyone better
quiet down, or they'd be paid a visit—individually—in their cells.
"This was greeted with jeers and catcalls," Quillen wrote, and the
guards retreated.

"We yelled back and forth about wreckin' the place," Quillen
later said. "That isn't something you just up and do. And the guys
in D—you knew that once they committed themselves, they were
going to do it."

Rage soon accelerated into destruction. Matches often came in
from the library hidden between the pages of a book. Knives were
more difficult, but shanks of steel were smuggled in and ground
down to sharp blades. Razor blades were also favorites. Once the
open defiance reached a pitch, violence erupted.

Men began ripping up their bedding, their mattresses and
throwing it out of their cells onto the flats.

Stroud could hear the commotion.

Then they began lighting fires and and flinging burning clothing out of their cells. In the midst of the mob violence, a convict bailed out the water in his toilet and flung it onto the floor. Once his toilet was empty, he stuffed mattress cotton in it and lit it. When it caught fire, he quickly flushed the toilet and stepped back. The cell block was blasted with an explosion.

"Utter chaos followed," Quillen remembered. In a frenzy of gleeful, bitter anger, he did like many others, rupturing his toilet, grabbing the bigger pieces and smashing his sink—pounding out all the rage of a frustrating, confined life. "All around me the same insane devastation was occurring," he said.

Smoke filled the upper tiers while water continued to pour down onto the flats. Coughing, screaming, convicts threw porcelain at the windows for more air.

The riot lasted most of the night. Broken pieces of toilet bowls and sinks, mattress ticking, books and burned clothing lay on the floor, soaking up the water.

"Believe it or not, I felt free and elated," Quillen remembered when he awoke the next day. The tension that had been building for weeks had now been released. The men began realizing, however, what they had done. D block reeked of smoke and humidity. Officers doubled up and began shifting men from one cell to another, assessing the damage and escorting them to inmate court, where Associate Warden E. J. Miller pronounced sentence.

Jim Quillen had been out of prison for more than thirty years when interviewed. As a convicted bank robber, escapist and kidnapper who was "always convicted with a gun," Quillen would remain ten years on "the Rock." But he turned his life around there. He became an alter boy for the priest, contacted his family and began working in the hospital. When he transferred to another prison later, he picked up skills as an X–ray technician and eventually became a licensed practical nurse. He was released, got married and raised a family. Later, he gained both a Presidential and a Governor's pardon, wrote a book about his life and frequently returned to the National Park on Alcatraz, signing books and talking about his experiences. He carried a piece of paper marked with the date he stepped on Alcatraz—just to remind him.

"I don't think there was a damn thing wrong with Stroud," he said, taking a long draw from a cigaret. "He was bored." By his inflection Quillen let it be known that that was no excuse.

"We were *all* bored."

Quillen and twelve others were punished for their night of rioting. He was required, at ten cents an hour, to pay for what he'd broken, and he lost seven–and–a–half years good time.

"If I'd'a gone to court, they wouldn't have given me seven–and–a–half years," he said.

But something else hardened him up real quick.

When he was escorted from his cell to go to the hole he passed by a cell in which Stroud had been moved and glanced in. He was shocked. Stroud was relaxing on his cot and his cell was intact. Later the old man admitted to Quillen that he hadn't gotten involved in the destruction—what was the point? Quillen felt used. He and others spent days in the hole on a restricted diet. Stroud had never joined in the disturbance which he had created.

Quillen was just a kid then, maybe even a little naive. Stroud was an old con. Stroud never went to the hole. Former prisoner Henry Brown had a theory. "The ones that do most of their time in the hole," he said, "those are the ones who don't learn how to manipulate."

Less than five days later, men saw another side to Robert Stroud few would have guessed even existed.

Following the noon meal on May 2, 1946, all was quiet. Most prisoners were out of the building at work; most officers were eating lunch or assigned to the factories. Stroud had not bothered to put on his shoes and was seated at his bench, writing. "Everybody used to lay down and take a nap after lunch," Quillen remembered. "And it got real quiet in there."

Suddenly, everyone heard scuffling, like two men fighting. Cons hit the bars.

"At first we thought they were working some guy over," Quillen said. "And then somebody yelled, 'No, it's in the gun gallery!'"

Running the width of the main cell house and through a door into D block, the gun gallery was a barred security walkway high on the wall, patrolled by an armed guard. It contained many of the important keys to the institution, including those to the outside. Until this moment the gun gallery had seemed impenetrable.

Prisoner Barnard Coy, serving a twenty–six–year sentence for bank robbery, interstate flight and auto theft, had spread the bars, surprised the gun gallery officer, Bert Burch, and choked him into unconsciousness. Coy passed down Burch's jacket, clubs, gas masks and keys, one Winchester bolt action rifle with fifty rounds of ammunition and one Colt .45 automatic with three clips, each containing seven cartridges. By then he had already unlocked the cell door of Joseph "Dutch" Cretzer, a bitter, handsome criminal since the age of fifteen, who had a thirty–year bank robbery and murder rap.

Within minutes Clarence Carnes, Marvin Hubbard and Miran Thompson were also released. Hubbard was serving a thirty–year kidnapping conviction and Thompson was serving ninety–nine years for kidnapping. Carnes, a twenty–year–old, was serving Life for murder and ninety–nine years for kidnapping. He already had at least one escape attempt on his record. A dirt–poor Choctaw Indian from Oklahoma, remorseful at his botched record but quiet and sullen, he was also conspicuously naive. Years later, he admitted that by stepping out of his cell on Alcatraz that day he had sealed his fate: although most prisoners remained an average of five years before transferring, Carnes remained on Alcatraz eighteen and was not transferred until two months before it closed in 1963.

Segregation was suddenly in turmoil as men tried to see along the sides of their cell fronts. When Cretzer entered D block with a Colt .45, word spread up and down the tiers like wildfire: "They got guns!"

Cretzer, Hubbard and Coy quickly captured Cecil Corwin, the D block Day Watch officer, and unlocked the cells on the top two tiers. Now Sam Shockley joined them. Testimony later revealed that Shockley had an IQ of between fifty–four and sixty–eight, was erratic, unpredictable, had hallucinations and broke down easily under pressure. His rap was Life for kidnapping and bank robbery. He was described as a "ranting wild man" during the revolt.

The armed convicts' purpose in entering D block had been to release Whitey Franklin, who, as an expert lock picker, could help them get out of the building. Although they had unlocked the solid cell fronts of all the isolation cells, they couldn't unlock the inner cell gates. Thus Franklin was forced to remain in his cell.

Although his cell door too had been unlocked, Stroud did not leave. But many others did. Several of them went to the D block door to peer out at what was now happening in the main cell house, but then quickly returned. Only four men walked through that door; Quillen was among them. "Hell, I'm twenty–five years old, I got forty–five years and a fifty–year detainer from California, already got an escape charge, my parents had disowned me, I hadn't received a letter or a visit for over seven–and–a–half years. What the hell have I got to lose?"

Curious, and believing the rumor that the prison armory had been taken, Quillen excitedly approached Cretzer to join up. By then, however, even the armed convicts realized it was all over.

Nine officers had walked in on the escape, had been captured and forced into two cells just outside the D block door. The convicts had already shot and missed several tower guards, but in doing so, had alerted those outside that an armed escape attempt was in progress. More importantly, however, the armed prisoners could not locate the yard door key. Without it, the six could not leave the building.

As Quillen approached, Cretzer nodded in the direction of his gun. "This is all I've got," he told Quillen nervously. "I don't think we're going to make it." He looked at Quillen hard and told him, "Go back in. We blew it."

Years later Quillen admitted that there was no point in "dying without a gun for a cause that had no hope of making it." As he walked back to D block, Officer Burch in the gun gallery regained consciousness and saw him enter his cell. It was one of the luckiest moments of Jim Quillen's life and completely serendipitous. Burch remembered in sequence that Quillen entered his cell seconds before the shooting started.

Robert Stroud's most illustrious forebear, John Franklin McCartney. He was a Civil War Captain in the Union Army, a lawyer and newspaper publisher, an early member of the Prohibition Party and the father of twelve children.

Robert Stroud, left, probably when he was about ten. By then, he claimed, he had already tried to kill his father. Tall, gangly, he was emotionally distant, garrulous and often sick. Reprinted from the *St. Louis Post Dispatch*

Three members of the Stroud family in Seattle, Washington, below, ten years after the family moved from the Midwest. Barely visible in the photograph is a small black dog Bobbie clutches to his side.

Massac County Historical Library

Stroud as he appeared in 1912 when he was twenty–two and was transferred to Leavenworth. Bright, egotistical, he needed to be challenged. His early Leavenworth years were marked with hostility and defiance; his original sentence and subsequent knifing had earned him ten more years at Leavenworth. He remained thirty.   National Archives/BOP

Warden Robert W. McClaughry, seated third from left, was warden at Leavenworth when Stroud arrived. McClaughry, who introduced fingerprint technology to federal prisons after seeing a demonstration at the St. Louis World's Fair, had also signed the Civil War discharge papers of Stroud's grandfather. Guard Andrew F. Turner, right, whom Stroud fatally knifed in 1916, in a formal photograph introduced as evidence.   National Archives

A Stroud painting hangs in the Mary Cotton Library in Sebetha, Kansas. A portrait of Queen Louise of Prussia, it's thought to be a copy from a picture. Stroud was a good artist as long as he had a model from which to copy. His mother claimed that he painted greeting cards, the sales from which helped support her. His talents faltered, however, when he worked without a model. JB

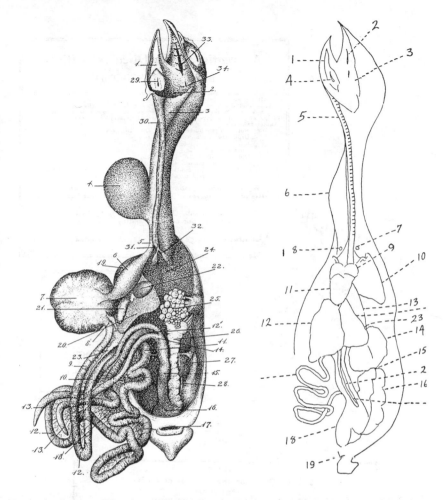

Drawings from Ward and Gallagher's *Diseases of Domesticated Birds,* top left, and Stroud's *Diseases of Canaries*, top right. Stroud's book appears to be a dumbed down version of Ward and Gallagher's. They were similarly organized, even some sentences were almost the same. Stroud's theories, however, were his own. Left, two drawings from *Stroud's Digest on the Diseases of Birds,* which illustrate his talent when he was copying, left, and when drawing freehand, right.

T.F.H. Publications

Examples of a small pamphlet which accompanied his bottled bird medicines, left, an ad for his first book, top right, an ad calling him "America's Foremost Authority on the Diseases of Canaries," and an announcement on his second book, *Stroud's Digest on the Diseases of Birds*, published when he was living in D block on Alcatraz.

The man who had enormous influence over Stroud's life—James V. Bennett, Director of the Federal Bureau of Prisons from 1937 until 1964. Bennett's first encounter with Stroud occurred at the USP Leavenworth in 1931. A progressive in many ways, he may have been shocked at the enormous latitude Stroud had been given at Leavenworth.

Alcatraz, known world–wide as America's most maximum–security federal penitentiary from 1934 until 1962. Stroud served seventeen years here—six years in D block and eleven in the prison hospital.

In a rare photograph, Alcatraz is shown at night, when Stroud often read by the exterior lights. In front of the cell house are the lighthouse keeper's residence, left, and the warden's residence. Below right is a recreation hall for the staff and a play area for island children.

Photo courtesy of Don Bowden; taken by his father, Ira L. Bowden, an officer on Alcatraz from 1958 until 1960.

A view of D block from the west gun gallery. Stroud resided in D 4, along the flats (but not one of the solid door cells which were for solitary confinement), cell 41 (top tier, far end) where he was during the 1946 escape attempt, and cell 42 at the end.   JB

The view from cell 42 along the top tier. Although the top tier cells faced the windows across the aisle with a view of the San Francisco skyline, the view was obscured by detention sash and dirty glass. Similarly, prisoners could not see other prisoners with whom they conversed.   JB

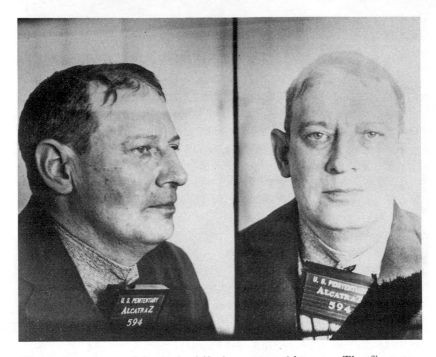

Three mug shots of Stroud while he was at Alcatraz. The first, top, was taken in December 1942 when he arrived. He was fifty-two years old and weighed one–hundred–eighty pounds. The second, to update his file, next page, was taken ten years later in 1952 when he was living in the prison hospital. The mug shots below were taken in 1956 when he was sixty-six years old. By then he was shaving his entire body and weighed about one–hundred–thirty–eight pounds.

San Francisco Maritime National Historical Park, top/ JB from a BOP Stroud file, bottom

By 1952 when this shot was taken, Stroud had been living in the prison hospital for four years. He was as depressed as he had been in 1916 when he killed Turner. Within a year of this photograph, he twice attempted to take his own life. He was also studying French at this time and writing his long manuscript on prison history.

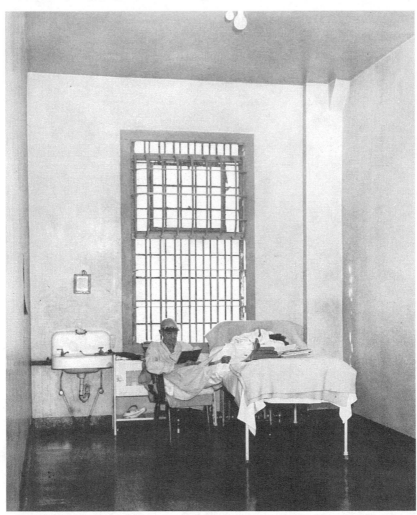

In a rare photograph, Stroud is shown seated in his hospital room on Alcatraz. The room was bare except for two beds—one, not shown, was his "count bed" near the door in which he slept, and the other, pictured here, was used as a desk. He is seated on a hard back desk chair similar to ones made by prisoners in federal prisons. Note the bed pan, below and to the right of his sink. Stroud used it for several years before attorney Stanley A. Furman complained.

The same room, a four-man ward room, shown here after the prison closed, was thirty-six by eleven feet and contained two light bulbs in the ceiling. A toilet was installed some time after 1956. This was Stroud's deepest lockdown in which he had no job and was forced to occupy himself by writing and studying for eleven years. He became eccentric at this time and sometimes despondent.   JB

Stroud in 1959 in Topeka, Kansas, when he was before Judge Walter A. Huxman on a motion to dismiss his 1918 conviction because of double–jeopardy and cruel and unusual punishment. Early in the hearings Stroud was transferred from the Alcatraz prison hospital to the Federal Medical Prison at Springfield, Missouri, where he was placed in a wing with other prisoners. It was the first time since March 1916 in which he lived in population with other prisoners.

Stroud, handcuffed, as he was attending one of the Becker hearings in 1962–63. The movie had been released and he was now world-famous. He had written, however, that he would delay his parole in order to revise his book, *Stroud's Digest on the Diseases of Birds*. He was never paroled.

One of the last photographs of Robert Stroud, taken in the visiting room at the Federal Medical Prison in Springfield, Missouri. Stroud is seventy-three. Attorney Richard M. English snapped the shutter while officers weren't looking; he wanted an image that would show Stroud in a more positive light than had the widely-printed mug shot of 1952. When the photograph was published, BOP director Bennett was so angered he attempted to have English investigated by the California Bar Association. Stroud was impressed with English's daring, and shows it in the photograph. Richard M. English

The armed convicts attempted to execute their nine hostages. Although several were seriously wounded, others were only superficially wounded, or missed being hit at all. Realizing that things had turned bad, Carnes, Thompson and Shockley skulked back to their cells. Coy, Cretzer and Hubbard decided to shoot it out. It would take two days for officers to regain control of the cell house.

Warden Johnston's description in his book of the 1946 armed escape attempt shows little of the chaos of the actual event as well as the panic of some of his own decisions. Despite the fact that the only possible guns in the cell house were a pistol and a rifle and that ammunition was limited, Johnston's first telegram to the media stated, "convict has machine gun in cell house." Either he was not thinking straight, or else wanted to exaggerate the danger. Moreover, he ordered a contingent of armed officers to the southwest hillside outside of D block, from where shots had been fired, and authorized them to shoot into D block. For the next twenty–four hours, officers used rifles, tear gas and grenades. Stroud later called the assault "promiscuous."

Stroud was still assigned to cell 41. But perceiving that many of the shots from outside the building were hitting near where he celled, he quickly moved down the line to cell 35. Burton Phillips was hidden behind a stack of law books. Quillen, Shockley, Jack Pepper, Bill Dainard and Ed Sharpe were huddled together, using their mattresses as shields. Sharpe testified that Shockley was so terrified that he had to be held down. Quillen remembered that one grenade hit a cell toilet. The concussion was so great, he said, you could see the metal walls expand. Water began flooding the cell and leaking over their tiers. "They're standing outside the windows calling you by name," Quillen said, "and if you answered, there'd be a grenade barrage. They would shoot right where your voice came from. Everybody was on the verge of going off the deep end."

"Kill that son–of–a–bitch when he steps out," one prisoner testified he heard an officer shout.

But some men had it much worse. In attempting to free Franklin, the armed convicts had opened all the closed–fronts cells. Thus the men inside, who had no bedding to hide behind, were suffering the worst of the flying shrapnel. They were totally vulnerable and screaming.

Officers and prisoners who had anything to do with the 1946 escape attempt remained bitter about it for the rest of their lives: prisoners had obtained guns; officers were killed; five of the six armed convicts were hunted down and killed, or executed; the one, Clarence Carnes, was given another Life sentence, and perhaps worse, became emotionally isolated from many prisoners because it was perceived that he had "stooled" his way out of an execution.

But none would be more bitter than the men in D block who were positioned like sitting ducks.

"Them bazooka shells cut through the bars and walls of the cell blocks like they was nothing," said James "Blackie" Audett in his book, *Rap Sheet*. "We could hear the screaming and yelling in D block."

"They were shooting at twenty–six unarmed guys!" Quillen roared. "Trying to kill us! This is your government at work!"

Lieutenant Bergen, and several others, volunteered later that night to go back into the gun gallery to provide information on the whereabouts of the armed convicts and the trapped officers. Within minutes of their assault on the gun gallery, officer Harold Stites was shot to death. Another officer was wounded in the arm. When additional men moved in to escort them out, two others were hit.

Many officers later felt that the only shooting going on came from the officers outside.

Bergen remained inside the cell house, laying low during the grenading. He was acutely aware of his own vulnerability—"like a fish in a barrel" he said later, and angered at the response of administrators. Bergen would have a long career on Alcatraz, considering it his best assignment. Arriving in 1939 he would remain until he transfered in 1955. He was mad as hell to have convicts controlling the cell house. But he thought the naked disregard for inmate safety—and *his* safety—was unwarranted. He could hear the panic, particularly from the men in isolation who were screaming with each explosion. But he could do nothing about it. No one could.

Bergen narrowed his eyes as he recounted what happened in the next few moments. As the shelling continued, one man stepped out of his cell on the third tier: Robert Stroud.

Bergen and Stroud had never talked much to each other, but they knew each other by reputation. As Bergen and officer Fred Mahan watched from the gun gallery, Stroud stood on the tier walkway and weighed his options.

"Incoming rifle grenades continued to explode," Bergen said. Then Stroud did what the lieutenant considered an amazing, foolish act; he climbed over the railing of the top tier walkway, climbed down to the second tier railing and jumped down onto the flats.

While Bergen watched, astounded, Stroud proceeded to close the solid doors of all six cells—one by one—thus shielding the men inside from the incoming grenades.

"He was doing this at great personal risk!" Bergen said. "And he didn't waste any time. He went back to his cell in the same way—climbing up to the railing of the second tier and pulling himself up to the top tier by muscular strength."

Stroud was fifty–six years old and conforming to type. It was the same thing he'd done on dozens of occasions when his brother, or stray dogs, or Kitty O'Brien, or small birds, or his mentally-diminished sister, Mamie, needed his help. He acted to protect them. He had always been moved by the powerlessness of the underdog.

"That person who is regarded as a monster by most people," Bergen said carefully, admiringly, "did the thing that none of the other younger inmates were willing to do. And he did it as easy as snapping your fingers."

Bergen was to have another surprise a few hours later. Shelling had continued throughout the night, although the nine hostages had by now been rescued. Bergen had remained inside in case the armed convicts showed themselves. Suddenly, Stroud called out to him, "Lieutenant, I want to talk to you."

"I'm listening," Bergen shouted back.

"There's no gun on this block," Stroud said.

"We think there is,' " Bergen told him.

"I'm sure there isn't," Stroud shouted. "They went out of here last night. You send people in here to inspect the block and I'll stand out here and be a sacrificial goat. You can go ahead and kill me if you find the guns."

Quillen remembered hearing Stroud's offer. "Stroud volunteered to strip his clothes off, walk to the middle of the flats and stand there, while officers searched, and if they found any [guns], shoot him. It was kind of dramatic!"

No one else said a word.

"Somebody's going to get killed," Stroud warned.

"And the conversation went back and forth for about fifteen minutes," Bergen remembered. Bergen hadn't seen the armed convicts in D block and he felt that they probably were no longer there. But he wasn't convinced the warden would listen to him—or Stroud—and stop the grenading. But he was just as anxious to get the firing stopped because he figured that the officers along the hill "were going to keep shooting through those windows until they finally got to us." Sensing that he had nothing to lose, he agreed.

"I called my contact in the front office—*not the warden! you don't talk to the warden!*—and I got through to somebody who carried the message to the warden."

To everyone's relief the shooting in D block abruptly stopped. It was about 1:00 p.m. on Friday. The assault on D block had continued since 2:00 p.m. the day before.

Almost fifty years later Bergen said with a wry smile that he thought the decision to stop shooting had already been made; there hadn't been return fire from D block for hours. He never told Stroud, however, letting him think that he had something to do with the decision.

By Saturday, Coy, Cretzer and Hubbard had been killed in the utility corridor. The riot and the escape attempt had ended.

Stroud had been right. There were no guns in D block.

And it appeared that he was right in thinking that they were shooting at him. "The Battle of Alcatraz" would serve to increase his paranoia of the Bureau of Prisons and the personnel who worked on Alcatraz.

Bergen gained a new respect for the old man. He felt that the barriers between a hard–nosed con and a hard–nosed guard had begun to tumble. Although it can be assumed Stroud felt some rapport with the lieutenant, he would have changed his tune had he known that one day a letter from Bergen would help to keep him in prison until the day he died.

The '46 escape attempt was not the last big event in Robert Stroud's life, but it was going to seem like it for a long, long time.

The new warden, Edwin B. Swope, would not take as kindly to Stroud as Johnston had and would isolate him further. Although the years ahead would be long and drawn out for Stroud, he was going to emerge a famous man and a hero to some.

꙼   ꙼

Part VII
Broken Promises

On December 2, 1948, Shockley and Thompson were executed in the gas chamber at nearby San Quentin State Prison for the murder of William Miller.

Clarence Carnes' life was spared because the prosecutor didn't think a jury would put to death a kid who was barely twenty years old. It was almost the only lucky break he ever had.

As a teenager Carnes and his partner had earned Life sentences for a gas station robbery that, in a panic, led to a killing. He then aggravated that with an escape attempt, in which he jumped in a car along with a surprised motorist (kidnapping), and inadvertently drove into Texas (crossing state lines to avoid prosecution), both which were federal crimes. He was sent to Alcatraz. At age nineteen, he was one of the youngest men ever there. His part in the '46 riot and escape attempt gave him another Life sentence.

Carnes would become a famous Alcatraz prisoner, but not until after he was finally paroled in the late 1970s. Although by then he'd been in prison since 1943, he didn't look like a typical maximum—security con; he had soft round features, salt and pepper hair, a modest, restrained demeanor. He eventually worked for Habitat for Humanity. Then Hollywood discovered him and made a movie about his life in 1980. But it was mostly downhill after that. In 1988 he stole a little money and crossed state lines to get back into prison—where he was most comfortable—and died of AIDS at the Federal Medical Prison at Springfield.

But in 1946, with already a year of Alcatraz behind him, he was still looking at seventeen more years on "the Rock." Eventually he became, along with Karpis and Stroud, among the three men who were there the longest.

Stroud had donated two hundred dollars from his *Digest* sales towards the prisoners' defense—so the story went—and when Carnes moved into D block, they had something to talk about.

By then the old man was approaching sixty, and writing his history of the federal prison system, a project that would become as important to him as his bird business.

Stroud conceived it as a thesis on good prison management. But it actually was a collection of stories he'd heard over the years from other prisoners, all loosely tied together with the theme that prisons were not harsh enough.

He felt that anyone first entering prison should go to a maximum security setting, and only by good deeds could he then go to less restrictive institutions. Stroud felt that "not one prison structure put up during the last fifty years is not a disgrace to civilization." He later wrote that he would solicit architecture departments of large universities throughout the world to "contact a top-notch graduate student who is willing to invest his spare time for from two to five years in order to take a chance on making himself the world's top architect in his field. . . . While the architect does the technical drawings, I will write the details of management." Stroud wanted to send his book to "every governor, every state attorney general, every cabinet member, every member of the judiciary committees of both houses of Congress and every prison organization throughout the world." Over the next ten years, he wrote approximately two-thousand pages.

Carnes knew about the old man but now met him for the first time. He was struck by Stroud's green eye shade, an item that normally would be contraband. He later described Stroud as stooped and careless in his appearance.

The two played chess together. They each had a homemade, numbered chess board, and they would quietly call out their plays. "I was eventually able to beat him," Carnes said. "And every time I beat him—*every time*—he'd make the point, 'after all, it was *only* recreation' to him.

"Stroud did have a tremendous ego and it's probably the reason he survived," Carnes deduced. "There were people who couldn't stand that place—the confinement and not being able to face another human being when they talked. Carnes thought that Stroud, on the other hand, actually thrived in segregation. "I heard him say that he didn't want to go in the general population," he said. "He would have a job and it would have taken his time. He would have had to get up at a certain time, stand for the count, go to meals and do the routine. Being in that cell, he didn't do any of that."

Carnes felt Stroud had read books on psychology but could only superficially relate it to himself. He thought Stroud's thinking was immature.

"He told me that when he first went into solitary, he made up his mind that he was going to maintain his individuality," Carnes said. "If he had stopped fighting administration he could have gotten out. They would have been glad to have taken credit for everything he did."

Particularly since the D block riot, officers figured Stroud for a chief agitator in segregation. But Carnes disagreed. "There was always someone down there who was a hard ass," he said recounting an incident in which three segregated prisoners became infuriated at an officer. "I did this myself, take a shit and a piss in the toilet and make a goo of it and put it in a paper cup [we] were allowed to have. And when the lieutenant opened the door, poured it right in his face." But Stroud was "too old," he said, to get involved in those kinds of hassles.

"You've got to have a certain amount of meanness or you won't survive," Carnes stipulated, "or be super sharp—or make the guards and *especially* the prisoners think you're mean."

Stroud had *that*, Carnes said. He recalled an incident in the yard one day when a kid asked the older man if he could borrow his handball glove. "'Why you son–of–a–bitch!'" Carnes quoted Stroud as saying. "He smacked him across the face. Guards didn't see it, but other cons helped the kid get up."

There were reasons why Carnes didn't assign to Stroud as much power over inmates as did administration. Stroud was often patronizing and he continued his homosexual counseling—two things that did not sit well with most cons.

"Old Creepy" Karpis, for example, thought Stroud "had a definite mental quirk." In his book, *On the Rock*, he wrote,

*His behaviour and statements in isolation convinced me
he was dangerous. I have vivid memories of his lanky form
and his unusually long arms hanging low and ape–like
fashion and the profanities and threats he uttered against
the guards and their families rush into my mind. He hated
Fatso Mitchell and would rave about how he would 'eat
up' the guard's little daughter before he tore her apart
giving half to each parent. His wild exclamations dwelt on
how, if he were released, he would grab little boys or girls
off the street, 'eat them up' and then kill them. I believed
him. They weren't just idle threats: he would have killed
or mutilated a child. He bragged of how he would show
society that they really owed him something. If I had the
responsibility of deciding whether or not to release Robert
Stroud I would have reached the same conclusion as the
parole board.*

Stroud may have been the author of his own reputation. "He
considers himself to be in a position of some influence," a written
report said of him during this time. Whether his power was actual,
or just perceived and bragged about, it worked against him. Stroud
may have told Carnes he didn't want to get out of segregation, but
he frequently made requests to authorities to get back to the main
population, and his perceived "influence" tipped the scales against
him. In July 1948, he told Alcatraz officials that he "feels certain he
can adjust himself in the main prison population." They disagreed
and he remained in seg.

"Next time you glance casually at Alcatraz," wrote famed San
Francisco columnist Herb Caen in 1947, "you might want to toy
with the thought that inside those wall[s] sits a prisoner named
Robert Stroud—who has been in isolation for twenty–nine years."

Caen had it wrong on two counts; Stroud had been in segregation—not isolation—and for thirty–one years. But Caen's sentiment was unmistakable and represented the growing discrepancy
between the public and private views of Robert Stroud.

That same year Stroud was written up on two disciplinary actions (the only disciplinary reports in his first twelve years there). In January, he was cited for "conspiring with an officer to smuggle out a letter." Addressed to Marcus, the letter asked that $50 be sent to the address of the officer. Although the amount of money was small, it was a serious offense.

Stroud was also written up for attempting to destroy a "filthy story" before it was discovered during a shakedown in his cell.

Although the rules on Alcatraz were more consistent than many prisons, a lot still depended on the officer in charge. It was obvious to many that Stroud was writing pornography. In his writings he had a preference for "plump," "angelic" boys with bright smiles and flashing thighs.

"Frankie Perkins, age nine, stirred, rubbed his sleep–filled big blue eyes, then stretched and yawned, displaying a perfect set of pearly–white teeth which gleamed from between his rather–full red lips," he wrote in one short story that was confiscated. He passed around stories to friendly officers and some cons. Those who couldn't stomach it, stopped right there, sensing what was coming. "I read it," Carnes said about one story, with a chuckle. "It was sick."

Ernie Yates, a prison officer on Alcatraz from 1947 until 1955, read some of his stories.

"I got to know Stroud reasonably well," he said. "You become a good judge of character when you hang around guys like that."

Yates, a red–haired, easy–going, confident man, took the job on Alcatraz after he left the military service in '47. He attended law school at night in San Francisco at the same time and eventually quit the civil service to became a lawyer. Interviewed in his Santa Monica office years later, he said that Stroud frequently handed over parts of his manuscript.

"Stroud decided one day he was going to write porno stories to end all porno stories," Yates began. "He wrote one about this family—brother, sister, dad and mom. And it wound up that each of 'em had a turn at the other, including father–son, son–mother, daughter–mother, brother–sister, the whole works. And I told him, 'Stroud, you're sick!' " Yates laughed, " 'you're just sick.' "

Mimicking Stroud's low voice and fast comment, Yates said,

" 'Oh listen, don't you think that goes on?' "

Yates was not the stereotypical prison officer; many were far more offended and not as forgiving. In the 1950s, even psychiatrists considered homosexuality to be deviant behavior. Some prison officers understood that most men did not go into nor come out of prisons as homosexuals, but practiced it inside out of emotional, physical and safety needs. While those men regarded it as a necessary response, they were in denial.

Stroud was not. He had no such boundaries. On numerous occasions to numerous officers he made references to the joys of homosexual sex.

Given Stroud's two write–ups in 1947, his annual report recommended that he "continue present program." It also said that he was "maladjusted with homicidal tendencies. Superior intelligence. Well oriented. Not psychotic. Adjusted to prison routine."

Stroud's pattern of court petitions, his verbal and written complaints to Washington, his petty infractions and serious disciplinary reports, his boasting and advocacy of his power and homosexuality, coupled with a history of violence and an ability to exert his will over powerful men, combined to keep him where he was. The opposition dug in its heels. And part of the reason lies in the new direction taken at Alcatraz.

In 1948 Warden Johnston retired and Edwin B. Swope took over as the second warden.

Swope was the subject of legendary stories within the federal prison system. Portly, with wide jowls and a pompous and blustery attitude, he was perfectly type–cast as the narrow–eyed warden of a super max pen.

He had been warden at New Mexico State Prison when he moved into the federal system in 1934 as associate warden at McNeil Island. He served six years there, was promoted to warden and transferred to the USP at Terre Haute, Indiana. He was then transferred to the boys training center in Englewood, Colorado, before being tapped for warden at Alcatraz.

Dollison, who transferred to Terre Haute after Swope had left, found it apparent that Swope had left a wide slick of malcontent in his wake.

Old "Square Deal Eddie," as officers and cons called him, was arbitrary, fearful and exacting. He was legend for riding rough–shod over his staff, pitting one man against another and plummeting morale. He rarely socialized with subordinates, flaunted island rules and did strange things. Later, when he moved off the maximum security prison island, Swope actually allowed a convict to carry his shotguns from his house to the truck.

With prisoners, he liked the good–cop/bad cop–tactic. He buddied up to them, calling them "M'boy," and letting them think he would approve their request. But he often instructed his associate warden to ignore anything he had promised. He instituted the "Alcatraz cocktail," food given to prisoners in the solitary cells. It allegedly had the same caloric content as food served on the main line, but was blended into a semi–solid mass, chilled in the re-frigerator and served in a cup. Swope overlooked the medical staff's liberal use of tranquilizers, which tended to subdue prisoners. When Dollison arrived later, he discovered that some prisoners were so medicated they couldn't run the Industries sewing ma-chines. Many had learned to hoard the pills to get high.

The new warden took a dim view of Stroud's extra privileges and immediately curtailed them. He stepped up cell shakedowns, confiscated Stroud's writings and stopped his letters to outsiders. By July 1948, Marcus wrote saying that the warden was turning back letters from bird lovers with a note saying that prisoners could not conduct business. Stroud explained to Swope that Bennett had given him permission to answer all letters regarding his book. Swope was deaf to the plea. As a result, Bergen said, Stroud threatened the warden so vividly that Swope believed he meant it.

"He used to pose as good ol' godfather Swope," remembered Bergen. "It didn't click with Stroud. He'd say, 'You rotten old son–of–a–bitch, if I ever get my hands on you . . .' That sort of thing." Swope, he said, was "deathly afraid" of Stroud. "And Stroud never let you forget he had murdered two people."

In fact Swope had to contend with one of the most famous stories concerning the Birdman. A letter arrived in the last weeks of

1949 asking Stroud to diagnose a sick bird. The warden returned the letter, denying correspondence. Days later, the same person sent another letter. It politely asked if the warden could relay a description of the bird's symptoms to the Bird doctor, get back his diagnosis and reply. The warden again refused.

Weeks later, a little package arrived, addressed to Swope. It was later revealed in a UPI wire service story that Minnie T. King of North Hollywood, California, who was the vice–president of the National Association of Canary Breeders, had sent it. Inside was the dead bird, with the note that said, "You killed it. You bury it."

The story, of course, traveled to Washington and Swope was asked about it. On February 23, 1950, he replied to Bennett, "The bird arrived and we gave it a decent burial."

If Swope was tightening Stroud's reins it was also because things were beginning to happen for the old man.

A Los Angeles bird enthusiast named Richard K. Polimer found his rare birds dying of a contagious disease. He was introduced to Stroud's *Digest*. Calling it in an interview almost fifty years later the "most comprehensive book" he'd found, he decided that his birds were dying of avian diphtheria. He took Stroud's advice, and was so impressed with the results that he wrote a letter of thanks to the author through the publisher.

"One day I got a letter postmarked 'Alcatraz'," he said, adding that he sometimes got letters from prisoners, so was only mildly puzzled. It was from Warden Swope stating that Stroud was a prisoner on Alcatraz and could not receive mail from outsiders.

Polimer was stunned. A film producer and agent, he represented several well–known authors whose books were made into films, among them Sir James Barry (*Peter Pan*), Theodore Dreiser (*An American Tragedy*) and Horace McCoy (*They Shoot Horses, Don't They?*). He began thinking of the dramatic possibilities.

Eventually he was able to contact Marcus, and they began talking about a possible movie. Marcus wrote Stroud, telling him about it.

On August 23, 1948, Stroud returned a letter to Marcus. "I

have taken four Luminals since reading your letter, and I am still so excited that I can't sit still. Yes, Marc, this looks like the money."

Luminal is a phenobarbital—a sedative—often with hypnotic side effects. Stroud had obviously been hoarding it.

He gave his brother carte blanche to make the best contract he could. "So hop to it and close the deal," Stroud instructed. "Get his name on the dotted line." But Stroud had very big demands. "To line up all the connections he has to get me out of here before he starts shooting," he wrote. ". . . Tell Richard [Polimer] to use all the angles he knows and get permission from Washington to see me. I can tell him things in five minutes more amazing than anything he has heard yet."

Stroud liked to think that a deal like this could get him out of prison. The presidential election campaign was in full swing by then and Harry S. Truman was making much of the "forgotten man." Stroud urged Marcus to fly to Washington to see Truman. He wrote, "and if the cards are thrown right in his lap Harry might think that it is better for him to get the credit for recognizing the forgotten man just before the election than for his successor to get it after January 1st."

He told Marcus to get to Truman's secretary and promise him votes in exchange for a pardon, luring his brother with the suggestion that he might actually get an interview with Truman himself.

That same day, August 23, 1948, Stroud wrote to his sister Mamie, boasting that the deal with Polimer "will run into real money . . . at least five figures to start . . . [and] it will open up to me several lines that may produce money running into seven figures." He promised his sister a down payment of "not less than ten or twelve thousand dollars." Then he told her, "If this goes through, and I don't think it can miss, I will probably be out before the election. If not, surely in January."

A red flag went up the pole on Alcatraz. One of the reasons why the super max pen had opened was to keep the media from popularizing the exploits of criminals. A film about a defiant agitator and double–murderer was a threat to the Bureau's ideal. Swope had the letters promptly returned to Stroud.

The next day, August 24, 1948, according to prison memos,

Stroud got involved in a segregation protest.

Prisoners, who were angry because administration had favored a black inmate over a white on a job as a clean–up orderly, decided to go on a hunger strike. Relations between them and officers deteriorated so badly, Dollison said later, that a "continuous stream of obscenties was directed at officers and especially the Associate Warden" whenever they entered the block.

Stroud wrote about the fracas in minute detail in a letter to U.S. Attorney Frank J. Hennessy. It was read, of course, and interpreted as another of his agitations. As a result, on August 31, 1948, prison officers escorted him from segregation upstairs to the prison hospital. "We passed word through the grapevine that Stroud was eating like heck up in the hospital," said Associate Warden Nova Stucker later, "and that broke up the strike."

But Stucker may not have known the half of it; given Polimer's interest in making a movie, the opportunity to bury "old birdseed" seemed golden.

Stroud was placed in a large four–man ward cell. It was the deepest lock down he had ever known, and would amount to isolation for the next eleven years. During most of those years he seldom went to the prison yard. Later, when he did go to the yard, he went alone.

Normally, only a doctor could place a prisoner in the hospital and only for the duration of his illness. Bergen insisted that administration could not have arbitrarily moved Stroud there without authorization. In fact, most officers believed Stroud was kept there because he was sick. Even among the general public who visit Alcatraz as a National Park more than thirty years later, it's commonly understood that Stroud was in the hospital because he was sick.

But prison reports tell a different story. While it was written up for the next several years that Stroud at age fifty–eight had "arteriosclerosis" and "spastic colitis," those were only secondary reasons. In 1950, the associate warden wrote,

> *Since this man has been confined in the hospital we have*
> *had very little trouble in the Treatment Unit and there*

*does not seem to be the leadership present to cause any
disturbance. This man has an exalted opinion of his own
importance and in a way he is shrewd and cunning.
However, it seems much better for the institution to keep
this man confined in the hospital where he has little
contact with other inmates.*

Bennett concurred. He wrote later in the Federal Prison Service Newsletter that "Stroud, because of his continued recalcitrance
and participation in an inmate strike and agitation of others, was
removed from his open–front cell in 'D' block to a separate outside
room in the hospital area." Clearly the prisoner was isolated with
the Bureau's full knowledge and cooperation.

Stroud's fate altered immediately upon entering isolation. He
became the only permanent resident and his human contact was
now limited.

The hospital was upstairs from the dining room. It was entered
through a locked door, up two flights of stairs, where the hospital
officer unlocked another gate, left and down a long hall. Stroud's
"cell," a long room eleven by thirty–six feet, was the third room on
the left. Besides several other similar rooms, there was an X–ray
room, a locked cell with a bathtub, a padded cell for violent or
suicidal patients, a physical therapy room, an operating room, a
room for the visiting dentist and a pharmacy.

His was a ward room, used to temporarily house as many as
four prisoners too sick to remain in the general population. It had
one dim light bulb hanging from the ceiling, a large window
opening comprised of small panes of glass and protected by bars, a
sink and a bed. There was no toilet. Stroud used a bed pan—for
possibly as long as eight years. Thus, orderlies or officers were
forced to empty it several times daily.

Stroud's room had a regular barred door and a wooden door.
Closing the outer door isolated Stroud. A confidential memo from
Swope on December 9, 1948 stated that he should never be turned
into the hall while other prisoners were there. In fact, during sick

call, Stroud's outer door was often closed, so that he would have no contact with other prisoners.

With few opportunities to go to the recreation yard and no job for eleven years, Stroud needed a high degree of self–motivation in order to survive. He did not fail. He worked on his prison manuscript, he read and he began studying languages—starting first with French and eventually expanding into Spanish and Italian. Over the years he read many books in French, writing once to a friend, "I'm getting pretty good at it. I am getting so I even dream in French." His knowledge of Spanish and Italian was much more limited.

The prison interior lights were shut off at 9:30 p.m. and officers tried to make him conform to prison rules. He grew more and more frustrated. In one incident he jumped out of bed and flipped on his light switch after an officer turned it off. "I put out his light and he leaped out of bed and switched it on again," officer Griffiths wrote. When he turned it off again, Stroud jumped up, turned on the light and said, "He didn't give a fuck what [the lieutenant] said the light stays on."

Stroud learned to work by the light of the floodlights outside the building and continued working at night.

A photograph from this period showed him sitting in a hard back chair in his cell, wearing a thin hospital gown, glasses and his green eyeshade. His bare feet were propped up on a bed that was stacked high with books, legal journals and scores of legal–sized yellow note pads. The cell actually contained two beds—the count bed nearest the door in which he slept and another near the window which he used as a desk.

"They catered to him a little bit," remembered Yates, "gave him his toys, let him read and write. He was getting along good."

Out of sympathy, some officers didn't close his outer door, Quillen explained. He went to the hospital several times while Stroud was there. "Now you could make the difference in Stroud's day whether you left that outer door open or closed," he said. "Some guards never thought about closing that door. We used to be able to walk up to the gate and talk to Stroud. They wouldn't let you stand there for an hour and talk, but you could go up and say, 'How you doin' Bob, what's goin' on?' Nobody bugged you.

"But then you could have some guy who was by–the–book and he'd close that door and Bob was back in isolation. And to him, you know, it was going to be a good day or a bad day. And Stroud could be very mouthy, very belligerent if things didn't go as he wanted them to."

Stroud did see two prisoner–orderlies, an Hispanic and a Japanese. Serving Life for murder, the Hispanic prisoner was an old friend from Leavenworth, who often mixed a special cream salve for Stroud's dry skin. The Japanese man, known as "Meatball," worked in the hospital under protective custody. An American citizen, he was inducted into the Japanese Army during World War II and eventually became head of a POW camp in which American servicemen were tortured. Amazingly, after the war, he returned to Los Angeles where he was spotted by a former captive. Tried and convicted, he eventually wound up on Alcatraz. Prisoners were patriotic; this man celled in the main population but had to be let out separately from everyone else for his own protection. Emotionally isolated from the rest of the population, he was safe in the prison hospital.

Stroud's hospital isolation had both a limiting and a freeing effect on him. He was now largely forgotten by most cons and not a part of the daily rumor mill. And convict rules were different here; he could talk at length with officers. He could sleep during the day and wait up for a favorite officer to talk to, or play chess with all night. He could expound on his theories, monopolize their time, show them his writings, predict his eminent release and rail and complain when he didn't get his way.

Many officers on Alcatraz in the 1950s were new to the prison service, often they were younger and more flexible. Some were local residents who thought Alcatraz might be an interesting job, and for them, it was their first prison. Stroud was a killer, but so were a lot of other guys and he was old; they felt they could handle him. To them, he was fascinating and unique, and Stroud was anxious to build on that picture.

There were the rules, however.

"They took all these precautions," remarked George De Vincenzi, skeptically. An officer on Alcatraz from 1950 until 1957,

De Vincenzi was a vigorous, confident, easy–going Italian-American who eventually quit the prison service and became a U.S. Customs Inspector in California. He worked several three–month shifts in the hospital and quickly developed a rapport with Stroud.

"We used to give him a bath," De Vincenzi remembered. "And we had to lock everybody up. Everything stopped."

Former officer Vernon A. Sendek, who worked on Alcatraz for three years in the early 1950s, distinctly remembered Stroud's Saturday baths. "I had to have three—no less than two and usually three—guards before I could open that door." They escorted Stroud to the tub room, where Sendek stood by. "Funny," he said, "I couldn't open his door with less than two guards but I stayed in the tub room alone with him."

While another officer shook down his cell, Stroud filled up the tub and began his weekly ritual of taking a long, hot bath. He liked to scrub down thoroughly and soak in the water as long as he could.

Stroud's eccentricities began to appear during this time. He started shaving his entire body.

"Stroud would shave his face first," De Vincenzi said, "then shave his head, then his body. It'd take two blades for him to do this. I used to kid around with him, and say, 'Damn it, Robert, hurry up! You're going into my lunch hour!'" Stroud would reply, "'Oh, give me a few more minutes.'"

Perhaps because of the shaving, Stroud developed sensitive skin and he spent time pouring skin softeners on his body.

"By that time, he had new slippers, socks, underwear and gown," said De Vincenzi. "Then we'd lock him up again. This would take about an–hour–and–a–half, every Saturday morning. Ritual."

"He read some place that bald men were more virile than men who kept their hair," said officer Bill Rogers. "And he decided that if he shaved his entire body he'd be a superman."

He also began drinking excessive amounts of tea at this time, maintaining that it eased his kidney problem. Officers would see him up late at night reading medical books and furiously writing notes to the staff "on little pieces of paper" about drugs he also thought he needed.

In addition to bowls of tea he also got extra soup. "Every Friday we had chowder and he loved it," said Sendek, who remembered that Stroud could eat "thirteen bowls" of it. "Being a thin man, when he'd get through, he'd look just like he was pregnant."

"Talk? Oh, yes, incessantly," said Sendek. "I don't think he ever trusted me, really, but he talked quite freely."

"He *did* talk," recalled De Vincenzi, with a chuckle. "He probably felt as long as he was talkin' that door would stay open."

Stroud corralled especially sympathetic officers by his door and told them stories about the old days.

"He talked your ear off," said Rogers. "He talked about his experiences at Leavenworth, and his hatred of all bureaucracies—which I'm almost inclined to agree—his early life."

At night, the hospital was deathly quiet and a little spooky. Doors on either side of a long hallway gave experienced officers the willies. An officer working the graveyard shift was locked alone in the hospital, connected only by the phone cord.

"The wind would howl through there, it'd just sing a song to you," recalled Jimmy Dukes, who worked on Alcatraz from the Spring of 1949 until August 1950 and had a turn in the hospital. A watchmaker by trade, Dukes had been laid off and took the civil service exam because he'd heard they were hiring. Later, he quit to join the Marines. Eventually he became a California Highway Patrol officer.

"Stroud wore bedroom slippers, and he'd come sliding across there," Dukes remembered. "He loved to talk. Every time I'd come through he'd want to talk. He *loved* prison. Now that's hard to say about anybody, but he had accepted that he would never get out. And he was proud of what he had done, of the problems he had caused, the changes he had caused. He loved to talk about it, loved to write about it, loved the old way of doing things."

"I thought he was kind of a nut," said Sendek.

"Friendly?" said Yates. "He'd stop me and I'd have to wave him off. Tell me how good he was.

"The man was pretty sharp," Yates reasoned. "He must have

had a couple of hundred pages written by then, telling his version of the prison service. He talked a little bit about everything—his ailments, about how he translated a medical book from French into English, about how he was going to get his brother over in town set up in business, just different things. He was an egotistical old man. Bright as a penny, but egotistical."

Not everyone was charmed. "I thought he was kind of an icky man, really," said former Alcatraz officer George Gregory. "He was a pain in the gluteus maximus. You didn't talk to him, you *listened.*"

"Extremely egotistical," Rogers agreed. "I used to go along with the old boy because I wanted somebody to talk to on the morning watch. In fact, I honestly think the man was insane. If you differed with him on anything, he became almost irrational, as if, 'Who are *you* to differ with *me*?'"

"I played checkers with him at night," remembers De Vincenzi. "He'd ask questions about my family—being of Italian heritage. I used to be careful though, because if the lieutenant was coming, I had to shut that door right away."

"He was a big talker—sure," agreed Furman. "I learned to get along with him by letting him talk. It was all interesting. But I don't suppose he was as interesting to them as to me."

Stroud grew particularly fond of Father Scannell, the Catholic priest who was assigned to Alcatraz. Scannell was a sympathetic, soothing man—very priest–like—but perhaps a little naive for a max pen. One officer remembered how Scannell became convinced of a con's claim of innocence and helped champion his transfer. Not long after, the prisoner committed murder.

Stroud often tried to dominate Scannell's time in the hospital. The effect was like being grabbed by the lapels and forced to listen to a long monologue. Scannell, pleasant to the end, found it difficult to extricate himself. The prisoner would regale him with stories, try out Latin phrases, ask questions of the man he would hint was the only intelligent man here. Questions that were only a wedge for another of Stroud's long–winded monologues.

"Stroud loved to talk to him," De Vincenzi recalled. "He'd say, 'Father Scannell come in yet?' I'd say, 'No, he hasn't,' and he'd say, 'Don't forget to get Scannell for me.' You know—in the meantime, Scannell'd come and gone.

"Stroud *never* let him go. And Scannell just got tired of it. He'd try and by–pass Stroud's cell door. He'd walk down the hall and crouch down—starting about three or four feet before Stroud's door—and *duck-walk* under that window until he got beyond the door. I seen him do that four or five times!"

Furman clearly remembered his client talking sarcastically about the "man of God crouched down on his knees" to get past his door. "He was amused, and half irate," Furman said.

"Stroud caught him once," De Vincenzi said, laughing. "His head was sticking up and he caught him!"

Stroud yelled at the priest. Trapped in his indiscretion, Scannell stood up and said lamely, "I was just kidding."

Older officers, especially, scrutinized Stroud because he had killed a guard with little provocation. Every man had read his file and knew, as Bergen said, that the killing was "never satisfactorily explained." While they may have been relaxed in their dealings with him, they were aware of his volatility. In at least one conversation, Bergen said, Stroud turned from "genial to *very* bitter." Bergen was not easily intimidated. "I got the hell out of there," he snapped. "And the next night he was back to his ol' genial self."

"He may [have] gotten along good for a long time," said Yates, "but it was there, you could tell it when you talked to him. The hatred was smoldering."

"I *never* lost the feeling that he could be dangerous," Bergen said. "With some people you just had that feeling when you were around them. He was mercurial."

Former officer John McGoran disagreed. "There were others I was more afraid of," he said. And then he recounted an incident. "He told me, 'I could kill you with just these two fingers,' " McGoran said, touching his first finger and thumb together. "It was just a conversation. Not a threat."

Yet even his lawyer was aware of his attitude.

"He was *bitter*!" Furman said, his words almost flying out of his mouth, but Furman felt it was "because of what they had done to him."

Increasingly unhappy about his brother's handling of his affairs, Stroud frequently berated him in person and in letters. "Now Marc," he wrote in one letter that was included in court records, "I have outlined some other great plans to you in the past and so far you have bungled every one of them. . . . I don't want any minute detail slighted and I don't want any lies, deception or evasions."

Stroud often included copies of letters in his court petitions. He would painstakingly copy them in his little print, leaving out portions that he felt were not pertinent. Honest to a fault—at times humorously high–minded—Stroud would explain these omissions. In one passage, he wrote, "The petitioner and his agent are brothers . . . and therefore enjoy the brotherly prerogative of insulting each other and of being brutally frank in their analyses of each others [sic] characters. At the time petitioner wrote his memo, he was very much aggravated and in a critical mood and . . . some definite slanderous paragraphs have been omitted [here]."

Stroud read Marcus very well. He was accommodating, obsequious and appeared slippery. By now he was fifty–two years old. Officers, lawyers, agents and writers who dealt with him give an amazingly consistent portrait of a "con man," a "blow hard," a pudgy man who was "a little sleazy" but "meant well." Both men sought fame and fortune, but the more intelligent brother issued his grandiose plans behind deep lock and the more inept had difficulty fulfilling them. "Marc's only trouble is mental laziness," Stroud wrote to a close friend. "Of letting himself be made a sucker by people who do not have a tenth of his real brains. A fault I once had to a very large degree, but which I got over, totally."

Marcus did his best to shield Stroud from the bad news—an attempt to cover himself and gain time, tactics which when discovered by Stroud made him seem all the more incompetent. "Marc comes up with the usual lying stories," Stroud wrote in another letter, "which I could see through without difficulty." But Marcus had to make a living and his brother's affairs were a constant interruption. He was caught between prison rules and his brother's continuous demands.

Although Stroud had given his brother carte blanche to negotiate a movie contract with Polimar, the eventual terms of the
agreement infuriated him. "Stroud announced that if he ever did get
out," Rogers recalled, "his first act was to kill his brother."

Stroud made incredible demands on Marcus. In July 1951, for
example, he wrote asking him to make two hundred copies of a legal
brief and a petition. Stroud was ignorant of the amount of work this
would take.

In the 1950s, copying documents was not the easy task it is
today. Documents were typed on a standard typewriter using a
stencil. Typing errors often had to be cut out of the stencil and
replaced with a taped splice—a messy, frustrating task. The stencil
was then mounted on an ink–filled drum or a mimeograph and
copies were cranked out by hand. If the stencil was damaged,
everything had to be retyped. Stroud's legal briefs and petitions
were often excessively long—numbering six to fourteen legal size
pages crowded with words—and often accompanied by long letters.

Marcus must have gasped when he got the instructions. Stroud
asked his brother to send forty copies to the Supreme Court, three
copies to the Solicitor General, two to Warden Swope, four copies
to himself, one each to J. Edgar Hoover, former President Herbert
Hoover, President Harry S. Truman, former warden James A.
Johnston, Leavenworth Warden Walter A. Hunter, Martin J.
O'Donnell, Fred Robertson, Judge Woodward, BOP official Austin
McCormick and the *Los Angeles Times*. He also wanted one copy
sent to each member of the House and Senate Judiciary Committees, especially Senator Joseph McCarthy.

McCarthy, of course, was then at the beginning of his notorious accusations in which he was falsely identifying prominent men
and women as communists and ruining their lives. Of McCarthy,
Stroud wrote, "He recently made the statement in a letter that
J.V.B[ennett] is guilty of more crimes than any man ever committed
to a federal penitentiary, and that if he ever got the chance, he would
put a number on his back."

That sentiment obviously appealed to Stroud, who tended to
align himself with whomever was big in the news—be it Hitler or
Joe McCarthy.

Stroud told Marcus, "This is very big . . . and at that price it will be cheap, for that will be the best money that you ever invested in my business, and it will get the best results we have ever obtained." He gave Marcus thirty days.

Marcus fumed. He was losing patience and replied that "for the past twenty years you have waged a losing battle." This lecture only deepened Stroud's disdain.

By this time Marcus was living in Sacramento, California, and working as a salesman. Occasionally he visited his brother on Alcatraz—a drive of some eighty miles, a boat ride and then a return by boat and by car. It took all day to visit Stroud for ninety minutes.

Yates recalled one visit between the two brothers about this time. "I had to take [Stroud] down to the visiting room," he began. The visitor sat in a room just outside the cell house. Through a window he could see the prisoner, who sat on the cell house side. Conversation was by telephone. Yates was stationed with Stroud, another officer with Marcus in the visiting room.

"The brother was trying to explain to Stroud that he couldn't quite make things fit yet," Yates said, "but he was working on it and things hadn't fallen into place. And Stroud got mad. He stood up, and just like that, he stepped back, took the phone and threw it against the window. He then turned around and said, 'This visit is over!' "

Yates was stunned. Like most Alcatraz prisoners, Stroud had few visits.

"And I said, 'Stroud, it's your brother. You're going to walk away?' And he said, 'He's *incompetent* as hell. He should be *killed*!' "

On January 14, 1950, Marcus had entered into a contract with Polimer for Stroud's life story. Polimer had subsequently assigned a writer for the screenplay. Stroud, however, was so unhappy with the terms of the agreement that he wrote to his lawyer, Jacques Leslie, who sometimes represented him as well as Polimer and was then acting as a go–between.

Stroud had a long memory and tended to collect injustices as proof of persecution. For two decades he had felt swindled by the publisher of his first book and he held the Bureau of Prisons responsible for not aiding him in going to court. Now it appeared that forces were conspiring to keep him from realizing further profits. The movie didn't look too promising.

In a letter that is by turns flattering, blustery, accusatory, boastful, contentious and raw, Stroud showed that although he had little understanding of the complexity of film production, he was nonetheless a confident negotiator who knew what he wanted. "Dear Mr. Leslie," he wrote,

It was with considerable gratification that I received from Mr. Marcus a copy of your recent letter. I had feared that Dick [Richard Polimer] *might close his option on December 15th . . .*

Of course, Mr. Marcus, much to my displeasure, was naive enough to accept all the synthetic enthusiasm and glowing promises at face value, and make a contract that could not by any stretch of the imagination be said to represent my best interests. Had I known the terms, I most certainly would have not permitted you to mess in my legal affairs in any way, but I have taken precautions to see that nothing of the kind happens in the future.

I do not like people whose promises cannot be depended upon, and I don't give any man a chance to lie to me more than twice. With these thoughts in mind, I have instructed Mr. Marcus not to renew that old contract with Dick at any price. That exclusive rights to the story of my life are not for sale.

You may inform Dick that exclusive rights to produce a picture based upon his own script may be acquired only under the following terms:

Fifty thousand dollars cash on the line upon signing of new contract.

Five percent of the gross at the box office, regardless of whether the picture earns a dime of profit.

The right to read script and demand deletion or correction of any sequence not conforming to actual facts.

Note that I do not say unfavorable. *There are many un-favorable incidents in my life, but I shall not object to any of them if truly presented. I shall object to inaccuracies, no matter how favorable, as I have no desire to be presented to the world other than as I am—merely an imperfect human being doing the best he can under difficult circumstances.*

The picture must be released not later than September 1, 1950, and in event of unavoidable delay I must be paid one thousand dollars per week for every week of delay beyond that date, in addition to royalty.

There must be a saving clause in the contract protecting my rights in any material not used in the script and in other version[s] of the same subject matter.

I have no objection to the publication of the story of your script in book form . . . as I realize that such a move would add considerably to the ease of financing, but I will demand a twenty percent royalty on the gross sale of the book; that is, twenty percent of the list price on every copy sold or distributed. If it is five dollars I will demand one dollar.

You can readly [sic] *see from the above that the situation no longer offers a buyers* [sic] *market, and even though it is none of your business, there is no reason why I should not tell you why, as the matters are not secret.*

[Here Stroud writes about three books being written by or about him. The first is a biography written by a friend of twenty–five years, which he claimed was already completed.]

Second I have completed a detailed study of my own life up to my thirteenth year, at which time I attempted to murder my father, and declared my complete emancipation from parental authority of any kind. This work will run to seven hundred pages and traces the development of an edipus complex and the resulting grouth [sic] *of antisocial tendencies. It covers all phases of child development, both subjectively and objectively, including home life, religion, schooling, the growth of the mind, with a completely frank discussion of the development of sex, the growth of the various ideas and the translation of subjective thought into objective action. This is the kind of book that few men could ever bring themselves to write, since it holds up the innermost recesses of the child's mind and emotions to public view. The* [manuscript] *has been read by two qualified men. One a profound student of criminal psychology, the other a man with twenty-five years experience in handling insane persons. Both have pronounced it an intensely absorbing work presenting a phase of human development never before treated with such thoroughness and sympathetic understanding. It is planned to bring this work out as a scientific monograph under the auspices of one of the societies devoted to such subjects. Both of the readers mentioned predict that it will prove a larger seller than the Kinsley Report* [sic], *in fact, it is a Kinsley Report dramatized and set to music, the music of beautifully flowing words.*

[Stroud then mentioned a third project, the first volume of his analytical history of the federal prison system, which he claimed would be ready for the printer in April.]

You can easily see that the publication of these works will greatly add to the value of my life story, and that is why I am not anxious to close any deal at this time. I am thoroughly convinced that as soon an [sic] *these works hit the market and the big companies realize the great mass of absorbingly dramatic material available, they will be bidding against each other and will not be talking in terms of less than half a million.*

As to your profound devotion to my legal interests, don't make me laugh! I might have a split lip, you know. Marc is no longer dumb enough to fall for that tripe even ... I know just how long those things take, I know that that petition you sent for my approval could have been drawn by any law clerk from my original papers in less than one hour. You did not even take the trouble to check up on the

*jurisdiction. I also thoroughly understand the character
of a man who would make his living by pulling such stunts.
And to me, it stinks. Therefore, when I am ready to begin
any new legal action, I will do it myself.*

   *Even so, since it appears that everything will shortly
work out to my best advantage, there are no hard feelings,
and I extend to you the best of good wishes for this bright
new year.*

   Sincerely,
   Robert Stroud, #594

In the meantime, Polimer was having his own troubles. "I
received a call from Washington," he recalled; it was Bennett.
Polimer was surprised and immediately intrigued. Bennett told him
he shouldn't make this film and invited him to Washington to see
Stroud's files.

   When they met, Polimer was impressed with Bennett, finding
him "very forthright, very honest." Bennett apparently opened the
Stroud files. Polimer spent hours delving into reports from wardens
and prison officers and he began to feel that he had been given a
false picture by Marcus. In fact he was completely turned around by
the experience. When located by phone years later, his first comments about Stroud were sharp and harsh, calling him a "vicious
murderer," a "bad egg" and announcing "to hell with him."

   He became convinced that he didn't want to make a film about
such a man and dropped the project. He did, however, agree to hand
off the idea to others and according to a later contract, was to be
given $3,000 if the movie was ever made.

   At the same time, Stroud complained to U.S. Attorney Frank J.
Hennessy that Swope had been returning his letters. He argued that
a movie about his life would sell "a million books" and was
"primarily an advertising project," therefore permitted in his
agreement with Bennett. When this failed to get him the desired
response, Stroud wrote up a petition for an injunction restraining
Swope from unlawful interference. *Stroud v. Swope* was filed in
June 1950, and included the impounded letters to Marcus, Mamie,

Jacques Leslie and Hennessy. The court did not agree with his premise, however, and ruled against him.

Stroud appealed the court's decision, alleging a "conspiracy" among prison officials Sanford Bates, James V. Bennett, Fred G. Zerbst, C.J. Shuttleworth and others to deprive him of the fruits of his labor.

But once again his prose only deepened his troubles. At one point he wrote about himself, ". . . and he firmly believes that, even though he is untrained in the niceties of civil pleading, his grasp of the fact[s] and his training as a researcher and writer in the evaluation and presentation of facts, makes him more capable of presenting this matter than any attorney could possibly be, even after months of study."

The Court of Appeals was even more harsh in its judgment. Agreeing with the lower court, it found the letters to be "defamatory, scurrilous and abusive" and stated that a busy court "should not be compelled to listen to such nonsense."

But even as that was occurring, Gaddis was publishing his first articles about the Birdman from Alcatraz.

The prisoner, however, did not know this.

By November 1951, he had been in isolation for three years. Almost sixty–two years old, having spent nearly forty–two years in prison, he was now marching towards the end of his life.

He was thinning dramatically, his bulk now whittled down to a boniness that was accentuated by his baldness and his wide wale fleshy ears. He had lost some of his muscle tone from lack of exercise and his skin was loose and flabby. He spent most of his time in a hospital gown and slippers.

Stroud had always lived with pride in his accomplish- ments and hope that the future would be full of opportunities. He wanted to be published again. He still believed he would be the subject of a major motion picture and finally vindicated—even released—triumphant at long last over his arch–enemy, Jim Bennett.

The snail's pace of progress, however, seemed shadowy and thin. Increasingly, he became depressed. Perhaps it had finally sunk

in that he had lost his bird business forever. Outside interest in his
Digest had waned and the film project was currently stalled—thus
the darkening fear that he might never get out. Alone much of the
time, he brooded, becoming ever more self–absorbed. His correspondence had withered to only three people—his brother, sister
and one long–time fan. It was a far cry from the hundreds of letters
he used to get in a year.

In fact, between February 1950 and March 1951 he sent only
two letters, both to his lawyer discussing his last will and testament—
further indication that he was severely disturbed.

"He got moody," said De Vincenzi. "He wouldn't talk sometimes, he'd just eat and drink his tea."

Stroud blamed his brother for his "feeble representation of my
affairs," he had said, and according to prison reports had severed all
relations with him in October 1951.

It was the most difficult time in his life since 1915–16. He was
gloomy, contemptuous and, according to the medical staff, unreasonable in his demands. His signature, which often reflected his
moods, was so scrambled it was unrecognizable. He felt, as he told
De Vincenzi later, that "there was nothing to live for." He knew the
Bureau had him in a vice grip. He wanted to embarrass them and
bring public criticism down on Alcatraz.

On November 15, 1951, he swallowed a large quantity of
Luminals, paregoric, potassium iodine and other pills and slipped
into unconsciousness.

On a routine count an officer found him semi–comatose and
"sluggish to painful stimuli." The medical staff went to work,
pumping his stomach.

On a thorough shakedown, several suicide notes were found in
his cell. They were addressed to prison administrators, the coroner,
relatives and his attorney, becoming the basis for the consensus that
Stroud had genuine intention of destroying himself.

Prison scuttlebutt—whether begun by Stroud or someone else—
had it from then on that he had written a lengthy thesis on toilet
paper—to reveal the corruption on Alcatraz—encapsulated it in the
fingers of a surgical glove and swallowed it whole, hoping that it
would be discovered upon autopsy. Indeed, this became one of the

most famous Stroud stories. In fact, he even wrote several versions
of it in his manuscript.

> *Now communication has always been the writer's specialty*
> *and he probably knows more ways of getting information*
> *and getting it out of the prison underground. In [one] case*
> *he put 192,000 words on six sheets of the thinnest legal*
> *tissue, cut into narrow strips. The strips were rolled into*
> *a tight cylinder, encased in a double layer of rubber with*
> *fingers cut from surgical gloves and swallowed by a*
> *prisoner the day he was due to be discharged.*

Compared with a typical paperback book of approximately
four–hundred–and–forty words per page, a 192,000–word manuscript is equivalent to a four–hundred–and–thirty–six page book.
That he smuggled written material out of prison is not questioned.
That he smuggled out a book–size manuscript in the fingers of a
surgical glove is fantasy. But as always, there was a snip of truth.
According to Swope, Stroud wrote "a note, enclosed it in a piece of
rubber glove and swallowed it, hoping that the coroner would
discover it." In essense the note said that Bennett was driving
him insane.

When Stroud regained consciousness, according to his prison
report, he bitterly cursed the staff for saving him.

Two months later he made a second attempt. This time he
wasn't as quiet. According to De Vincenzi, Stroud took advantage
of a new officer, asked for a razor to shave and then slashed himself
in both groins. He was bleeding profusely when he stood naked at
the barred door of his room and shouted out that he "would be dead
within ten minutes!"

"With his usual egotism," his report stated, "Stroud declared
that he had intended to cut his femoral arteries and accomplish a
rapid exsanguination. However the attempt was feeble, and there
were no untoward affects from the lacerations." For all his bragging,
Stroud could not find his femoral arteries.

The prisoner's sense of humor was intact here as well. According to the prison report, he had left another message to the

coroner, writing on the skin of both thighs, that Bennett was driving him insane and his mistreatment should be investigated.

Swope had had enough.

Writing to Bennett about the incidents, he said Stroud had "openly boasted that he wouldn't hesitate to take human life if necessary." He requested that Stroud be sent to the Medical Center at Springfield. Bennett declined, saying, "I don't think any more can be done for him at Springfield than you can do at Alcatraz." That meant: continue present program.

That year Stroud refused to go before the Classification Committee—a new method of evaluating prisoners yearly by group interviews—saying to the associate warden, "There is nothing I can get out of the committee, so why bother?"

The committee recommended that he remain in the hospital, not only to keep him from committing suicide, but because the "antagonistic and anti–social prisoner will be isolated and unable to agitate and create discord among other inmates."

He was now watched more closely; cell checks occurred more often.

In 1953, it was reported that "his adjustment is very poor. He keeps his ward and person just clean enough to get by."

According to the annual prison evaluation, several Congressional members had written letters urging prison administrators to allow him to revise his book. "Brother Stroud is certainly causing a great deal of correspondence," Bennett wrote to Swope in February 1953. When they asked him to outline his needs, administrators decided that "the amount of materials he stated he needed would have placed the institution in the same condition that made his transfer to Alcatraz in 1942 necessary."

Growing more desperate, Stroud tried another route. In September 1953, he wrote the FBI and Director Bennett saying that he had a "fool–proof solution for ridding the country of communist agents." Anti–Communist fervor was at its peak in 1953; Ethel and Julius Rosenberg were executed that year; Morton Sobell was convicted and would soon arrive on Alcatraz. Senator McCarthy was receiving headlines for his accusations and still one year from Congressional censure. Stroud offered to reveal his plan "in exchange for his freedom."

There is no response in his file from anyone regarding this offer.

Stroud again refused to go to the Classification Committee meeting, stating that he was being kept in isolation for "personal vindictiveness." It may have been true, but Stroud's attitude continued to contribute to, and justify, his predicament.

A cantankerous individual [the 1953 report stated] *who must be watched closely. He seems to be brooding and moody over confinement but there appears nothing can be done regarding program change in his case. Shrewd, calculating and dangerous character, who at times tries to provoke discord between inmates and officers. An egotist who states definitely that he is an atheist, believing in nothing. Very bitter against those responsible for his custody. Recommendations: Continue present program.*

Arthur M. Dollison stepped onto Alcatraz in October 1953. He was forty–four years old, conservatively dressed in a gray overcoat over a suit and tie and a brown hat. He had thinning, almost white hair, light blue eyes and a ruddy complexion. He was now a fifteen–year veteran with four prison posts behind him.

After training at Leavenworth in 1938, he transferred as a junior officer to the Federal Jail and Correctional Institution at Ashland, Kentucky, which was mostly filled with bootleggers and moonshiners. Returning to Ashland after the war, he saw his career opportunities limited as a prison officer and moved into Federal Prison Industries, Inc. That led him to Terre Haute, Indiana, and finally to Alcatraz.

Dollison hadn't considered Alcatraz when he wrote "West Coast" on his transfer request because a colleague had just moved there in his position. But his colleague quit the prison service after only two weeks on Alcatraz and Dollison was shoveled into his place. He was somewhat apprehensive about reporting to work on the prison island and bringing his family to live there.

"The Rock" was almost as infamous among prison employees as it was in the general public. Media hype, and ex–Alcatraz officers' exaggeration of the dangers, made it seem pretty bad. The fact that the prison was rarely mentioned in training classes and in Bureau meetings only added to the mystery. The reasons would become clear as Dollison settled into work as Industries office manager: Alcatraz was a singularly unique penitentiary. Conditions elsewhere simply did not apply here. Where at Terre Haute, for example, there were three inmate counts a day, on Alcatraz there were twelve.

He checked in at the dock office, was told to pass through the metal detector and instructed to board a little blue bus for the trip up to the prison. The bus stopped first at the basement entrance of old Sixty–four building where officers who had changed from civilian into prison clothing were let aboard.

Two men were laughing and talking loudly about "what a sonofabitch the Captain is," and Dollison looked up, surprised. As they sat down, one told a story about an incident that had occurred the day before. He had had a dental appointment in the city and needed to be relieved early so he could get there in time. He informed the captain that he would need an early relief. The captain nodded, stone–faced. At noon he reminded him. Ten minutes before the boat departure, with no relief in sight, he called the captain's clerk to ask what the hell was going on. "Where's my relief?"

"Didn't the captain tell ya?" the clerk replied, and in a mocking tone, said, "He called your dentist and cancelled your appointment."

The other officer burst out laughing and agreed that the captain was a sonofabitch. The humor was lost on Dollison, however. That they talked so openly in the presence of a stranger—someone who could be from the Bureau, or a prisoner's visitor—was shocking and made him wonder just what kind of institution Alcatraz was.

A few minutes later in Warden Swope's office, Captain Philip R. Bergen walked in and introduced himself.

Bergen, who had arrived in 1939 as a senior officer and had risen from lieutenant to become captain of the guards, was perfectly typecast. He was tough, flinty and realistic. Many thought that Alcatraz was more than a a job to him—it was his life. But from his perspective he was head of security in a prison filled with men who were security risks and staffed by some who were "just filling a uniform." He was generally disliked, which didn't bother him and some lieutenants, whom he had risen above, were jealous. Almost everyone agreed, however, that he was intelligent, security–minded and consistent.

Dollison found Bergen to be "a husky, sober–faced, quiet individual who had no time for amenities with an unproven outsider." He was perfunctory; he told Dollison that he would take him on a brief tour of the prison, merely pointing out some of the differences between Alcatraz and other institutions. With that, they were let into the cell house.

Although both were men of integrity, they could not have been more unalike.

Dollison was quiet, introspective and objective, a gentleman. Warm but cautious, he didn't exhibit his emotions. He had grown up in Cambridge, Ohio, the only child of a straight–laced newspaper editor and his wife—as upper crust as you could get in a tiny pottery and glass factory town. He thought he would enter business.

Bergen was opinionated, passionate and blunt. He had grown up in Chicago in the '20s when Capone was at the height of his power. He was a tough Irish kid from a tough Irish neighborhood near the mansion where "Scarface" kept his family. Pimps and whores, bootleggers and gangsters were frequent residents. He spoke their language and he could get physical if need be. His ambition had been to be a police officer.

Both men had been forced into the prison service by the depression.

Years of conditioning in their different jobs had jostled each man's attitude even further apart. Dollison worked in Industries, where he tried to help prisoners get skills. Bergen worked in the correctional force, where he met the day–to–day bitterness that greeted a line–staff officer of a super max pen.

To Bergen, Dollison was "not quite tough enough."

To Dollison, Bergen "was a little rough."

Bergen would stay two more years, a total of fifteen years on Alcatraz, considering it his best assignment. Dollison would stay nine, rising to become superintendent of Industries in 1958, considering it his "most interesting" prison. Eventually both men became associate wardens—Bergen at La Tuna, Texas, in 1955, and Dollison at Alcatraz in 1961.

In many respects Alcatraz resembled Bergen far more than Dollison.

As far as Robert Stroud was concerned, Dollison would have much less to do with him than Bergen. They would meet, maybe, once or twice yearly at the Classification meetings, but Dollison rarely spoke at the meetings outside of a question or two. Stroud wasn't considered employable and Dollison was mostly looking for men to work in Industries. By the time he became the associate warden of Alcatraz, and might have had a direct affect on Stroud's fate, the prisoner had been gone for three years.

Nonetheless, Dollison and Bergen shared similar feelings about Stroud; he was dangerous, manipulative and could kill again. For Bergen, it was a knowledge gained from personal encounters. For Dollison, it was the sheer weight of institutional opinion.

As early as 1949, articles about the "Canary Expert" living on Alcatraz had begun appearing in newspapers around the country. After hearing the story from his agent, Thomas E. Gaddis, a parole officer and college instructor, began researching the prisoner's unusual life.

In 1952, he requested permission to see Stroud's prison file. Request denied. He asked for permission to visit Stroud on Alcatraz. Request denied. Gaddis grew suspicious, feeling like he was on to something.

The Bureau of Prisons was not without its own perverse sense of humor when it came to Stroud. Still operating on the idea that no information would emerge about any prisoner, and at the same time attempting to put the best face on federal prisons, bureaucrats had written pamphlets about each institution to be given to dignitaries when they toured. Gaddis got the one about Alcatraz. In it Stroud cropped up—unnamed—as a "Typical Case History."

*Alaska's gold rush spawned many a desperado, but none
more callous of human life than Jack, who, at the age of
19, in a quarrel over the favors of a prostitute, shot and
killed a bartender. At the McNeil Island Penitentiary,
where he was committed to serve a twelve–year sentence
for this offense, he soon assaulted and severely wounded
another inmate with a knife. He received only a six–month
sentence for this, but was transferred to the Leavenworth
Penitentiary for more secure custody. It was not long
until his murderous nature again asserted itself. He knifed
an officer to death in the prison dining room in the
presence of twelve hundred other inmates. For this crime,
he was three times tried and each time sentenced to death,
but the President commuted the sentence to life imprisonment. Jack boasted that he had made five other daggers,
one of which, he said, had been used in the murder of a
fellow inmate. There was considerable evidence that he
had been plotting an organized mutiny and murder of
prison officials as part of a general escape plan, and,
because of his homicidal tendencies, he was placed in
segregation. Later, murderous weapons were found in his
possession and he was transferred to Alcatraz. It is still
necessary to keep him in segregation.*

That was the entire description. No mention of his two published
books or his unusual twenty–two–year bird research. Stroud was
hardly "typical." Anyone favorably impressed with his accomplishments would have been incensed at the deception. Gaddis felt
that the Bureau of Prisons was hiding something.

He published his first national article on Stroud, "The Bird
Man of Alcatraz" in *Cosmopolitan* magazine in May 1953.

Until now publicity for Stroud was amateur and regional.
When Gaddis stepped onto the stage, however, he had refined the
techniques of Elizabeth and her son, and was giving Stroud
something he had never had before: a national audience. In Gaddis'
words, by 1953 Stroud had "been in isolation for thirty–seven
years." That was patently untrue. Stroud had been in isolation for

five years. He had been in *segregation* for thirty–seven.

Cosmopolitan was not the *Cosmo* of today, but it did trade on the romantic. It's clear from Gaddis' later publishing of the Birdman's story that the article is a work–in–progress. His timing of events is off, minor details are in error and his descriptions are imagined. Kitty O'Brien was described as a "long–legged dance hall girl with an Irish complexion and a temper to match." The current Stroud is an avuncular "tall old man who wears a green eyeshades cap, like an aging baseball umpire."

The article was accompanied by drawings depicting various scenes in Stroud's life. In one, an attractive, scantily–clad woman is being kissed by a tall, dark Yukon minor—her fishnet–dressed leg lifted in high sexual gratification. The caption reads: "In a roaring frontier town he fell in love with a dance–hall girl, killed his first man and kissed his last woman."

Gaddis was onto something; no one would do more for the marketing of the Birdman than he would.

Naturally, Marcus and Gaddis found their way towards one another like lemmings to the sea.

Later Captain Bergen would echo the common opinion among officers that Stroud himself had written much of Gaddis' book. Gaddis had no access to prison reports, nor to Stroud, nor to officers who knew him, yet had sprinkled accurate quotes throughout the book. How else could he have obtained so much information?

But in fact, Gaddis, who later also wrote a Master's thesis about Stroud, would eventually receive a bundle of approximately twenty–one–hundred letters written by him and another eighteen–hundred written to him from Elizabeth, Mamie, Marcus, Della Jones and long–time correspondent and fellow bird breeder Fred E. Daw, among others. They described everything Stroud had done. Stroud and Gaddis, of course, were never permitted to write to one another, but that did not prohibit them from communicating.

In April 1953, Gaddis signed a contract in collaboration with Marcus. Gaddis accepted $2,400 from him to deliver a publishable manuscript by December 31, 1953. He also agreed to "conduct a

publicity and propaganda campaign to further our mutual interests."
Thus, by contract, Gaddis had seriously compromised his objectivity
as a biographer.

By 1954, however, Gaddis was still toiling on the manuscript,
and Stroud was becoming ornery and vocal about the delay. Over
the course of 1954, Stroud wrote monthly letters to his friend Fred
Daw complaining about Gaddis' inability to finish the book. According to Stroud's recitation of Marcus's comments, Gaddis'
writing "lacked drama," was "overwritten" and "too fancy." Stroud
rightfully understood that a powerful story did not need fancy
prose. But he also imagined that he could control everyone and
when it became apparent that he could not, he attacked.

In an April 13, 1954, letter, Stroud wrote mischieviously that
Marcus had said, "as a writer, Tom stinks, and what is worse he took
a batchelor's [sic] degree in writing and imagines that he can write
so you can't tell him anything."

Now Gaddis' college degree became Stroud's monthly tirade.
"I could have written the book in French in less time than he has
taken and he is a college graduate," Stroud wrote.

Stroud was also focused on the money to be made. In letters to
Daw, he threw a lot of figures around, thinking that the book would
generate $10,000 in magazine serial sales, that if it became a best-
seller in hardback "it will probably run the softback up to three-
hundred years," that softback sales would generate $150,000, that
the movie could push sales up to a quarter of a million and beyond.
He always mentioned taking care of Mamie. Mamie came first, even
before Marcus.

By that summer, Marcus and Gaddis were feuding. According
to the Stroud brothers the problem seemed to rest on the fact that
Marcus didn't have a college degree therefore Gaddis refused to
listen to his advice on how to write the story. Stroud fumed from
behind bars. The delay was frustrating. At some point that summer
the rift between the writer and the brother became so gaping that
Stroud intended to get to the bottom of it. He instructed Daw to
write Gaddis to tell him that he was "plenty sore at the delay." He
asked Daw to pose thirteen questions to Gaddis so he could decide
who was lying, his own brother or Gaddis. Daw refused to inter-

vene. Stroud angrily wrote back using one of his his typical thun-
derbolt reversals,

> *Because our friendship has always rested on complete*
> *faith and complete frankness, I finally made up my mind*
> *to tell you just how I feel—for I don't think that any other*
> *basis of friendship is possible. . . . I have received a good*
> *hard kick in the face from the only person who could ever*
> *have possibly [done] it under any circumstances, and it is*
> *only because I cannot convince myself that the kick was*
> *intentional that I have taken the trouble to write at all. I*
> *hope this finds you well and all things going well with you,*
> *As ever, Bob.*

By October, Stroud was urging Marcus to file a law suit.

Poor Tom Gaddis. He was having trouble writing what would
become the biggest book of his life. He felt increasing paronoia
over the Bureau of Prisons and Bennett, who in the 1950s seemed
as powerful as J. Edgar Hoover. And he had to contend with the
clamorous, ambitious, irrational Stroud brothers.

"Roosevelt committed many crimes against the American
people and against humanity," Stroud announced in an October
1954 harangue, "but one of the worst was the G. I. bill; for it led to
many young people being overeducated and made into misfits. Tom
was one of these."

Gaddis was also concerned about the potential lawsuit. He
mentioned the dilemma to his acquaintance and attorney, Stanley
A. Furman, who like everyone became intrigued with the story.

Furman would eventually become the most successful of
Stroud's string of lawyers. A bantam–weight, understated, quietly–
teasing and bright lawyer, Furman had the exact qualities to cope
with Stroud's emotional extremes. He had graduated from Harvard
Law School in 1937 and had moved his practice to Beverly Hills,
California, where he specialized in real estate and contracts. Although it was Furman's recollection that the issue centered around
Gaddis' depiction of the Stroud family relationships, later court
records revealed that the Stroud brothers perceived that Gaddis had

entered into a contract with Random House without them and had received an advance which he had not shared with them. Furman advised Gaddis and Random House to hold the profits in escrow in case Marcus did sue.

After years of toiling in a makeshift workroom in his garage, Gaddis published his book in 1955. Not a true biography, but a narrative using dramatized quotations mixed with authentic quotes, it left an indomitable impression of Man Against The System. It was probably one of the most influential books on a prisoner ever written. School kids carried it in their back pockets. Newspaper columnists wrote essays about it.

This is where many of the myths about Robert Stroud achieved their greatest push; where he was described as a man with a "third-grade education," who exhibited "meticulous personal habits." Gaddis alluded to the probability that Stroud was a genius, and reprinted at face value Stroud's more outrageous claims, such as his numerous cures, and his building a microtome " 'that will give me cuts down to two micrones . . . equal to 1/12,000 of an inch.' "

The writer inserted his own dramatic claims and outrageous generalizations, that Stroud "was living on a commuted sentence, in solitary for life," or that "It has long been known that policemen and guards incline toward cultivating flowers and pets as a way of 'getting unwound' from the tension of the big house."

In his breathless, dramatic tone, he referred to Stroud as journeying "with the smoking torch of Freud through the caves of his own fearsome personality." He wrote that "Stroud loved to open the breeding cages and let nature take its hot avian course." Yet he stripped Stroud and Della Jones of any feeling, writing about their first meeting: "Middle-aged, with sex a remote memory, they soon found themselves talking excitedly about their common interest."

Stroud was depicted as an abused child of an alcoholic father and a dominant, manipulative mother, but there the facts ended and fiction began to play. His two killings and prison stabbing were shielded in a fog of drama that mostly relieved him of blame. Over and over Gaddis stressed Stroud's will, concentration, creativity and fighting spirit against all odds.

"He had triumphed over prison torpor and educated himself," Gaddis wrote. "He had supported his mother from a solitary cell. He had gone forward through a series of mind–cracking crises to become a bird scientist whose contributions to bird pathology and therapy had saved thousands of dollars, an estimated fifty thousand birds and uncounted human heartaches in the lives of bird–lovers throughout the world."

That fifty thousand birds owed their lives to Robert Stroud was a statement of which Elizabeth would have been proud.

What emerged was a portrait of an aging prisoner–statesman who was dedicated, immaculate, noble and moral, who was completely rehabilitated yet still under the thumb of a brutal prison system.

Although Gaddis accurately portrayed Stroud's bird studies at Leavenworth, what the public remembered, and still remembers, was Alcatraz. The island prison played a major role in the depiction of the Birdman and the book may have played a major role in the fate of that prison. While Alcatraz had been the fictional scene of numerous grade B movies since the mid–1930s, now with the publishing of a book in the 1950s about one of its oldest and most maligned prisoners, the public's reaction began to shift; Alcatraz began to seem like an unnecessarily brutal penitentiary.

By 1955, when the book was published, Stroud had been "in solitary" for "forty years." Reviewers were quick to understand that the book was about, as one wrote, the "thrilling evidence of the indomitableness of the human spirit." Yet that subtlety was lost as good reviews poured in, assuring the book of a wider audience. Translated into German, French, Italian and Hebrew, it captured the emotions of millions of people. Newspapers throughout the country began serializing it in daily installments. The story was inspirational, and despite the histrionics, a very good read.

Now that there was a national audience, things began to change. For the first time, Stroud was no longer directing the actions of others. Increasingly, people on the outside were calling the shots. And as his life story became more popularized, the old band wagon was heaved out of the barn.

An editorial in a 1956 issue of *American Cage Bird* magazine stated that the prisoner was now "forty years in solitary" and that it's time "we wake up and realize that what is happening to Robert Stroud could happen to any one unfortunate to be in prison." It called his treatment by the federal prison Bureau "inexcusably cruel," his rehabilitation "remarkable" and suggested that readers write to President Dwight D. Eisenhower and Vice President Richard M. Nixon urging his release.

Prison officers were sarcastic about the dramatization. The Birdman they knew was egotistical, hostile, homicidal and not very clean. "His quarters must constantly be checked for contraband," a prison report indicated in March 1955. "If permitted the inmate would live in filth." But if officers felt defensive, Alcatraz administrators were caught in the middle. For the first time the Classification Committee in 1955 felt that Stroud's continued isolation in the hospital was not ideal, but they recommended no change.

"He frequently attempts to prescribe medication for himself," his annual report stated in 1956. "Frequent examinations by medical officers have not revealed any significant medical findings. On occasion he presents a hostile attitude towards members of the medical staff." Stroud boasted that "eventually he will be released by Executive Clemency," the report continued. It recommended, "that he continue with his present program."

Comments in his file the next year seem even more contradictory than usual. "This man still is as unrealistic in his thinking as usual and he is very untidy in his quarters in the hospital," the January 1957 prison report began its final paragraph.

He spoke frankly at the meeting where he protested his segregated status as 'unjustifiable cruelty.' He thinks he should be permitted to converse and associate with other people. He said that he now is feeling better since he is being provided with a diet including more cheese and buttermilk and he seemed more pleasant than usual when he was interviewed. The Committee recommended no change in program.

In the meantime, Marcus did sue, and Furman, representing Gaddis, began seeing Stroud in late 1956. The island prison was Furman's first maximum security prison, and he described it as "an overwhelmingly depressing experience." He flew into San Francisco, caught the island boat at the foot of Van Ness Avenue, was driven up to the cell house at the top of the island and escorted into the Warden's office. Paul J. Madigan was the stout, ruddy–faced man who stood to greet him.

An unruffled, pipe–smoking, devout Irish Catholic with a thorough prison background, Madigan had replaced the mercurial Warden Swope in January 1955. Genuinely appreciated by many prisoners and most of the staff, Madigan had acquired the affectionate names "Prayin' " or "Promisin' " Paul because of his well–known Catholicism and his tendency to agree to most requests. His niceties were legend.

"Christ, Madigan would promise to put strippers in your cell if you asked him," Quillen said once. Dave Beck, famed Teamsters president who served five years at McNeil Island when Madigan was there, described the warden's relationship with prisoners as not unlike an elder professor beloved by his undergraduates. He was genuine, honest, steady; a worker. While James V. Bennett had a McNeil Island cruiser named after him, Madigan's namesake, appropriately, was a tugboat.

Madigan's reputation was solid. In 1941, as Captain on Alcatraz, he had calmly convinced four life–timers during an escape attempt in which he was tied up, that their saws were useless against the window bars and they would soon be discovered anyway. The four—among them Arnold Kyle, Joe Cretzer and Sam Shockley— gave up. Such cool stood well with cons and guards, all of whom liked a good yarn.

Madigan's prayers paid off in other ways as well. He was transferred before the disastrous '46 escape attempt in which he easily might have been wounded or killed, returned later as warden, then was transferred from "the Rock" just before its final difficult year.

Yet Madigan was hardened by years of prison work and often viewed prisoners in black and white. Harshly–worded comments appear in several prisoners' files, or in letters to Washington, like one in which he defines several Alcatraz cons as "a group of psychopaths who have no reasoning power."

Furman and Madigan had lunch together in the Alcatraz dining room before the attorney met Stroud. Later, after Stroud gave Furman a leather–bound copy of his book containing the bitter dedication, Madigan asked to see it, "took a razor blade," Furman said, "cut that page out, and gave the book back."

In fact, Furman and Madigan side–stepped one another in a continual dance of procedural maneuvers. Madigan filed at least one letter in 1956 in which he refused permission for the attorney to see Stroud and summarily eliminated him from the correspon– dence list. Then Furman announced he was now representing Stroud as his lawyer. Yet Furman felt no animosity for Madigan; he felt the warden thought of himself as a civil servant conducting the rules of the system. Despite the professional tug of war Furman called him "very protective," and felt that Madigan was on Stroud's side.

Furman was shown into the visiting room and Stroud was escorted from the hospital. The attorney saw a man of sixty–six years, who was thin, bald and pale. He had on wire rim glasses and his eyes were piercing.

"At first we were formal," Furman recalled. "I decided to call him Mr. Stroud, until he told me otherwise. And he said, 'I haven't heard *Mister* Stroud since I saw my own father.'

"He told me, 'Be very careful what you say—this is being taped,' and he whispered it to me through both hands. And I said I wasn't going to whisper to someone who wasn't [yet] my client."

At first Stroud was cordial, but serious, Furman said. Gaddis later wrote in a newsletter that Furman showed him some of the reviews of the *Birdman of Alcatraz*, but not the book itself. (The Bureau's refusal to allow Stroud to read the book was based on the rule that prisoners couldn't read nor write about crime, criminals or men in prison.)

Stroud relaxed and became more friendly, Furman remembered. "His conversation was brighter, his gestures wider." He must have become excited about the book, of which he knew only a little. Later, a prison report stated that Stroud hoped he would "receive a considerable sum from royalties" from the book.

He was perhaps disappointed. The Stroud–Marcus suit against Gaddis was settled out of court, but of course there were court fees. Eventually the author's profits were divided among Furman, Gaddis, Stroud, Marcus and an agent named George Landy. Stroud was apparently able to buy a color television set for his sister. A "small amount," according to Furman, went towards the "Committee for the Release of Robert Stroud," which was then being organized.

Furman began representing Stroud. He developed a three–pronged procedure of attacking Stroud's case in the courts, with publicity and with applications for Executive Clemency.

As Gaddis' book became more popular, however, the Bureau of Prisons, through Madigan, began to cast its long shadow over their relationship.

The era of prisoners' rights didn't begin until long after Robert Stroud was dead; during this time prison officials were often unsympathetic toward attorney-client relationships. There were attempts to wear Furman down through interference, semantics, silence, delays and confusion. And it was difficult for the attorney to see through the haze of prison bureaucracy to determine exactly who was at the bottom of it.

He had asked Stroud to outline the pattern of his relationship with the Bureau. The attorney received a twenty–five page report from Stroud, but a subsequent one–hundred–and–seven page document Stroud wrote was confiscated.

Madigan wrote that he felt the document was irrelevant to Stroud's current confinement, since it contained "many fancied grievances and extraneous material covering the period since 1920."

Furman protested to the U. S. Attorney General and the President of the United States that the confiscation was a flagrant disregard of attorney-client privilege. He never received it.

Then, in 1958, Director Bennett visited Alcatraz and saw Robert Stroud, bringing with him the world–famous psychiatrist Karl Menninger. According to one source Menninger and Stroud spent about an hour–and–a–half together, but Menninger later wrote that he only spent a "few minutes" with Stroud. Although a report was rumored to have been made, both Menninger and Bennett were evasive about its contents and indeed, even its existence. Much later, George Reed, the Chairman of the U.S. Parole Board, wrote that Menninger's "report indicated that Stroud was still an extremely dangerous man. . . . He was an absolute individualist, determined to live by his own impulses and prone to violence when challenged." Dr. Charles E. Smith, Assistant Medical Director for the Bureau of Prisons, accompanied Menninger and later said that no formal examination was given to Stroud and no report was made, but everyone felt Stroud was psychotic. Whether the Menninger report existed or not, the innuendo was used against Stroud and Furman had no recourse.

By now Stroud was again pinning his stated hopes to getting a release. Furman had gently cautioned him that he would never get out if he didn't change his attitude towards officials and become more pleasant and cooperative. Stroud took his advice, writing later, "It will be much easier to sell my ideas to the world if I restrain myself," he wrote.

He was once again busy preparing a petition for Executive Clemency and preparing arguments for an upcoming court battle over his solitary confinement order.

In December 1957, the *Scientific American* magazine article appeared. A science magazine which adapted its tone for a wider audience, *Scientific American* usually included one article celebrating an amateur inventor or scientist. Although the article on Stroud was ostensibly written by an editor of the magazine, C. L. Strong, it consisted largely of quoted material from Gaddis or his book. Morton Sobell, about the only prisoner on Alcatraz who subscribed to the popular scientific magazine, was astonished to discover that the article had slipped by the prison censors.

"In population no one ever talked about him," Sobell said, "and that article gave me more information than I had ever known."

Sobell, an engineer with two master's degrees, was almost as equally famous as Stroud; he had been convicted with the Rosenbergs in 1953 for espionage and would serve eighteen years in prison, almost six of them at Alcatraz. Sensing that Washington would get wind of the article and send prison officers to look for it, he devised a fake magazine "route list," crossing off names of inmates who had ostensibly already seen the magazine, tore out the article and had it smuggled up to Stroud. He considered this his "biggest coup" on Alcatraz.

This was the first glimpse that Stroud got of Gaddis' book.

Four months later, in April 1958, a *Newsweek* magazine article entitled "Scholar on Alcatraz" called the Birdman an "eminent scientist," and stated that he was allowed only to talk to the prison chaplain "a couple of times a month."

In June, *The New York Mirror Magazine* wrote in the "The Strange Saga of the Caged Birdman" that a presidential order decreed he would "spend the rest of his natural life in solitary confinement."

By now the Birdman's story began to assume a life of its own.

That same month the Los Angeles *Mirror News*, in an error-filled, emotional outpouring, announced, "There's a living–dead victim of our savage, medieval penology of half a century ago surviving in Alcatraz prison." Calling the Stroud story an "almost unbelievable case" of how "this buried–alive prisoner, cut off from all contact with humankind for so long," whose sentence was commuted to "solitary confinement" by President Wilson, from which "there was no provision for parole."

This writer really got worked up. "This savage law," he wrote, "has since been rewritten but Stroud is still its victim. . . . Not even our most depraved criminals face such inhuman punishment as Stroud has endured for forty–two years." Who could conclude otherwise? "Efforts should be made to obtain his release from solitary," it concluded.

Inside Detective chimed in with an article entitled, "Forty–one Years in Solitary Confinement." Stroud was said to be "one of the world's foremost authorities on bird pathology; a brilliant man, a genius perhaps. But he's kept alone, shunned, concealed; sentenced to serve out his life as a complete outcast."

This magazine's appeal to disgruntled male readers was obvious. "His father was a moderately prosperous coal merchant. His mother was a domineering woman who despised her husband and did not rest until she had kicked him out and donned the pants in the family."

Even Gaddis acknowledged that Stroud's father was a drunk who beat the kid. But in the mens' magazines of the 1950s every woman was suspect. To wit: "But his mother complex soon guided him into the arms of a dancehall tart exactly twice his age." Stating that he had not "had a woman since 1909," the article furthered other myths. "He is forbidden to talk with the guards or orderlies. Once or twice a week, two guards march him down the hall to take a shower—in silence."

In October '58, *Coronet* magazine published an article in which Gaddis asserted that while most prisoners faced with the thought of isolation until death would turn into "human vegetables," Stroud had instead become a "genius–scientist."

The Bureau of Prisons was by now trying to contain the monster.

By June 1958, Stanley Furman submitted an application for Executive Clemency—Stroud's fifth petition since 1915.

The document, written by Stroud and sent on June 27 to U.S. Pardon Attorney Reed Cozart, stated seven reasons why the prisoner deserved to be released by President Eisenhower: he had a record of non–violence since 1920 and had recognized then that violence was not the proper solution (Stroud explained in the petition, "His sometimes irritating manner of expression should not be allowed to obscure this long record of non–violent behavior"); he had been kept "in a solitary cell since 1916," over forty years, and had paid his debt to society; he was a scientist, a linguist and had employment available to him on the outside; he was sane, intelligent, industrious, with "quiet, studious, scholastic, scientific habits"; he was old and had been confined to Alcatraz prison hospital since 1948 for "ill health"; and his remaining years could be devoted to socially worthwhile activities.

The petition carried with it letters from several prominent supporters, hundreds of letters from average citizens and tens of thousands of signatures from concerned citizens.

People were passionate about obtaining freedom for the Birdman.

A man wrote to the White House in 1958, "The whole case has been well–documented and written up by Thomas E. Gaddis, *Birdman of Alcatraz*, and no one in the Federal Prison System has even dared to try to challenge this set of facts."

A women who read the *Coronet* article wrote to Eisenhower, "I dare to say that if there were more Robert Strouds outside prison walls today, this world would be a better one in which to live."

In a hand–written note to "Ike," a man referred to Stroud as "the eminent bird pathologist and bacteriologist in solitary confinement" who "for the last fifteen years has been denied the right to improve himself."

Another wrote, "I have just finished reading *Birdman of Alcatraz*. This prisoner has evidently made quite positive contributions to society from within prison. He has also pinpointed the cause of his crime. And he has paid his debt to society—forty–two years in solitary. Why isn't it possible to pardon him!"

"Dear Mr. President," wrote a man named McKee, "I just this moment finished reading *Birdman of Alcatraz*. I WAS SHOCKED . . . . . . This, right here in America, what a tragedy. . . . . This man must be freed!"

One prominent letter came from Raymond E. Baglin, an insurance agent from Manchester, Connecticut, who operated a large aviary and offered Stroud employment and living quarters.

Furman, in fact, was able to get offers of temporary residence from the American Friends Service Committee in Los Angeles, and permanent residence and a job from Harry Rumberger of Jeanette, Pennsylvania. These proposals were essential before release would be considered. When U.S. Pardon Attorney Cozart wrote asking for more information about Stroud's proposed "aftercare," it instilled a feeling in Furman and Gaddis that he was seriously considering recommending a clemency—a feeling that would soon betray them.

Procedure required the Department of Justice to review the application for merit before sending it to President Eisenhower—a little like the fox being asked to rate the chickens for desirability.

In Stroud's case, Justice at first refused to act on Executive Clemency because of a "general rule" that clemency could not be recommended while the applicant was subject to release by the Board of Parole. With further inquiry Furman uncovered no such "general rule" but was told that this has been the "practice" of the Justice Department.

In fact, Stroud had just been turned down by the Parole Board. The chairman, George Reed, personally visited Stroud in March 1958—three months before the Executive Clemency application was submitted. Reed, a religious conservative and a long–time parole board member, stated in his book that he was convinced that Stroud was trying to hypnotize him by "weaving back and forth like a pendulum" with a "deliberately hypnotic tone of voice." Reed claimed others had filed similar reports but nothing of this sort was found. Nonetheless, Stroud's perverse sense of humor and his manipulation of authorities probably earned him more than a few outrageous claims (either that or he had been hoarding Luminals again).

Since Stroud, like all prisoners, was subject to annual review by the Parole Board, then he could never be recommended for clemency—a nice bureaucratic catch–22.

In his petition Stroud had cautioned the U.S. Pardon Attorney that he was considered by the Bureau to be a guard–killer and a source of danger, annoyance and irritation. "[Their] record is unquestionably distorted and prejudiced," he warned.

But he was barking up the wrong tree. Reed Cozart was quite familiar with Stroud. He had been present at Leavenworth in 1942 when the prisoner was transferred to Alcatraz.

In a dissenting memo to Attorney General William P. Rogers, he wrote, "I saw the knife that was secreted under a table in his quarters. Certainly, the knife was not there for his self–defense, and I recall at that time that the employees believ[ed] that he would kill under the slightest provocation." Cozart wasn't sure if it were still true today, he wrote, but he didn't want the responsibility of finding out.

In a later memo to Attorney General Robert F. Kennedy, Cozart wrote further. "I knew Stroud personally about a year before his transfer to Alcatraz. I supervised his vast correspondence at that time, and was instrumental in finding out that he was smuggling letters out of the institution." The Pardon Attorney had followed Stroud since then, adding, "I have never talked with a warden or other prison employee who had contact with Stroud, who considered him to be a normal prisoner. He has always been considered to be dangerous, vindictive and likely to kill again."

Stroud remembered Cozart equally well. "Reed Cozart is one of the men responsible for me being sent to Alcatraz," he wrote. "I always thought very little of him."

Dissenting recommendations also came from the Bureau, Warden Madigan, Captain Bergen, Ida M. Turner—the Leavenworth guard's widow, now in her 70s—and Director Bennett.

The Bureau's memo was a matter–of–fact listing of Stroud's two killings and knifing, his bird studies which had required unusual administrative accommodations, his agitation on Alcatraz, the smuggling of manuscripts and letters at both Leavenworth and Alcatraz, his violence against himself and threats to others.

Madigan's memo was thoughtful, sympathetic and almost approving. He noted that Stroud's behavior had improved. He concluded,

I do not feel Stroud has ever felt remorse for anything he has done to others. He is highly egotistical and self–centered, but perhaps many of us would react the same way were we to be as closely confined for forty years as has Stroud. He has now advanced to the stage that he has self control. He does not lose his temper and he accepts denials of requests with grace. . . . Before clemency is considered I believe he should be transferred to Spring-field and placed in population to note his reaction. He has not had a job for forty–two years. It would all be foreign to him. . . . If he responds properly perhaps some thought

could be given to clemency if someone were to look after
him after release.

Bergen's letter to the Pardon Attorney was far more condemning, but he had transferred from Alcatraz in 1955—several
years before Stroud's change in attitude. He wrote that Stroud was
a "very dangerous influence," and, what had much weight in the
1950s and '60s, that Stroud was a "self–professed homosexual,"
who "openly advocates and promotes . . . homosexuality."
Moreoever, he concluded in a strong warning, "I believe his hate for
Mr. Bennett is so intense and so bitter that he will attempt to kill or
injure [him] if he is ever given the opportunity."

Bennett thought that Stroud was "too old to commit a serious
crime of violence," but "doubt[ed] his capacity to abide faithfully
by any conditions or restrictions placed upon his movements if
released." He claimed at this point that he would "raise no objec-
tions to the commutation of his sentence" but he felt that since there
were so many others who were more deserving that he "could not
consistently recommend Stroud's release."

The public's passion, based on Gaddis' infatuation with the
Birdman, could not meet the opposition's arguments. The Bureau
held all the cards. Stroud did not get his Executive Clemency.

By 1957–58 Furman began visiting Stroud with another purpose in mind. A film production company had engaged two men to
write a film script based on Stroud's life and he was asked to learn
details of Stroud's character and living arrangements.

Stroud became "hyped up" at the possibility of a new movie
project, the attorney said.

The Justice Department somehow got wind of it and made an
unusual move. According to a letter Furman wrote to Special
Council David W. Kendall, Attorney General William P. Rogers
called the motion picture studio in August and Bennett *visited* the
studio in September 1958 to ask that the film project be dropped.
Furman was incensed. He asked Kendall for a special Presidential
commission to investigate the Bureau's behavior. Kendall declined.

Public pressure was mounting for Stroud's transfer, however. Alcatraz was by then receiving scores of letters protesting the sixty–eight–year–old man's continued incarceration in the maximum security pen.

Yet the bureaucratic mill turned very slowly. Despite the constant good reports on his behavior, his status as an isolated prisoner continued throughout 1958.

Stroud bragged that the efforts of his lawyer would one day get him out of prison. When asked what he would do if released, he told the MTA that he would go to Los Angeles to contact his attorney concerning the royalties due him on the book. He also told officers that he expected to continue with aviculture, starting where he had left off in Leavenworth.

Benjamin Wolfman, the contract doctor that year, reported that Stroud was improving and was "cheerful, alert and cooperative." For the first time, it was recommended that Stroud might return to the general prison population after a period of medical observation at Springfield Medical Prison.

There was one minor change that year. In the summer of 1958, Stroud was allowed to go to the prison yard for one hour a week, with the result, as his '58 prison report stated incredulously, that there had been a "distinct improvement" in his physical condition and he had been "cheerful, cooperative and courteous."

His housekeeping was still considered "very poor." He didn't seem under stress. He did not appear before the Classification Committee.

> *He informed one of the Lieutenants that he had nothing to add to what he said last year but, oddly enough for him, he stated that he has no complaints to make and he expressed his satisfaction with the quality of the food, and he paid the Chief MTA a compliment in expressing his opinion that this official is the best MTA who has been at the institution since Stroud's arrival. The Committee recommended that he continue with his present program.*

Furman thought that it was quite a coincidence that just after

breakfast on February 25, 1958—less than two weeks after he wrote
to Special Council Kendall—that Warden Madigan asked Stroud,
"What would you think about a transfer?"

Stroud wrote a long letter to Furman about the conversation.
"'I'm thinking about Springfield,'" Madigan apparently said.
"'No! I want no part of that place,'" Stroud wrote that he replied.

The Medical Prison for Federal Prisoners in Springfield was
situated on a 440–acre tract of beautiful farm land near the Ozark
region of southern Missouri. Since 1933 a medical prison for
psychiatric prisoners, short–term surgical, long–term sick and
elderly prisoners, it had a mixed reputation among prisoners for
freedom and mistreatment. Yet prisoners at Springfield were housed
in wards with rooms and doors. The grounds were lush and accessible
to most. Stroud would be in a unit along with other men.

He was fearful that such a transfer, however, would relieve the
Bureau of its oafish reputation in regards to him, or that he would
be considered "bugs." He told the warden that he didn't trust the
men in the Bureau.

"I can't say about that," the warden replied, "But I think your
fears are groundless. I can tell you this. The idea did not originate
with the Bureau. It originated locally, simply because we think it
would be best for you. I wrote Mr. Bennett. He told me if you want
it and if you promise to cooperate he will be inclined to approve it."

In fact, Bennett was bowing to considerable nation–
wide pressure.

Alcatraz committee members had been urging Washington to
transfer Stroud to Springfield. Bennett had turned them down as
early as 1952. Cozart had written in '58 that Bennett still thought
Stroud "can receive better care at Alcatraz" and "is not approving
that recommendation." Even as late as January 1959, Bennett
would not approve a transfer. But with articles, editorials, letters to
Congress, petitions—and now Madigan's push—Bennett was beginning to reconsider.

Stroud agreed to think about it. He told Madigan, "you know
my friends are making great efforts to get me out. Whether I do or
not, I am inclined to play the string out as she lies." But just weeks
earlier he had written to Furman that he was uncertain he would

even accept the requirements of parole and certainly he would
"never agree to accept any job in advance of release."

Madigan told him to think it over. "Whether you get out or not,
you will at least have the best medical attention and much more
pleasant living conditions."

One of Stroud's last Alcatraz reports said of him, "He does not
act like a man who has had a terrible sentence. He has grown used
to it, perhaps." Not surprisingly it was stated that he had been more
content than previously since being given a part–time job. He had
actually said he would welcome a *full–time* assignment. When interviewed at the Classification Committee he was pleasant. The
Committee was surprised.

By now Stroud had just turned sixty–nine. He was in good
health and had been for several years. His attitude had improved,
not only because of the book and the movie which were again
moving forward, but because of his work assignment. "However,"
the January '59 report continued,

> *He cannot be expected to live many years longer and
> several of the Committee members expressed concern
> over the possible reaction of the public, especially on the
> part of the various individuals who have enough interest,
> probably mainly sentimental, in his case to write the
> institution pleading for his release, and the Committee
> agreed that the institution and the Bureau might be con-
> siderably less subject to criticism on the part of some
> individuals in the general public were he to expire in a
> Public Health Service Hospital, rather than in a maximum
> custody institution. The members of the Committee agreed
> unanimously that Stroud should be transferred from
> Alcatraz before long . . . to Springfield.*

❧   ❧

Part VIII
Marketing the Birdman

I t turned out that Bennett was concerned about the scrutiny
surrounding the Birdman not only because the sentiment might
sway a future Attorney General or a President to release him,
but also because he was standing on legal quicksand. He had
already made inaccurate and false statements about Stroud.

In February 1956, for example, Bennett wrote to Senator Paul
H. Douglas who had inquired about Stroud. In recapping the story
of Stroud's second killing at Leavenworth, Bennett wrote, "For this
he was tried three times and three times sentenced to death, but in
1920 this was commuted to life and the then Attorney General
ordered that he be kept in isolation."

Three paragraphs later, Bennett wrote, "Because of his sentence, he is not eligible for parole consideration."

Aside from the cavalier dismissal that Stroud was "three times
sentenced to death," as well as the inaccuracy that Stroud was
ineligible for parole, Bennett was making two substantial statements. He was stating first that Stroud was indeed given an unusual
sentence by Palmer and secondly, that it was still being faithfully
carried out.

If there's any doubt about Bennett's meaning, it can be dispelled
by the statement in a form letter sent to private citizens, now
contained in the U.S. Pardon Attorney files. Bennett wrote that
"The then Attorney General directed that Mr. Stroud should
thereafter be confined in isolation."

Clearly, Bennett was still following Palmer's Life in solitary
confinement ruling. Yet, events would soon transpire to force him
into a hasty retreat.

In 1959, while still on Alcatraz, Stroud petitioned the court on
a motion to dismiss his sentence. This came about because of the

1957 Supreme Court case, *Green v. United States*, in which *U.S. v. Stroud* had been mentioned in the dissenting opinion.

"Stroud asked me to come to Alcatraz," Furman explained later in *Life* magazine, "and as soon as he saw me he said, 'I'm out! The Supreme Court reversed itself in the Green case!' . . . I hadn't even heard of it, but he'd gotten all the details, somehow, on the prison grapevine, and he had immediately seen the implications."

Briefly, in the Green case, the defendant had been convicted of second degree murder in which the jury had been silent on a first degree murder charge. Green appealed his conviction and the judgment was reversed on insufficient evidence, and remanded, whereupon at a second trial Green was convicted of first degree murder and sentenced to death.

The Supreme Court eventually reversed this decision, saying that Green was "forced to run the gauntlet once on the [first degree murder] charge and the jury refused to convict him" on that charge. They reasoned, therefore, that a second trial constituted violation of the Constitutional amendment against double jeopardy and that he should not have been retried and convicted.

In researching the deciding opinion, justices cited Stroud's 1918 case as "clearly distinguishable," since Stroud was retried for first degree murder after appealing a prior guilty conviction on the *same* offense—namely, first degree murder.

In a dissenting opinion Justice Felix Frankfurter called the Stroud case, "of special relevance," saying that it was "scarcely possible to distinguish" the difference between the Green case, in which the defendant on appeal from a conviction of a lesser offense is then convicted of a greater offense, from the Stroud case, in which the defendant on appeal from a murder conviction without capital punishment is then convicted with capital punishment.

In a later interview Furman agreed that, "Frankfurter's prestige was such that it might open the door."

Stroud decided that his writ should be directed not at the Ninth Circuit—San Francisco—where he was unknown to the courts, but to the District of Kansas, where he was quite well known.

Writing his petition from his cell on Alcatraz, he argued that his solitary confinement sentence was and is illegal because it violated the Constitutional amendment against cruel and unusual punishment. He also argued that his third murder trial put him in double jeopardy as similarly happened in the Green case. The petition was signed and notarized by Alcatraz Associate Warden Olin G. Blackwell on June 24, 1959, and submitted to the court.

Even though administrators on Alcatraz had agreed unanimously back in January '59 that Stroud should be transferred to Springfield, he was still there in June. Stroud had tried to negotiate his transfer conditions—he didn't want to be moved in irons, he wanted to travel by airplane and he wanted assurance that he would get his diet. Madigan had told him to "forget about a transfer."

This petition may have stoked the flames under the Bureau's grate, however, because three weeks after the associate warden notarized it, on July 15, 1959, Stroud was transferred to the Medical Center for Federal Prisoners at Springfield, Missouri. Thus by the time the court hearing took place, Stroud was out of isolation on Alcatraz and living in a ward with other prisoners in Springfield. That move killed his argument of cruel and unusual punishment.

Furman handled the case in Topeka, Kansas; U. S. Attorney Wilbur G. Leonard stood for the government's side. The hearing was presided over by Judge Walter A. Huxman.

Stroud became excited when he heard that Huxman would be presiding; he wrote Furman that Huxman had known about him for forty years and had come to Leavenworth "more than once" to see his birds. "He likes a good show when he has a case where he thinks a man has been badly treated and he can put one on I know." In another letter to Fred Daw Stroud had promised, "when I step out of that courtroom Fred, I will surely be free."

True to Stroud's assessment, Huxman devoted much of the hearing to questioning the government lawyers on the confinement issue. His questioning put Bennett on alert.

During the case, attorney Wilbur Leonard wrote Bennett on December 9, 1959, about Huxman's questioning of Attorney General Palmer's 1920 ruling. The judge asked whether it was contended that Stroud was maintained in solitary confinement. "We advised the Court," Leonard wrote to Bennett, "that we would not consider solitary confinement a part of the sentence. . . Thereupon the Court, in substance, stated it was a good thing we took this position because had it been otherwise Stroud would walk out of the court room a free man."

Stroud, who was sitting in the courtroom, must have grinned.

"It was our distinct impression that all Judge Huxman intended," Leonard continued in his letter, "was that if the Government was of the opinion that Stroud would be held in solitary confinement because the Attorney General in 1920 said [he] should, that the Court would consider such a sentence to be cruel, unusual and inhuman . . ."

On December 16, 1959, Bennett replied,

I note that you quote in your letter an order of the Attorney General of the United States, dated April 18, 1920, which directed that Stroud's sentence of Life Imprisonment should be 'served in solitary confinement in the isolation building within the walls of the U.S. Penitentiary at Leavenworth, Kansas.'

We have searched our files and those at Springfield with reference to such a directive and are unable to find it. Will you please let us know where you found this order.

Bennett explained that Stroud's files contained a 1917 letter from Assistant Attorney General Larrin Graham which stated that he should be placed in segregation and given no opportunity to obtain another weapon, but that *that* certainly wasn't the order in question. He also stated that *"we have not over the years followed any Attorney General's Order but . . . handled . . . Stroud in accordance with our regular procedures . . ."*

"That's odd," Bergen said later when he was shown Bennett's statement. "It's quite obvious that he wasn't handled according to regular procedures."

Had Stroud been handled like other federal prisoners, there would have been no bird research after 1930, he would not have remained idle in segregation for the next twelve years without cause, he would not have remained in Alcatraz D block for six years without being tried out in the general population, he would not have been allowed to publish one book while at Alcatraz, nor write another, nor would he have been held in isolation in the hospital for eleven years. Stroud had *never* been handled in accordance with regular procedures. Said Bergen: "It was generally understood by everyone that he was going to be there for the rest of his life."

Bennett ended his letter with a fatuous comment aimed at shrouding his complicity: "I will certainly appreciate," he empathized, "learning more about the Attorney General's Order of April 18, 1920."

On January 14, 1960, Bennett again wrote Leonard. "So far as the order entered by the Attorney General dated April 18, 1920, is concerned, we have made an exhaustive search of all available records in the Stroud case and have been unsuccessful to locate it."

Indeed, no such order has ever surfaced. Court records from the Huxman case refer to records from the 1943 *Stroud v. Johnston* case, which refer to records allegedly contained in Stroud's Alcatraz records, but which are not documented in the case file. Of Stroud's prison records that have been released, no documentation suggests that such an order was ever formally issued. Neither has Palmer's telegram ever surfaced. That it was sent, and what it contained, was reported in the newspapers in 1920; how it disappeared later is fodder for a brief, but fascinating, speculation.

In his opinion filed on January 19, 1960, Judge Huxman ruled on both counts. On the double jeopardy issue he found "much force" to Frankfurter's comment, but would not overrule the Supreme Court decision in *U.S. v. Stroud* when *Green v. U.S.* had not overruled it.

As to the confinement issue, the judge agreed with Stroud's contention that *if* a ruling of solitary confinement had ever been made, it was "illegal and void" and "constituted punishment in excess." He chastised the Ninth Circuit court for its decision in *Stroud v. Johnston*, and ruled that *if* Attorney General Palmer had ordered Stroud to solitary, it was an "unwarranted assumption of power." Huxman complimented Stroud's "thorough, exhaustive and able brief" but stated that since the government said that it had no intention of imposing solitary as a part of his sentence, then the argument was no longer at issue.

Stroud reacted in typical fashion. He announced that he was going to circumvent the Appeals Court and take his case straight to the Supreme Court. They did appeal to a higher court and it was within the context of this appeal in February 1961, that U. S. Attorney Wilbur G. Leonard revealed that when Stroud was asked what he would do if he got out, he had replied that he wanted "to kill a number of others on his list, and he had so short a time" in which to do it.

Huxman's decision was upheld.

After forty–three years the "solitary confinement" charge had been legally laid to rest. Both parties had used the phrase for four decades to further their own cause—Stroud by relying on the emotional impact of the words to whip up support for his martyrdom; Bennett by denying that the prisoner was held in solitary "in the ordinary sense of that term," yet approving his isolation and justifying it with Palmer's telegram.

In the end, by his denials and maneuvers, Bennett snatched satisfaction from the jaws of justice; Stroud was out of segregation and no decree could be found. Ostensibly the prisoner had lost— this time with his strongest argument. Yet Stroud must have been pleased. The decision was actually a draw. The Bureau of Prisons had succeeded in preventing him from being released, but he had finally broken away from Palmer's long, personally motivated, underhanded, illegal reach.

Stroud had arrived at Springfield on July 15, 1959, and was placed on close security. By then he appeared frail, elderly and pale. He was still a heavy smoker and according to some sources he finished off two packs of cigarets daily. Initial medical exams, however, uncovered no major physical disorders. The next four years were probably his happiest since Leavenworth. The Medical Center was the antithesis to Alcatraz; it was warm, breezy, lush with lawn and bustling with medical personnel and prisoners.

All was not ideal, however.

The medical prison had its own particular kind of punishments. Since prisoners were sent there for surgery, psychiatric observation or recovery during long illness, there were ways to make them uncomfortable. Whether by default or design, doctors sometimes withheld pain killers on the pretext of not wanting to create drug addicts. Admittedly a difficult call, nonetheless the results were often painful for prisoners seeking relief. On the other side, there were "lots of crazies," officer Rex Plank has said. Lots of violent crazies. Doctors used tranquilizers to keep them subdued and abuses occurred. "Building 10 was really bad," said a former Springfield resident about the psych ward. "I know one man who was actually killed by a psychiatrist. They put him in a padded cell. He was dehydrated. Within days he was dead."

More than one prisoner has said that while he didn't see much brutality at Alcatraz, beatings and chokings were common at Springfield. Indeed, another officer informally said that an acceptable form of controlling an inmate at Springfield was to "choke him out. It scares 'em. They don't go off on you again." Another officer, who worked for many years at Alcatraz and retired out of Springfield, also talked about this form of control. But that was for younger prisoners, not for old hands like the Birdman.

Stroud was euphoric at his new circumstances. He wrote to Fred Daw on July 23, 1959, "You can imagine what a pleasure it was to me to lie on the grass for the first time since 1914."

The euphoria was anticipated. Morton Sobell once said that a transfer from Alcatraz to any *other* maximum security prison required more adjustment than moving from a medium security institution to freedom. Stroud's isolation on "the Rock" made his transfer to Springfield radical in the extreme. He saw his first television set, ate meals with other men, had more access to the news, telephones, radio—he could even leave his room. Within a month he was given a job in the library. Stroud wrote Furman three days after he arrived,

> *Imagine how it feels to me to be able to sleep without a*
> *door being locked on me, to talk to whom I please,*
> *privately if I wish and if I want to be alone, to be able to*
> *close my door and know that I will not be disturbed. . .*
> *There are so many surprises here that I will never be able*

to outline them all to you . . .

He felt a renewed sense of importance,

For this is a hospital, and there are many cases here, I've found some already, very pitiful cases, where an hour's talk at a bedside of a lonely and suffering human being can give a new hope and where hope is impossible, much courage. And I've already had the pleasure of seeing smiles replace a look of despair, courage replace hopelessness . . .

However heroic he thought of himself, others were to tell a different story. The first year his prison report agreed that he "is somewhat of a hero to other inmates" yet "treats them in a patronizing manner." To officers, as he always had, he maintained a "superior, egotistical attitude." By the time Morton Sobell arrived in 1962– 63, he found that "most of the inmates didn't like him; he boasted openly that he was a pederast, and they felt that this wasn't good for the public image of the convict." One former Springfield prisoner, Joseph Duhamel, who was fascinated said, "He talked so continuously, I could hardly get a word in edgewise." There was also the sloppy habit of eating with his fingers, which Sobell felt alienated others.

Within days the new prisoner was given a battery of tests, including the Wechsler Adult Intelligence Scale, the Rorschach Method of Personality Diagnosis, the House–Tree–Person Figure Drawings and the Minnesota Multiphasic Personality Inventory.

"First, I completed my psychological test yesterday," he wrote to Furman on July 28, 1959. "The tests were rather extensive, and in my case required three days to complete and on the mental score, I made a total IQ score of one–hundred–thirty–nine plus a fraction."

Indeed, he scored "very superior intellectual functioning" on the Wechsler, with a verbal scale of one–hundred–and–thirty–nine and a full scale of one–hundred–and–thirty. The wide difference was felt to be due to age and impairment of visual–motor skills.

"I also took about a four–hour personality test here for the first time. I do not know the score on that yet but will bet that it was equally high, because my mind was hitting on all cylinders." He was right. He scored "equally high" in "severe personality malintegration."

In the Rorschach he showed a "compulsive need to do the big thing in an intellectual sense," had a "much too ready tendency to superimpose generalizations on the facts whether they fit or not," his ability to recognize and solve everyday problems was impaired, his value system was built entirely around a drive for intellectual achievement and nondependence upon others, he was not socially adaptable and had a "clearly indicated" deficiency in capacity for empathy.

"I am virtually sure that I have made a favorable impression on every man I have met here," he wrote to Furman. In another letter he revealed, "One of the doctors told a guard that I was one of the most interesting men he had ever talked to and that in one short talk I have given him many new ideas, and that he just wished he had time to listen to me for days."

The House–Tree–Person and the Minnesota Multiphasic corroborated the diagnosis: strong need to control, hostile and withdrawn, sex role confusion, acute sensitivity to criticism, general personality disorganization (so much so, noted the test–giver, that it interfered with the test), heightened self–preoccupation, poor judgment and perspective and a high degree of egocentricity.

In all likelihood Stroud remained ignorant of the diagnosis. He wrote to Furman that he had "more peace of mind than I have enjoyed in many years." He praised the administration throughout the letter. He knew that management read every word, and no doubt his repetitious compliments were meant to be seen: " . . . everyday I am amazed by the consideration and politeness with which I am treated." In the same letter he wrote, "I have seen so much bad management in my life, that it is a pleasure to see good management." A few paragraphs later he wrote, "I am frequently amazed by the general high quality of the administration and the unfailing politeness of almost everyone, official and inmate alike."

The MMPI further corroborated the diagnosis of a "profoundly and significantly disturbed" personality, a "psychopathic deviate" who was impulsive and paranoid. In short—the perfect profile of a sociopath.

In a small way, Stroud's ability to abruptly change course mid–letter was evidence of his personality disorder. His extreme juxtapositions were almost comical. In one letter to Fred Daw written days after he transferred to Springfield he was commiserating presumably about Daw's wife, who had had a stroke;

> *I certainly hope that it is not too bad a one, but should it be serious enough to incapacitate for the rest of her life, for both her sake and yours I hope that it is rapidly fatal. That may seem ruthless on my part, Fred, but for years I have faced the fact that I am going to die that way, and it is my most ardent wish that when that time comes, it will either be heavy enough to kill me at once or that it will leave me the use of one hand long enough to get a knife in it. I will do the rest.*
>
> *Things with me are going wonderful. I have been changed to new and larger quarters, [and] I have the run of an enormous ward. . . . I have my own desk, lamp, and radio connection. I can see T.V. every evening and night, but never look at it. I prefer visiting with my friends. I have met more men and talked more in the last three weeks than the previous fifty years. So, I've been on a visiting spree.*

Overt acts of violence by Stroud were not in evidence at Springfield. Yearly evaluations still remarked on his egotistical nature, his grousing and defiance, but there were no violent episodes. In fact he appeared "calm," "more settled" and "seemed to adjust well to others." That first year his work reports were above average, except for "quality of dependability," for which he was given an "average." Reports noted his lack of interest in language study; in

September he began a Spanish class but dropped it in November. He was not considered a custodial or behavioral problem.

Although he did circumvent the rules increasingly over the next four years, his defiance was petty, almost childlike. The most significant act was being caught naked in February 1960 with another inmate. When discovered, Stroud immediately admitted that he was about to have sex and it was his idea. He was segregated for three days, then released to the ward.

As he became more used to his surroundings, however, he was written up more. In 1961 he had one adverse behavior report, but in '62 he had four. Although minor (possession of lewd writings, food and poker chips in his room), nonetheless his pattern of breaking rules steadily worsened. That year he also made an "unauthorized telephone call" outside the prison. Although years later telephone use by prisoners would be common and allowable in many institutions, it was unheard of during Stroud's time.

"It used to make him livid as hell," when his room was checked for contraband, said Bob Cron, an officer who worked at Springfield at the time. Officers would find "mostly fruit," Cron said, and although Stroud would "act insulted, a little surly, saying things under his breath, he knew it wouldn't do him any good to go off."

Typically, others felt differently. "I found him delightful," said Sobell years later. "He was impish, effervescent. He enlivened my experience."

Sobell had been transferred to Springfield for stomach ailments. A stocky man, with a wild shock of white hair and a liberal, East Coast intellectual demeanor, Sobell sought out Stroud to tell him about the *Scientific American* caper. Both prisoners were knowledgeable and well read, and they developed an immediate rapport. While Sobell didn't share Stroud's bitterness, he did share his cynicism. He recounted a conversation with Bennett years before, in which he expressed concern over a rumor that had him on a transfer to Alcatraz. Bennett looked him in the eye and said, "We don't send a man like *you* to Alcatraz." As director of the Bureau and the self–described "talent scout" for Alcatraz, Bennett had to have known that one of the nation's biggest celebrity–prisoners was going to Alcatraz. Dollison, who said that Bennett "approved every move to and from Alcatraz," agreed.

The two prisoners began a friendship which lasted until Stroud's death. They met most mornings and talked about their cases, current events, science and history. Sobell didn't find him to be antagonistic or quick to anger. "No, no, our discussions were not debates," he explained. "We sought to clarify." There was no question of his brilliant mind, yet Sobell sensed Stroud's truncated feel for time; he talked about historical events, "as if they were the present." He remembered Stroud's droll humor and cited the time he once said he hoped the *Birdman of Alcatraz*, "would be a cell out."

The book *was* a sell—out, but not the way Stroud hoped. By 1958, interest in the Birdman was so awakened that Gaddis and Furman organized a "Committee for Release of Robert F. Stroud."

Gaddis began sending out periodic bulletins to private individuals and news releases to the media. The bulletin was a folksy newsletter designed to keep the public informed and interested enough to send money to further the cause.

In his 1958 pocketbook edition of the *Birdman of Alcatraz*, Gaddis took up a comparison between Stroud and Nathan Leopold, one—half of the Leopold—Loeb team whose thrill—killing of a fourteen—year—old boy had riveted the nation in the 1920s. A famous book, *Compulsion*, had been written about the case. The comparison, written originally by Stroud, (his hand—written document later showed up in his pardon file), attempted to show how Stroud had been retained in prison while Leopold was eventually released. "Stroud had already lived behind bars for fifteen years before Leopold spent his first hour in jail," the document stated. Gaddis said that Leopold was paroled after thirty—three years, yet Stroud remained in prison. This became a new tack in the move for the prisoner's freedom. "Leopold became a valuable teacher and master of languages," Gaddis wrote, "Stroud became a scientist and an international authority on bird diseases. Leopold's privileges were increased. Stroud was separated from his birds and placed in Alcatraz, where he has been kept alone for fifteen more years." In Gaddis' new edition, he urged people to write to their

Congressional representatives. They did. Many letters in Stroud's
last two petitions for executive clemency included the comparison
between Leopold and Stroud.

Gaddis didn't pretend to be unbiased and he used his influence
where he could. One of the committee's honorary members was
Mrs. Art Cohn, whose husband was a columnist for the *San Francisco Examiner*. About 1958, Cohn wrote an editorial in support of
Stroud's clemency. In a confusing opening paragraph, he said:
"Robert Stroud has murdered two innocent men. He is an uncompromising nuisance. And if there is any justice, President Eisenhower
will sign commutation papers three weeks hence freeing him from
Alcatraz." He continued, "Why has this man been kept in isolation
from his fellow man for more than four decades? . . . He has not
committed an act of violence in thirty–eight years."

By now the pattern begun years ago by Elizabeth, Robert,
Della and others was engraved in the public mind; Stroud had been
in solitary, his killings were justified or minimized, his rehabilitation was absolute and the federal prison bureau was brutal. And
because the Bureau maintained a policy of silence about its prisoners—a policy that in Stroud's case was fast becoming a liability—
no corrections or refutations appeared. The old bandwagon had
been spruced up for a parade.

But there were holes in Gaddis' assumptions. He took everything Stroud said at face value, never considering that the prisoner
might be exaggerating. He got half the story and thought that the
other half validated it. More importantly, he erroneously assumed
that Stroud's medical research was valid and distinguished. Although pathologists as yet knew little about avain diseases, scientists could have informed Gaddis, even then, that Stroud's research
methods were shaky and poorly conceived. (In fact, it appears that
no reporter ever investigated Stroud's research methods by inter-
viewing medical researchers.)

But paramount in Gaddis' errors was a basic illogical foundation. He flaunted Stroud's intellectual achievements as proof that
he was rehabilitated. People conduct research and write books from
their intellectual abilities; they kill from their emotional disabili-
ties. Intellectual achievement does not necessarily compensate

for—nor repair—emotional defects. Gaddis was blinded by the heroic story, by Stroud's will and stamina and his vast ability to blame others for his situation.

Others fell in line behind him. *Life* magazine published a leading article on the Birdman in April 1960, entitled "Prodigious Intellect in Solitary." It stated that Stroud "has not raised a hand to another man since 1916," yet allowed that he was "one of the most cantankerous old men alive in the world today." The article referred to a "feud" between Bennett and the prisoner as a "remorseless contest of wills," yet called Bennett "a decent and honorable man," whose handling of the Stroud case, nonetheless, raised questions. Although it was balanced, it continued to herald Stroud's veterinary achievements, calling his *Digest*, "the most authoritative and comprehensive work on the subject ever published."

In July '61, radio announcer and columnist Paul Coates, in a column entitled "Time May Be Running Out for the Birdman of Alcatraz," minimized Stroud's first murder as an "Alaskan dance hall brawl." Stating that Stroud had "spent nearly all of the next half century in solitary confinement," he urged Stroud to be freed, or warned that "his case could develop into an embarrassing 'international crisis'."

In August 1961, a *Los Angeles Mirror* editorial urged that "further imprisonment for the seventy–one–year–old convict is vicious and vengeful, a return to the medieval brutality of exacting the last full measure of suffering from gaol inmates." (Stroud was hardly suffering "medieval brutality" at Springfield). Saying that "Richard [sic] Bennett, director of federal prisons, has spearheaded the vindictive campaign to keep the old convict behind bars," the editorial urged Kennedy to overrule Bennett and grant clemency "to a man who has long since paid his debt for youthful transgressions."

Each president, including Wilson, Hoover, Roosevelt, Truman, Eisenhower and Kennedy, got letters about Stroud from an increasingly concerned public.

"Dear President Kennedy," wrote a woman in 1961, "You

could make yourself even more popular with the American public if you'd exert what influence you can in the project of freeing Robert Stroud from prison."

"Dear President Kennedy," another wrote, "It would be an act of the greatest kindness and humanity if, in the midst of world problems, you could give a few moments of your attention to the case of Robert Stroud." "Abolition of Alcatraz is not enough," a man, who obviously thought Stroud was still on Alcatraz, wrote to Kennedy, "I urge you to obtain the release of Robert Stroud. Continued imprisonment of this man is not only morally reprehensible, but also deprives our nation of incalculable scientific achievement."

By May 1, 1961, a man named Herbert Axelrod wrote to Stroud asking about a possible revision of his *Digest*. Axelrod, who had probably heard about the impending Hollywood movie starring Burt Lancaster, owned T.F.H. Publications which published pet books largely for a non–professional audience. Although he wanted Stroud to revise his book, he offered in the meantime to "grind out" 1,000-2,000 copies to "cash in" on the publicity. That was an approach destined to appeal to Robert Stroud.

By return mail Stroud suggested additional laboratory work would not be necessary, but that Axelrod needed to secure permission for him to have special books placed in his room. He also hinted to Axelrod that he would need to get out of prison, because "I have grave doubts" that Springfield is a suitable place to write. He then indicated that his only problem was that someone else owned the copyright to the book.

The same day he wrote to Frank Dittrich, of *All Pets* magazine, who in 1950 had paid Marcus $625 for the copyright.

Stroud told Dittrich that "the Hollywood people seem to be going all out," and therefore "a lot of people [are] trying to climb on the gravy train." He asked what Dittrich's plans were concerning the book.

"My present plans," Stroud told Dittrich, "which are naturally only tentative, do not contemplate my remaining in the United

States more than three or four months following release, but there is nothing I can foresee at this time which would prevent me from devoting some time to this book and with a little research on modern drugs I am certain that I can turn out a very creditable piece of work."

Stroud was dreaming. Advances in antibiotics and the study of diseases had moved way beyond his already weak capabilities.

On May 24, he wrote Axelrod that he was forced to work with Dittrich, "a fine man who has been a loyal friend for many years." The same day he wrote Dittrich, saying that he could do a revision in ninety days. "And, should my parole be granted, I would myself insist that the effective date be set back until the work is completed."

Obviously, Stroud was high on thinking that he would soon get out. So confident, that on May 28, he repeated to Furman, that although he hadn't heard from the parole board, "I would defer my release, if offered, until the work is finished." Stroud was again dreaming, but the statement illustrated his extreme egocentricity— thinking that the U.S. government would continue to pay for him to remain in prison even after parole.

Bennett was notified of the negotiations, and on June 14 he sent a memo permitting Stroud to negotiate only with Dittrich. Bennett further stated that Furman could not negotiate this book— that his participation was limited to questions of custody—that Gaddis was not on the approved visiting list and "under no circumstances is any of this group to be permitted to correspond with, or visit or negotiate any contract with Stroud without previous approval." Bennett had had it with Stroud, his books and supporters, and he was still able to call the shots.

By September, however, it was clear that Dittrich was not interested in a revision as Stroud outlined it. It sounded hasty and haphazard, and Dittrich was probably concerned about publishing a less than sterling resource on bird care. "I want to know the score," Stroud demanded in a letter when he obviously hadn't heard from Dittrich, "if I do not hear from you promptly, I shall write the whole thing off." Dittrich replied that he would need to have a professional approve the final text and that if someone else wanted to publish it, he wouldn't turn a deaf ear on it.

That day Dittrich went from being a "fine . . . loyal friend" to being a "stuffed shirt who lacks imagination," and a man of "boorish temperament." Stroud offered Axelrod the deal. The same day he wrote to Furman announcing that he'd heard that Axelrod was a weekend guest of President Kennedy along with Frank Sinatra and Peter Lawford, "another reason why I prefer to do business with him."

With this new wrinkle, however, Springfield administrators began turning back Stroud's letters. Figuring that this was a delaying tactic, a litigious feeling overcame Stroud and he began casually referring to himself in letters as "the movant." It was this issue that eventually drove him to his final court battle with the Bureau.

The buzz around Hollywood at that time was that the new Burt Lancaster film, *Birdman of Alcatraz,* was going to be a classic. Even though the movie was still in the editing stage, people were very excited.

Gaddis had already taken one trip across the country with his wife and two children in the summer of 1961, giving news conferences along the way in "support for Stroud and the motion picture which is going to free him." Phyllis Gaddis, then fifteen, remembered the family camping out in their old beat up station wagon, then occasionally waltzing into plush hotels where the studio paid the bills.

Lancaster, Gaddis and Furman joined forces in the Spring of 1962. They held news conferences in San Francisco, Chicago, New York and Washington, D.C., with the triple purpose of selling the book, the movie and the man. The specter of the Birdman caged in solitary confinement hung over the news conferences like a pall at a funeral. In a Hearst headline service Lancaster was quoted as saying Stroud should be paroled and that he had been in solitary confinement forty–two years. It's unclear if Lancaster believed what he said, or was humping for the film. It *was* clear that it was not hurting the film's popularity.

A special viewing was held in Washington, D.C., for interested congressmen.

In an April 27, 1962, *Washington Daily News* article, "Should the Birdman be Uncaged?" in which Lancaster, Furman and Gaddis are all cited, Furman admitted that the prisoner is an "overt homosexual but doubted he would prey on society." This appeared to be the first revelation of its kind by the Release Committee members.

Stroud's homosexuality had been mostly eliminated from the Birdman portrait. Gaddis may have been ignorant of it early on, but by April '62, when news of it had become so widespread that reporters were asking about it, Gaddis was publicly blaming the prison system for its origin. He had already seen a handwritten document by Stroud telling of his early homosexual activities and he knew that Stroud had recently been caught naked with a young prisoner. In his September 1962 Committee bulletin he chose to publicly admonish the federal prison system for leaking the news "in the effort to discredit the character of Stroud and the work of the Committee."

The point is not Stroud's homosexuality per se. Stroud never tried to hide it. And once Stroud was dead, Gaddis was far more forthright about his homosexualty—and his preference for boys. The point was that it was necessary while Stroud was alive for Gaddis to keep the Birdman's story simple and pure so that it could be swallowed whole by the public.

Something else came up in the news conference which sent a mixed message. One of Stroud's first letters written from Springfield was read, in which he stated,

> *If I had no hope of doing greater things than any I've done in the past, I now know that I could in a very short time build for myself right here just as happy and satisfactory a life as anywhere on earth, and it would not be a useless life either.*

Was Stroud again hinting that he didn't want to get out of prison? That he was happy where he was? That at age seventy–two, after more than fifty years in prison, life on the outside would be too difficult an adjustment?

The media attention that began in the 1930s reached a peak in the summer of 1962 when millions poured in to see the movie. Gaddis' misguided ideals, which lifted Stroud's life story onto an heroic pedestal, along with the participation of Furman and Burt Lancaster—an enormously popular actor who personified honesty and integrity—now combined to mislead an emotionally manipulated public. Together they confused the issues and combined profit with clemency.

Tables were set up by Committee members outside theatres where the movie was playing. When people poured out, impressed with the performance and charged with feelings of injustice, they signed petitions by the thousands. Over six linear feet of paperwork is contained in Robert Stroud's pardon attorney files now in the National Archives, at least five feet containing *tens of thousands* of signatures, many of them grabbed in just this manner.

Furman, in an interview thirty years later, was not apologetic and in fact took a slightly amused stance at his methods for getting Stroud's case heard. He was not motivated by the wish to free Stroud, he said. He simply wanted to get Stroud's case heard. "I didn't think he would get *out*," Furman explained, almost exasperated at the question. "I thought the odds were very strongly against it. The bureaucracy would have risen in its wrath. I just wanted him to get his chance to speak his piece."

The height of confusion about the Birdman can be summed up in a film review published in an unknown newspaper and attached to a letter in the pardon attorney files. The article is a mixture of movie review, political outrage and advocacy journalism. In the midst of comments about actors, the director and screenwriter, the reviewer wrote, "I hope it will help but it does not place enough blame, it seems to me, upon the old–fashioned and vengeful attitude by federal prison authorities who have kept this man behind bars when horrible child murderers, prisoners, rapists, and vicious criminals, even traitors to the country, many of them not rehabilitated like Stroud, have been paroled. . . . If you think Stroud deserves the few years he has left on the outside (he is in his middle seventies), why not drop a post card to Attorney General Robert Kennedy or to United Artists saying so."

Gaddis himself was now reaching an almost–religious fervor

about Stroud which showed in his writing. "Four decades in solitary, hungering year after year through his twenties . . . thirties . . . forties . . . fifties . . . into the slow freeze of his sixties," he wrote in one Committee bulletin. "A man of iron endurance whose deepest wish is to be released," said another. The Committee solicited funds for a Robert Stroud Research Foundation, "and these pledges and more to come are kept in a file marked 'Hope' for the old prisoner."

"If we all act," a June 10, 1962, bulletin promised, "Stroud will go free this year." It's not clear what prompted Gaddis to write this. Three months before, on April 26, 1962, Attorney General Robert Kennedy had announced that he was not recommending commutation. Another executive clemency bid loomed but it was doubtful Kennedy would change his mind. And the Parole Board was not going to overrule him. The case was dead.

Nonetheless, people's reaction to Kennedy's announcement was swift and passionate. A woman wrote: "I have been following the Robert Stroud case for over ten years. . . . Newspaper stories concerning your investigation of the case say that Stroud still possesses 'anti–social attitudes' and a 'hostility to those around him.' Ought we not to marvel, instead, that this man did not lose his sanity *completely* in forty–two years of solitary confinement? What ought one learn from forty years of solitary? Good social attitudes?"

Another man wrote a three–page, legal–sized, single–spaced typewritten letter to the Attorney General in which he in part said,

Do you assert, sir, that you know better than does Mr. Stroud where his best welfare lies after fifty years of Federal Penitentiary home cooking? Or are you simply telling us that this is the way it is going to be because you have spoken? Are you telling us that the case is finally closed and that we had better not inquire further into it? May we all relax now and worship at the church of our choice next Sunday and think fine thoughts about the marvelous precision of U.S. Justice as personally administered by you and your employee, Mr. James V. Bennett.

. . . The Birdman would not crawl. He would not lick spittle and smile. Remember, kind sir, here is a man who

has suffered severely for his crime. He did it. He suffered.
He was the man. He was there. And he is here now. He is
the man who found himself in the fire of redemptive love
for the beating hearts and wings of sparrows. Hawks
don't truckle. They never cringe. Hawks are not romantic.
They are very fierce, extremely practical, and they pos-
sess their being in fire, in the valance and violence of
facts, not rosy sentiments.

To say that Gaddis was responsible for all this misguided passion is overstating the case. Nonetheless, by quoting from Stroud's letters, by printing news of the latest petitions, the latest paperback, braille and foreign editions of his book, by reporting the latest Bureau gaffs and eventually the latest stories about the heady news conferences with the star, Gaddis had driven into the land of conflict of interest.

Furman defended Gaddis as being "just as bitter as Stroud" in his feelings against prisons in general. To Gaddis, Stroud was the capstone of the Bureau's indifference. Gaddis' eldest daughter, Phyllis Gaddis, tacitly agreed. She described an idealistic man who became increasingly more adamant in his belief in Stroud as the Bureau threw up more obstacles. She described an almost bunker–like mentality as Gaddis began publishing the articles, that "everyone knew there was a lot of danger," in doing the story because of Bennett's perceived power. "People kept walking backwards," she said, and it only made her father more determined to get the story out.

Even though Gaddis wrote in the September 20, 1962, bulletin that he attempted "in all areas to preserve the integrity of the story," that could no longer be determined. The myth of Robert Stroud was now inextricably linked with the profits from the Birdman book and the movie.

This did not go unnoticed in governmental circles. "The latest diatribe of brother Gaddis," U.S. Pardon Attorney Cozart wrote in a memo attached to a bulletin by Gaddis then making its rounds in the Justice Department. "I still believe he is making a good living from Stroud's plight." Perhaps it wasn't fair or accurate. But whether Gaddis was beating the drum for Stroud, or for himself, could no longer be distinguished.

As the Hollywood Birdman did time on movie screens throughout the country in the summer and fall of 1962, hundreds of letters poured into the U.S. President's office.

"Dear President Kennedy," wrote a woman in September, "I have just finished reading *Birdman of Alcatraz* and am sickened and terrified to find that such a thing could happen to a human being in these United States."

A man named Montgomery wrote to the president, "if what I've heard is true, there never has been a man more rehabilitated."

A five-page, single-spaced typewritten letter written to President Kennedy in October, 1962, attempted to outline the high numbers of people who should be in prison instead of Stroud, including unethical physicians who "killed or crippled by unnecessary operations and toxic drugs," drug companies who pushed vaccinations, Jonas Salk whose vaccine was known to cause polio and paralysis, companies who pushed alcohol, chemicals, cigarets, those involved in organized crime and elected politicians who got Americans into wars. The writer concluded, "Why bother to punish the smaller crimes if you are going to allow the larger ones free rein? . . . Stroud is potentially a better and safer citizen than a great many out of prison."

"Dear President Kennedy," another man wrote in November, 1962, "I have just finished reading *Birdman of Alcatraz*. Why has this man had to stay in prison for such a long time? . . . If this man were set free I am certain he would commit no crimes."

At this time, Richard M. English became a part of Furman's team, working on the case the last eighteen months of Stroud's life. English saw Stroud at Springfield several times and found an old, very independent, "law and order" man, with a keen sense of humor. It was obvious to him that Stroud was a conservative Republican. "Completely opposite from my political beliefs," English said, chuckling. "I'm a liberal Democrat. And Mr. Stroud was completely conservative. Bob Stroud believed in the death penalty. I do not. He was a backer of Eisenhower, which I particularly was not."

The attorney found Stroud to be extremely knowledgeable about the world. "And he was quite a firm person," he said. "He came across as having his mind made up—you weren't going to budge him from that."

During one of these visits to Springfield, English borrowed a camera, and positioning himself behind a column where guards couldn't easily see him, he snapped five or six photographs. Stroud was wearing his eye shade and looked at English admiringly, almost impishly. "He thought that was fantastic," English said. "He wanted to stand up and applaud."

The photograph was reprinted around the nation, and Bennett was so angered that he wrote to the California Bar Association asking that they investigate the attorney. They declined.

English did his best to get Stroud out of prison. He traveled to Washington and spoke to Bennett about Stroud's rehabilitation and once spoke to ex–president Harry S. Truman by phone.

He tells the anecdote with perfect timing.

> *Truman said, when I talked to him, 'Well, what was he accused of young man?' And I said, 'Well, he was accused of murder.' He says, 'Well, he should have been hung.' And I say, 'Well, Mr. President, he wasn't hung.' About twelve seconds later I said, 'Well, he wasn't.' And he says, 'Well, I think he shoulda' been.'*
> *That ended that conversation.*

As if the movie had not been enough to severely corrode the already tarnished image of Alcatraz, on June 11, 1962, a spectacular escape attempt occurred.

Frank Morris and John and Clarence Anglin had broken through their cell walls at the air ducts, climbed the pipes in the utility corridor, broken through the roof, climbed down the building and the hill to wade in the waters of San Francisco Bay. They were never seen again.

The escape attempt involved one of the largest manhunts since the Lindbergh kidnapping and much speculation as to the security worthiness of the old and decrepit prison facility.

Estimates in 1961 to rehabilitate the island prison came in at about $4 million. Since there was diminishing support in Congress for Alcatraz—given the film about Stroud and now an escape attempt in which prisoners could not be accounted for—the decision was made to close it.

In what Gaddis accurately portrayed as a "backstairs campaign," the Bureau now let loose its prized Stroud prison reports. Perhaps there was nothing left to do; in the history of the federal Bureau of Prisons, no single prisoner had caused such a stir. The Birdman of Alcatraz was now the most famous prisoner in America, indeed, in the world. Eve Edstrom, a *Washington Post* writer, was given access to selected Stroud files in preparation for a series of articles that began in July 1962.

For the first time Stroud was depicted accurately as a bright, willful, but manipulative man who had killed twice and threatened others. The articles indicated that Stroud's bird work was unique and that the Bureau had gone out of its way to accommodate him. The articles indicated that far from being a maligned prisoner, Stroud had actually gained more privileges than others. Judging from the Stroud quotes, Edstrom saw many of his letters, parts, or perhaps all, of his voluminous prison manuscripts, yearly prison reports, court proceedings and old newspaper clippings. The articles were straightforward, using many of Stroud's own comments. This portrait was far more complicated than the book or movie and not as flattering.

The articles were reprinted in the *Congressional Record* on July 25, 1962, and the Bureau sent copies to people who had written protest letters.

Not everyone was convinced that Edstrom was unbiased. "Anyone with human perception could see the articles were slanted," wrote one man to the Department of Justice. Admitting that the articles' slant was the opposite of the movie, he concluded, "The journalist's miscomprehension of this matter may be spiritually, if not legally, a greater evil than Stroud's crimes. . ."

Also weighing in against the Birdman was a decidedly negative look by Charles Remsberg for *True* magazine in July 1963, entitled, "The Phony Fairy Tale of 'The Birdman of Alcatraz.' "

Remsberg fought to get access to the Stroud file, based on the access already granted another reporter. Although he included much of the same material as did Edstrom, he condemned Stroud by his very tone. He referred to Stroud's work on bird diseases as a "convenient camouflage for a moonshine still . . . and a smuggling racket." Stroud himself was a "self–admitted sex deviate who must be closely watched to make sure he does not contaminate younger inmates," who openly engages in "degenerate sex acts despite his age and infirmities."

The article seems bound to bring out the worst in *True* men's fears.

Gaddis referred to these less romantic pictures as "cheap, sensational attacks." Bennett, rightly or wrongly, was gaining the upper hand.

Furman and English, and now a young Springfield, Missouri attorney named Charles Dudley Martin, were working on the Stroud case. But the old man was winding down. Since the fall of 1961 he had had several minor heart incidents. He wrote Furman about one incident in which he had an "all gone feeling in the pit of my stomach and almost fell down."

Stroud had always been difficult because of his hypochondria and his presumed knowledge. This had not changed. He "has a number of complaints which fit no pattern of any known organic disease," wrote a Springfield doctor, and has "rather rigid pseudoscientific ideas." Said another report, "Stroud has acquired throughout the years many bizarre beliefs surrounding his health not supported by any scientific facts. These include the intake of large quantities of tea daily in order to avoid 'uremia;' [a] daily consumption of raw vegetables, raw meat on occasions; and an assortment of self–prescribed medications for various symptoms, and shaving regularly his entire body."

Little evidence of actual health problems existed. He did not have nephritis or kidney disease which he claimed. There was no evidence that he was going blind, which cropped up as a fact in articles written in 1930–31, and again in a *Saga* magazine article in 1963: ". . . he is not receiving the medical treatment which he thinks he needs," former prisoner Duhamel wrote. "He has a serious gall bladder condition. He is going blind and both his hands are wracked with arthritis."

Another Springfield document reported,

The patient gave a history of TB as a child although there is no evidence by X–ray that the patient ever had TB. There was a questionable history of heart disease in the past; numerous EKGs had always been negative. According to the patient he had a stroke in 1941 and was paralyzed in the right facial area and right arm. There was again no objective evidence that this happened. The patient also claimed an old history of pellagra in 1950; this diagnosis was not confirmed by his attending physician. In 1942 a poorly functioning gall–bladder was noted by X–ray but there was no other objective evidence of gall–bladder disease.

Because of his age, however, doctors were now taking him more seriously. "I really think that the trouble is that my new assistant insists on doing all the hard work," Stroud wrote to Furman about his first heart incident. He worked in the inmate library as a bookbinder, where he was considered skillful but careless and indifferent, so he was assigned with another inmate. He explained that he mostly sat, lettering books.

When I sit down the circulation is always poor, and that causes my blood pressure to go up . . I told him today that I had to spend more time on my feet. I've walked at least

*ten to fifteen miles today and am not really tired, so I'm
sure I will be o.k. but I was very much pleased by the
promptness with which they took care of me.*

That Stroud had walked so far on a day in which he was having
what doctors called ventricular contractions was exaggeration.

In December 1961, he had episodes of angina pain. By October
'62, when he wrote his last petition for executive clemency, giving
"ill health" as one reason for wanting release, the old man was
experiencing a general deterioration in his physical condition.

In his last months Stroud took up leather craft and made several billfolds and cases—one reportedly for a blind girl who had
written him, another for Furman.

Yet his hatred still smoldered. He stated that it was his mother
who had caused most of his problems. "He described his mother as
the aggressor," Dr. Moreau, M.D. wrote in a Springfield report,
"and said that she had ruined his life and his father's life, driving
his father to drink. He spoke of her with marked hostility."

Stroud also blamed prison authorities for making him a pederast.

"His judgment is poor and insight into his own interpersonal
relationships is impaired," the doctor concluded. "His attitude is
hostile and ego–defensive."

Yet, as always, Stroud could be magnanimous. In what was one
of his most generous last acts, he had written a letter to a thirteen–
year–old boy which summed up his philosophy of life. The boy,
Dennis Norton, had read Gaddis' book and, wanting to help, had
circulated a petition in his neighborhood. As thanks, Stroud made
him a billfold and they corresponded through his lawyer. Attorney
English had a pamphlet designed which included the letter. If
Stroud had a creed, this was it:

*There is just one thing about your note that I do not like.
You say that you know that you will never reach the
heights in your studies that I have reached in mine. Now,
I do not like to see a young person sell himself short.
Modesty may be all right on occasion, but in my opinion
it is often a virtue of dubious value. Always tell yourself*

that you are as good as anyone that breathes; that you have two hands and a brain, and a little time in which to use them. But they are enough, and no one has any more. And if you train and force them to serve you well, you can reach any height to which you aspire. But to waste any of them is to betray yourself.

Few persons, not insane, would ever think of cutting their hands off or cutting their throats, but you will see thousands of them whose only ambition is killing time. Do not ever permit yourself to fall into that group, for really, Dennis, the wasting of time when one has so little of it before him is just as much a form of suicide as cutting your own throat.

. . . And, Dennis, if there is any greatness or virtue in my life, it is not my work with birds. It is the fact that I have never joined that group. I have demonstrated time and again that no man ever is or ever can be defeated until he, himself, quits fighting. I have spent my entire adult life in prison and forty–seven years of that time locked in a cell alone. Most persons look upon my life as very sad, but no one has ever seen me give up to sadness. I have spent a lot of time locked up, but I have never wasted that time.

I have never served time, as that term is usually understood, because I have made that time serve me, and I have never been able to find enough of it to do all the things that I wanted to do.

In December 1962, another escape attempt occurred on Alcatraz. John Paul Scott and Darl Lee Parker had escaped from a cell house basement window and slipped into the water. Parker was quickly found clinging to a nearby rock. Apparently, he could not swim. Scott, however, drifted all the way to the Golden Gate Bridge, a long and treacherous float. Although he made it to shore alive, he was semi–conscious and unable to get out of the water to walk away. Within twenty–four hours he was returned to Alcatraz.

Four months later, in March 1963, Alcatraz was closed.

Robert Stroud's prison life had strangely paralleled the old cell house on Alcatraz. He had been imprisoned in 1909 when the cell house was being built by military prisoners. And he would die the year it closed.

In fact, Stroud outlived Alcatraz by only a few months. After his final court case before Becker wound down, there was little left to fight. And he seemed increasingly unable to battle even minor infections. On November 18, 1963, he suffered chest pains radiating into the arm. Sobell understood it to be a heart attack.

Two days later he returned early from work feeling poor and a physician was called. "I don't want to see those fucking doctors," Sobell remembered him saying.

Perhaps anticipating that the end was near, Stroud handed an unfinished thirty–two page letter to a prisoner to send to Judge Becker; the letter, later included in Becker's file, was a rambling, anecdotal account of how prisons systematically hindered prisoners from mounting their court cases.

The next morning, on November 21, 1963, Stroud did not meet Sobell at the usual time for breakfast. Sobell walked into his room to check on him.

"I was the one who found him," he said. "His eyes were open; I picked up his hand."

In what may have been the kindest act accorded him in his seventy–three cantankerous years, one without strings—as if a god gently reached down to touch him, saying, *You're done now—* Robert Franklin Stroud had died peacefully in his sleep, the way he wanted.

Sobell walked quickly to the attendant. "When I told him, the guard said, 'No, can't be, can't be. I just checked him.' And I said, 'Check him again.'"

Telegrams were sent to Bennett, Judge Becker, to Stroud attorneys, his remaining family members and a news release was prepared. There was talk around the institution about Stroud and his fifty-four years behind bars. Seasoned prison officers know that a man who can take a twelve-year manslaughter sentence and turn it into a fifty–four year death sentence does not really want to get out of prison. But there were admiring comments, too. Comments about his will, his stamina, his intellect.

"He made the most of it," Sobell said philosophically. "It was a life. [Going to prison] wasn't the end of life. It was just a different life."

Not long after that Reed Cozart got a letter from a Stroud fan named Francine, who wrote, "It sure is shocking to know that he passed so sudden. A lot of people sure are going to miss him, I sure am. He made me realize that just being a plain prisoner inside a prison does not mean that you can't make something of yourself."

&. &. &.

Epilogue

Robert Stroud remained in prison from August 30, 1909, until November 21, 1963, a total of fifty-four years and almost four months—perhaps one of the longest continuous federal sentences ever served. He remained on McNeil Island for three years, in Leavenworth for thirty, on Alcatraz for seventeen and at Springfield for four years.

Death came early in the morning on November 21, 1963. Many people read the obituary on November 22nd, but when John F. Kennedy was assassinated just before noon that day, it quickly overshadowed news of Stroud's death.

Stroud's body was claimed by the family and taken to Metropolis, Illinois. Cousin Howard Faughn, Jr., presided over the funeral. Mamie, who was still living in Metropolis, attended, but Marcus did not. Faughn had never met his cousin and knew little about him outside of the book and movie. He said a few words about Stroud's life being a lesson in how someone "can start out at the very bottom and make something out of his life." Stroud was buried near his mother a respectable distance from the McCartney family plot.

Mamie died at age eighty-seven on April 10, 1969, and she was buried on the other side of Robert. Marcus died in Honolulu, Hawaii, where he was living, at age seventy-eight on April 19, 1976. His body was cremated.

Many people believed that had Kennedy and Stroud lived, the president might have commuted the prisoner's sentence. It seems unlikely, however, that he would have overruled the advice of his brother the Attorney General, as well as the U.S. Pardon Attorney, the U.S. Parole Board chairman, the Bureau of Prisons director and F.B.I. director J. Edgar Hoover, who certainly would have joined the cause.

Many also believed that Stroud wanted to get out of prison. It was hard to imagine that he didn't want to live free. Yet his pattern of inappropriate and darkly comical statements—his explanation that the "meat" he wanted to cut was the hospital orderly, for example, or his assertion that he could easily make decisions even when life and death were at stake, and had done so many times, his comment that he had many people on his hit list—were virtual assurances that no official would take the responsibility of authorizing his release.

Moreover, just when freedom was occasionally within his grasp, Stroud would perversely push it back, as when he wrote to his attorney that he would remain at the Medical Center in order to revise his *Digest* even if paroled .

Stroud first became eligible for parole in 1937. With good behavior and a permanent move from segregation to the main population, eventually he could have been paroled—other men convicted of murder had been, even those convicted of killing prison officers. Good behavior over a period of years, a good work record, transfer to less maximum–security institutions, eventually work–release, a half–way house and a job offer was the normal path. The modern Bureau of Prisons might have looked more favorably upon Stroud had he opted for it.

Instead, Stroud maneuvered the Bureau into an antagonistic response and eventually the two entities became locked in a stalemate. To paraphrase Richard English, the Bureau won. They did not let Mr. Stroud get out of prison alive.

The question of whether Stroud would kill again is not so easily determined.

In 1969, six years after Stroud died, District Court Judge James C. Logan wrote a dissertation about him entitled *Analysis of a Murderer*. Logan did a content analysis on Stroud's writings, listing often repeated words such as "mother," "father," "brother," "sister," "prostitutes," "self," "girls," "boys," "laws," etc., noting how many and what kinds of descriptions accompanied each. For example, Stroud mentioned his mother many times in his autobiography, referring to her sixty-seven times as dominant, thirty-one times as someone who was negative towards her husband, twenty-two times as strict, nineteen times as someone who belittled him, fifteen times as a liar and five times as seductive. The picture that emerges is undeniably consistent.

Logan then asked three sets of judges to analyze the words and descriptives—one group of men who had known Stroud, another who had not known him and a third set of lawyers who were sophisticated in criminal law and criminology. Only the first group knew whose writings they analyzed. Logan hypothesized that Stroud was a homosexual and could have committed other violent acts. Although the issue of homosexuality probably wouldn't be included in such an analysis today, the question of Stroud's propensity for violence is still quite important.

Logan found a "striking degree of unanimity" among all three sets of judges that Stroud was homosexual, sociopathic and predisposed to criminal behavior.

That was the same conclusion prison psychiatrists had drawn.

The problem there, however, was that Stroud was diagnosed as a sociopath by a government agency whose actions were sometimes suspicious. And, by the time of the diagnosis, the myth of the Birdman was so entrenched in the public's consciousness that people were unwilling to believe he was a sociopath; instead they could only suspect that a maligned government agency had coerced its own psychiatrists—or at least the power of suggestion had intimidated them—into issuing a diagnosis that would support its ultimate conclusion.

Stroud, however, exhibited nearly every characteristic associated with sociopathic personalities.

The label of sociopath, like "psychopath" (they are used interchangeably), is no longer the preferred descriptive and has largely been replaced by the all inclusive "anti-social personality."

As early as 1948 researchers found that such children associated with weaker or younger children with whom they are persistently aggressive and could intimidate.

Others had defined the personality as asocial, aggressive, highly impulsive, remorseless and unable to form lasting bonds of affection with other human beings. Studies have consistently shown that sociopaths have little ability to change their behavior following punishment, are vain, emotionally immature, narcissistic, have a marked absence of anxiety or guilt, a lack of insight and an inability to delay satisfaction. They are frequently callous and are scarred by disturbed early parent-child relationships.

Wright, in 1965, concluded that the sociopathic personality disorder usually involves a mother who overwhelms her son with indulgence and solicitude, while the father is distant, highly successful, driving and critical.

The current definition of a sociopath by the American Psychiatric Association is someone who is chronically anti-social, often in trouble with the law, who profits neither from experience nor punishment, who is frequently callous, hedonistic and has an ability to rationalize anti-social acts so that they appear warranted, reasonable and justified.

Dennis Doren, in *Understanding and Treating the Psychopath*, described the traits as emotionally immature, self-centered, lacking a moral sense, unable to experience guilt, lacking control over impulses, lacking a sense of responsibility, unable to form meaningful relationships, chronically anti-social, unable to learn from experience to change behavior and undeterred by punishment.

Interestingly, Doren noted that, like Stroud, "psychopaths usually attempt to interact with the highest person in charge."

In writing his book for professional therapists, he suggested that psychopaths tend to think of others as "typically someone [they] considered the cause of all their problems, or at least someone who could remedy all of [their] problems."

He noted they were typically hypochondriacs and tended to complain of inaccessible pain such as headaches or stomach aches.

Lee N. Robins, Ph.D., who wrote *Deviant Children Grown Up*, a study of the life course of some five hundred patients who were restudied thirty years later, found that, "the combination of multiple anti–social symptoms plus an alcoholic father yields the highest rate of sociopathy which we have yet encountered."

Robins found that the mother's behavior may aide in the development of a sociopath, but if the father didn't have serious behavior problems, her's alone would not encourage anti-social tendencies in the children.

Physical abuse is relatively common among those with anti-social personality traits. Psychoanalyst, Alice Miller, in her book *For Your Own Good, Hidden Cruelty in Child-Rearing and the Roots of Violence,* said that "We punish our children for the arbitrary actions of our parents that we were not able to defend ourselves against."

That was Frank and maybe Elizabeth too.

"When a person can not talk about the cruelty endured as a child because it was experienced so early that it is beyond the reach of memory," Miller wrote, "then he or she must demonstrate cruelty." And that was Robert.

Stroud's anti-social traits could be checked off on a list. He was almost pathologically self-centered, impulsive, hypochondriacal, manipulative, violent and expressed feeling no remorse for his killings. He tended to blame everyone else and went straight to the top with his problems. He had little insight into his behavior and, by his repeated threats and callous comments, warned that his behavior had not changed.

Moreover, throughout his life Stroud seemed intent on provoking authorities to retaliate. He was antagonistic, he threatened, intimidated and tried to humiliate those in high position, and this did not go unnoticed.

Both Gaddis in his thesis, and Logan in his, noted that segregation, as Logan wrote, "contributed favorably to [Stroud's] self-actualization in a paradoxical way."

Stroud had discovered the same thing: that his excessive sentence was one-half of what made him famous. Clearly, late in life, he enjoyed the challenges of potentially gaining his freedom, more than the thought of freedom itself.

Predicting human behavior is not easy and, given Stroud's rather mild reaction to living in relative freedom the last four years at Springfield, it can be quite arrogant as well.

But freedom for a man who had lived in such captivity for half a century would truly have become a frustrating experience. Five decades had elapsed since Stroud walked as a free man, and with them had come technological and social changes which would have been an almost unsurmountable challenge for someone unaccustomed to even deciding when to eat, what to wear and where to go. Stroud had become virtually institutionalized.

With release he would have required constant care, and given his massive ego, eventually he would have become a very poor guest. Freedom and frustration could have quickly led to violence.

Sociopaths often kill over incidents from which the rest of us walk away.

The gravity of releasing an institutionalized sociopath is easily illustrated by a similar case in the 1970s and '80s, when writer Norman Mailer became involved through correspondence with a prisoner named Jack Henry Abbott.

Mailer was at that time writing his prize-winning book about Gary Gilmore, *The Executioner's Song*. Abbott and Gilmore were spiritual brothers of Stroud's—both had long criminal, sometimes violent records, both had been confined to penal institutions much of their adult lives.

Gilmore eventually was executed by the state of Utah and Mailer's book about it was brilliant. Through Mailer's involvement, however, Abbott was able to publish a book about prison called *In the Belly of the Beast*. Despite its dubious merit, the book became a best–seller briefly in 1980. Abbott was embraced by the New York literati and largely because he had the support of such idealistic champions, he was given a release from prison in 1981.

Within six weeks of his release he got into an argument with a twenty-two-year-old waiter, fatally stabbing him in the heart from behind.

At issue was whether Abbott could use the employee's restroom facilities.

Most psychiatrists, criminal psychologists, psychiatric nurses, and criminologists state emphatically that violent anti-social personalities mostly cannot be turned around once they leave their mid-teen years. Mailer had made the common mistake that Stroud's legions of supporters had made—of using intellectual achievement to predict a change in behavior.

Robert Stroud may not have ever killed again. But he had always threatened to do so, even late in life and he had killed two men early in life. He had never left any doubt as to what he might do when crossed.

Nor were his dubious accomplishments in avian medicine an inducement to consider him rehabilitated.

In the end the real Robert Stroud was much more fascinating than either the book or the movie portrayed. He was far more complicated, intense, diabolical, perverse, deadlier and funnier.

The fictional portrayals of Robert Stroud proved to be ultimately more dangerous, however—precisely because they were so simple.

&ae;   &ae;   &ae;

Source Notes

Introduction

1   But not until three decades . . . .: The U.S. Penitentiary at Alcatraz Island closed and Robert Stroud died in 1963; the island became part of the Golden Gate National Recreation Area in 1972.

1   I asked a National Park ranger . . .: Rex Norman was the NPS ranger.

2   In '46, nine . . .: Prison reports, court records, numerous book citations.

2   "A boat pulled out . . .": Testimony, *U.S. v. Shockley, Carnes and Thompson.*

3   He wrote later . . .: Stroud letter to Chief Judge William H. Becker, November 1963, Becker files.

Part I - Grand Illusion

5   Sitting in the court room . . .: Phyllis E. Gaddis interview, Summer 1992.

5   For the last decade, however . . .: T.E. Gaddis, *Birdman of Alcatraz.*

6   Fifty-four years old . . .: Phyllis E. Gaddis, Summer 1992.

6   A former probation . . .: O'Neil, "Prodigious Intellect in Solitary," *Life*, April 1960.

6   The old man turned . . .: *Ibid.*; Stanley A. Furman interview, 1990-92.

6   Although the bailiff quickly . . .: Phyllis E. Gaddis, 1992.

6   By 1962, the Birdman of Alcatraz . . .: Stroud entered prison in Aug. 1909.

6   His first book, *Diseases of Canaries* . . .: Stroud, *Diseases of Canaries*; 1933, "The first publication exclusively on treatment of birds was by a Leavenworth Prison inmate," Assn. of Avian Veterinarians.

6   His second, *Stroud's Digest* . . .: Stroud, *Stroud's Digest on the Diseases of Birds.*

7   In 1957 the prestigious . . .: C. L. Strong, "The Strange Story of Robert Stroud . . ." *Scientific American*, Dec. 1957.

7   *Newsweek* in 1958 . . .: "Scholar in Alcatraz," *Newsweek*, April 7, 1958.

7   Prominent articles . . .: O'Neil, "Prodigious Intellect in Solitary," *Life*, April 1960.

7   Titles like . . .: John Muth, "The Strange Saga of the Caged Birdman," *New York Mirror Magazine*, June 8, 1958; T.E. Gaddis, "The Agony of the Caged Birdman," *Coronet*, Oct. 1958.

7   "[Stroud] faced the prospect . . . ": *Coronet, Ibid.*

8   Actors Burt Lancaster and . . .: Furman, July 1990, Feb. 1991, March 1992; Phyllis E. Gaddis, 1992; news clippings, April 1962.

8   Lancaster was said to . . .: "The Role that Touched His Heart," *San Francisco Examiner Pictorial Living*, date unknown, PA files.

9   It even may have had a subtle . . .: Movies and overly dramatic news stories beginning in the 1930s had made Alcatraz seem unnecessarily harsh, even brutal. By 1955 Gaddis pictured a bright, rehabilitated scientist in his sixties who was in "solitary confinement" there. At the same time the prison infrastructure was corroding. Finger to the wind, the Bureau of Prisons no longer presented Alcatraz as an important prison during its request for funding before a Congressional committee in 1961. By '62 when the movie was released, public sentiment was decidedly against keeping Alcatraz open. It closed in March 1963.

9   He had been transferred . . .: Stroud declared that he discovered thirteen diseases in a letter to Dennis Norton, Jan. 24, 1963, reprinted in a pamphlet by Committee to Release Robert F. Stroud members; referenced by Richard M. English; copy also in PA files.

10   "I have seen the *Birdman* . . .: *Stroud v. Mayden and Nicholas.*

10   "I wish you would release . . .: *Ibid.*

10   Among them was a young man . . .: Richard M. English interview, April 2, 1990.
10   "There were many women . . .": Becker Oral History.
10   Stroud had gone to court . . . [until] He also claimed . . .: Memorandum and Order,
        March 8, 1963, *Stroud v. Mayden and Nicholas*; Bill Snyder, "Birdman Wins One
        Point in U.S. Court Hearing," *Springfield (Mo.) Daily News,* Nov. 8, 1963.
11   This court appearance . . .: List of Proceedings, *Stroud v. Mayden and Nicholas.*
11   Initially he had represented . . .: Furman, 1990-92.
11   "Stroud was having the time . . .": *Ibid.*, March 1992.
11   Judge Becker later said . . .: Becker Oral History.
12   Furman felt he . . .: Furman, 1990-91.
12   Furman asked if Stroud . . .: Becker Oral History.
12   "No, since the invention . . .": *Ibid.*
12   "You could see the air . . .": *Ibid.*
12   In 1909, for example . . .: "Both are Held Without Bail," *Daily Alaska Dispatch,*
        Jan. 21, 1909, Alaska Historical Library.
12   Similarly, after the 1916 murder . . .: Stroud letter to Frank Stroud, April 7, 1916, *U.S.
        v. Robert Stroud.*
12   It was what . . .: T.E. Gaddis, "Birdman of Alcatraz," *Cosmopolitan*, May 1953.
12   According to U.S. Attorney . . .: Wilbur G. Leonard letter to the Solicitor General,
        Feb. 14, 1961, *U.S. v. Robert Stroud.*
12   "He got into trouble . . .": Furman, 1990-1992.
13   They could no more . . .: Stroud to Daw, March 21, 1942, "Impounded," PA files.
13   When interviewed thirty years later . . .: Furman, March 1992.
13   "Some of them didn't . . .": Becker Oral History.
13   At recess Stroud ordered . . .: *Kansas City Star*, Nov. 26, 1959.
13   The old man picked up his food . . .: Morton Sobell interview, Aug. 1991.
13   "His table manners . . .": Bill Rogers interviews, 1979.
13   "He'd lived by himself . . .": Clarence Carnes interview, March 1984.
13   Sobell regularly ate with . . .: Sobell, Aug. 1991.
13   Even Stroud admitted . . .: T.E. Gaddis, Committee Bulletin #4, Sept. 26, 1958,
        Committee for the Release of Robert Stroud, PA files.
14   For years he claimed . . .: Appl. for Commutation, Oct. 5, 1915, PA files.
14   Doctors found no evidence . . .: Annual Parole Review, Feb. 6, 1963, Logan, p. 648.
14   "Within the last . . .": Swope's memo to BOP Director James V. Bennett, Nov. 24,
        1950, BOP Stroud files.
15   About his teeth . . .: Swope memo to Bennett, Nov. 24, 1950, *Ibid.*
15   In one memo . . .: W. J. Keenan, MTA, USPHS, Alcatraz to the Associate Warden,
        Oct. 2, 1950, *Ibid*; capitalization of "HE" original to the memo.
15   In a report . . .: Swope memo to Bennett, Jan.15, 1952, *Ibid.*
15   He shaved his entire . . .: Rogers; George De Vincenzi interviews, 1990, 1991; Ernie
        Yates interviews, Jan. 1990, Feb. 1991; prison memos.
15   In fact, the man . . .: List of Proceedings, *Stroud v. Mayden and Nicholas.*
16   The U.S. Parole Board in 1962 . . .: Joseph P. Henderson, "A Question of Freedom
        for the Aging Birdman," *Kansas City Star,* Nov. 18, 1962.
16   "He was just a homicidal . . .": Alcatraz prison officer said this to author at a reunion
        of former employees in July 1991.
16   Writing in the third person . . .: Robert F. Stroud, "Comparison of Robert Stroud with
        Nathan Leopold," Stroud's hand-written and typed versions, date unknown, PA files.
17   "Stroud was such a floozy . . .": Philip R. Bergen interview, Jan. 1990.
17   Only two years before the Becker . . .: Special Progress Report, Federal Medical
        Prison at Springfield, Missouri, March 16, 1960, Logan, p. 644.
17   Reports stated . . .: Special Progress Report, *Ibid.*
17   Officials were anxious to suppress . . .: Robert F. Stroud, "Looking Outward, An

Historical and Analytic Study of the Federal Penal System from the Inside," unpublished manuscript quoted by permission of Charles Dudley Martin, Administrator W.W.A. of the Robert F. Stroud estate.

17   "A little blond . . .": *Ibid.*
17   In another passage he wrote . . .: *Ibid.*
18   In the Becker hearings . . . "indescribable filth . . .": Attachment entitled "Frankie," *Stroud v. Mayden and Nicholas.*
18   In a chilling passage . . .: Stroud, "Looking Outward."
18   "The man who can fight . . .": *Ibid.*
19   In other less reasonable words . . .: *Ibid.*
19   He could say . . .: Stroud to Axelrod, Oct. 7, 1961, *Stroud v. Mayden and Nicholas.*
19   "Hell, they didn't want Robert . . .": Joe Landers interview, July 1991.
19   He called him . . .: Stroud, "Looking Outward."
20   Later, by inference, he . . .: Petition for Writ of Habeas Corpus, *Robert Stroud v. James A. Johnston.*
20   By 1962, he'd headed up . . .: Bennett became director of the BOP in 1937.
20   In 1931, when Stroud was . . .: Bureau Memorandum, July 28, 1931.
20   By 1962, Stroud's supporters . . .: English, Furman, T.E. Gaddis.
20   "I spent some two-and-a-half . . .": English, April 2, 1990.
21   In 1958 Stroud's attorneys initiated . . . : James V. Bennett memo to Pardon Attorney Reed Cozart, Sept. 12, 1958, PA files. Interestingly, in an April 1960 *Federal Prison Service Newsletter*, the official bi-monthly BOP newsletter, Bennett stated, "I have never, as a matter of fact, made any recommendation to the Parole Board of [sic] anyone else for or against parole or pardon of Stroud."
21   They were able to show . . .: *Stroud v. Mayden and Nicholas.*
21   Stroud believed . . .: Correspondence, *Ibid.*
21   Although Bennett permitted . . .: Bennett memo to Dr. Settle, June 14, 1961, *Ibid.*
21   Stroud had two publishers . . .: Correspondence, *Ibid.*
21   When the approved publisher . . .: Axelrod letter to Stroud, May 15, 1961, *Ibid.*
21   Bennett curtly removed . . .: Bennett memo to Dr. Settle, June 14, 1961, *Ibid.*
22   "He has never so much . . .": Respondant's Suggestions, June 9, 1962, *Ibid.*
22   Stroud's plan for revising . . .: Stroud's correspondence, *Ibid.*
22   Although this was the crux . . .: Order on the Supplemental Complaint, *Ibid.*
22   "My motion is so drawn . . .": Stroud letter to Furman, April 10, 1962, *Ibid.*
22   At his second hearing . . .: Order on the Supplemental Complaint, *Ibid.*
22   Becker overruled . . .: *Ibid.*
22   Stroud accused the Bureau . . . [until] He alleged . . .: Supplemental Complaint, *Ibid.*
23   From his point . . .: BOP Summary Statement, July 10, 1958, PA files.
23   Bennett even . . .: Corey, "He Took the Bars Off Prisons," *Nation's Bus.*, July 1944.
23   In the course of two . . . [until] Becker did not . . .: List of Proceedings, Orders, *Stroud v. Mayden and Nicholas.*
23   "In some instances . . .": Memorandum and Order, March 8, 1963, *Ibid.*
23   Only one copy of his manuscript . . .: *Ibid.*
24   Bennett subsequently . . .: Bennett memo to Warden, Nov. 4, 1963, *Ibid.*
24   And while revision . . .: Robert F. Stroud, *Digest*, (T.F.H. Publications, 1964).

Part II - The Prevailing Winds

25   One, taken around 1900 . . .: Postcard photographs, circa 1900, Seattle, Wash., referenced by Paul Fellows.
25   The family's new house . . .: King County Department of Assessments, Real Property Characteristics, Lot 18, Seattle, Wash.
25   Not photographed . . . was Marcus . . . nor Frank Stroud . . .: In T.E. Gaddis' *Birdman*

of Alcatraz, Stroud's father, Benjamin Franklin Stroud, is called "Ben," however he is mentioned by name only a few times in Elizabeth's letters, and once in a McCartney family history and in all instances he is called "Frank."

26   In one letter she described . . .: E. J. Stroud letters, circa 1900, Massoc County Historical Society.

26   She wrote about Mamie . . .: *Ibid.*

26   Elizabeth didn't use the term . . .: *Ibid.*; Furman, Harold Faughn interviews.

26   Elizabeth complained modestly . . .: *Ibid.*

26   Frank had had typhoid . . .: *Ibid.*

26   Then Frank had invested money . . .: *Ibid.*

26   "I do not anticipate a fortune . . .": *Ibid.*

26   In a letter written on New Year's Day . . .: *Ibid.*

27   And Bobbie? . . .: *Ibid.*

27   A few months after her father . . .: Smith, *History of Southern Illinois,* in biography of his son, Marcus McCartney; Elizabeth McCartney's birthdate is in question; some records indicate she was born in 1862 or '63, however, her death certificate lists birthdate as Nov. 3, 1860 and her tombstone lists 1860 as her date of birth.

27   Thus, at the age of four . . .: Letters to McCartney dating 1865 and 1868 indicate the two children were living with friends and relatives; Paul Fellows.

27   Even then she was . . .: Letter to McCartney from his sister, Sept. 10, 1865.

27   Eventually, McCartney married again . . .: Minnie Leukins, a German immigrant, G.W. Smith, *History of Southern Illinois,* pp.1566-1569.

28   He became a prominent . . .: *Ibid.*; news clippings from the *Metropolis Times,* 1868; *Massac Journal,* 1982; *Metropolis Promulgator,* Cent. Ed. 1965.

28   In one delicious slander . . .: "McCartney's Vanity," *The Metropolis Times,* Sept. 17, 1968, Vol. 2 No. 27.

28   When he died . . .: Fellows interview, Jan. 1990.

28   And Elizabeth . . .: Family member interview, Jan. 1990.

29   In Stroud's interpretation . . .: Stroud letter to E. J. Stroud, March 25/26, 1916; testimony, *U.S. v. Robert Stroud.*

29   Elizabeth defiantly left home . . .: 1880 Census, Jackson Precinct, Massoc County, IL, p. 4, Ed. 62, Elizabeth, age 18; Henry Casper Shaffer, 30; married less than one year; no accounting for her age discrepancy; Shaffer's name has been spelled Schaefer in T.E. Gaddis' *Birdman of Alcatraz.*

29   The Shaffer marriage . . .: *Jane E. Shaffer v. Henry C. Shaffer*; possibly to cloud her identity Elizabeth had switched her first and middle names.

29   Minnie was born . . . : 1900 census, King County, Seattle, Wash.

29   Mamie Emma, born . . .: International Genealogical Index, Batch 7509004-1058035, serial 55.

29   Even before she was born . . .: *Shaffer v. Shaffer.*

29   Divorce proceedings began . . .: *Ibid.*

29   Elizabeth took her two children . . .: *Ibid.*

29   Disappointed, socially . . .: *Shaffer v. Shaffer*; *B. F. Stroud v. E.J. Stroud.*

29   "I have quite a distinct recollection of it . . .": Testimony, 1917, *U.S. v. Robert Stroud.* Minnie's married name is not included here to protect her family. Under oath in 1917 she gave a false last name.

30   "My father was a wastrel scion . . .": Stroud, "Looking Outward."

30   Born in 1858 . . .: 1900 Census, King County, Seattle Wash; Death Certificate #28-012225, March 8, 1928, Bureau of Vital Statistics, California. The Stroud family is large and numerous efforts at genealogical research elicited almost no information on Benjamin Franklin Stroud or his ancestors.

30   He studied briefly . . .: Stroud, "Looking Outward."

30   "He was a nice-looking . . .": Testimony, 1916, *U.S. v. Robert Stroud.*

31   Frank found a job . . .: Polk's Seattle City Directory, 1901.
31   But things changed suddenly . . .: Testimony, 1916, *U.S. v. Robert Stroud.*
31   "[He] became very . . .": Exec. Clem. Appl., by E. J. Stroud, Wilson papers.
31   She was more bold . . . [until] "Whenever I would submit. . .": Testimony, 1916, *U.S. v. Robert Stroud.*
32   "I have a very distinct recollection. . .": Testimony, 1917, *Ibid.*
32   They remained married. . .: *B.F. Stroud v. E.J. Stroud.*
32   "After these relations . . . [until] "Yes, Sir . . .": testimony, 1916, *U.S. v. Robert Stroud.*
32   Elizabeth delivered her third . . .: No birth certificate was found, leading to the assumption that the baby was born at home, common among poorer families at the time; birthdate from Stroud, "Looking Outward."
33   "When the child was born . . .": Exec. Clem. App. by E. J. Stroud, Wilson papers.
33   "Taught to hate father . . .": Stroud, Comparison with Nathan Leopold, PA files.
33   He had convulsions while teething . . .: Testimony, 1916, *U.S. v. Robert Stroud.*
33   "As he grew . . .": Exec. Clem. App., by E. J. Stroud, Wilson papers.
33   In truth two deeply . . .: Lee N. Robbins, Ph. D., *Deviant Children Grown Up.*
33   It's well established . . .: *Ibid.*
33   "He violently hated his father . . .": Stroud, "Looking Outward."
34   Elizabeth, on the other hand . . .: A consistent pattern of guilt and emotional manipulation could be discerned from comments she and Robert made in letters, by obvious omissions in her otherwise genteel letters and by her later behavior.
34   "My every thought was tempered . . .": Eve Edstrom, "Stroud Says Mother Ruined Life She Helped Save," *Washington Post* series, July 1962.
34   Relatives have called Minnie's . . .: Hazel Larson interview, Jan. 1990; Trousdale, Jan. 1990.
34   In 1932, when she . . .: Death Certificate, Wash. State Department of Health. She died March 20, 1941 and had been committed 8 years, 10 months and 17 days.
35   Written in 1921 . . . : BOP Stroud files.
35   Furman remembered . . .: Furman, Aug. 5, 1990.
35   "She stared a lot. . .": Faughn, Dec. 1989.
35   Mamie remained dependent . . .: Death Certificate #69-020654, April 10, 1969, Illinois Department of Vital Records.
35   "The child was never . . .": Exec. Clem. App., by E. J. Stroud, Wilson papers.
36   It's been hinted . . .: Stroud talked frequently to prison officers and wrote about incest; "tension which stemmed from the possibility of incest," T.E. Gaddis, "The Evolution of a Personality Under Correctional Stress;" Logan, "Analysis of a Murderer," (but much of his information was taken from Gaddis' works). Gaddis may have known more than he described in his book and thesis, or he may have been influenced by his era, in which mothers were often blamed for their delinquent children.
36   Years before Frank died . . .: In Polk's 1910 Seattle City Directory and in Polk's 1922 Kansas City Directory, Elizabeth is listed as a widow; opening statement of defense attorney, 1918, as "a widow's son," *U.S. v. Robert Stroud.*
36   More telling, after . . .: "Wid of Robert," Polk's Kansas City Dir. 1933, 1934.
37   On his death certificate . . .: "Widower," Death Certificate #28-012225, March 8, 1928; Bureau of Vital Statistics, California.
37   Elizabeth promoted . . .: Exec. Clem. Appl., by E. J. Stroud, Wilson papers.
37   Although Bobbie had remained . . .: International Genealogical Index, #8225001-94.
37   Marcus was a chubby . . .: Elizabeth letter to relatives, Jan. 1, 1900.
37   Now Bobbie could see how . . .: Numerous references by Stroud and Gaddis.
37   At age ten he contracted typhoid . . .: Testimony, 1916, *U.S. v. Robert Stroud*; Exec. Clem. Appl., by E. J. Stroud, Wilson papers.
38   If the little kid brought home . . .: T.E. Gaddis, "The Evolution of a Personality . . .," Logan, p. 466.

38   Once after Frank knocked him . . .: Edstrom, "That the Birdman of Alcatraz Really Feathered His Nest," *Washington Post* series, July 1962; actual quote that he "had come up out of the dust. . . ", Stroud, "Looking Outward."

38   About the time Bobbie . . .: Edstrom, "Stroud Says Mother Ruined Life . . ." *Washington Post, Ibid.*

38   He'd also tried to kill himself . . .: Stroud, Comparison with Nathan Leopold, PA files.

38   As a kid he delivered . . .: T.E. Gaddis, "The Evolution of a Personality . . ."; Polk's Alaska-Yukon Directory, 1917-18.

38   In the 1920s he was on the fringe . . .: Furman, Jan. 1990; "The Great Marcus," BOP Stroud files.

38   In the early 1940s . . .: *Ibid.*

38   He moved frequently . . .: *Ibid.*

39   Out of embarrassment . . .: Furman, 1990; L.G. Marcus letterhead, *Ibid.*

39   Although no one could . . .: Family member, Jan. 1990.

39   Eventually he lost touch . . .: Death Certificate, April 19, 1976, Office of Health Status Monitoring, Honolulu, Hawaii; funeral announcement, April 24, 1976, *Honolulu Star Bulletin.*

39   Robert Stroud derided . . .: Ernie Yates interview, Jan. 1990; Bergen, Jan. 1991; letters to Fred Daw and others, i.e., Nov. 16, 1954, Gaddis Collection.

39   He was focused . . .: T.E. Gaddis, *Birdman of Alcatraz* (Comstock).

39   It was always said that he quit school in the third . . .: ". . . even when he refused to go to school after the third grade," T.E. Gaddis, "The Birdman of Alcatraz," *Cosmopolitan*, May 1953; "He had a third grade education," C. L. Strong, "The Amateur Scientist," *Scientific American*, Dec. 1957; "He was a boy of 19, with a third-grade education . . .," Art Cohn, date unknown, PA files; "He had only three years of grammar school, but he earned college-extension diplomas . . .," "Scholar in Alcatraz," *Newsweek*, April 7, 1958; "Stroud had entered prison with a third grade education," Muth, "The Strange Saga of the Caged Birdman of Alcatraz," *New York Mirror Magazine*, June 3, 1958; "Yet his education ended at the third grade," "41 Years in Solitary," *Inside Detective*, date unknown, PA files; prison reports.

40   Because, from what Elizabeth has said . . . what Stroud later testified . . .: Testimony, 1916, *U.S. v. Robert Stroud.*

40   At age thirteen . . .: Fred Robertson letter to Pardon Attorney James A. Finch, Wilson papers; testimony, 1916, *U.S. v. Robert Stroud.*

40   He wrote that he was . . .: Stroud, Comparison with Nathan Leopold, PA files.

40   He later testified . . .: Testimony, 1916, *U.S. v. Robert Stroud.*

40   At fourteen . . .: Robertson letter to Pard. Att. Finch, Feb. 2, 1920, Wilson papers.

40   Then around the age of . . .: Testimony, 1916, *U.S. v. Robert Stroud.*

40   About the same time . . .: *B. F. Stroud v. Elizabeth J. Stroud.*

40   Elizabeth had been augmenting . . .: *Ibid.*

40   The separation left Bob . . .: Edstrom "Stroud Says Mother Ruined Life. . .," *Washington Post* series, July 1962.

41   But now, away from her . . .: Alice Miller, *For Your Own Good.*

41   In one article . . .: Duhamel, Spivak, Stroud, "My 53 Years in Jail!" *Saga*, Sept. 1963.

41   In 1905, the Metropolis, Illinois, newspaper . . .: Paul Fellows.

41   Bob spent a lot of time . . .: Stroud letter to Fred Daw, July 2, 1954, Gaddis Collection.

41   "Had I stayed a little longer . . .: *Ibid.*

41   "I was married before . . . ": Faughn, Jan. 1990.

42   "On the way to jail" . . .: Stroud, "Looking Outward."

43   "Why, myself and another . . .": Testimony, 1916, *U.S. v. Robert Stroud.*

43   By 1907 Bob . . .: Exec. Clem. Appl., by E. J. Stroud, Wilson papers.

43   Elizabeth sent two postcards . . .: Massoc County Historical Library.

43   Stroud said later . . .: Testimony, 1916, *U.S. v. Robert Stroud.*

43   He had other reasons . . .: *Ibid.*
43   Prison records indicate . . .: Edstrom, "Stroud Says Mother Ruined Life . . .,"
      Washington Post series, July 1962.
43   Elizabeth Stroud said . . .: Exec. Clem. Appl., by E. J. Stroud, Wilson papers.
43   Stroud contracted . . .: Duhamel, Spivak, Stroud, "My 53 Years in Jail!" *Saga*, Sept.
      1963.
43   He began to buy stolen . . . [until] Convicted, he served . . .: Testimony, 1916, *U.S.*
      v. Robert Stroud.
43   In 1908 John Franklin McCartney . . .: *Metropolis Promulgator*, 1965 Centennial
      Edition; Paul Fellows.
43   Elizabeth had filed . . .: *E.J. Stroud v. B. F. Stroud*; *B. F. Stroud v. E.J. Stroud.*
44   Finally, in 1909 . . . [until] Elizabeth filed . . .: *Ibid.*
44   Indeed, he had purchased . . .: *Ibid.*
44   In the 1909 decree . . .: *Ibid.*
44   According to a city directory . . .: Polk's 1910 Seattle Directory.
44   Frank moved to California . . .: Death Certificate 28-012225, March 8, 1928,
      California.
44   When he received . . .: Logan, p. 475.
44   "If it had not been for the help . . .": B. F. Stroud letter to John E. Raker, Wilson papers.
44   Frank wrote to his son . . .: Correspondents, USP Leavenworth, BOP Stroud files.
44   In an amusing note . . .: Stroud, "Looking Outward."
44   Frank's last years . . .: Property, Precinct, Court, Marriage and Cemetery Records, El
      Dorado County, Calif.; 1928 California Death Certificate 28-012225, March 8, 1928.
44   According to federal prison . . .: Logan, p. 617.
44   Indeed, Stroud wrote . . .: Stroud to Daw, June 18, 1954, Gaddis Collection.
45   But a California . . .: Death Certificate 28-012225, March 8, 1928, California.
45   A tiny note . . .: BOP Stroud files.
45   There is no record . . .: Extensive search at various probable El Dorado County
      cemeteries elicited no burial information.
45   He was seventy years old . . .: Death Certificate 28-012225, March 8, 1928,
      California; *Mountain Democrat*, March 9, 1928.
45   He probably ate poorly . . .: Prisoner Commitment Log, McNeil Island, 1909;
      testimony revealed he began using morphine when he was eighteen, 1916, *U.S. v.*
      Robert Stroud.
45   In Juneau he and Kate . . .: "F.K.F. Von Dahmer Killed in a Quarrel," *Daily Alaska*
      Dispatch, Jan. 19, 1909, Alaska Historical Library.
45   Dahmer was an unknown . . .: Affidavits, Stroud Case File.
45   According to the *Daily Alaska Dispatch* . . .: "F.K.F. Von Dahmer Killed in a
      Quarrel," *Daily Alaska Dispatch*, Jan. 19, 1909, Alaska Historical Library.
45   The legend from . . .: T.E. Gaddis, *Birdman of Alcatraz* (Comstock), p. 18-20.
45   The rap from U.S. prison reports . . .: "started pimping for a woman of the streets,"
      1937 Special Admission Summary USP Leavenworth, Logan, p. 615-616; Stroud
      revealed that she was a prostitute, testimony 1916, *U.S. v. Robert Stroud.*
45   For whatever reason . . .: "F.K.F. Von Dahmer Killed in a Quarrel," *Daily Alaska*
      Dispatch, Jan. 19, 1909, Alaska Historical Library; Stroud later testified that the
      murder occurred at around 9:00 p.m., testimony 1916, *U.S. v. Robert Stroud.*
46   He never adequately explained . . .: Stroud claimed Dahmer reached behind him and
      he thought Dahmer had a gun—at odds with the path of the bullet in the victim's body.
46   But shots were heard . . .: Neighbor William Dickinson heard shots and ran out of his
      house in time to see Stroud, "F.K.F. Von Dahmer Killed in a Quarrel," *Daily Alaska*
      Dispatch, Jan. 19, 1909, Alaska Historical Library; he was also listed as a witness.
46   An autopsy, conducted by . . . [until] A reporter . . .: U.S. Attorney John J. Boyce letter
      to the U.S. Attorney General concerning Stroud's probable self-defense plea, DOJ

files; "F.K.F. Von Dahmer Killed in a Quarrel," *Daily Alaska Dispatch*, Jan. 19, 1909, Alaska Historical Library.

46 The money involved . . .: "Both are Held Without Bail," *Daily Alaska Dispatch,* Jan. 21, 1909, Alaska Historical Library.

46 He explained nonchalantly . . .: Stroud, "Looking Outward."

46 Both Stroud and Kitty . . .: Stroud Case File.

46 She told authorities . . .: *Ibid.*

47 Stroud claimed the killing . . .: *Ibid.*

47 According to the *Daily Alaska Dispatch* . . .: "Both are Held Without Bail," *Daily Alaska Dispatch,* Jan. 21, 1909; "Is Continued Until Monday," *Daily Alaska Dispatch*, Feb. 5, 1909. Alaska Historical Library.

47 "I had a great many interviews . . .: Thomas R. Lyon's letter to Attorney General A. Mitchell Palmer, Dec. 11, 1919, Wilson papers.

47 He once faced a prison . . . : Psychiatric Summary, Jan. 7, 1943, Logan, p. 620.

47 Later still, staff . . .: Report, FMC Springfield, March 16, 1960, *Ibid.*, pp. 642-645.

48 Gaddis even . . .: T.E. Gaddis, "The Evolution of a Personality . . .," p. 53.

48 The man "with the character . . .": Stroud, "Looking Outward."

48 Upon learning of her son's . . .: "Is Continued Until Monday," *Daily Alaska Dispatch*, Feb. 5, 1909, Alaska Historical Library.

48 Later, she called him . . .: Edstrom, "Stroud Says Mother Ruined Life . . .," *Washington Post* series, July 1962.

48 "My poor boy . . .": *Ibid.*

48 On Friday, Feb. 5, 1909 . . .: "Is Continued Until Monday," *Daily Alaska Dispatch*, Feb. 5, 1909, Alaska Historical Library.

48 After Elizabeth arrived . . .: Stroud Case File.

48 Valdez was a remote . . .: Dean K. Dawson, Ref. Asst., AARC, Juneau, suggested that Valdez was an odd choice which could afford a chance for escape.

48 The court agreed . . . [until] Abruptly his attorneys waived . . .: Stroud Case File; Gaddis may not have seen the Alaska court records because he stated that "A change in venue set the case for disposition in Skagway," T.E. Gaddis, *Birdman of Alcatraz* (Comstock), p. 24; Later he wrote, "After some delays and a change of venue to Skagway . . .," T.E. Gaddis, "The Evolution of a Personality . . .," p. 49.

49 First Degree Murder . . .: Acts of Congress and Treaties relating to Alaska, Alaska Criminal Code, Chap. 429, Title One, Chap. One, Section 4, 1906, Dean K. Dawson, Alaska Historical Library.

49 Stroud was also . . .: T.E. Gaddis, *Birdman of Alcatraz* (Comstock), p. 23-24.

49 The prosecution's evidence . . .: Stroud Case File.

49 Manslaughter in Alaska . . .: Acts of Congress and Treaties relating to Alaska, Criminal Code, Chap. 429, Title One, Chap. One, Section 4, 1906, Alaska Hist. Lib.

49 Stroud was given twelve . . .: Prisoner Commitment Log, U.S.P. McNeil Island, Wash. 1909; court records.

49 For Elizabeth McCartney Shaffer Stroud . . .: *B. F. Stroud v. Elizabeth J. Stroud.*

Part III - Meet John Pain

51 In the Commitment . . .: Prisoner Commitment Log, U.S.P. McNeil Is., Wash. 1909.

51 The clerk thought a moment . . .: *Ibid.*

51 Thirty years later in a short story . . .: Stroud, "The King's English," *The Atlantan,* USP Atlanta, Ga., Aug. 1939.

51 He described him . . .: *Ibid.*

51 They shoved the property . . .: Property Release, Aug. 30, 1909, USP McNeil Island, Wash., BOP Stroud files (see front page for signature).

51 He was number 1853 . . .: Prison violation file, Nov. 11, 1912, *Ibid.*

52 McNeil Island, in Puget . . .: John Roberts, "Sixty Years of a Proud Tradition," *Federal Prison Journal*, Summer 1990. Only the USPs at Leavenworth, Kansas and Atlanta, Georgia predated it. The jail had been in operation since 1875.

52 By the time Stroud arrived . . .: Paul W. Keve, *The McNeil Century*.

52 Ten years before . . .: *Ibid.*

52 Stroud was led through . . .: Stroud, "Looking Outward."

52 He was racked . . .: *Ibid.*

52 "Only directly in front . . .": *Ibid.*

52 ". . . At least nineteen hours . . .": *Ibid.*

53 Except one thing that . . .: Paul W. Keve, *The McNeil Century*, quoting Stroud manuscript, "Looking Outward."

54 When Bob Stroud entered McNeil . . .: Numerous Stroud letters show his English grammar was poor.

54 "Hard as some of those . . .": Stroud, "Looking Outward."

55 Before 1930, when . . .: John Roberts, *Federal Prisons Journal*, Summer 1990.

55 Director Bennett allowed Stroud to write . . .: No documentation was found, but it was known among staff and prisoners that Stroud had permission to write his manuscript, and such a privilege needed Bennett's approval.

55 Instead, he wrote . . .: Stroud, "Looking Outward."

56 But the entrepreneurial sort. . .: *Ibid.* The actual quote, "He has won more privileges, both for himself and others, than any other federal prison inmate. He has abolished, amended, or rewritten more rules and regulations by the simple process of . . ."

56 In those days, convicts . . .: Rules and Regulations, USP McNeil.

56 The lucky, the wealthy and . . .: Stroud, "Looking Outward."

56 Silence was observed . . . [until] Either could do a lot of damage . . .: Rules and Regulations, USP McNeil Island; Paul W. Keve, *The McNeil Century;* Stroud, "Looking Outward."

57 The McNeil Island Rulebook . . .: Rules and Regulations, USP McNeil, p. 37.

57 For a convict . . . [until] Solitary confinement . . .: Alexander Berkman, *Prison Memoirs of an Anachist*; Frank Tannenbaum, *Wall Shadows, A Study in American Prisons* ; Al Jennings and Will Irwin, *Beating Back.*

57 At McNeil at this time . . .: Keve, *The McNeil Century.*

57 Stroud agreed . . .: Stroud, "Looking Outward."

58 Wardens and their assistants . . .: Marvin Orr interview, 1981; Bergen, 1981.

58 "The King," as cons . . .: Keve, *The McNeil Century;* Stroud, "Looking Outward."

58 One employee called him . . .: Paul Keve, *The McNeil Century;* Stroud, "The King's English," *The Atlantan.*

58 Halligan was rumored . . .: Keve, *Ibid.*

58 Stroud saw him as . . . [until] "If they shook . . .": Stroud, "Looking Outward."

59 "It was looked upon almost . . ." [until] But with the influx . . .": *Ibid.*

59 "[It] might force him out at any time . . .": *Ibid.*

59 Prisons were strapped . . . [until] It wasn't personal . . .: Keve, Tannenbaum, Berkman, Jennings and Irwin.

60 Stroud told of one . . . [until] "Paper, however . . .": Stroud, "Looking Outward."

60 He also began to read . . .: Stroud's testimony, 1916, *U.S. v. Robert Stroud.*

60 Combining karma, past . . .: Bruce F. Campbell, *Ancient Wisdom Revised, A History of the Theosophical Movement.*

61 "On one occasion he come in . . .": Testimony, 1916, *U.S. v. Robert Stroud.*

61 According to Gaddis' . . .: T.E. Gaddis, "Evolution of a Personality . . .," p. 50.

61 Gaddis essentially blamed the prison . . .: *Ibid.*

61 In Gaddis' popular . . .: T.E. Gaddis, *Birdman of Alcatraz* (Comstock), p. 27.

61 According to cross-examination . . .: Stroud's testimony, 1916, *U.S. v. Robert Stroud.*

62 He wrote that . . .: Halligan to LaDow, Nov. 11, 1911, DOJ files.

62   On November 1, 1911, Stroud struck Henry . . .: Halligan letter, *Ibid.*; 1937 Prison report, Logan, p. 615-616.

62   A physician reported that . . . [until] He sutured them . . .: W. Bond letter to Halligan, Nov. 11, 1911, DOJ files.

62   Stroud reportedly told . . .: Halligan letter, DOJ files.

62   Halligan also said . . .: *Ibid.*

62   "Stroud borrowed . . .": Stroud, Comparison with Nathan Leopold, PA files.

62   Stroud was reduced . . .: Halligan letter, DOJ files.

63   "It would be appreciated . . .": Halligan letter, April 1, 1912, BOP Stroud files.

63   Stroud was given six months . . .: Testimony 1916, *U.S. v. Robert Stroud;* 1935 Special Admission Summary, Logan, p. 615.

63   "If anyone had told . . .": Keve, *The McNeil Century,* quoting "Looking Outward."

63   On September 5, 1912 . . .: Prison reports, BOP Stroud files.

63   Stabbings at Leavenworth . . .: Ranson, *Tuberculosis in Penal Institutions.*

63   The warden was a uniformed . . .: Photograph, National Archives; Jack Cope, *1300 Metropolitan Avenue*; U.S. Penitentiary Clippings, Kansas State Historical Library.

64   The two men actually had . . .: Discharge papers of John F. McCartney, Aug. 12, 1865, signed by R. W. McClaughry, Paymaster of U.S. Army; news clippings, *Kansas City Star,* May 11, 1933.

64   He called him . . .: Synopsis of Chapters, Stroud, "Looking Outward," file unknown, NARA, NA–PSR.

64   McClaughry's guards were armed . . .: Stroud, "Looking Outward."

64   McClaughry was replaced. . .: T.W. Morgan, warden from 7-1-13 until 10-31-18, Jack Cope, *1300 Metropolitan Avenue.*

64   Morgan reflected the future . . .: *Ibid.*

64   He called him . . . [until] "I was in no hurry . . .": Stroud, "Looking Outward."

65   In one document . . .: Synopsis, Stroud, "Looking Outward.

65   But he sometimes took credit . . .: *Ibid.*

65   Within four months . . .: Dec. 13, 1912, BOP Stroud files..

65   Two months later . . . [until] The following September . . .: *Ibid.*

65   In his manuscript . . .: Stroud, "Looking Outward."

66   After their meeting . . . [until] One year later . . .: BOP Stroud files.

66   By 1915 Stroud was working . . .: *Ibid.*

66   Other reports indicate that Stroud . . .: Remsberg, "The Phony Fairy Tale of The Birdman of Alcatraz," *True,* July 1963.

66   When Morgan introduced . . .: Stroud's testimony, 1916, *U.S. v. Robert Stroud.*

66   Elizabeth told a Kansas City reporter . . .: A.B. MacDonald, "The 'Canary Prisoner' Is To Lose The Birds That Have Been His Only Companions for Years," *Kansas City Star,* Oct. 4, 1931; "High honors . . .": *Topeka Journal,* April 30, 1955.

66   Stroud's grasp of . . .: Testimony, 1916, *U.S. v. Robert Stroud.*

66   Elizabeth, who had moved . . .: Elizabeth remained in Alaska at least until 1917-18, Polk's Alaska-Yukon Gazetteer; Oct. 4, 1931, *Kansas City Star.*

67   In 1915, he wrote to . . .: Stroud letter to E. J. Stroud, March 25/26, 1916; testimony, 1916, *U.S. v. Robert Stroud.*

67   In a letter to Minnie . . .: Stroud letter to Minnie, Sept. 19, 1915; Wilson papers.

67   In this early . . .: Stroud, Appl. for Commutation, Oct. 5, 1915; PA files.

67   After he was turned . . .: Stroud to Minnie, Nov. 23, 1915, Wilson papers.

68   ". . . I can't live this way . . .": Stroud letter to E. J. Stroud, Oct. 10, 1915, *Ibid.*

68   Elizabeth asked him to be . . .: "Guard Murdered in Cold Blooded Manner by Convict," *Leavenworth Times,* March 28, 1916.

68   "Mother I should feel very badly . . .": Stroud letter to E. J. Stroud, March 25-26, 1916, *U.S. v. Robert Stroud.*

69   At noon the next day . . .: "In the presence of almost 1,500 prisoners," "Guard

Murdered . . ." *Leavenworth Times,* March 28, 1916; "about 1,500 prisoners,"
Morgan's letter to the U.S. Attorney General, March 28, 1916, file unknown; Captain
Purcell said the dining room only held 1,200 seats and only "about 1,000" were there
at the time, testimony, *U.S. v. Robert Stroud.*

69 Hidden beneath his prison coat . . .: *Ibid.*
69 The dining room was approximately . . .: *Ibid.*
69 Stroud was seated . . .: "Guard Murdered . . ." *Leavenworth Times,* March 28, 1916;
testimony, *Ibid.*
69 Captain John M. Purcell. . .: *Ibid.*
69 Legend has it that the band . . .: T.E. Gaddis, *Birdman of Alcatraz* (Comstock) p. 44.
69 The most consistent version . . .: Testimony, *U.S. v. Robert Stroud.*
69 "He had fruit, candy, nuts . . ." [until] "Mr. Turner leaned over . . .": Stroud statement
at court 1916-18, Wilson papers.
70 In *Birdman of Alcatraz* . . .: T.E. Gaddis, *Birdman of Alcatraz* (Comstock), p. 37.
70 According to testimony, however . . .: Testimony, 1916, *U.S. v. Robert Stroud.*
70 "Damn!" exclaimed Bergen . . .: Bergen, Feb. 1, 1990.
70 Evidence was introduced . . . [until] Convicts apparently spread the rumor. . .:
U.S. v. Robert Stroud.
70 "Stroud kept watching . . .: T.E. Gaddis, *Birdman of Alcatraz* (Comstock), p 39.
70 Years later Elizabeth . . .: A.B. MacDonald, "The 'Canary Prisoner' Is to Lose . . .,"
Kansas City Star, Oct. 4, 1931.
70 He was asked . . . [until] A. "No sir . . .": Testimony, *U.S. v. Robert Stroud.*
71 Stroud raised his hand . . . [until] No one was sure . . .: Testimony, *Ibid.*
71 In testimony later, Stroud . . .: Testimony, *Ibid.*
71 The encounter lasted less . . . [until] "I turned around . . .": Testimony, *Ibid.*
71 His aim was deadly . . .: W.J. Pollard and Dr. W.F. Rohoblt testimonies, *Ibid.*
71 It struck Tuner's heart . . .: Testimony, *Ibid.*
71 Alarmed, nearby prisoners stood up . . . [until] Guard Turner . . .: Testimony, *Ibid.*
72 "We came cheap . . .": Bergen, Feb. 1990.
72 "I guess you know . . .": Stroud letter to Marcus, March 29, 1916; testimony, *U.S. v.
Robert Stroud.*
72 He explained later . . .: Testimony, *Ibid.*
72 "What about your conscience . . ." [until] "Because I don't see . . .": *Ibid.*
72 "The guard took sick . . .": Stroud letter to Frank Stroud April 7, 1916, *Ibid.*
72 Boyle was to ask . . . [until] "Your own higher . . .": Testimony, *Ibid.*
73 "Now don't worry . . .": Stroud letter to E. J. Stroud, March 31, 1916, *Ibid.*
73 As she had done before . . .: Elizabeth remained in Kansas City temporarily during
the trials, 1916-1918; and took up permanent residence at least in 1920 until 1935,
Polk's Kansas City Directory.
73 Although Morgan reportedly . . .: E. J. Stroud letter to Secretary Tumulty, April 10,
1920; Wilson papers; Faughn, Dec. 1989.
73 "I've succeeded in raising money . . .": E. J. Stroud letter to Tumulty, April 10, 1920,
Wilson papers.
73 She sold her house . . .: *Ibid.*
73 According to a family . . .: R.E. Robertson letter Feb. 10, 1920, Wilson papers.
74 The first trial began . . .: C.B. Ames, Office of the Attorney General, March 29, 1920,
PA files.
74 "Is there any . . ." [until] "They have absorbed . . .": Testimony, *U.S. v. Robert Stroud.*
74 A few questions later . . . [until] Stroud replied, "Some . . .": *Ibid.*
75 He admitted that his . . .: *Ibid.*
75 Although psychiatrists . . . [until] During the trial . . .: Testimony, *Ibid.*
75 Five doctors for the defense . . .: *Ibid.*
75 Dr. Lindsay L. Milne's testimony . . . [until] The doctors testified . . .: *Ibid.*

75   "He is a law . . .": *Ibid.*
75   The psychiatrists' comments . . .: *Ibid.*
75   He wrote that Stroud . . .: Robertson letter to Pardon Attorney Finch, Feb. 2, 1920, Wilson papers.
75   In another letter . . .: Robertson's letter to Finch, Feb. 25, 1920, *U.S. v. Robert Stroud.*
76   In the trial . . . [until] Robertson had shown . . .: Testimony, *U.S. v. Robert Stroud.*
76   Guard E.E. Whitlatch . . . [until] Another guard named Beck . . .: Whitlatch testimony, 1916/17/18; Beck testimony 1916/18, *U.S. v. Robert Stroud.*
76   He was pronounced . . .: Ames memo to the President, March 20, 1920, PA files.
76   Boyle uncovered an error . . .: Stipulation of Facts, Nov. 1959, *U.S. v. Robert Stroud.*
76   This time, Whitlatch testified . . .: Testimony, *U.S. v. Robert Stroud.*
77   Warden Morgan, for example . . . [until] The prosecution suspected . . .: Arthur M. Dollison manuscript; personal collection of the author.
77   At the same time, Stroud claimed . . .: Stroud, "Looking Outward."
77   U.S. Attorney Fred Robertson . . .: Robertson letter, date unknown, BOP Stroud files.
77   In the second trial . . .: "Statement as to Pardons of Certain Witnesses," 1917, *U.S. v. Robert Stroud.* Prisoners Riley, Costello, Elliott, Burton and Tyson were all handed pardons "in the presence of the jury."
77   Stroud was convicted again . . .: Stipulation of Facts, Nov. 1959, *U.S. v. Robert Stroud.*
77   According to Gaddis and Judge . . .: T.E. Gaddis, "Evolution of a Personality . . .," p. 67; Logan, "Analysis of a Murderer," p. 476.
78   A third and final trial . . .: *Ibid.*
78   In this trial . . . [until] "I have not been memorizing . . .": *Ibid.*
78   "On that double hand-hold . . ." [until] "For myself it matters . . .": Stroud's statement before sentencing, 1918, Wilson papers.
78   "Jury out less than one hour . . .": Warden Morgan telegram sent to Atlanta, date unknown, BOP Stroud files.
78   On June 28, 1918, it was ordered . . .: *U.S. v. Robert Stroud.*
78   Elizabeth took . . .: On Nov. 24, 1919, Supreme Court affirmed the judgment, Stipulation of Facts, Nov. 1959, *U.S. v. Robert Stroud.*
78   Woodrow Wilson was by then bedridden . . .: Wilson collapsed after a speech in September, 1919, and never recovered, but served out his term until President Warren G. Harding was inaugurated in 1921.
78   His wife, Edith Bolling Wilson . . .: Elizabeth Stroud wrote to Secretary Tumulty, Tumulty wrote to Mrs. Wilson, and Robert Stroud wrote to Tumulty thanking him for his interception, Wilson papers. A later article again mentioned Tumulty but not Mrs. Wilson, "The 'Canary Prisoner' is to Lose . . .," *Kansas City Star*, Oct. 4, 1931. Nothing in these sources indicate Mrs. Stroud either wrote to, or saw, Mrs. Wilson, as Gaddis reported and the movie depicted.
79   She did get to presidential . . .: "came to my office last week," Tumulty letter to Mrs. Wilson, April 6, 1920, Wilson papers.
79   Elizabeth's case rested . . . [until] "With the money she had . . .": Wilson papers.
79   Tumulty quoted him saying . . .: Tumulty's memo on the Stroud case, date unknown, item #246543-5, Wilson papers.
79   Palmer stated his main . . .: A. Mitchell Palmer letter to Tumulty, Jan. 31, 1920, *Ibid.*
80   Wilson signed Stroud's commutation . . .: *U.S. v. Robert Stroud.*
80   "At first, five minutes walking . . .: Stroud, "Looking Outward."
80   On Saturday, April 17, 1920 . . . [until] "Yet he can't be . . .": "Stroud Won't Be Hanged," *Kansas City Star*, April 17, 1920.
81   The next day . . .: "Stroud To Be Isolated," *Ibid.*, April 18, 1920.
81   "It will be hard . . .": "Death Sentence Is Commuted to 'Life In Prison'," *Leavenworth Times*, April 17, 1920.
81   In June 1917, Assistant Attorney . . .: Asst. Att. Gen. Larrin Graham letter to Warden

Thomas W. Morgan, June 7, 1917, Warden's Notebook, BOP.

82   High-toned, moralistic and . . . [until] Coben described him . . : Stanley Coben, *A. Mitchell Palmer: Politician.*

82   Historian Richard Gid Powers was . . .: Powers, *Secrecy and Power.*

82   Despite the accusations . . .: Coben, *A. Mitchell Palmer.*

82   The prisoner's commutation bid . . . [until] A. Mitchell Palmer . . .: Eliot Asinof, *1919, America's Loss of Innocence.*

83   In fact, Palmer had his eyes . . .: Coben, *A. Mitchell Palmer.*

83   It was Palmer who gave . . .: *Ibid.*

83   Acting within a presidential . . . [until] He tried to recoup his . . .: *Ibid.*

84   It was an old, favorite. . . [until] When he would retire . . .: *Ibid.*

84   Although Life in solitary . . .: No crime is punishable by "solitary confinement" in the strict and practical sense of the phrase.

Part IV - Cage Bird

85   In 1920, the Leavenworth . . . [until] The second floor . . .: Ralph Chaplin, "Share My Cell!" *Forum, The Magazine of Controversy,* Dec. 1929, p. 321-326.

85   "Pretty rough solitary . . .": Bergen, Summer 1992.

85   "There was a small drain in the floor . . .": Arthur M. Dollison, unpublished manuscript, personal collection of the author.

86   These cells were filled with . . .: Stroud, "Looking Outward."

86   Even Stroud "could wake up the whole . . .": *Ibid.*

86   Stroud wrote that he . . . [until] "Had he ever gotten. . .": *Ibid.*

86   When the Great War waged . . .: Many Conscientious Objectors wrote about their prison experiences, e.g. Alexander Berkman, *Prison Memoirs of an Anarchist*; Philip Grosser, *Uncle Sam's Devil's Island, Experiences of a Conscientious Objector in America During the World War*; and numerous articles in *The Nation, Survey,* etc.

87   Other Lifers had had pets before . . .: Idleness among prisoners wasn't uncommon in the last century and even in the first decades of the 20th Century. Lifers, especially, were allowed to keep canaries, mice, or, even as late as 1980 at Lorton, near Wash., D.C., cats. Some prisons even in the 1980s, such as Lima State Hospital for the Criminally Insane, have tried introducing animals to calm inmates and help establish bonds; see "Pets Help Break Through Defenses," *Columbus (Ohio) Citizen Journal,* Aug. 25, 1981.

87   Later one of . . . [until] Stroud felt that soil . . .: Stroud, *Digest* (T.F.H.), p. 167.

87   He built his first bird . . .: A.B. MacDonald, "The 'Canary Prisoner' is to Lose . . .," *Kansas City Star,* Oct. 4, 1931.

87   A former county . . .: August V. Anderson, warden from 4-1-19 until 5-1-21; William I. Biddle, warden from 6-1-21 until 12-15-26, Jack Cope, *1300 Metropolitan.*

87   A familiar face . . . [until] Kansas also became the second . . .: "Biddle will be Warden of the Federal Prison," *Topeka Capital,* April 22, 1921; "Sage of Leavenworth Times Writes '30' to Active Career," *Kansas City Star*; Jesse A. Hall and Leroy T. Hand, *History of Leavenworth, Kansas*; "William Biddle Dies," *Kansas City Star,* Sept. 29, 1947; Death of W.I. Biddle," *Tonganoxie Mirror,* Oct. 2, 1947, Ks. St. Hist. Soc.

88   On his first day June 1, 1921 . . . [until] By mid-1925 . . .: Jack Cope, *1300 Metropolitan Avenue.*

88   Yet Biddle, in an April . . .: Biddle to Moore, April 6, 1925, BOP Stroud files.

88   Ever the publicist . . . [until] Biddle conducted these tours . . .: Stroud, "Looking Outward." Although relatives were contacted and attempts were made to find an autobiography by, or a biography about, Biddle, no corroborating evidence was found to support Stroud's story.

89   By 1922, he was getting . . .: BOP Stroud files.

89   According to a Stroud . . .: Stroud to Warden Hudspeth, March 17, 1937, *Ibid.*
89   Stroud joined an active coterie . . .: *Roller Canary Journal and Bird World*, 1928-32, Edited by Edward J. Powell (Kansas City, Missouri).
89   "I was on my way . . .": Stroud, "Looking Outward."
90   When Elizabeth moved to Kansas City . . .: Polk's Kansas City Directory, 1920.
90   Elizabeth worked . . .: E. J. Stroud to Fletcher, Aug. 27, 1919; Sept. 9, 1920, etc., BOP Stroud files.
90   In beautifully, hand-written . . .: E. J. Stroud to Biddle, Dec. 17, 1923, *Ibid.*
90   ". . . But, as I am sure you . . .": E. J. Stroud letter to Biddle, Dec. 1923, *Ibid.*
90   "My dear Mr. Biddle . . .": E. J. Stroud to Warden Biddle, Dec. 17, 1923, *Ibid.*
91   In a letter to Biddle's . . .: E. J. Stroud letter to T.B. White, April 11, 1927, *Ibid.*
91   In 1927, she wrote . . .: E. J. Stroud letter to T.B. White, 1929, *Ibid.*
91   Stroud began experimenting . . .: Stroud, *Digest* (T.F.H.), p. 341.
91   He became so . . .: Stroud to Foley Advertising, Jan. 6, 1931, BOP Stroud files.
91   He began buying seed . . .: "Fancy Pedigreed Glucke Roller Weanlings and the very best of recleaned Bird seed," ad by Robert Stroud, *Roller Canary Journal and Bird World*, Sept. 1932.
91   Probably his greatest initial accomplishment . . .: Stroud letter to Foley Adv. Agency, Jan. 6, 1931, BOP Stroud files; Stroud, *Diseases of Canaries*, p. 51, 139; Stroud, *Digest*, p. 345.
92   "Sir," he addressed . . .: Stroud to White, March 29, 1929, BOP Stroud files.
92   Although years later . . .: Edstrom, "That Birdman of Alcatraz Really Feathered His Nest," *Washington Post* series, July 1962.
92   He built cages of out cardboard . . . [until] Some were . . .: A.B. MacDonald, "The 'Canary Prisoner' Is To Lose . . .," Oct. 4, 1931, *Kansas City Star*.
92   By February 1930, he was . . .: Stroud request, Feb. 1930, BOP Stroud files.
92   In 1931 he requested material . . .: *Ibid.*
92   From common canaries . . .: Stroud advertisement, *Roller Canary Journal and Bird World*, Sept. 1932.
92   Later, an avid friend named Fred Daw . . .: Daw letter to BOP, 1939; BOP Stroud files.
93   Describing the conditions in his cell . . .: Stroud, "Looking Outward."
93   "This prisoner, Stroud . . .: Guard Andrews note to White, undated, BOP Stroud files.
93   When he didn't get . . . : Stroud to Hudspeth, Sept. 4, 1939; *Ibid.*
93   By now he was selling his good stock . . .: Stroud letter to Sanderson, Jan. 5, 1932, BOP Stroud files; Show quality birds at $25 . . .: Stroud, "Looking Outward."
94   Later he bragged . . .: *Ibid.*
94   He claimed that in one three–month . . .: *Ibid.*
94   "He has a great variety . . .": Zerbst to Leach, 1933, BOP Stroud files.
94   There were problems . . .: Stroud, "Looking Outward."
94   It's likely that the first diseases . . .: Drs. James M. Harris, D.V.M., Robert Schmidt, D.V.M., Ph.D., Brian Speer, D.V.M., interviews, 1990-1993.
94   With few quarantine methods . . .: *Ibid.*
94   *Canary Birds*, written by Mary Wood . . .: Mary Wood, *Canary Birds, A Manual of Useful and Practical Information.*
95   In *The American Bird Fancier* . . . [until] Rich food was also . . .: Daniel Jay Browne, *The American Bird Fancier.*
95   In *Canaries and Cage Birds* . . . [until] "If the bird is about . . .": George Henry Holden, *Canaries and Cage Birds.*
96   Stroud ordered the Farmer's . . . [until] As a rule . . .": Farmer's Bulletin #1337, "Diseases of Poultry," Department of Agriculture, 1925.
96   One prominent medical veterinarian . . .: A. R. Ward and B.A. Gallagher, D.V.M., *Diseases of Domesticated Birds.*
96   The first disease . . .: Stroud, *Diseases of Canaries*, p. 101, footnote.

96 Like nearly all . . .: Ward and Gallagher, *Domesticated Birds*, p. 252.
96 The disease struck suddenly after Christmas . . .: Stroud, "Some More About Septic Fever," *Roller Canary Journal and Bird World*, Jan. 1932.
97 "Every time he passed the bird cage . . .: Stroud, "Looking Outward." Stroud also wrote nearly the same comment in his *Digest*, "I have had birds die in my hand when their death brought me greater sadness than that I have ever felt over the passing of a member of my own species. "
97 It was this disease . . .: Stroud, *Diseases of Canaries*, p. 101, footnote.
97 In Ward and . . . [until] There was no . . .: Ward and Gallagher, *Domesticated Birds*, see "Infectious Necrosis of Canaries," synonym: septic fever, pp. 252-4.
97 Later, his supporters assumed . . .: "From 1930 on, Stroud was allowed to possess a veritable arsenal—scalpels, scissors, ice pick, chisels, claw hammers . . .," O'Neil, "Prodigious Intellect In Solitary," *Life*, April 1960.
97 Yet, according to . . .: Cozart to Att. Gen. William P. Rogers, Oct. 7, 1958, PA files.
97 "In at least ninety percent . . .": Stroud, *Digest,* p. 314.
97 In later writings, he advised . . .: Stroud, *Ibid.*, p. 313.
98 He didn't know that . . .: Drs. Harris, D.V.M., Schmidt, D.V.M., Speer, D.V.M., interviews, 1990-93.
98 In one of his . . .: Stroud, *Diseases of Canaries*, p. 97, footnote; also Stroud, "Some More About Septic Fever," *Roller Canary J. and Bird World*, Jan. 1932.
98 He also later suggested that psittacosis . . .: Stroud, *Diseases of Canaries*, p. 108; Stroud, *Digest*, p. 31; note that by this time the name of the disease, septic fever, has been changed to avian diphtheria.
98 He wrote that the disease . . .: Stroud, *Digest*, p. 30-31.
98 He suggested breeders . . .: Stroud, "More About Septic Fever," *Roller Canary Journal*, Jan. 1932, pp. 5-6.
99 Other treatments included . . .: Stroud, *Diseases of Canaries*, p. 111.
99 "Stroud's Specific" was a . . . [until] Selling for two dollars . . .: Stroud, "Stroud's Specific, A Remedy for Avian Septicemias Affecting Poultry and Pet Birds, Directions for Use," 14-page pamphlet, BOP Stroud files.
99 He asked for and obtained permission . . .: "Stroud's Specific for Avian Septicemias," Letterhead, Feb. 1931.
99 On his letterhead, he . . .: *Ibid.*
99 In a 1931 letter . . .: Stroud letter to Foley Advertising, Jan. 6, 1931, *Ibid.*
100 And although he was no longer . . .: Stroud, *Digest*, p. 366.
101 In ads he urged readers . . .: "foremost authority," Stroud ad, *American Canary and Cage Bird Life*, date unknown, p. 9, accompanying article on "Apoplectiform Septicemia," PA files; "I can save you money! I can save your birds!" ad, *Roller Canary Journal*, Sept. 1932; "America's greatest authority on bird diseases," ad, *American Canary Magazine*, Dec. 1943.
101 "The real reason my stuff . . .: Stroud letter to Daw, marked March 21, 1942, "Impounded," PA files. Stroud frequently repeated comments in letters and manuscripts and literary license is used here with this quote.
101 In one reply he suggested . . .: "Our Forum," *Roller Canary J.*, July 1932, p. 16-17.
101 The main ingredient . . .: Description, *The Merck Index*.
101 Potassium chlorate . . .: *Ibid.*
101 Potassium permanganate . . .: *Ibid.*
101 Hydrogen peroxide . . .: Peroxide, *Academic American Encyclopedia*, 1991.
102 The 1989 paperback . . .: T.E. Gaddis, *Birdman of Alcatraz* (Comstock), cover.
102 A mass murderer who hated . . . [until] Thus Panzram . . .: T.E. Gaddis and James O. Long, *Killer, A Journal of a Murderer.*
102 Panzram was scared . . . [until] In Aug. 1930. . .: Stroud, "Looking Outward."
103 As many as one hundred . . .: Letters to and from Stroud, BOP Stroud files.

103   Pet store owners, "American bird breeders . . .": Stroud, *Digest,* p.161.
103   Every letter required . . .: Special Purpose Requests with signatures, BOP Stroud files.
103   Stroud was also sending and receiving . . .: BOP Stroud files.
103   He was frequently boxing up birds . . .: *Ibid.*
103   "Stroud had his light on . . .": Bill Sugg interview, 1979.
104   He could be comically . . .: Stroud to Bullock, Dec. 31, 1931, BOP Stroud files.
104   "See what can be done . . .": F. Lovell Bixby letter to warden, ca. 1931- 33, *Ibid.*
104   Each bird was shipped . . .: Stroud letter to Sanderson, Jan. 5, 1932, *Ibid.*
104   "Now Sir, the people to whom . . ." [until] "You will have to . . .": Stroud letter to Warden White, June 20, 1929; White's reply, June 23; *Ibid.*
106   The Bureau sent . . .: Bureau Memorandum, July 28, 1931.
106   In the summer of 1931. . .: BOP Stroud files.
106   He was carrying "between . . ." [until] "My cell is lined . . .": A.B. MacDonald, "The 'Canary Prisoner' Is To Lose . . .," Oct. 4, 1931, *Kansas City Star.*
106   Stroud, who has been . . .: *Ibid.*
106   "He has been born again . . .": *Ibid.*
107   Stroud later claimed . . . which compared with . . .: Remsberg, "The Phony Fairy Tale . . ." *True,* July 1963 (Mr. Remsberg had access to the Stroud files); Consumer Price Index, U.S. Bureau of Labor Statistics, U.S. Commerce Department (dollar comparisons for 1931-1991).
107   Elizabeth called her son . . . [until] She said that he painted . . .: *Ibid.*
107   The *Star* article . . .: *Ibid.*
107   Indeed, Powell had . . .: E. J. Powell letter, date unknown, BOP Stroud files.
107   A subscriber to Powell's magazine . . .: "Romance of the Canary Breeder," *St. Louis Post Dispatch,* Nov. 19, 1933.
107   Some time after that . . .: *Ibid.*
108   "Bob killed the guard in prison . . ." [until] "He wouldn't . . .": *Ibid.*
108   Later, when it became important . . .: *Ibid.*
108   But, according to Della's son . . .: Fred L. Jones interview, 1980; "took an apartment . . . where Stroud's mother lives," *Ibid.*
108   Unlike the movie heroine . . .: Jones, 1980.
108   Her letters were . . .: BOP Stroud files; Richard M. English collection.
108   In a letter to Warden White . . .: Jones to White, Feb. 10, 1931, *Ibid.*
108   Throughout the years from 1929 . . .: List of correspondents, BOP Stroud files.
109   Moreover, they frequently . . . [until] "Four available OK . . .": *Ibid.*
109   "It is three weeks since you . . .": Stroud telegram to Della Jones, 1929, *Ibid.*
109   Much later, when . . .: Hudspeth letter to Asst. BOP Director Hammack, Aug. 21, 1939, *Ibid.*
109   "Surely, you all know Robert . . ." [until] "Now what are you going . . .": Della Jones, "An Appeal for Justice For One Who Has Given Years of Valuable Service to the Canary Breeder," *Roller Canary Journal,* Oct. 1931, PA files.
110   Two months later . . . [until] "He has asked simply . . .": "How The Hidden Life of the Astonishing Canary Convict Was Disclosed," *Denver Post,* Dec. 20, 1931.
111   That plus a tiny but passionate . . . "the tambourine jangle . . .": Remsberg, "The Phony Fairy Tale of The Birdman of Alcatraz," *True,* July 1963.
111   He wrote up a petition . . .: Letters referring to the petition, letters signed by Della Jones, E.J. Powell, and congress members attesting to letters and signatures sent from the public, Fall 1931, PA files.
111   The petition asked . . .: "Petition for the Investigation of the Case of Robert Stroud with view to Clemency," to Herbert Hoover, exact date unknown, 1931; file unknown.
111   Stroud's argument . . . [until] "We feel that the claims . . .": *Ibid.*

112 "Why is that man in prison?" [until] "Oh *Please . . .*": BOP Stroud files.

113 Born in Silver Creek, New York in 1894 . . .: James V. Bennett, *I Chose Prison*; Herbert Corey, "He Took the Bars Off Prisons," *Nation's Business*, July 1944; House Congressional Record, Aug. 19, 1964.

113 A little naively . . .: James V. Bennett, "The Federal Penal and Correctional Problem," 1928; reprinted in the House Congressional Record, Aug. 19, 1964.

113 Although the Bureau . . . [until] In 1934, Alcatraz . . .: John Roberts, BOP Archivist, *Federal Prisons Journal*, Summer 1990.

113 By 1944, under Bennett's . . .: "Prison Work as a Career," Study course, BOP, 1944.

113 When he finally retired . . .: Includes penitentiaries, federal correctional institutions, camps, half-ways house and jails, John Roberts, Archivist, BOP, Nov. 22, 1993.

113 Bennett would institute . . . [until] At the end of his career . . .: John Roberts, BOP Archivist, *Federal Prisons Journal*, Summer 1990; James V. Bennett, *I Chose Prison;* Herbert Corey, "He Took the Bars Off Prisons," *Nation's Business*, July 1944; House Record, Aug. 19, 1964.

114 "It is this moment . . ." [until] In writing about . . .: Bennett, *I Chose Prison.*

114 He was hidden "deep inside. . .": Bergen, Nov. 29, 1989.

114 One of his first administrative orders. . .: Dollison interview and manuscript.

115 White wrote to an inquiring citizen . . .: White to Saye, Oct. 7, 1931, *Ibid.*

116 Two weeks later White wrote . . .: White to Strong, Oct. 14, 1931, *Ibid.*

116 Days later, White . . .: White statement, *Kansas City Star*, exact date unknown, *Ibid.*

116 "He was getting pretty cocky. . .": Bergen, Jan. 1990.

116 On October 31, 1931, White sent a . . .: White letter to Bates, Oct. 31, 1931; PA files.

116 In November 1931 . . .: Bates to Pardon Attorney Finch, Nov. 3, 1931; *Ibid.*

116 Finch replied . . .: Finch memo to Bates, Nov. 3, 1931; *Ibid.*

116 Massive appropriations . . .: John Roberts interview, 1991; Bergen interviews.

117 In the face of this . . .: Roberts, *Ibid.*; Bergen, *Ibid.*; T.E. Gaddis; Stroud.

117 He referred to 1931 . . . [until] He was selling . . .: Stroud letters to Shopp; Minor; Bullock; Gerard, Dec. 31, 1931; Sanderson, Jan. 5, 1932; BOP Stroud files.

118 "The skeleton of a bird. . .": Robert Stroud, *Diseases of Canaries*, p. 3.

119 "The female generative organs. . .": Ward and Gallagher, *Domesticated Birds*, p. 16.

119 "The female canary has a single ovary . . .": Stroud, *Diseases of Canaries*, p. 24.

119 "The feathers are . . .": Ward and Gallagher, *Domesticated Birds*, p. 17.

119 "The feathers of a bird . . .". Stroud, *Diseases of Canaries*, p. 26.

119 In another example Stroud copied . . .: "Skeleton of a Canary" illustration, Stroud, *Diseases of Canaries*, p. 5; "The skeleton of a fowl" illustration, Ward and Gallagher, *Diseases of Domesticated Birds*, p. 2.

120 By 1933, however, Dr. H. E. Moskey, D.V.M. . . .: No letter from Moskey turned up in the released Stroud files, nor were any government documents located attesting to this ruling. Moskey's name is included in the list of Stroud correspondents in 1931, however, when Moskey was the veterinarian of the Food, Drug and Insecticide Administration. Various statements by Stroud, Maude Foote and others state that Moskey had ruled that the bottled bird cures were worthless; Stroud, "Exec. Clem. application," Janaury 23, 1934; PA files; Maude Foote letter to President Truman, March 8, 1951, *Ibid.*

120 Stroud received no money . . . [until] "I think that this just . . .:" Stroud to Social Service Unit, May 1939; BOP Stroud files. Stroud's comments of Powell as a "crook" and that he had been "gypped" appear in the same files.

121 In the first sentence . . .: Stroud, *Digest*, 1944, p. v.

122 In January 1934 . . .: Stroud, Exec. Clem. Appl., Jan. 23, 1934, PA files.

122 One letter . . . [until] "But because they . . .": Della May Stroud letter, Nov. 1, 1933, *Ibid.* Comparison of Stroud's and Jones' letters shows distinct differences.

122 He wrote that . . . [until] His years . . .: Stroud, Exec. Clem. Appl, *Ibid.*

123   Herbert Sanborn, Professor of Philosophy . . .: Herbert Sanborn letter to Senator
      McKellar, Dec. 3, 1931, PA files.
123   A man named Lewis . . .: Lewis letter to Roosevelt, Nov. 27, 1933, *Ibid.*
123   He wrote up a contract declaring . . .: Stroud, Marriage Contract, Nov. 15, 1933;
      U.S. v. Robert Stroud.
123   "I am in love with Robert Stroud . . .": "The Romance of the Canary Breeder," *St.
      Louis Post Dispatch*, Nov. 19, 1933.
123   She immediately began . . .: Numerous documents were signed Della May Stroud or
      Mrs. Robert Stroud.
123   Stroud based the legality of his marriage . . .: Stroud, Exec. Clem. application, Jan.
      23, 1934; PA files.
124   Della's son, Fred Jones . . .: Jones, 1980.
124   The marriage worried . . [until] "Robert Stroud not . . .": BOP Stroud files.
124   Calling her "my constant aid . . ." [until] "In the present . . .": Stroud, Exec. Clem.
      application, Jan. 23, 1934; PA files.
125   She stated that . . .: "The Romance . . ." *St. Louis Post Dispatch*, Nov. 19, 1933.
125   "I am sorry Mrs. Stroud feels . . .": *Ibid.*
125   In 1934, Zerst . . .: Zerbst to Finch, Feb. 14, 1934, PA files.
126   How she thought of him . . .: "wid of Robert," Polk's 1933, '34 Kansas City Directory.
126   Both women moved from their . . .: *Ibid.*
126   Elizabeth seemed to have . . .: Death Certificate, Elizabeth J. Stroud, #31299, Aug.
      19, 1938, Illinois Department of Public Health-Division of Vital Statistics.
126   He claimed to a . . . : Special Progress Report, Aug. 19, 1959, Logan, p. 639.
126   Correspondence between Della and Stroud . . .: BOP Stroud files.
126   Della eventually stopped writing . . .: Jones, 1980.
126   Although Leavenworth . . .: Asst. BOP Director Bixby letter to Zerbst, Aug. 9, 1935,
      BOP Stroud files; Apparently the Leavenworth Classification Committee voted to
      send Stroud to Alcatraz, but Bixby "could not properly make a favorable recom-
      mendation" to the director, and the matter was dropped.

Part V - Cell House Suite

127   By 1935, the Leavenworth Birdman . . .: Weight based on admissions information at
      Alcatraz. Stroud's weight changed significantly throughout the years. He claimed
      that at times in Leavenworth his weight reached 210 pounds and was 185 when he
      left. By the time he was in the Alcatraz hospital he weighted 138; Stroud to Daw, June
      18, 1954, Gaddis Collection.
127   He was judged to be college equivalent . . .: Leavenworth Prison Report, July 25,
      1935, Logan, p. 613.
127   The petitions and the articles . . .: Documentation doesn't reveal when Stroud got his
      second cell. Dollison, Bergen, Stucker, Gregory, Karpis, etc., attest to this fact.
127   He was astonished to . . .: Alvin Karpis as told to Robert Livesey, *On The Rock.*
127   Weslyan University . . .: Stroud received the microscope on April 15, 1936, BOP
      Stroud files.
127   According to Bergen . . . [until "He looked like . . .": Bergen, Dec. 1, 1989.
128   Mabel Walker Willabrandt . . .: Stroud, "Looking Outward." Only Stroud's story tells
      of her visits, but she oversaw the Bureau of Federal Prisons which may have
      necessitated visits, and she was from Kansas.
128   Later, he had also caught . . .: Curt Jentry, *J.Edgar Hoover, The Man and the Secrets*;
      supported by Leavenworth correspondents list, BOP Stroud files.
128   "He was an historical . . ." [until] "And we knew . .": Bergen, Dec. 1, 1989.
129   Using glass, half-inch . . .: Stroud letter in *Scientific American*, Dec. 1957.
129   A micron is one-millionth of a meter . . .: *American Heritage Dictionary*, Houghton-

Mifflin, 1976.
129 Judging from . . . [until] "Freehand drawing by the. . .": Stroud, *Digest*, p. 168.
130 In his second book, he also wrote . . .: *Ibid.*, p. 148.
130 In 1937 he was granted . . .: BOP Stroud files.
130 In 1938 there was a note from . . .: *Ibid.*
130 He wrote that he had been . . .: Stroud, "Looking Outward."
131 But officers worried . . .: *Ibid.*
131 Nor could he resist boasting . . .: *Ibid.*
131 "His cell was always dirty . . ." Nova Stucker interview, 1980.
131 In a letter . . .: Stroud to Daw, March 21, 1942, "Impounded," PA files.
132 Art Dollison . . . [until] "The only thing . . .": Dollison manuscript.
132 "The impression I had . . .": Bergen, Dec. 1, 1989.
133 In 1936, for example . . . [until] "Those who are not . . .": Zerbst letter to Asst. Director Bixby, Jan. 30, 1936, BOP Stroud files.
133 "Unquestionably, Stroud . . .": BOP Summary Statement, July 10, 1958, PA files.
133 In fact Stroud frequently . . .: ". . .he would complain bitterly and report each instance to Washington." Leavenworth Prison Report, Oct. 13, 1942, Logan, p. 619.
133 "This man has had numerous complaints . . ." [until] "There is nothing . . .": Leavenworth Prison Report, July 25, 1935, *Ibid*, p. 611.
134 Aspergillus has been known . . .: Drs. Speer, Schmidt, and Harris, D.V.M. interviews, 1990-93.
134 Psittacosis is a serious disease . . .: Dr. Julius Schachter, Ph.D., interview, 1993.
134 In 1942 he complained often . . .: Prison Report, Jan. 14, 1942, Logan, p. 618.
134 That year, for example . . .: Leavenworth Prison Report, July 25, 1935, *Ibid.*, p. 612.
134 Although it appears that . . .: Asst. Warden's Record Card, BOP Stroud files.
135 "Stroud will always. . .": Prison Report, July 25, 1935, Logan, p. 616.
135 In a comment that was . . .: BOP Summary Statement, July 10, 1958, PA files.
135 "Owing to the fact that he . . .": Prison Report, July 25, 1935, Logan, p. 612.
135 Similarly, another . . .: Alcatraz Progress Report, March 21, 1952, *Ibid.*, p. 626.
136 When Bennett became director . . . [until] "Big men do not . . .": Edstrom, "That Birdman of Alcatraz Really Feathered His Nest," *Washington Post* series, July 1962.
136 Stroud wanted a guard . . .: BOP Stroud files.
136 Always pushing . . .: Edstrom, "That Birdman . . .," *Washington Post* series, July 1962.
136 Stanley Furman noted that Stroud . . .: Furman, Feb. 12, 1991.
136 That same year . . .: Parole Progress Report, Nov. 24, 1936, Logan, p. 614.
136 A 1936 annual report . . .: *Ibid.*
136 According to Gaddis. . .: T.E. Gaddis, *Birdman of Alcatraz* (Comstock), p. 186.
136 According to *Washington Post* reporter . . .: Edstrom, "Research by Stroud Results in New Book," *Washington Post* series, July 1962.
137 "I am neither a moron nor a sycophant . . .": O'Neil, *Life*, April 1960.
137 His father had died . . .: Death Certificate 28-012225, March 8, 1928, Bureau of Vital Statistics, California.
137 Letters to and from . . . [until] Coincidentally or not . . .: Leavenworth correspondents list, BOP Stroud files.
138 On August 3, 1938 . . .: *Ibid.*
138 Elizabeth died on August 19, 1938. . .: Death Certificate #31299, August 19, 1938, Department of Public Health-Division of Vital Statistics, Illinois.
138 He could now study . . . [until] two thousand sections. . .: Stroud, *Digest*, p. 239.
139 In text that eventually . . . "We all stand on the shoulders . . .": *Ibid.*, p. ix.
139 "Those of you who are not . . .": *Ibid.*, p. 69.
139 "Much of our craving for drink . . .": *Ibid.*, p. 398.
139 In one footnote he said . . .: *Ibid.*, p. 270.
139 Of one, Dr. Durant, he wrote . . .: *Ibid.*, p. 236.

139   He was critical of veterinary . . .: *Ibid.*, p. 23 and p. 50.
139   "It may interest some readers. . .": *Ibid*, p. 168.
139   In one passage . . . "These symptoms are so realistic . . .": *Ibid.*, p. 261.
139   "The best course. . ." *Ibid.*, p. 30.
140   "A child may like and need candy . . .": *Ibid.*, p. 355.
140   In writing about mating birds . . .: *Ibid.*, p. 60.
140   "Years of work . . .": *Ibid.*, p. 312-3; repeated in his manuscript.
141   On Dec. 1, 1941, he wrote . . .: Special Purpose Letter request form, BOP Stroud files.
141   On January 3, 1942 . . .: *Ibid.*, Jan. 3, 1942.
141   ". . . And if the condition is what . . .": *Ibid.*, circa 1941.
141   On Feburary 20, 1942 he wrote . . .: *Ibid.*, Feb. 20, 1942.
141   "There is one essential . . .": Stroud letter to Daw, marked March 21, 1942, "Impounded," PA files.
142   No matter how many . .: Dr. James Harris, D.V.M. interview, June 1993.
142   Briefly, Robert Koch . . . : Dr. Harris, D.V.M., *New Standard Encyclopedia.*
143   Stroud claimed . . .: ". . . and I had the good luck of discovering cures for 13 of their diseases," Stroud to Dennis Norton, Jan. 24, 1963, reprinted in a pamphlet by Committee to Release Robert Stroud members, Richard M. English.
143   To illustrate his challenges . . . [until] Clustering like this is common . . .: Drs. Schmidt, Harris, Speer interviews, 1990-93.
144   He called it . . . [until] He wrote in his . . .: Stroud, *Digest*, pp. 30-47.
145   Dr. Robert Schmidt . . . [until] "Psittacosis is not . . .": Dr. Schmidt, 1990-93.
145   Psittacosis . . . [until] Although the . . .: Dr. Schachter, Ph.D., 1993.
145   Other diseases Schmidt recognized . . .: Dr.Schmidt, 1990- 93.
146   Dr. Brian Speer, D.V.M., felt . . . [until] Yet he persistently . . .: Dr. Speer interviews, 1990-93.
146   Stroud claimed in his second book . . .: Stroud, *Digest,* pp. 201-5.
146   In the 1957 *Scientific American* article . . .: C.L. Strong, "The Strange Story of Robert Stroud . . .," *Scientific American*, Dec. 1957.
146   In this example . . . [until] Stroud then . . .: Stroud, *Digest*, pp. 169-176.
147   "The finest laboratory equipment . . .": *Ibid.*, p. 314.
147   "I'd be very suspicious . . ." [until] He thought perhaps . . .: Speer, 1990-93.
147   He theorized that the hemorrhages . . .: Stroud, *Digest*, pp. 8-18.
148   "A lot of what he saw . . ." [until] Moreover, bacteria . . .: Schmidt, 1990-93.
148   Aspergillus is a fungus . . .: Stroud, *Digest*, pp. 18-28.
148   "It is possible to cure . . ." [until] "I claim priority . . .": *Ibid.*, p. 25.
148   Sir William Henry . . . [until] In fact, anthraquinone . . .: "Perkins," "Dyes, "History of Chemistry," "Gentian Violet" from *Academic American Encyclopedia*; interviews with Anna Scott, president of Noremco, former manufacturer of Gentian Violet mold inhibitor; Robert Fudge, pharmacist and Associate Medical Director of Adria Labs, manufacturer of Adrimycin, a bone marrow suppression treatment for cancer; Dr. James Sun of Union Carbide; Dr. Russell Steiner, Ph.D., retired Vice-President of Research and Development at Crompton and Knowles Corp.
149   Secondly, birds don't usually . . .: Speer, 1990-93.
149   Letter poured into . . . [until] "He really requires . . .": BOP Stroud files.

Part VI - The Birdman of Alcatraz

151   He had just won . . .: Stroud, "The King's English," *The Atlantan*, Aug. 1939.
151   Buoyant, he worked . . . [until] "The book is coming first rate . . .": Stroud letter to Fred Daw, marked March 21, 1942, "Impounded," PA files.
151   Senior Officer Bergen . . . [until] War fever . . .: Bergen, Dollison interviews.
152   Early in the morning . . .: Edstrom, "Research By Stroud Results in New Book,"

Washington Post series, July 1962.
152 A special medical report . . . [until] At the bottom of the report . . .: Special Progress Report, Oct. 13, 1942, Logan, p. 619.
152 "By slow degress he . . .": BOP Summary Statement, July 10, 1958, PA files.
152 A list dated Dec. 21, 1942 . . . [until] "All the alcohol was . . .": *Ibid.*
153 Stroud had boasted . . .: Edstrom, "Research By Stroud Results in New Book," *Washington Post* series, July 1962.
153 The 1942 report . . .: BOP Summary Statement, July 10, 1958, PA files. Stroud's manuscript also contained references to his stills.
154 "I'd lived in the . . ." [until] "For years . . .": Jim Quillen interview, Jan. 1990.
154 An Army fort dating . . . [until] And while most men saw . . .: Alcatraz Post Records.
155 Eight years after Alcatraz opened . . . [until] "He is well nourished . . .": Stroud arrived Dec. 19, 1942, USP Alcatraz Psychiatric Summary, Jan. 7, 1943, Logan, p. 620.
155 Creases between his eyes . . .: Alcatraz arrival mug shot.
155 "Very, very pale . . .": Bergen, Dec. 1989.
155 Although at age fifty-two . . .: Alcatraz Commitment Record.
156 By then, Alcatraz . . . [until] In fact his name would be . . .: News clippings, 1934-63; Alcatraz Neuro-Psychiatric Examination of Alphonse Capone; Karpis, *On The Rock*; Warden James A. Johnston, *Alcatraz Island Prison;* Roy Gardner, *Hellcatraz*; Gentry, *J. Edgar Hoover*; BOP statistics on prisoners; *Alcatraz Rules and Regulations.* Fifteen-hundred-and- seventy-six numbers were issued on Alcatraz, but only 1545 men served time there (some returned and were given a second number; "Blackie" Audett served three times there and was given three separate numbers).
158 Stroud was quickly . . . [until] Although he . . .: Quillen, Carnes, Bergen, Dollison, Orr, Gregory, etc., and *Ibid.*
160 The warden was a tough . . . [until] Staff would number . . .: Johnston, *Alcatraz Island Prison*; Barbara Johnston Ford, Bergen, Quillen, San Francisco newspaper clippings, photographs,*Who's Who in America*, Vol. III 1951-1960.
161 "Damn near as many guards . . .": Henry Brown interview, 1980.
161 Johnston reconstructed . . .: Johnston, *Alcatraz Island Prison*; Bergen, 1993.
162 Johnston brought back . . .: Several other books, especially some written by former prisoners, exaggerate the number of years the silent system was in effect. Silence between prisoners as a rule was only in effect from 1934 until sometime in 1938, when it was no longer enforceable.
162 During one of these episodes . . .: Bergen, Barbara Johnston Ford interviews.
162 Phillips was worked over pretty good . . .: Dollison manuscript.
163 Stroud was racked into a cell . . .: BOP Stroud files.
164 His eyeglasses were confiscated . . .: *Ibid.*
165 But it could be worse . . . [until] By then, Stroud . . .: Dollison, Bergen, Quillen, Carnes, Brown, trial transcripts, prison reports, etc.
166 To some officers . . .: *Ibid.*
166 Indeed, in his book . . .: Bennett, *I Chose Prison.*
166 Stroud bitterly believed . . .: *Robert Stroud v. Edwin B. Swope.*
166 Within six months he had filed . . .: *Robert Stroud v. James A. Johnston.*
166 Although Alcatraz associate . . .: Prison report, March 17, 1944, BOP Stroud files.
166 *Stroud v. Johnston* stated that . . .: Transcript of Record, *Stroud v. Johnston.*
166 He later wrote to his brother . . .: Stroud letter to Marcus, Oct. 11, 1947, exact file unknown.
166 In *Stroud v. Johnston* . . . : Petition for Writ of Habeas Corpus, *Stroud v. Johnston.*
167 He further argued . . . [until] In Dec. 1943 . . .: Transcript, *Stroud v. Johnston.*
168 He worked when others slept . . .: Bergen and others interviews.
168 "I've heard guys argue for one week . . .": Clarence Carnes interviews, 1979.
168 Listening to cons discuss . . .: Petitioner's Reply to Respondent's Suggestions . . .,"

Stroud v. Mayden and Nicholas.

168 A month after he arrived on Alcatraz . . .: Stroud, "I Wonder," *American Canary Magazine*, Jan. 1943, pp. 18-19.

168 "Many years before . . ." [until] On the same page . . .: *Ibid.*

169 Marcus had by now changed . . .: Letterhead, BOP Stroud files; Advertisements, *American Canary Magazine*, Oct. 1943, p. 21.

169 After the early 1920s . . .: BOP Stroud files.

169 It appeared in a later . . .: Stroud to Furman, Oct. 2, 1958, Gaddis Collection.

169 Yet Stroud was critical . . .: Bergen, George De Vincenzi, Yates interviews.

169 In a variation on . . .: Stroud letter to Daw, May 11, 1959, Gaddis Collection.

169 Two more articles . . .: Bertha Marie Hayden, "I Wonder Too," *American Canary Magazine*, Feb. 1943, pp. 20-21; Frank Lipp, "Don't We 'All Wonder Too' ?" *American Canary Magazine*, April 1943, p. 14.

170 "The sooner the money . . .": Ad, "Stroud's Digest On The Diseases of Birds Will Soon Be Ready For Delivery," *American Canary Magazine*, April 1943, p. 14.

170 An announcement . . .: L. G. Marcus, "We Apologize," *American Canary Magazine*, June 1943, p. 17.

170 In September, an ad guaranteed . . .: Ad, "Stroud's Digest," *American Canary Magazine*, Sept. 1943, p. 34.

170 In October, the ad . . .: Ad, "Stroud's Digest," *American Canary Magazine*, Oct. 1943, p. 21.

170 In a March 1944 memo . . . [until] Stroud was still proving . . .: Prison report, March 17, 1944, BOP Stroud files.

170 A favorable article on him . . .: Corey, "He Took the Bars Off Prisons," *Nation's Business*, July 1944, pp. 60-65.

171 In years to come he would show . . .: "Bennett sometimes displays this weapon to visitors in his office," O'Neil, "Prodigious Intellect in Solitary," *Life* , April 1960.

171 The *Kansas City Star* called . . .: "Prison Bird Man Publishes Story," *Kansas City Star*, Feb. 5, 1944.

171 "To all of my friends," . . . [until] "I have no desire to name . . .": Stroud, "Dedication," as it appeared in the first edition of *Stroud's Digest on the Diseases of Canaries,* (Webb Pub., 1944), provided by Anne Diestel, BOP Archivist, Wash., D.C.; Furman, 1990-92; L.G. Marcus, wrote to Johnston in Feb. 1944 that he had "finally prevailed on [Stroud] to allow me to eliminate the dedication page which I have always believed to be in bad taste," BOP Stroud files.

172 Despite the dedication . . .: *Biological Abstracts*, 1944, p. 991, Citation 9003.

172 More than a decade . . .: C. L. Strong, "The Strange Story of Robert Stroud . . .," *Scientific American*, Dec. 1957.

173 In fact, some of his descriptions . . .: Speer, 1990-93.

173 In his glossary . . .: Stroud, *Digest*, p. 460.

173 They were concerned . . .: Drs. Speer and Schmidt.

174 The *Journal of Avian Diseases* . . .: *Journal of Avian Diseases*, American Association of Avian Pathologists, Vol 1, College Station, Texas, 1957.

174 In fact, veterinarians . . .: J.R. Brownell, MS., D.V.M., *The Diagnosis and Treatment of Cage Bird Diseases in the Veterinary Practice.*.

174 Veterinarians who specialized . . .: Assn. of Avian Veterinarians History, Linda R. Harrison, editor, *J. of Assn. of Avian Veterinarians,* Lake Worth, Florida.

175 Robert Stroud went to his death . . .: Stroud frequently referred to himself as the "most unusual researcher the world has produced since Louis Pasteur" and it appeared in ads, *American Canary Magazine*, January 1943, p. 19.

175 And specialists today . . .: Drs. Speer, Schmidt, Harris interviews.

175 James M. Harris, D.V.M. is one . . .: Harris, 1990-93.

175 "He hit very clearly . . .": Speer, 1990-93.

176 Stroud was not an avian pathologist . . .: "Robert Stroud's Letter to Dennis Norton," four-page brochure, PA files.
176 Nonetheless, Stroud is still somewhat . . .: Harris, 1990-93.
176 Its publication coincided . . .: Many letters are contained in his files from people who referred to articles they had seen, or sent copies in with the letters.
177 Then a tiny pamphlet . . . [until] "This does not . . .": "The Life Story of Robert Stroud," National Bird Protective League, Minneapolis, Minn., circa 1945.
177 Stroud's book . . .: Letters, BOP Stroud files.
177 Jim Quillen met Stroud . . . [until] It didn't take . . .: Quillen interview, Aug. 1992.
179 Besides Stroud, Franklin . . . [until] Altogether . . .: Dollison notes, De Nevi, *Alcatraz '46*, Johnston, *Alcatraz Island Prison,* etc.
179 "Stroud was great at . . .": Bergen, Dec. 1989 and Feb. 1990.
180 An angry MTA . . . [until] Broken pieces of . . .: Quillen, Aug. 1992; BOP Stroud files.
180 "When they're making noise . . .": Bill Long interviews, 1979-81.
182 "The ones that do . . .": Brown, 1980.
182 Following the noon meal . . . [until Although it can be assumed . . .: Interviews with Carnes, Bergen, Quillen, Lieutenant Isaac Faulk, Dean Burch, former officers Fred Mahan, Marvin Orr, Irving Levinson, Barbara Johnston Ford; Johnston, *Alcatraz Island Prison*; Audett, *Rap Sheet*; Howard, *Six Against the Rock*; Karpis, *On The Rock*; De Nevi, *Alcatraz '46;* newspaper accounts; court records, *U.S. v. Shockley, Carnes and Thompson.*

Part VII - Broken Promises

191 On November 2, 1948 . . . [until] It was almost . . .: *Ibid.*
191 As a teenager Carnes . . . [until] In 1988 he stole . . .: Carnes biographical information from personal contact over a ten year period from 1978-88; death information from his former parole officer, Joseph Brandenberg, Kansas City, Missouri.
192 Stroud conceived it . . .: *Robert Stroud v. Edwin B. Swope.*
192 He felt that anyone first entering prison . . .: Stroud, "Looking Outward."
192 Stroud felt that . . . : Stroud to Furman, Oct. 2, 1958, Gaddis Collection.
192 He later wrote that . . . [until] He determined that . . .: Stroud letter to Furman, Oct. 2, 1958. *Ibid.*
192 Carnes knew about . . . [until] "He smacked him . . .": Carnes, 1978-82.
193 In his book, *On the Rock* . . .: Karpis, *On The Rock*, p. 267.
194 "He considers himself to be . . .": Special Progress Report, USP Alcatraz Island, Oct. 24, 1947, Logan, p. 621.
194 In July 1948, he told the Alcatraz . . .: Special Progress Report, USP Alcatraz Island, July 16, 1948, *Ibid.*, p. 622.
194 "Next time you glance casually . . .: Caen, "It's News to Me," *San Francisco Chronicle*, December 1947.
195 In January, he was cited . . . [until] Stroud was also written . . .: Special Progress Report, USP Alcatraz Island, July 16, 1948, Logan, p. 622.
195 "Frankie Perkins, age nine, stirred . . .": Stroud, "Frankie," date unknown, pornographic story submitted to court, *Stroud v. Mayden and Nicholas.*
195 "I read it . . .": Carnes, 1978-82.
195 "I got to know Stroud. . ." [until] " 'Oh Listen, don't . . .' ": Yates, Jan. 1990.
196 Given Stroud's two write-ups in 1947 . . .: Special Progress Report, USP Alcatraz Island, Oct. 24, 1947, Logan, p. 621.
196 In 1948 Warden Johnston retired . . . [until] It allegedly had. . .: Interviews with Bergen, Dollison, Carnes, De Vincenzi, George Gregory, Levinson, Mahan, Mawbreys, Orr, Quillen, Sobell, Roberts, Yates; *New York Times* Obituary, Dec. 26,

1955.
197   When Dollison arrived . . .: Dollison interivews.
197   By July 1948, Marcus wrote saying . . .: Marcus letter to Stroud, July 29, 1948, *Stroud
        v. Swope*; Bennett return letter to Marcus, September 14, 1948, BOP Stroud files.
197   "He used to pose as good . . ." [until] "And Stroud never . . .": Bergen, Dec. 1989.
197   In fact Swope had to contend . . . [until] "The bird arrived and . . .": I grew up hearing
        this famous anecdote and it was very satisfying to discover that it had actually
        happened; the first person to remind me of it was former Alcatraz prisoner Ben
        Rayborn in *Forum, California Attorneys for Criminal Justice* (Nov./Dec. 1978); Jean
        Long, Alcatraz island postmistress and wife of former Officer William Long,
        remembered getting the package and talking to Warden Swope about it; Minnie T.
        King letter to Swope, Feb. 18,1949 and Swope letter to Director Bennett Feb. 23,
        1949, BOP Stroud files; "Canary Expert Only Sees Gulls Over Alcatraz," *New York
        Herald Tribune*, March 20, 1949.
198   A Los Angeles bird . . .: Richard K. Polimer interview, July 1991.
198   On August 23, 1948 Stroud returned . . . [until] He told Marcus . . .: Stroud letter to
        Marcus, Aug. 23, 1948, *Stroud v. Swope*.
199   The same day, August 23 . . . [until] Then he told her . . .: Stroud letter to Mamie, Aug.
        23, 1948, BOP Stroud files.
199   Swope had the letters . . .: *Stroud v. Swope*.
199   The next day, August 24, 1948 . . .: BOP Summary Statement, July 10, 1958, PA files.
        Strike began Aug. 24 and ended when Stroud went to the hospital on Aug. 31, 1948.
200   Relations between . . .: Arthur M. Dollison manuscript.
200   Stroud wrote about the fracas . . .: Stroud letter to U.S. Attorney Frank J. Hennessy,
        Aug. 25, 1948, *Stroud v. Swope*.
200   As a result, on August 31, 1948 . . .: BOP Summary Statement, July 10, 1958, PA files.
200   "We passed word through . . .": Stucker, 1980; BOP Summary Statement, *Ibid*.
200   Normally, only a doctor could . . .: Bergen, 1989-90.
200   While it was written . . .: Prison Reports, 1948, '49, '52, Logan, p. 622-25.
200   In 1950, the associate warden . . .: Special Progress Report, 1950, *Ibid*., p. 624.
201   He wrote later . . .: Bennett, *Federal Prison Service Newsletter*, Director's Page,
        April 1960.
201   A confidential memo . . .: Swope memo to Madigan, Dec. 9, 1948, BOP Stroud files.
201   In fact, during sick call . . .: Bergen, Yates, De Vincenzi, John McGoran, Landers,
        Levinson, etc.
202   Over the years he read . . .: Stroud letter to Daw, June 2, 1954, Gaddis Collection.
202   In one incident . . .: Stroud disciplinary report, June 19, 1951, BOP Stroud files.
202   "They catered to him a little . . .": Yates, Jan. 1990.
202   "Now you could make . . ." [until] "And Stroud could be very . . .": Quillen, Jan. 1990.
203   The Hispanic man was . . .: De Vincenzi, 1990-91.
203   The Japanese, known as "Meatball" . . .: Dollison, De Vincenzi, Gregory, Bergen,
        etc.; Commitments to the USP at Alcatraz, California.
203   Many officers . . . [until] Many were local . . .: Dollison interviews.
203   "They took all these precautions . . .": De Vincenzi, 1990-91.
204   "We used to give him a bath . . .": *Ibid*.
204   "I had to have three. . . ":Vernon A. Sendek interview, 1992.This was done with the
        approval of authorities; Captain Phil Bergen memo to Cell house Lieutenant, Dec. 22,
        1952, BOP Stroud files WDC.
204   "Stroud would shave his face first . . ." [until] "Ritual . . .": De Vincenzi, 1990-91.
204   "He read some place . . .": Bill Rogers interviews, 1978-79.
204   Officers would see him . . .: Yates, 1990-92.
205   "Every Friday we had chowder . . .": Sendek, 1992.
205   "Talk? On yes, incessantly . . .": *Ibid*.

205 "He *did* talk . . .": De Vincenzi, 1990-91.
205 "He talked your ear off . . .": Rogers, 1978-79.
205 "The wind would . . ." [until] "He loved . . .": Jimmy Dukes interview, Dec. 1990.
205 "I thought he was kind of a nut . . .": Sendek, 1992.
205 "Friendly? . . ." [until] "Bright as a penny . . .": Yates, 1990.
206 "I thought he was . . .": George Gregory, July 1982.
206 "Extremely egotistical . . .": Rogers, 1978-79.
206 "I played checkers with him . . .": De Vincenzi, 1990-91.
206 "He was a big talker . . .": Furman, 1990-92.
206 Stroud grew particularly . . . [until] "'I was just. . .'": De Vincenzi, 1990-91.
207 Every man had read . . .: Bergen, 1989-93.
207 "He may [have] gotten along good . . .": Yates, 1990.
207 "I *never* lost the feeling . . .": Bergen, 1989-93.
207 "There were others . . .": John McGoran interview, Aug. 1992.
207 "He was bitter! . . .": Furman, 1990-92.
208 "Now Marc," he wrote in one letter. . .: Stroud letter to Marcus, date unknown, Petitioner's Exhibit B, *Stroud v. Swope.*
208 In one passage he wrote . . .: *Ibid.* p. 13.
208 "Marc's only trouble is mental laziness . . .": Stroud to Daw, Oct. 29, 1954, Gaddis Collection.
208 "Marc comes up with the usual lying . . .": Stroud to Daw, Aug. 13, 1954, *Ibid.*
209 "Stroud announced that if he ever did . . .": Rogers, 1978-79.
209 Stroud made incredible demands . . . [until] "This is very big . . .": Stroud letter to Marcus, July 1, 1951, BOP Stroud files.
210 He was losing patience . . .: Marcus letter to Stroud, Aug. 4, 1951, Ib*id.*
210 By this time Marcus was living . . .: *Ibid.*
210 "I had to take [Stroud] down . . ." [until] "And he said . . .": Yates, Feb. 14, 1990, BOP Stroud files. Files confirm that in 1951 an extra officer was stationed nearby during his visits "due to Stroud's violent outbreaks in the past few days."
210 Polimer had subsequently . . .: Polimer letter, Nov. 27, 1992.
211 Now it appeared . . .: Petition for an Injunction, *Stroud v. Swope.*
211 "Dear Mr. Leslie . . ." [until] "Even so, it appears . . .": Stroud letter to Jacques Leslie, Jan. 14, 1950, Exhibit A, *Ibid.*
214 "I received a call . . ." [until] He became . . .: Polimer, Aug. 19, 1991.
214 He did, however, agree . . .: *Marcus, Stroud vs. T.E. Gaddis.*
214 At the same time . . . [until] Agreeing with the lower court . . .: *Stroud v. Swope.*
215 He was thinning dramatically . . .: Associate Warden's Record Card with photograph from 1952, BOP Stroud files.
216 His correspondence . . .: Special Progress Report, March 21, 1952, Logan, p. 625.
216 In fact between February 1950 . . .: *Ibid.*
216 "He got moody . . .": De Vincenzi, 1990-91.
216 Stroud blamed his brother . . .: Special Progress Report, March 21, 1952, Logan, p. 625.
216 He felt, as he told De Vincenzi . . .: De Vincenzi, 1990-91.
216 On November 15 . . . [until] They were addressed . . .: Special Progress Report, March 21, 1952, Logan, p. 626.
216 Prison scuttlebutt . . .: This story was well known by everyone on Alcatraz. Confirmed also by Swope's letter to Bennett, Jan. 15, 1952, BOP Stroud files.
217 "Now communication has always been . . .": Stroud, "Looking Outward."
217 According to Swope . . .: Swope letter to Bennett, Jan. 15, 1952, BOP Stroud files.
217 When Stroud regained consciousness . . .: Special Progress Report, March 21, 1952, Logan, p. 626.
217 According to De Vincenzi . . .: De Vincenzi, 1990-91.

217 He was bleeding . . . [until] According to the prison report . . .: Special Progress Report, March 21, 1952, Logan, p. 626.

218 Writing to Bennett . . .: Swope to Bennett, Jan. 15, 1952, BOP Stroud files.

218 He requested that Stroud . . . [until] Bennett declined . . .: Special Progress Report, March 21, 1952, Logan, p. 626.

218 That year Stroud refused to go before . . . [until] It was recommended . . .: *Ibid.*

218 In 1953 it was reported . . .: Special Progress Report, April 3, 1953, Logan, p. 627.

218 "Brother Stroud is certainly. .": Bennett letter to Swope, Feb. 25, 1953, original file unknown.

218 When they asked him . . .: Special Progess Report, April 3, 1953, Logan, p. 628.

218 In September 1953, he wrote . . . [until] Stroud offered to reveal . . .: Special Progress Report, May 28, 1954, Logan, p. 629.

219 Stroud again refused to go . . . [until] Recommendations: Continue . . .: Special Progress Report, April 3, 1953, Logan, p. 628.

219 Arthur M. Dollison stepped . . . [until] For Dollison it was the sheer. . .: Dollison, Bergen interviews, Dollison manuscript.

222 As early as 1949 . . .: *New York Herald Tribune*, March 20, 1949; many articles around the nation were cited in letters, PA files.

222 After hearing the story . . .: Phyllis E. Gaddis, Summer 1992; Phyllis E. Gaddis, Epilogue, *Birdman of Alcatraz* (Comstock), p. 253.

222 In 1952, he requested permission . . .: Gaddis letter to Swope, June 9, 1952; return letter from Swope, BOP Stroud files.

222 Gaddis grew suspicious . . .: Phyllis E. Gaddis, 1992; Furman 1990-92.

223 "Alaska's gold rush spawned . . . [until] "It is still necessary . . .": "U.S. Penitentiary, Alcatraz Island, California," published after 1958 and "Alcatraz," published after 1960 (when Stroud had already departed for Springfield), BOP, Department of Justice.

223 He published his first . . . [until] "In a roaring frontier . . .": T.E. Gaddis, "The Birdman of Alcatraz," *Cosmopolitan*, May 1953.

224 But in fact, Gaddis . . .: T.E. Gaddis, "Evolution of a Personality . . .," p. 17.

224 In April 1953, Gaddis signed a contract . . . [until] He also agreed . . .: *Marcus, Stroud vs. T.E. Gaddis*, contract marked "Exhibit A."

225 By 1954, however, Gaddis . . .: Stroud letters to Daw, 1954, Gaddis Collection.

225 According to Stroud's recitation . . .: *Ibid.*.

225 In an April 13, 1954 letter . . .: Stroud letter to Daw, April 13, 1954, *Ibid.*

225 "I could have written. . .": Stroud to Daw, Feb. 23, 1954, *Ibid.* It's often assumed that Stroud could speak three or four languages. It's not known how well he knew French, Italian and Spanish, and possibly even Latin, but in letters he wrote about books he read in French, often relating the plots. He admitted that his knowledge of Italian, Spanish and Latin was not as good as French. His verbal skills in any language were probably lacking because he rarely had a chance to converse.

225 Stroud was also focused . . .: Stroud to Daw, June 2, 1954, Gaddis Collection.

225 According to the Stroud brothers . . .: Stroud letters to Daw, *Ibid.*

225 He instructed Daw. . . [until] "As ever, Bob . . .": Stroud letters to Daw, Aug. 13, 1954; Sept. 16, 1954, *Ibid.*

226 By October Stroud was . . .: Stroud letter to Daw, Oct. 3, 1954, *Ibid.*

226 "Roosevelt committed . . .": Stroud to Daw, Oct. 29, 1954, *Ibid.*

226 Gaddis was also concerned about . . .: Furman, July 20, 1990.

226 A bantam-weight, understated, quietly–teasing . . .: *Ibid.*

226 Although it was Furman's . . .: Furman, 1990; *Marcus, Stroud v. T.E. Gaddis.*

227 Furman advised Gaddis. . .: Furman, *Ibid.*

227 After years of toiling in a makeshift . . .: Phyllis E. Gaddis, Summer 1992.

227 This is where many of the myths . . .: T.E. Gaddis, *Birdman of Alcatraz* (Comstock),

p. 8: "He was educated to the third grade . . .," p. 181: "that will give me cuts down to two micrones . . . ."

227 "A man of meticulous personal habits . . ." *Ibid.*, p. 90.

227 Gaddis alluded to . . .: *Ibid.*, p. 111.

227 The writer inserted . . .: *Ibid.*, "on a commuted . . .," p. 103; "It has long . . .," p. 106.

227 In his breathless, dramatic . . .: *Ibid.*, p. 193.

227 He wrote that "Stroud loved to open . . .": *Ibid.*, p. 105.

227 Yet he stripped Stroud and Della Jones . . .: *Ibid.*, p. 141.

228 "He had triumphed . . . [until] He had gone . . .": *Ibid.*, p. 186.

228 By 1955, when the book was published . . .: T.E. Gaddis,"Breeding Problems Deal Stroud a Hard Blow," *Detroit Free Press*, Feb. 5, 1956, serialization of the book.

228 Reviewers were quick to . . .: Croswell Bowen, *New York Times*, Oct. 2, 1955.

228 Translated into German, French. . .: T.E. Gaddis, Committee for Release of Robert F. Stroud, Bulletin #12, June 28, 1961.

229 An editorial in a 1956 issue . . .: Bertha Marie Hayden Boyd, "Canary Culture," *American Cage Bird Magazine*, pp. 29-30.

229 "His quarters must . . .": Special Progress Report, March 18, 1955 Logan, p. 630.

229 "He frequently attempts to prescribe . . .": *Ibid.*, pp. 631-2.

229 "This man still is as unrealistic . . ." [until] "The Committee recommended . . .": Special Progress Report, Jan. 15, 1957, Logan, p. 632a.

230 The island prison was . . .: Furman, 1990-91.

230 An unruffled, pipe-smoking . . . [until] "He was very protective . . .": Dollison, Bergen, Quillen, Furman; also Paul W. Keve, *The McNeil Century*; John D. McCallum, *Dave Beck*; BOP Stroud files.

231 "At first we were formal . . ." [until] "He told me . . .": Furman, July 20, 1990.

231 Gaddis later wrote . . : T.E. Gaddis, "The Evolution of a Personality . . ." Stroud asked Judge Becker to allow him to read the book, which was granted by the BOP.

232 "His conversation . . .": Furman, July 20, 1990.

232 Later a prison reported stated . . .: Annual Review, Jan. 30, 1959, Logan, p. 636.

232 The Stroud-Marcus suit against . . .: *Marcus, Stroud vs. T.E. Gaddis.*

232 He had asked Stroud to . . .: Furman, 1990-92; Furman letter to Att. Gen. William P. Rogers, July 23, 1958, *Stroud v. Mayden and Nicholas.*

232 Madigan wrote that . . .: *Ibid.*

233 According to one source . . .: Menninger letter to Babyak, June 21, 1978.

233 Much later, George . . .: George Reed, *Fear No Man.*

233 Dr. Charles E. Smith . . .: Cozart memo to Att. Gen. Rogers, Oct. 7, 1958, PA files.

233 Furman had gently cautioned him . . .: Furman, 1990-92. Prison reports indicate in the late 1950s that Stroud took this advise to heart.

233 "It will be much easier to sell my ideas . . .": Stroud letter to Furman, Oct. 2, 1958, Gaddis Collection.

233 In December 1957 . . .: C.L. Strong, "The Strange Story of Robert Stroud . . ." *Scientific American*, Dec. 1957.

233 Morton Sobell, about the only . . . [until] He considered this . . .: Sobell, Aug. 1991.

234 Four months later . . .: "Scholar on Alcatraz," *Newsweek*, April 7, 1958, pp. 27-28.

234 In June, *The New York* . . .: Muth, "The Caged Birdman of Alcatraz," *The New York Mirror Magazine*, June 8, 1958.

234 That same month . . . [until] "Efforts should be made . . .": "A Prisoner Buried Alive," *Los Angeles Mirror News*, June 28, 1958.

235 *Inside Detective* chimed in . . .: Coburn, "41 Years in Solitary," *Inside Detective*, 1958, PA files.

235 In Oct. '58 *Coronet* . . .: T.E. Gaddis, "The Agony of the Caged Birdman," *Coronet*, Oct. 1958.

235 By June 1958, Stanley . . .: Petition for Exec. Clem., June 27, 1958, PA files.

236 The petition carried with it . . .: *Ibid.*
236 A man wrote to the White . . .: Beardslee letter to Adams, Sept. 23, 1958, *Ibid.*
236 A woman, who read . . .: Roberts letter to Eisenhower, Sept. 19, 1958, *Ibid.*
236 In a hand-written note . . .: Hakala letter to Eisenhower, March 12, 1957, *Ibid.*
236 Another wrote . . .: Hongaard letter to Eisenhower, Jan. 27, 1959, *Ibid.*
236 "Dear Mr. President . . .": McKee letter to Eisenhower, March 28, 1959, *Ibid.*
236 One prominent letter came from . . . [until] Furman, in fact . . .: Raymond E. Baglin letter to Furman, March 3, 1958, *Ibid*; other letters, *Ibid.*
236 When U.S. Pardon Attorney . . .: Cozart letter to Furman, July 16, 1958, *Ibid.*; Furman's correspondence to Senator Long, *Stroud v. Mayden and Nicholas.*
237 In Stroud's case, Justice . . .: Cozart to Furman, Nov. 12, 1958; Furman reply Dec. 12, 1958; Cozart response, Dec. 15, 1958; *Stroud v. Mayden and Nicholas.*
237 Reed, a religious conservative . . .: Reed and Hunt, *Fear No Man.* No other reports like this were found in Stroud's file, however O'Neil had reported, "At Alcatraz he formed the habit of grasping his barred door while talking, and rocking himself endlessly back and forth like a bemused zoo chimp," although the source is not cited. O'Neil, "Prodigious Intellect in Solitary," *Life*, April 1960.
237 "[Their] record is . . .": Stroud, Petition for Exec. Clem., 1958, p. 5., PA files.
237 In a dissenting memo . . .: Cozart memo to Att. Gen. Rogers, Oct. 7, 1958, PA files.
238 In a later memo . . .: Cozart to Att. Gen. R. F. Kennedy, Aug. 16, 1961, PA files.
238 Reed Cozart is one of the men . . .": Stroud letter to Furman, Oct. 2, 1958, Gaddis Collection.
238 Dissenting recommendations . . .: PA files.
238 He concluded "I do not feel Stroud . . ." [until] "If he responds . . .": Madigan letter to Bennett, July 25, 1958, *Ibid.*
239 Bergen's letter . . . [until] Moreover . . .: Bergen to Cozart, July 18, 1958, *Ibid.*
239 Bennett thought . . . [until] He claimed . . .: Bennett to Cozart, Sept. 12, 1958, *Ibid.*
239 By 1957-58 Furman began visiting . . .: Furman, 1990-92.
239 According to a letter . . .: Furman to Special Council Kendall, Feb. 13, 1959; response to Furman March 9, 1959, *Stroud v. Mayden and Nicholas.*.
240 Stroud bragged that . . .: Special Progress Report, July 25, 1958, Logan, p. 634-5.
240 Benjamin Wolfman . . .: *Ibid.*, p. 635.
240 He informed one . . .: Special Progress Report, Jan. 31, 1958, *Ibid.*, p. 633a.
240 Furman thought that it . . . [until] "He told me if you want it . . .": Stroud to Furman, Feb. 26, 1959, Furman to Kendall, Aug. 13, 1959, *Stroud v. Mayden and Nicholas.*
241 Bennett turned them . . .: Swope to Bennett, Jan. 15, 1952, BOP Stroud files.
241 Cozart had written . . .: Cozart memo to Att. Gen. Rogers, Oct. 7, 1958, PA files.
241 Even as late as January 1959 . . .: Annual Review on Stroud, Jan. 30, 1959.
241 He told Madigan . . .: Stroud to Furman, Feb. 26, 1959, *Stroud v. Mayden and Nicholas.*
241 But just weeks . . .: Stroud letter to Furman, Feb. 5, 1959, Gaddis Collection.
242 Madigan told him . . .: Stroud to Furman Feb. 26, 1959, *Stroud v. Mayden and Nicholas.*
242 One of Stroud's last . . .: Annual Review, Jan. 30, 1959, Logan, p. 637.
242 Not surprisingly it was stated . . . [until] When interviewed . . .: *Ibid.*
242 "However," the January '59 report . . .: *Ibid.*

Part VIII - Marketing the Birdman

243 In February 1956 . . . [until] Three paragraphs later . . .: Bennett letter to Senator Paul H. Douglas, Feb. 7, 1956, Richard M. English; copy resides in PA files.
243 Bennett wrote that . . .: Bennett form letter, undated, PA files.
243 In 1959, while still . . .: Stroud, "Motion to Vacate Judgment and to Dismiss

Indictment," filed July 1, 1959, *U.S. v. Robert Stroud.*

243 This came about because . . .: *Green v. U.S.*

244 "Stroud asked me . . .": O'Neil, "Prodigious Intellect in Solitary," *Life*, April 1960.

244 Briefly, in the Green case . . . [until] In a dissenting opinion . . .: *Green v. U.S.*

244 In a later interview Furman agreed . . .: Furman, 1990-92.

244 Stroud decided that . . .: O'Neil, "Prodigious Intellect . . .," *Life*, April 1960.

244 Writing his petition from . . .[until] The petition was signed . . .: Stroud, "Motion to Vacate Judgment and to Dismiss Indictment," *U.S. v. Robert Stroud.*

245 Stroud had tried to negotiate . . . [until] Madigan had told him . . .: Madigan letter to Bennett, Feb. 26, 1959, BOP Stroud files, WDC, researched by Anne Diestel.

245 This petition may have stoked . . .: Petition signed June 24, 1959; Stroud transferred July 13, 1959; Special Progress Report, Feb. 10, 1960, Logan, p. 640.

245 Stroud became excited when he . . . [until] "He likes a good show . . .": Stroud letter to Furman, July 28, 1959, *U.S. v. Robert Stroud..*

245 In another letter . . .: Stroud to Daw, Aug. 5, 1959, Gaddis Collection.

245 During the case, attorney . . .: Leonard letter to Carl F. Zarter, Dec. 9, 1959, with copy to James V. Bennett, *Ibid.*

246 On December 16, 1959, Bennett . . . [until] He also stated that "we have not over the years . . .": Bennett letter to Leonard, Dec. 16, 1959, *Ibid.*

246 "That's odd," Bergen . . .: Bergen, July 19, 1991, in which he was asked: "Did you understand that Stroud was in solitary for life? " Answer: "It was generally understood by everyone that he was going to be *there* for the rest of his life."

247 Bennett ended his letter . . .: Bennett letter to Leonard, December 16, 1959. *U.S. v. Robert Stroud.*

247 On Jan. 14, 1960, Bennett again . . .: Bennett letter to Leonard, Jan. 14, 1960. *Ibid.*

247 In his opinion . . .: Judge Walter A. Huxman, "Opinion," *Ibid.*

248 He announced that he was . . .: Annual Review, Feb. 1960, Logan, p. 640.

248 They did appeal to a higher court . . .: U.S. Court of Appeals, Tenth Circuit, hearing Sept. term, 1960, *U.S. v. Robert Stroud*; Wilbur G. Leonard letter to the Solicitor General, Feb. 14, 1961, *Ibid.*

248 Stroud had arrived . . .: Special Progress Report, Feb. 10, 1960, Logan, p. 640.

248 He was still a heavy smoker . . .: Duhamel, Spivak, Stroud, "My 53 Years in Jail!" *Saga*, Sept. 1963.

249 Whether by default or design . . .: Interviews with Morton Sobell, Clarence Carnes, Bob Cron, Rex Plank, etc.

249 "Building 10 was really bad . . .": Anonymous,1991.

249 Indeed, another officer . . .: Anonymous.

249 He wrote to Fred Daw . . .: Stroud letter to Daw, July 23, 1959, Gaddis Collection.

249 Morton Sobell once said . . .: Sobell, Aug. 1991.

249 Stroud wrote to Furman three days . . . [until] "And I've already . . .": Stroud letter to Furman, July 18, 1960, BOP Stroud files.

250 The first year his prison report . . .: Annual Review, Feb. 1960, Logan, p. 640.

250 By the time Morton Sobell arrived . . .: Sobell, Aug. 1991.

250 One former Springfield prisoner . . .: Duhamel, Spivak, Stroud, "My 53 Years in Jail!" *Saga*, Sept. 1963.

250 Within days . . .: Psychological Examination, Aug. 19, 1959, Logan, p. 638-639a.

250 "First, I completed my . . .": Stroud letter to Furman, July 28, 1959, file unknown.

250 Indeed, he scored . . .: Psychological Exam, Aug.19, 1959, Logan, p. 638.

251 "I also took a four-hour personality . . .": Stroud to Furman, July 28, 1959, file unknown.

251 He scored "equally . . .": Psychiatric Exam, Aug. 18, 1959, Logan, p. 638.

251 In the Rorschach he showed . . .: *Ibid.*

251 "I am virtually sure that I have made . . .": Stroud letter to Furman July 28, 1959, file

unknown.

251   In another letter he revealed . . .: Stroud to Furman, July 18, 1959, BOP Stroud files.

251   The House-Tree-Person and the . . .: Psychiatric Exam, Aug. 18, 1959, Logan, p. 639.

251   He wrote to Furman . . . [until] A few paragraphs later . . .: Stroud to Furman, July 28, 1959, file unknown.

252   The MMPI further corroborated . . .: Psychiatric Exam, Aug. 18, 1959, Logan, p. 639.

252   In one letter . . .: Stroud to Daw, Aug. 5, 1959, Gaddis Collection.

252   Yearly evaluations . . .: Springfield Progress Reports, 1959-63, Logan, pp. 638-650.

253   The most significant act . . .: Special Progress Report, March 16, 1960, Logan, p. 643.

253   In 1961 he had one . . .: Special Progress Report, Feb. 3, 1963, Logan, p. 647.

253   "It used to make him . . .": Bob Cron interview, 1992.

253   "I found him delightful . . ." [until] As director of the Bureau . . .: Sobell, Aug. 1991.

253   Dollison, who said that . . .: Dollison interviews.

254   The two prisoners . . . [until] He remembered Stroud's . . .: Sobell, Aug. 1991.

254   Gaddis began sending out . . .: "Committee for Release of Robert F. Stroud," Bulletin #4, T.E. Gaddis, chairman, Furman, treasurer, PA files.

254   In his 1958 pocketbook edition . . .: T.E. Gaddis, *Birdman of Alcatraz* (Signet); Meyer Levin, *Compulsion*.

254   The comparison, written originally . . .: Stroud, Comparison with Nathan Leopold, date unknown, hand-written and typed versions, contained in PA files.

254   "Leopold became a valuable teacher . . .": T.E. Gaddis, *Birdman of Alcatraz* (Comstock), p. 249.

255   Many letters in Stroud's . . .: PA files.

255   About 1958, Cohn . . .: Art Cohn, "Free This Man!" exact date unknown, *Ibid.*

256   *Life* magazine . . .: O'Neil, "Prodigious Intellect in Solitary," *Life*, April 1960.

256   In July '61, radio announcer and columnist . . .: Paul Coates, "Time May Be Running Out for the Birdman of Alcatraz," July 4, 1961, newspapers unknown, PA files.

256   In August 1961 . . .: Editorial, "Bird Man Deserves Freedom," *Los Angeles Mirror*, Aug. 3, 1961.

256   "Dear President Kennedy," wrote . . .: Steele letter to President Kennedy, July 4, 1961, PA files.

257   "Dear President Kennedy," another . . .: Cameron letter to President Kennedy, Aug. 4, 1961, *Ibid.*

257   "Abolition of Alcatraz is not . . .": Hickman to Kennedy, July 24, 1962, *Ibid.*

257   By May 1, 1961, a man named Herbert . . .: Stroud return letter to Axelrod, May 7, 1961, *Stroud v. Mayden and Nicholas.*

257   Although he wanted . . .: Axelrod letter to Stroud, May 15, 1961, *Ibid.*

257   By return mail Stroud suggested . . .: Stroud letter to Axelrod, May 7, 1961, *Ibid.*

257   The same day he wrote to Frank . . . [until] "My present plans . . .": Stroud letter to Frank Dittrich, May 7, 1961, *Ibid.*

258   On May 24, he wrote Axelrod . . .: Stroud to Axelrod, May 24, 1961, *Ibid.*

258   The same day he wrote Dittrich . . .: Stroud letter to Dittrich May 24, 1961, *Ibid.*; Agreement between Marcus and Dittrich on May 12, 1950, *Ibid.* Stroud had apparently never seen the agreement Marcus made with Dittrich; although sale of the copyright amounted to $625, plates, outstanding books, packing boxes and other items Marcus sold him amounted to a total of $3,802. The agreement also gave Dittrich an option on any future pet books that Stroud might produce. When Dittrich supplied a copy of the agreement to Stroud, Stroud became livid, writing on May 24, 1961, that ". . . it verifies once again, that Marcus robbed me right and left while handling my affairs," then in a letter written the same day to Axelrod, he referred to Marcus as a "venile agent."

258   So confident, that on May . . .: Stroud letter to Furman, May 28, 1961, *Ibid.*

258   Bennett was notified . . .: Bennett memo to Dr. Settle, June 14, 1961, *Ibid.*

258   By September, however, it . . . [until] "I want to know the score . . .": Stroud letter
      to Dittrich, Sept. 17, 1961, *Ibid.*
258   Dittrich replied that . . .: Stroud letter to Axelrod Oct. 7, 1961, quoting Dittrich Oct.
      3 letter; *Ibid.*
259   That day Dittrich went . . .: Stroud, Oct. 7, *Ibid.*
259   Figuring that this was a . . .: *Stroud v. Mayden and Nicholas.*
259   The buzz around Hollywood . . .: T.E. Gaddis, Committee Bulletin #13, Nov. 10,
      1961, PA files.
259   Gaddis had already taken . . .: *Ibid.*
259   Phyllis E. Gaddis, then fifteen . . .: Phyllis E. Gaddis, Summer 1992.
259   Lancaster, Gaddis and Furman . . .: T.E. Gaddis, Committee Bulletin #14, June 10,
      1962, PA files.
259   In a Hearst headline service . . : Barbara Kober," 'Birdman' Flies Into Controversy,"
      Hearst Headline Service, *San Francisco Examiner*, prob. date April 27, 1962, *Ibid.*
259   A special viewing was held in Washington . . .: T.E. Gaddis, Committee Bulletin #14,
      June 10, 1962, *Ibid.*; Furman interview.
260   In an April 27, 1962 *Washington Daily News* article . . .: George Clifford, "Should
      the Birdman Be Uncaged?" *Washington Daily News*, April 27, 1962. *Ibid.*
260   He had already seen . . .: Stroud had written his Nathan Leopold-Robert Stroud
      comparison at least as early as 1958, because Gaddis quoted from it in his March 1958
      "Author's Note to the Signet Edition" (Comstock, 1989). In it, Stroud wrote of his
      early sexual experiences and his subsequent preference.
260   In his September 1962 Committee bulletin . . .: T.E. Gaddis, Committee Bulletin #15,
      Sept. 20, 1962, under the question "Is Stroud homosexual?" Gaddis wrote, "The
      Prison Bureau, in the effort to discredit the character of Stroud and the work of the
      Committee, has attacked this prisoner as 'homosexual.' They know that the Ameri-
      can public knows little about what happens in prison. The distortion of personality
      which decades of imprisonment puts upon men twists their impulses. There are few
      who have escaped. Stroud is no exception. . . "
260   And once Stroud was dead . . .: T.E. Gaddis, "The Evolution of a Personality . . ." in
      which he wrote, "He had learned the practice of pederasty, and may have had a
      number of such experiences."
260   One of Stroud's first letters . . .: Stroud letter to Furman, July 18, 1939, BOP Stroud
      files. Also quoted by George Clifford, "Should the Birdman Be Uncaged?" *Wash-
      ington Daily News*, April 27, 1962.
261   Tables were set up by Committee members . . .: Furman, July 20, 1990; T.E. Gaddis,
      Committee Bulletin #14 June 10, 1962, where he states "We are hoping to get some
      free literature about Robert Stroud into every theatre in the country which shows
      'Birdman of Alcatraz.'" In Bulletin #17 June 20, 1963, Gaddis wrote: "For instance,
      you may be able to get many, many signatures from people in the theatre lobbies, who
      have just seen the picture."
261   He was not motivated . . . [until] I just wanted . . .: Furman, Feb. 12, 1991.
261   In the midst . . . [until] "If you think Stroud . . .": Hazel Flynn, " 'Birdman' Is Odd
      Role for Lancaster," newspaper unknown, date unknown, PA files.
262   "Four decades in solitary, hungering year . . .: T.E. Gaddis, Committee Bulletin #9,
      date unknown, *Ibid.*
262   "A man of iron endurance whose deepest wish . . .": T.E. Gaddis, Committee Bulletin
      #11, Jan. 14, 1961, *Ibid.*
262   The Committee solicited funds . . .: T.E. Gaddis, Committee Bulletin #4, Sept. 26,
      1958, *Ibid.*
262   "If we all act . . .": T.E. Gaddis, Committee Bulletin #14, June 10, 1962, *Ibid.*
262   It's not clear what prompted . . .: Attorney General Robert Kennedy memo to U.S.
      Attorney F. Russell Millin, April 26, 1962, *Ibid.*; copy also contained in BOP Stroud

files; Associated Press, "Bobby Balks on Freeing Stroud," April 26, 1962.

262 A woman wrote . . .: Marshall letter to Robert F. Kennedy, May 12, 1962, PA files.

262 Another man wrote a three-page . . .: Whitnah to Robert F. Kennedy, April 27, 1962, *Ibid.*

263 Furman defended Gaddis as being . . .: Furman, Feb. 12, 1991.

263 She described an . . .: Phyllis E. Gaddis, Summer 1992.

263 Even though Gaddis . . .: T.E. Gaddis, Comm. Bull. #15, Sept. 20, 1962, PA files.

263 "The latest diatribe of . . .": Cozart memo to Executive Assistant to the Attorney General Andrew R. Oehmann, hand-written, exact date unknown, *Ibid.*

264 "Dear President Kennedy" wrote a woman . . .: Gordon letter to President Kennedy, Sept. 22, 1962, *Ibid.*

264 A man named Montgomery . . .: Montgomery to Kennedy, Dec. 1, 1962, *Ibid.*

264 A five-page, single-spaced typewritten . . .: McBean to Kennedy, Oct. 15, 1962, *Ibid.*

264 "Dear President Kennedy . . .": Knudsen to Kennedy, Nov. 25, 1962, *Ibid.*

264 At this time, Richard M. English. . . [until] "That ended that . . .": English, April 2, 1990; State Bar of California (John S. Malone) letter to Richard M. English, May 13, 1964 stating that there were insufficient facts to warrant disciplinary action in the matter of Mr. James V. Bennett, copy provided by English.

265 As if the movie had not been . . .: For a more complete retelling of the Morris-Anglin escape attempt, see Babyak, *Eyewitness on Alcatraz.*

266 Estimates in 1961 . . . [until] Almost two months later . . .: Dollison interviews.

266 In what Gaddis accurately portrayed . . .: T.E. Gaddis, Committee Bulletin #15, Sept. 20, 1962, PA files.

266 Eve Edstrom, a *Washington* . . .: Edstrom, "Birdman of Alcatraz," *Washington Post* series, July 1962.

266 The articles were reprinted . . .: The articles were led with a paragraph citing Senator Edward V. Long, chairman of the Senate Judiciary Subcommittee concerned with federal prisons, as the man who provided official records, court proceedings and other data for the article. *Senate Congressional Record*, July 25, 1962.

266 "Anyone with human perception . . .: Eigen letter to Cozart, Sept. 27, 1962, *Ibid.*

267 Also weighing in against the . . .: Remsberg, "The Phony Fairy Tale . . ." *True,* July 1963.

267 Remsberg fought to get . . .: Remsberg to Bennett, July 13, 1963, PA files.

267 Gaddis referred to these . . .: T.E. Gaddis letter to Committee members asking for donations to "lay this matter personally before the Attorney General." Date unknown but probably summer 1963, *Ibid.*

267 Since the Fall of '61 . . .: Narrative Summary, Nov. 21, 1963, Logan, p. 649.

267 He wrote Furman about one incident . . .: Stroud letter to Furman, Oct. 16, 1961, *Stroud v. Mayden and Nicholas.*

267 He "has a number of complaints . . .": Annual Review, Feb. 10, 1960, Logan, p. 641.

267 Said another report . . .": Annual Parole Review, Feb. 6, 1963, Logan, p. 648.

268 There was no evidence . . .: Duhamel, Spivak, Stroud, "My 53 Years in Jail!" *Saga*, Sept. 1963.

268 Another Springfield . . .: Narrative Summary, Nov. 21, 1963, Logan, p. 649.

268 "I really think that the trouble . . ." [until] "I've walked at least . . .": Stroud letter to Furman, Oct. 16, 1961, *Stroud v. Mayden and Nicholas.*

268 He worked in the inmate library . . .: Prison reports, Logan, pp. 638-650.

269 In December 1961, he . . .: Narrative Summary, Nov. 21, 1963, Logan, p. 649.

269 By October '62, when he wrote . . .: Stroud, Petition for Exec. Clem., Oct. 19, 1962, PA files.

269 His last months Stroud took up . . .: Springfield prison reports, Logan, pp. 638-650; Furman, 1990-92.

269 "He described his . . .": Special Progress Report, March 16, 1962, Logan, p. 642.

269 Stroud also blamed prison authorities . . .: *Ibid.*, p. 644.
269 "His judgment is poor . . .: March 16, 1962, *Ibid.*, p. 644.
269 In what was . . . [until "I have never served time . . .": "Robert Stroud's Letter to Dennis Norton," Committee for Release of Robert Stroud, pamphlet quoting Stroud letter to Dennis Norton, Jan. 24, 1963, with biographical information on Norton, Richard M. English; copy contained in PA files.
270 In December 1962, another escape . . .: For complete details of the Scott-Parker escape attempt on Dec. 16, 1962, see Babyak, *Eyewitness on Alcatraz.*
270 Four months later . . .: The last day prisoners resided on Alcatraz was March 21, 1963.
271 On Nov. 18, he . . .: Narrative Summary Nov. 21, 1963; Sobell, Aug. 10, 1991.
271 Perhaps anticipating that the end . . .: Tyler letter to Becker, December 28, 1963; Becker's reply, Becker files.
271 The next morning . . . [until] "And I said . . .": Sobell, Aug. 10, 1991.
272 "He made the most . . .": Sobell, Aug. 10, 1991.
272 Not long after that Reed . . .: Ceriani letter to Reed Cozart, Dec. 3, 1963, PA files.

Epilogue

272 Cousin Howard Faughn . . .: Faughn, December 1989.
273 Mamie, died at age . . .: Death Certificate, April 10, 1969, Illinois Vital Records.
273 Marcus died in Honolulu . . .: Death Certificate, April 19, 1976, Office of Health Status Monitoring, Honolulu, Hawaii; funeral announcement, April 24, 1976, *Honolulu Star Bulletin.*
274 In 1969, six years after . . .: Judge James C. Logan, "Analysis of a Murderer."
275 As early as 1948 . . .[until] Wright in 1965 . . .: Karpman, Wright, Fosch and Wortis cited in Logan, p. 97-98.
276 The current definition . . .: Logan, p. 90-91
276 Dennis Doren . . .: Dennis Doren, *Understanding and Treating the Psychopath.*
276 Lee N. Robins, Ph.D., who . . .: Lee N. Robins, Ph.D., *Deviant Children Grown Up.*
277 Psychoanalyst, Alice . . .: Alice Miller, *For Your Own Good, Hidden Cruelty in Child-Rearing and the Roots of Violence.*
278 The gravity of releasing . . .: See, for example, M.A. Farber, "The Detective and the Fugitive: How Jack Abbott was Found," *New York Times,* October 11, 1981; "Proteges in Prison," *Washington Post,* January 21, 1982; Jonathon Yardley, "Risking Society for Literature," *Washington Post,* January 25, 1982. Incidentally, almost the same thing happened to writer William Styron, whose incarcerated protege escaped from prison and kidnapped and raped a woman. More recently, in late 1993, Steve Kroft interviewed writer-prisoner Kody Scott (*a.k.a.* Sanyika Shakur) for CBS's "Sixty Minutes," who wrote *Monster: The Autobiography of an L.A. Gangmember* (Grove/Atlantic, 1993). Scott, interviewed in prison, admitted on televison that he had killed many times. The underlying dilemma being presented was: how can someone who admits his killings, blames it on society and defends his argument so eloquently *not* be rehabilitated.
278 Most psychiatrists, criminal psychologists . . .:See, for example, Dennis Doren, *Understanding and Treating the Psychopath*: "If the therapist's goals are to make the psychopath into an upstanding citizen who will care about others, feel what others feel and feel guilty when he hurts someone (i.e., to increase his superego functioning, to use psychoanalytic terminology), the therapy is doomed to failure. I have never seen it happen. Nor have I ever heard of it happening."

Bibliography

Books, Manuscripts, Dissertations, Pamphlets

Abbott, Jack Henry, *In The Belly of the Beast*, New York: Random House, 1981.

Asinof, Eliot, *1919, America's Loss of Innocence*, New York: Donald I. Fine, Inc., 1990.

Alcatraz Rules and Regulations, Washington, D.C.: Bureau of Prisons.

Audett, James "Blackie," *Rap Sheet*, New York: William Sloane and Co., 1954.

Babyak, Jolene, *Eyewitness on Alcatraz*, Berkeley, CA: Ariel Vamp Press, 1988.

Bennett, James V., *I Chose Prison*, New York: Knopf, 1970.

Denevi, Don, with Carnes, Clarence and Bergen, Philip R., *Alcatraz '46*, San Rafael, CA: Leswing Press, 1974.

Berkman, Alexander, *Prison Memoirs of an Anachist*, New York: Mother Earth Publishing Association, 1912.

Biological Abstracts, Philadelphia, PA: Biosciences Information Service, 1944.

Browne, Daniel Jay, *The American Bird Fancier, or How to Breed, Rear, and Care For Song and Domestic Birds with their Diseases and Remedies*, New York: C.M. Saxton, Barker, 1860.

Brownell, J.R., MS. D.V.M., *The Diagnosis and Treatment of Cage Bird Diseases in the Veterinary Practice*, Iowa: Iowa State University of Science and Technology, 1968.

Campbell, Bruce F., *Ancient Wisdom Revised. A History of the Theosphical Movement*, Berkeley, CA: University of California Press, 1980.

Coben, Stanley, *A. Mitchell Palmer: Politician*, New York: Columbia University Press, 1963.

Cope, Jack, *1300 Metropolitan Avenue*, Kansas: U.S.P. Leavenworth print shop, 1964.

Dollison, Arthur M., "Alcatraz," unpublished manuscript.

Doren, Dennis, *Understanding and Treating the Psychopath*, New York: Wiley, Interscience Publication, 1987.

Earley, Pete, *The Hot House, Life Inside Leavenworth Penitentiary*, New York: Bantam, 1992.

Frisch, Otto Von, *Canaries, a Complete Pet Owner's Manual*, Hauppauge, New York: Barron's Educational Series, 1991.

Gaddis, Thomas E., *Birdman of Alcatraz*, New York: Random House, 1955; Sausalito, CA: Comstock Editions, 1989.

————, *"The Evolution of a Personality Under Correctional Stress,"* Dissertation in partial fulfillment for a Doctor of Education, University of Oregon, 1964.

————, and Long, James O., *Killer: A Journal of Murder*, (Includes excerpts from Carl Panzram's autobiography), Mattituck, New York: Amereon House 1987.

Grosser, Philip, *Uncle Sam's Devil's Island, Experiences of a Conscientious Objector in America During the World War*, self-published, 1933

Hall, Jesse A., and Hand, Leroy T., *History of Leavenworth, Kansas*, Topeka, KS: Historical Publishing Co., 1921.

Holden, George Henry, *Canaries and Cage Birds*, New York: G.H. Holden, 1888.

Howard, Clark, *Six Against the Rock*, New York: Dial Press, 1977.

Jennings, Al, and Irwin, Will, *Beating Back*, New York: D. Appleton and Co., 1914.

Jentry, Curt, *J. Edgar Hoover, The Man and the Secrets*, New York: W.W. Norton, 1991.

Johnston, James A., *Alcatraz Island Prison*, New York: Charles Scribner's Sons, 1949.

Karpis, Alvin, as told to Livesey, Robert, *On The Rock*, Beauford, S.C.: Beauford Books, Inc, 1980.

Keve, Paul W., *The McNeil Century, The Life and Times of an Island Prison*, Chicago, IL.: Nelson-Hall 1984.

Levin, Meyer, *Compulsion*, New York: Simon and Schuster, 1956.

Logan, Judge James C., *"Analysis of a Murderer,"* Dissertation in partial fulfillment for Doctor of Philosophy, Lawrence, KS: University of Kansas, 1969.

Mailer, Norman, *The Executioner's Song*, Boston: Little, Brown, 1979.

McCallum, John D., *Dave Beck*, Mercer Island, Washington: Writing Works, 1978.

The Merck Index, An Encyclopdia of Chemicals, Drugs and Biologicals, Rayway, N.J.: Merck and Co., Inc., 1989.

Miller, Alice, *For Your Own Good, Hidden Cruelty in Child-Rearing and the Roots of Violence*, Translated by Hildegarde and Hunter Hannum, New York: Farrar, Straus, Giroux, 1983.

Powers, Richard Gid, *Secrecy and Power, The Life of J. Edgar Hoover*, New York: The Free Press, 1987.

Quillen, James, *Alcatraz Inside*, San Francisco, CA: Golden Gate National Park Association, 1991.

Reed, George, with Hunt, Dave, *Fear No Man*, Eugene, OR: Harvest House, 1987.

Robins, Lee N., Ph.D., *Deviant Children Grown Up, A Sociological and Psychiatric Study of Socipathic Personality*, Baltimore, MD: Williams and Wilkins Co., 1966.

Rules and Regulations, USP McNeil Island, Washington, 1911.

Smith, George Washington, *History of Southern Illinois*, Chicago, IL.: Lewis Publishing Co., 1912.

Stroud, Robert F., *Diseases of Canaries*, Kansas City, MO: Canary Publishers, 1933.

——————, *"Looking Outward, An Historical and Analytic Study of the Federal Penal System from the Inside,"* unpublished manuscript quoted by permission of Charles Dudley Martin, Administrator W.W.A. of the Robert F. Stroud estate.

——————, *Stroud's Digest on the Diseases of Birds*, St. Paul, Minn.: Webb Publishing Co., 1944; Neptune City, N.J.: T. F. H. Publications, 1964.

Tannenbaum, Frank, *Wall Shadows, A Study in American Prisons*, New York: G.P. Putnam's Sons, 1922.

Ward, A.R., and Gallagher, B.A., D.V.M., *Diseases of Domesticated Birds*, New York: MacMillan Co., 1920.

Wolman, Benjamin B., *The Sociopathic Personality*, New York: Brunner/Mazel, 1987.

Wood, Mary, *Canary Birds, A Manual of Useful and Practical Information*, William Wood and Co., 1869.

Court Records

Jane E. Shaffer v. Henry C. Shaffer, for April term of Massac Circuit Court, Massoc County, IL., 1885.

Elizabeth J. Stroud v. B.F. Stroud, April 1907, Superior Court, King County, Wash.

B. F. Stroud v. Elizabeth J. Stroud, Oct. 28, 1909, Superior Court, King County, Wash.

Criminal Case #4287, *U.S. v. Robert Stroud*. Criminal Case Files 1861-1959, U.S. Dist. Court for the Dist. of Kansas, First Division, Topeka, Kansas. RG 21, Records of the Dist. Courts of the United States, National Archives and Records Administration, National Archives-Central Plans Region. *See also* Precedent Case Files 1917–1975. U.S. Attorney for the Dist. of Kansas. RG 118, Records of the U.S. Attorneys and

Marshalls, NARA, NA-CPR; *See also* "Motion to Vacate Judgement and to Dismiss Indictment," filed July 1, 1959.

Case #10527, *Robert Stroud v. James A. Johnston*, Records of the U.S. Courts of Appeals for the Ninth Circuit. RG 276, National Archives and Records Administration, National Archives-Pacific Sierra Region.

Case #12595, *Robert Stroud v. Edwin B. Swope*, Records of the U.S. Courts of Appeals for the Ninth Circuit. RG 276, NARA, NA–PSR.

Case #30316-G, *U.S. v. Shockley, Carnes and Thompson*, U.S. Dist. Court for Northern California, Criminal Case files. RG 21, National Archives and Records Administration, National Archives-Pacific Sierra Region.

Civil Case #13564, *Stroud v. J.A. Mayden and R.S. Nicholas*. Civil Case Files 1938-1972, U.S. Dist. Court, Western Dist. of Missouri, Western Division. RG 21, Records of the Dist. Courts of the United States, National Archives and Records Administration, National Archives-Central Plains Region.

L.G. Marcus, Robt. F. Stroud v. Thomas E. Gaddis, Complaint No. 656586, filed Feb. 28, 1956, California Superior Court, Los Angeles.

Green v. U.S., 78S, Ct. 221, Decided December 16, 1957, West, Vol. 78, p. 221.

Administrative and Archival Files

Administrative Files of Chief Judge William H. Becker, 1961-1976, RG 21, U.S. Dist. Court, Western Dist. of Missouri. National Archives and Records Administration, National Archives-Central Plains Region. *(Becker files)*

Records of the Office of the Pardon Attorney, RG 204, National Archives and Records Administration, NA–WDC. *(PA files)*

U.S. Dist. Court Judge William H. Becker, an oral history interview conducted by Fredrick M. Spletstoser, April-July 1989. Archives of the U. S. Dist. Court for the Western Dist. of Missouri. *(Becker Oral History)*

Collection #HDC-553, Robert F. Stroud file, U. S. Department of Justice, Federal Bureau of Prisons, Golden Gate National Recreation Area, Historic Documents Department, San Francisco Maritime National Historical Park; Record file at the Bureau of Prisons, Washington, D.C. *(BOP Stroud files)*

Executive Clemency application to Woodrow Wilson by Elizabeth J. Stroud, #5164 R. F. Stroud, Presidential Papers of Woodrow Wilson. *(Wilson papers)*

Robert Stroud, Case File No. 606-B, U.S. District Court, Series 112, Case Files, Box 5235. RG 506, Alaska Archives and Records Center, Juneau, Alaska. *(Stroud Case file)*

Department of Justice files #145161 Box 552. National Archives and Records Administration, National Archives-Washington, D.C. *(DOJ files)*

U.S. Penitentiary Clippings, Vol. 1, 1899-1963, Kansas State Historical Society, Topeka, Kansas. *(USP Clippings)*

Index to Memorandums, Circulars, Bulletins, and Manual Bulletins, National Archives and Records Administration, National Archives, Washington, D.C. *(Index to Memorandums)*

Thomas E. Gaddis Collection, Special Collections, Boston University. *(Gaddis Collection)*

Medical and Post Records, Alcatraz 1860-1933, National Archives and Records Administration, National Archives, Washington, D.C. *(Med. & Post Rec.)*

Acknowledgments

Few long-term projects are completed without assistance from professionals, friends and strangers who help in the research, listen to ideas and suggest options that are often hidden.

First, I wish to thank Charles Dudley Martin of Springfield, Missouri, who, as the Administrator With Will Attached of the estate of Robert F. Stroud, allowed me to view and quote from Stroud's prison manuscript, "Looking Outward." This offered an unparalleled view into Stroud's early prison years as well as his psyche. Judge James C. Logan also permitted quotes from his dissertation on Stroud's life and writings, "Analysis of a Murderer." Most importantly, Judge Logan included Stroud's prison records which presented another window on the prisoner's behavior as well as attitudes of those who wrote up the reports.

Without the assistance of these two men—both of whom spent time and money to obtain private and public documents—my task would have been much more difficult.

Paul Fellows, a writer and researcher in Metropolis, Illinois, generously helped with research at the Massoc County Historical Library. Several family members granted interviews, their curiosity and their innate appreciation of history at times at odds with the embarrassment of dredging up unpleasant family history, and I wish to thank them. Among them are the late Virginia Trousdale, cousin to Robert Stroud, Hazel Larson, a relative by marriage and Harold Faughn, a cousin.

John Reichert, who alerted me to the Woodrow Wilson papers; Allen Jensen, formerly an National Park Ranger on Alcatraz who filed a Freedom of Information Act request; John Roberts, Chief Archivist at the Federal Bureau of Prisons, Washington, D.C.; Anne Diestel, a former National Park Ranger on Alcatraz and now a BOP archivist; Erica Toland, Assistant Archivist at the San Francisco Maritime National Historical Park; and Stephen Haller, Park Historian of the Golden Gate National Recreation Area, all helped with Stroud prison records.

Others who were an enormous help include: Mark Corristan at the National Archives–Central Plains Region; Bobbie Prey, Managing Editor of the Kansas State Historical Society in Topeka, Kansas; Waverly Lowell, Director of the National Archives-Pacific Sierra Region; Dean K. Dawson, Reference Associate at the Alaska Archives and Records Center in Juneau; and Dr. Angel Kwolek-Folland, professor of history at the University of Kansas in Lawrence, Kansas.

Many people aided me in gaining an understanding of veterinary medicine in the 1920s, '30s and '40s, among them Peter Berg, Chief of Special Collections at Michigan State University; Drs. James M. Harris, D.V.M.; Robert Schmidt, D.V.M., Ph.D.; Brian Speer, D.V.M.; Richard B. Davis, D.V.M., M.S.; Linda R. Harrison, editor of the *Journal of the Association of Avian Veterinarians*; and Dr. Julius Schachter, Ph.D., professor of Epidemiology, University of California—San Francisco, and director of the Chlamydia Research Lab at San Francisco General Hospital.

Also invaluable were Phillip R. Bergen, Al Bloomquist, Henry Floyd Brown, John Brunner, the late Clarence Carnes, Bob Cron, George De Vincenzi, Jimmy Dukes, Isaak Faulk, Phyllis E. Gaddis, George Gregory, Al Kaeppel, Joseph Landers, Irving Levinson, William and Jean Long, Fred Mahan, Pat Mahoney, John McGoren, the late Marvin Orr, Rex Plank, Jim Quillen, Richard K. Polimer, Benjamin "Benny Denny" Rayburn, the late William "Bill" Rogers, Pat Bergen Rothschild, Vernon A. Sendek, Morton Sobell, the late Nova Stucker, Jan Moore Tarantino, Richard Waszak and Ernie Yates. Don Bowden was especially kind to lend me his photograph.

Reference librarians at the Berkeley Public Library; the San Francisco Public Library and the University of California Main, Law, Bio–Sciences, Social Science and Government Documents libraries were always helpful.

I'd like to thank the staff of the Golden Gate National Park Association for their on–going support, as well as Stan Zbikowski, Retail Manager, GGNPA—who always goes to bat for me—Marianne Galante, Lorna Garano, Ellen "Sam" Raher, Jeff Ullman, David Vignol, Tim Wade and the late James Draper. Naomi Torres, Supervisory Park Ranger, Lori Thomsen, John Cantwell and Phil Butler, as well as all the National Park Rangers on Alcatraz, were especially encouraging.

David Adams and India Ingargiola generously shared their ideas which resulted in the cover. David Bullen—as always—graciously incorporated those ideas into a beautiful cover design.

Special thanks goes to Gilda Waldman and Mary Ellen Brinkerhoff who helped with the financial arrangements; Ken Fox, whose long talks were invaluable; Laurie Harper of Sebastian Agency, a literary agent who is a good listener, a good editor and, more rare, a terrific talker who also has something to say; my brother, Philip F. Dollison, and sister, Corinne Dollison Edwards, who were loaded with encouragement, perspective and photographs.

Lynn Cullivan and Lyn Gray were especially plucky and painstaking as content and copy editors.

Finally, I wish to single out several friends who by their wit, charm, strength and eloquence have encouraged me throughout this long process. Donna Middlemist, a volunteer National Park Ranger on Alcatraz for many years, whose enthusiasm and generosity are legendary. Without Donna's loyalty and support the discovery process wouldn't have been as exciting nor would I have been able to flesh out the important ideas. Nicki Phelps, Golden Gate National Park Association, Alcatraz Project Manager, "Queen Bee" and personal friend whose extensive knowledge of family systems, innate ability to pluck out a buried lead, wit and *merciless* badgering were an enormous help. Nicki entertained and educated me, listened and, above all, talked—and I love every minute of it. Finally, Marla Eisenberg, *aka Tess*, who listened to hours of Stroud stories and became a ruthless critic, who thought up the title, helped with the photographs, fed the puppies and is a consistent, loyal friend. Without Marla's enormous talents and encouragement, the path would have been far narrower and not so fun.

Index

Abbott, Jack Henry, 278
acquired immune deficiency syndrome, (AIDS) 191, *see* disease, discovery of, adrimycin, 149
Agura, 74
All Pets magazine, 257
Alcatraz, USP, 1, 7, 9, 14, 17, 47, 113, 121-122, 123, 125, 126, 127, 128, 131, 135, 152, 176, 181, 191, 194, 198, 199, 200, 203, 210, 216, 218, 219, 221-222, 223, 228, 230, 234, 235, 237, 238, 240, 244, 245, 246, 249, 253; description, 153-155, 158-159, 220, 241, 257, 273; classification committee, 218, 219, 229, 242; escape attempts, 156, 265-266, 270, *see also* '46 escape attempt; privileges and rules at, 159, 161-162; types of prisoners, 157; silent system, 162
"Alcatraz Cocktail," 197
Alien Property Bureau, 82
American Association of Avian Pathologists, 174
American Cage Bird, 229
American Canary and Cage Bird Life, 100
American Canary Magazine, 168
American Friends Service Committee, 236
American Psychiatric Association, 276
American Trust Co. 161
Anderson, Warden A.V., 81, 83, 87, 130
Anglin, John and Clarence, 265
Anthony, "Colonel" D.R., 88
anthroquinone violet dye, 148-149
anti-social personality, *see* sociopath
apoplectiform disease, 99
apoplectiform septicemia, 99, 100, 119, 138, 147, 172-173
arguments for release, 112
aromatic cascara, 119
Ashland, Kentucky, FCI, 151, 219
aspergillosis, 100, 133, 138, 148-149
aspergillus, 91, 133, 148
Association of Avian Veterinarians, 174
Atlanta, USP, Georgia, 54, 78, 106, 113
Audett, James "Blackie," 122, 157, 186
autopsies, 97-98, 147
avian diphtheria, 98, 138, 144-145, 172
avian diseases, 94
avian septecemias, 100
Axelrod, Herbert, 257-258

bacteria, *see* disease, discovery of
bactcrial poisoning, 100
Baglin, Raymond E., 236
Bailey, Harvey, 122
baldness in birds, 100
Barker, "Doc," 157, 158, 179
Barry, Sir James, 198
Bates, Albert, 122
Bates, BOP Director Sanford, 106, 110, 113, 116, 215
"Battle of Alcatraz," *see* '46 escape attempt
Baudelaire, 54
Beck, Dave, 230
Beck, guard, 76, 78, 79
Becker, Judge William H., 10, 11, 12-13, 19, 23, 271
Bennett, BOP Director James V., 19-21, 23, 55, 112, 117, 136, 137, 149, 160, 166, 170-171, 197, 201, 209, 214, 215, 218, 226, 230, 232, 238, 239, 241, 243, 245-246, 247, 248, 253, 255, 256, 258, 265, 267, 273; career, 113-115; description, 20, 113
Benny, Jack, 22, 23
Bergen, Philip R., 17, 70, 72, 85, 114, 116, 127-129, 132, 151, 155, 165, 179-180, 186-189, 197, 200, 207, 220-222, 224, 238, 239, 246-247
Berta, Charlie, 122
Biddle, Warden William I., 35, 87-88, 90, 103, 106
bindle stiffs, 42
Biological Abstracts, 172
bird breeding business, 92
bird cages, 87
bird sales, 93-94, 117, 149
bird seed, 91, 130
bird, migraine headaches, 139
bird mating, 140
bird pox, 145, *see also* avian diphtheria
Birdman of Alcatraz, book, *see* Gaddis, Thomas E.
Birdman of Alcatraz, film, 5, 6, 174; description, 8–9, 10, 15, 16, 259, 261
blackjacks, 115
Blackwell, Associate Warden Olin G., 245
blood pooling, 148
Boggs, Dr., 45
Bonnie and Clyde, 105

Boyle, General Louis C., 31-32, 74, 76
Bright's Disease, 14, 67
"Broadway," 159
brooder pneumonia, 142
Brown, Henry Floyd, 161, 182
Browne, D.C., 95
Burch, Bert, 183, 184
Bureau of Prisons, 11, 14, 18, 21, 22, 55,
    104, 105, 116, 117, 120, 121, 123, 124,
    126, 128, 132-133, 136, 137, 152, 163,
    164, 166, 167, 169, 211, 216, 220, 222,
    223, 226, 231, 232, 233, 235, 238, 241,
    245, 248, 253, 263, 266, 274; initial
    goals of, 113; number of prisons, 113;
    Bureau memo forbidding business, 106,
    115-117

Caen, Herb, 194
Caldwell, Erskine, 168
canaries, 89, 107
Canary Journal, 120, *see also Roller*
    Canary Journal and Bird World
canary necrosis, 99
"Canary Prisoner," 106
Capone, Alphonce "Scarface," 114, 157-
    158, 221
Carnegie Institution, 150
Carnes, Clarence, 13, 165, 168, 183, 185,
    186, 192-194, 195
Carr, U.S. Parole Board Executive Ruby
    M., 136
Carter, James, 155
Chase, John Paul, 157
chemical dyes, 148-149
Chicago White Sox, 82
chlamydia, 145
cholera, 99
citric acid, 99
Civil War, 27, 64
Cline, Royal, 166
Coates, Paul, 256
Coben, Stanley, 82
Code of Napoleon, *see* Stroud, marriage
Cohen, Mickey, 157
Cohn, Art, 255
"Committee for the Release of Robert F.
    Stroud," 232, 254, 260, 261, 262
Commonwealth Club, 161
Congressional Record, 266

Conscientious Objectors, 86
contagious pneumonia, 99
control center, 178
Cordova, Alaska, 43, 45
Coronet, 7, 235, 236
Cosmopolitan magazine, 224
Cox, Dr. O.H., 134
Coy, Bernard, 183, 185, 188
Cozart, U.S. Pardon Attorney Reed, 235,
    236, 237-238, 241, 263, 272, 273
Cretzer, Joseph "Dutch," 183, 184, 185,
    188, 230
Cron, Robert, 253
crystal violet, 149

D block, 1, 160, 163-166, 192-193; riot
    incident, 178-182; '46 escape attempt,
    183-189
Dahmer, F.K.F. Von, (a.k.a. Charlie
    Dahmer), 45-49, 67
Daily Alaska Dispatch, 45, 46
Dainard, William, 179, 185
Daw, Fred E., 92, 224, 225, 245, 249, 252
"Decline," 94
dehydrated sodium phosphate, 99, 101
Dempsey, Jack, 168
Denver Post, 110-111
Department of Justice, 237, 239, 263, 267
De Vincenzi, George, 203-204, 205, 206-
    207, 216, 217
diarrhea, 95, 143
disease, discovery of, 142-149
Dillinger, John, 105
Diseases of Canaries, 6, 118-120, 121, 123,
    138, 150, 173
Diseases of Domesticated Birds, see Ward
    and Gallahger
Dittrich, 257-258
Dollison, Arthur M., 1, 85, 132, 164, 196,
    197, 200, 219-222, 253-254; description
    of, 132, 219
Doren, Dennis, 276
Douglas, Senator Paul H., 243
Dreiser, Theodore, 198
Dukes, Jimmy, 205
Duhamel, Joseph, 250, 268
Dulaney, Kate, 43, 45; *see also* O'Brien,
    Kitty
Durant, Dr., 139

Edstrom, Eve, 136, 266
Eisenhower, President Dwight D., 229,
    235, 237, 255, 256, 265
El Dorado County Hospital, 45
Electronic Radio and Television Institute,
    169
Emporia Gazette, 106
Englewood, Colorado, boys training center,
    196
English, Richard M., 10, 20, 264-265, 267,
    269, 274

Farmer's Bulletin, 96
Faughn, Howard, 41, 273
FBI agents, 155, 165
Federal Bureau of Investigation, 105, 218
Federal Prison Industries, Inc., 113, 115,
    219
Federal Prison Newsletter, 201
Field, Betty, 9
Finch, U.S. Pardon Attorney James A., 116,
    125
fingerprint identification, 64
Fleish, Louis, 179
Floyd, "Pretty Boy," 105
Folsom State Prison, 160
'46 escape attempt, 182-189, 230, *see also*
    Stroud, Robert F.
fowl cholera, 100, 138
fowl paralysis, 138, 142, 147
Frankfurter, Justice Felix, 244, 247
Franklin, Rufus "Whitey," 165-166, 167,
    179, 184, 185
fungus, *see* diseases, discovery of
Furman, Stanley A., 5, 8, 10, 11-13, 21, 22,
    23, 136, 176, 206, 207-208, 230, 231-
    232, 235, 237, 239, 240, 241, 245, 249,
    250, 251, 258, 259-261, 263, 264, 267,
    268, 269; description, 226

Gaddis, Martha, 5
Gaddis, Phyllis E., 5, 259, 263
Gaddis, Thomas E., 5–8, 11, 12, 23, 45, 48,
    146, 147, 172, 215, 222-224, 225, 226,
    230, 232, 234, 236, 239, 255-256, 258,
    259-261, 263-264, 266; *Birdman of
    Alcatraz* book, 5, 7, 11, 13, 16, 22, 61,
    70, 102, 174, 227-228, 231, 232, 234,
    236, 254, 264; "Evolution of a

Personality Under Correctional Stress,"
    61, 277; *see also* "Committee for the
    Release of Robert F. Stroud"
Gardner, Roy, 122, 157
gentian violet, 148
Ghandi, Mahatma, 5
Gilmore, Gary, 278
Goddard, Dr. Clarence C., 75
"goon squad," 180
Graham, Asst. Attorney General Larrin, 81,
    246
Great Depression, 105, 120
Great War, 82, 86
Gregory, George, 206
Green v. U.S., 244
Grove, Jimmy, 179
gun gallery, 183

Habitat for Humanity, 191
Halligan, Warden O.P., (a.k.a. "the King"),
    58-59, 61-63, 151
Harris, Dr. James, D.V.M., 174, 175-176
Harvard Law School, 226
head lice, 143
hemorrhagic septicemia, 100, 138, 146, 172
Hennessy, U.S. Attorney Frank J., 200,
    214, 215
Henry, Adolph E., 61-62
Hitler, Adolph, 138, 141-142, 209
the "hole," 163
Hope, Bob, 22, 23
Hoover, Anne M., 128
Hoover, President Herbert C., 110, 111,
    209, 256
Hoover, FBI Director J. Edgar, 20, 83, 128,
    155, 158, 209, 226, 273
House-Tree-Person Drawings, 250, 251
Hubbard, Marvin, 183, 185, 188
Hugo, Victor, 54
Hunter, Walter A., 209
Huxman, Judge Walter A., 245-246, 247

ich, 148
immune system diseases, *see* diseases,
    discovery of
"In Paradise," 69
insanity defense, 75
Inside Detective, 234
Interstate Casket Co., 90

Jefferson. SS, 48
Johnston, Ida Fulton, 162
Johnston, Warden James A., 155, 156, 160, 160-163, 178, 179, 185, 196, 209
Jones, Della May (nee Stroud), 107-109, 110, 111, 112, 115, 116, 122, 125, 126, 137, 169, 224, 227, 255; marraige of, 123, 124
Jones, Fred, 108, 124
Journal of Avian Diseases, 174

Kansas City Star, 80-81, 106-107, 111, 171
Kansas State Agricultural College, 66, 107
Kansas State Penitentiary, 88
Karpis, Alvin "Old Creepy" Karpowitcz, 127, 128, 157, 158, 191, 193-194
Katella, Alaska, 43
Kelly, George "Machine Gun," 79, 122, 157
Kendall, Special Counsel David, W., 239-240, 241
Kennedy, President John F., 9, 24, 256, 259, 264, 273
Kennedy, U.S. Attorney General Robert F., 238, 261, 262, 273
Keve, Paul W., *The McNeil Century*, 57
King, Minnie T., 198
Koch, Robert, 142
Koch's Postulate, 142
Kuhn, Dr. William F., 75
Kyle, Arnold, 230

Lancaster, Burt, 5, 8, 10, 15, 19, 20, 21, 24, 102, 174, 257, 259-261
Landers, Joseph, 19
Landy, George, 232
LaTuna, Texas, FCI, 222
Lawford, Peter, 259
Leavenworth, USP, Kansas, (The "Big Top"), 1, 12, 14, 15, 44, 54, 62-63, 69, 73, 78, 80, 103, 106, 113, 120, 122, 126, 128, 131, 132, 134-135, 149, 151-152, 158, 160, 167, 209, 219, 228, 237, 243, 245, 273; description of, 63, 69, 90; population of, 88, 117; segregation, 85, 127
Leavenworth Times, 81, 88
Leonard, U.S. Attorney Wilbur G., 12, 245-245, 248
Leopold, Nathan, 254

Leslie, Jacques, 210; letter to, 211-214, 215
Lewis, Judge James, 78, 81
Lewis, Joe, 168
Lewisburg, USP, Pennsylvania, 113, 128, 151
lice, 91
Life, 7, 244, 256
Logan, Judge James C., "Analysis of a Murderer," 77, 274-275, 277
Long, William, 180
"Looking Outward," 17, 23-24, 55, 213; description of, 192
Los Angeles Times, 209
Los Angeles Mirror, (also *Mirror News*), 234, 256
Louisiana Purchase, *see* Stroud, marriage of
Luminal, 199, 216, 237
Lyons, Thomas R., 47

Madigan, Warden Paul J., 161; description, 230-231, 232, 238-239, 241-242, 245
Mahan, Fred, 187
Mailer, Norman, 278
malaria, 148
Malden, Karl, 8-9
Maltzer, Chief Medical Officer, 15
Manson, Charlie, 158
Marcus, Lawrence G., 39, 137, 169, 177, 195, 197, 198-199, 208-209, 210, 211, 214, 216, 224, 224, 225, 232, 257, 273; *Marcus, Stroud v. T.E. Gaddis*, 226, 230, 232; *for early childhood references see* Stroud, Marcus
Martin, Charles Dudley, 267
Martin, Mary, 40
McCain, Rufus, 179
McCarthy, Senator Joseph, 209, 218
McCartney, Captain John Franklin, 27-29, 41, 43, 64
McCartney, Minnie, 27
McCartney, Marcus, 27
McClaughry, Warden Robert W., 63-64
McCormick, Austin, 209
McCoy, Horace, 198
McDonald, A.B., 106
McGoran, John, 207
McKean, Guard, 86
McNeil Island, USP, Washington, 51, 52-53, 54, 56, 61, 63, 106, 113, 151, 223, 230, 273; Commitment Log, 51;

Rulebook, 57
"Meatball," 203
medical technical assistant, 178-181, 240
Menninger, Karl, 233
Merck's Drug Index, 101
methelene blue, 148
Metropolis, Illinois, 28, 41, 43, 126, 137, 273
Miller, Alice, 41, 277
Miller, Associate Warden E.J., 166, 170, 181
Milne, Dr. Lindsay L., 75
Minnesota Multiphasic Personality Inventory, 250, 251-252
Missouri, University of, 141
Mitchell, Guard, 194
Moreau, Dr. L., 47, 269
Morgan, Warden Thomas W., 65-65, 66, 73, 78, 87, 153
Morris, Frank, 265
Moskey, Dr. H.E., D.V.M., 120
"mules," 56
multiple sclerosis, *see* diseases, discovery

National Archives, 261
National Association of Canary Breeders, 198
NBC (National Broadcasting Company), 22
National Bird Protective League, 177
Nation's Business, 170
Nelson, "Baby Face," 105
New Mexico State Prison, 196
Newsweek, 7, 234
Nixon, Vice President Richard M., 229
Norton, Dennis, 269

O'Brien, Edmund, 9
O'Brien, Kitty, 45-49, 187, 224, *see also* Dulaney, Kate
O'Donnell, Martin J., 209
opium, belladonna and brandy, 96

Pain, John, 51, 61
Palmer, Charles Stroud, 84
Palmer, U.S. Attorney General A. Mitchell, 79-89, 81-84, 166, 243, 245, 247, 248
"Palmer Raids," 83
Palmer, Obadiah, 84
Panzram, Carl, 86, 102-103
paramyxo family virus, 147

pararosaniline, 148
parasitic, *see* diseases, discovery of
pardons of prisoners, 77
Parker, Darl Lee, 270
Pasteur, Louis, 169, 175
"pathological candor," 12
Pearson Paper Box Co., 90
"Peckerwood Hill," 63
Pepper, Jack, 185
"Perkins, Frankie," 195
Perkins, Sir William Henry, 148
peroxide of hydrogen, 99, 101, 119
petitions, *see* Stroud, petitions
Phillips, Burton, 162, 167, 179, 185
Plank, Rex, 249
Polimer, Richard K., 198, 199, 200, 209, 210, 211, 214
Pollock, Judge John C., 76
potassium chlorate, 99, 101, 119
potassium permanganate, 99, 101, 119
Powell, E.J., 107, 111, 120-121
Powers, Richard Gid, 82
pox virus, 146, 173
pneumonia, of birds, 142; of Stroud, *see* Stroud, illnesses
prison conditions, 55-58; contract labor, 59; medical conditions, 57-58; offenses in, 59, 60
prison guards, 56; clubs of guards, 56-57
prison names, 164
prisoner businesses, 59-60
Prohibition Party, 28
Prohibition, 82, 105
psittacosis, 98, 99, 134, 138, 141, 144, 145, 173
Purcell, Captain John M., 65, 69, 71-72
"Purple" Gang, 179
Purvis, Melvin, 155

Quillen, James, 154, 159, 165, 178-182, 184-186, 188, 202, 230

Raker, Representative John B., 44
Random House, 227
"Red Scare," 83
Reed, U.S. Parole Board Chairman George, 233, 237
Remsberg, Charles, 111, 267
ringworm, 143
Ritchey, Dr. Romney M., 157

Ritter, Thelma, 9
Robertson, Fred, 40, 75-76, 209
Robins, Lee N., Ph. D., 276
Rogers, William (Bill), 13, 204, 205, 206, 209
Rogers, U.S. Attorney General William P., 237, 239
Roller Canary Journal and Bird World, 89, 98, 100, 107, 109, 111
roller canaries, 92
Roosevelt, President Franklin D., 123, 226, 256
Rorschach Method of Personality Diagnosis, 250, 251
Rosenberg, Ethel and Julius, 218, 234
Rumberger, Harry, 236
rump gland, *see* uropygial
rupture, 95

sadism, 173
Salk, Jonas, 264
Sanborn, Dr. Herbert, Ph.D., 118, 123
San Francisco Examiner, 255
San Quentin, California State Prison at, 160, 191
Savalas, Telly, 8
Scagway, Alaska, 48
Scannell, Father, 206-207
schistosomiasis, 148
Schmidt, Dr. Robert, D.V.M., Ph.D., 144-145, 148, 174
Scientific American, 7, 146, 172-173, 233-234, 253
Scott, John Paul, 270
Seagoville, FCI, Texas, 113
Seattle, Washington, 31
Sendek, Vernon A., 204, 205
septic fever, 96, 99, 100, 123, 138, 144
Shaffer, Henry C., 29
Shaffer, Mamie Emma, 25-27, 29, 35, 73, 90, 137, 199, 214, 224, 225, 273
Shaffer, Minnie, 25-27, 29, 30, 32, 34-35, 67, 68, 137
Shaffer v. Shaffer, 29
Sharpe, Ed, 185
shiv, 23, 153, 171
Shockley, Sam, 179, 183-184, 185, 191, 230
Shuttleworth, Deputy Warden C.J., 130, 215

Sinatra, Frank, 259
Sloane, Dr. L.O., 46
Smith, Dr. Charles E., 233
Sobell, Morton, 13, 218, 233-234, 249, 250, 253, 271-272
sociopathic personality, 34, 275-279
sodium citrocarbonate, 99, 101
sodium perborate, 99, 101, 119
sparrows, 87
"Special Purpose Letter" form, 103, 140-141
Speer, Dr. Brian, D.V.M., 146, 147, 173, 174, 175-176
Springfield, Federal Medical Center, 7, 9, 13, 14, 17, 22,47, 113, 128, 191, 218, 240, 242, 245, 248, 250, 252, 253, 257, 260, 265, 268, 273; description, 241, 248-249
Stites, Harold, 186
Strong, C.L., 233
Stroud, Benjamin Franklin, 25-27, 29, 31, 32, 38, 40, 43-45, 73, 117, 137; description of, 30, 73; personality, 36, 277
Stroud, Benjamin and Sarah, 30
Stroud, Daniel, 84
Stroud, Elizabeth McCartney Shaffer, 25-26, 30, 31, 33, 35, 40, 42, 43, 48, 49, 66, 67, 73 68, 70, 76, 77, 78, 90, 106-107, 109, 177, 228, 255, 268; break with son, 125-126; death of, 138; letters from, 26, 90, 224; personality, 28, 34, 36-38, 90, 274, 277; testimony, 31-32, 61
Stroud, Mamie and Minnie, *see* Shaffer
Stroud, Marcus, 25-27, 37-38, 69; personality of, 38; *see* Marcus, L.G. *for later references*
Stroud, Robert S. Research Foundation, 262
Stroud, Robert F.,
    bookbinder, 268
    as a boy, Part II
    as conservative, 168, 192
    attitude about brother, 169, 208
    attitude about father, 30, 33, 38
    attitude about life, 139-140
    attitude about mother, 34, 126
    birth, 32-33
    breaking prison rules, 61-62, 65, 72, 131, 152-153, 195, 202, 253

Stroud *(cont.)*
  celebrities, 128
  cell conditions, 93, 127-128, 131-132,
    133-134,152-153, 167
  chemicals, use of, 129
  cleanliness, 93, 133, 218, 229
  comments on Bennett, 19-20
  complaints about, 135, 150, 219
  complaints of, 121, 133, 134, 139, 166,
    170, 171-172
  claims and convictions of, 43, 112,
    115, 120, 122, 123, 227, 269-270
  correspondents, 103, 137, 140-141,
    149-150, 216, 236, 256-257, 262-
    263, 264
  Dahmer killing, 45-49
  death of, 272, 273
  depression of, 67-69, 72, 216
  description of, 5, 45, 51, 75, 127, 155,
    192, 215, 248
  drawings, 66,119, 127, 138, 151
  eating habits, 13–14
  eccentricities, 15, 204
  '46 escape attempt, 1-3, 187-188
  green eye shade, 128, 192, 224
  homosexuality, 15-17, 195-196, 239,
    253, 260, 267, 275
  honesty, 12, 104, 119, 120
  hypochondria, evidence of, 14-15, 107,
    11, 133, 151, 170, 178-182, 229,
    267-268
  illnesses, 33, 37, 40, 134, 139, 200,
    267-269, 271
  I.Q. evaluations, 127, 250
  isolation, 200-201, 202-203, 215, 223-
    224
  knifings, 61-62
  languages, 202, 252-253; *see also*
    Source note 225, p. 306
  law suit, see *Marcus, Stroud v. T.E.*
    Gaddis
  Life in solitary confinement, 1, 6, 8,
    80-84, 99, 107, 110, 132, 152, 160,
    163, 166, 168, 177 245, 246, 248;
    see also U.S. v. Stroud, Palmer, A.
    Mitchell, *Stroud v. Johnston*
  marriage of, 123-124
  microscope, use of, 127-128
  microtome, use of, 129
    moonshining business and

Stroud *(cont.)*
  letter–kiting, 152-153, 267
  morphine, use of, 43, 61
  myths about, 106-107, 111-112, 122,
    227, 229, 234-235, 255, 256, 263
  parole eligibility, 20, 136-137, 274
  petitions of, 1915 Application for
    Commutation, 14, 67
    1920 Petition for Commutation, 31,
      33, 79, 82
    1931 Petition with a View Towards
      Clemency, 111
    1934 Executive Clemency Appl.,
      122, 124
    1958 Petition for Executive
      Clemency, 21, 232, 235, 239,
      254
    1962 Petition for Executive
      Clemency, 9, 254, 261
  personality, 22-23, 39, 42, 66, 137,
    138-139, 250-252, 269, 274-275
  pornographic stories, 17-18, 168, 195
  prison reports, 104, 126, 127, 134-135,
    152, 155, 170, 194, 195, 199, 200,
    216, 219, 224, 229, 240, 242, 250,
    252-253, 266, 268
  privileges, 88-89, 117, 103-104, 127,
    129-130, 132, 136, 151, 152, 167,
    197
  psychological tests, 250-252
  schooling, 39-40, 54, 61, 66, 127
  sense of humor, 62, 217, 237
  sexual attitudes, 15-18, 40, 66, 193
  smuggling, 122, 217
  suicide attempts, 15, 216-218
  testimony of, 43, 72
  threats, 64, 65, 66 67-68, 77, 193, 197,
    207, 209, 210, 239
  Turner killing, 69-72, 177
  "Typical Case History," 222-223
  veterinary research, 22, 142-149, 173-
    175, 255
Stroud, E.J. v. Stroud, B.F., 43
Stroud v. J.A. Mayden and R.S. Nicholas,
  10-12, 17, 18, 21-22, 259
Stroud v. Johnston, 166-167, 247
Stroud v. Swope, 214-215
Stroudsburg, Pennsylvania, 84
Stroud's Digest on the Diseases of Birds, 6,
  7, 11, 21, 24, 66, 100, 138-140, 150,

151, 170, 171-175, 177, 191, 198, 216, 231, 256, 257-259
"Stroud's Effervescent Bird Salts," 99, 146
"Stroud's Specific," 99, 100, 101, 120, 146
"Stroud's Salts No. 1," 99, 146
St. Louis Post Dispatch, 111, 123
Stucker, Nova, 131, 200
sulfanilamide, 147
sweating disease, 95
Swope, Edwin B., 189, 196-198, 199, 201, 209, 217, 218, 220, 230

Terre Haute, USP, Indiana, 196, 219
tetracycline, 145
"The King's English," 151; *see also* Pain, John
Theosophy, 60, 74
Thompson, Miran "Buddy," 183, 185, 191
"Time's Square," 159
Topeka Journal, 66
Treatment Unit, *see* D block
triclomoniasis, ("canker") 145
True magazine, see Remsberg, Charles
Truman, Harry S., 199, 209, 256, 265
Tumulty, Presidential Secretary Joseph, 78-79
Turner, Guard Andrew F., 69; Gaddis' description of, 70; trestimony about, 70
Turner, Ida M., 238
typhoid septic enteritis, 99

University of California, 175
uropygial gland, 95
U.S. Bureau of Efficiency, 113
U.S. Customs, 204
U.S. Pardon Attorney, 20; *see also* Cozart, Reed
U.S. Parole Commission, (U.S. Parole Board), 16, 20, 136, 237, 262, 273
U.S. Supreme Court, 78, 209, 244
U.S. v. Robert Stroud, 31, 74-78, 244

Valdez, Alaska, 48
Vanderbilt University, *see* Sanborn
Veterinary Practice Act, California, 174
virus, *see* diseases, discovery of
vitamin A deficiency, 145
Vleit, Sarah Van, 84

Waley, Harmon, 179

Wallace, prisoner, 70
Ward, A.R., and Gallagher, B.A., D.V.M., 96, 97, 98, 118-119, 145
"Warden Johnston" boat, 162
Washington Daily News, 260
Washington Post, 136, 153, 266
Wechsler Adult Intelligence Scale, 250
Weslyan University, 127
Westman and Battan, 62
Weyerhaeuser, 179
White, Warden Thomas B., 91, 92, 104-105, 106, 110, 115-116
White, William Allen, 106
Whitlatch, Guard E.E., 71, 76-78, 79
Willabrandt, Assistant U.S. Attorney General Mabel Walker, 128
Wilson, Edith Bolling, 78-79
Wilson, President Woodrow, 28, 33, 67, 78, 80, 82, 256; *see also* petitions, *under* 1920 Petition for Commutation
Winchell, Walter, 155
Woldman, Dr. Benjamin, 240
Wolfe, Thomas, 168
Wood, Mary, 94-95
World War II, 138, 151, 203
Wright, 276

Yates, Ernie, 195-196, 202, 205-206, 207, 210
"yeggs," "dips," "hop heads," and "moochers," 53
Young, Henry, 179

Zerbst, Deputy and Warden Fred G., 66, 124, 125, 133, 215
Zulu witch doctor, 175

Jolene Babyak is a nationally–televised author and speaker about Alcatraz, where she lived as a child. A member of the Authors Guild and the San Francisco Convention and Visitors Bureau, she frequently makes Alcatraz presentations and is a special guest author on the island several days a month.

To inquire about speaking engagements, please call: 510-654-4849

You may also want to order:

Eyewitnesss on Alcatraz
> An oral history about the prisoners, officers and families who lived on Alcatraz when it was a federal prison. With 76 photographs.
> **ISBN O-9618752-0-8**   **$12.95**

Birdman, The Many Faces of Robert Stroud
> **ISBN 0-9618752-2-4**   **$13.95**

Breaking the Rock, The Great Escape from Alcatraz
> After months of digging through concrete, stealing supplies to make life vests and a raft, four convicts placed dummy masks in their beds and broke "The Rock". Three were never seen again. Using eyewitness accounts, FBI documents and crime scene analysis, she uncovers the REAL story of how they did it.
> **ISBN 0-9618752-3-2**   **$14.95**

Add $6.00 for shipping and handling. Send check:
Ariel Vamp Press, P.O. Box 3496, Berkeley, CA 94703.
Phone: 510–654-4849, FAX: 510-547-0335